A New Economic Theory of Public Support for the Arts

Should the arts receive public support? Can the arts survive in a modern capitalist society? Can economics shed light on the nature of public support and whether there is a rationale for public intervention? This book undertakes to examine these questions as it explores the ways government and public resources are used to support the arts.

This book applies a Veblenian approach to understanding economic development to investigate public support for the arts in an effort to determine whether this approach can elucidate economic rationales for public support. It begins by providing basic information on public support for the arts by surveying support in the United States and Australia. The book then provides an overview of the topic from the neoclassical perspective. Finally, the work presents Veblen's ideas on economic development and applies these to an analysis of public support for the arts.

This book will be of interest to researchers concerned with cultural and institutional economics as well as political economy.

Arnaldo Barone is Research Associate, Victoria Institute for Strategic Economic Studies, as well as Senior Strategic Adviser, at Victoria University, Australia.

Routledge advances in heterodox economics

Edited by Wolfram Elsner
University of Bremen
and
Peter Kriesler
University of New South Wales

Over the past two decades, the intellectual agendas of heterodox economists have taken a decidedly pluralist turn. Leading thinkers have begun to move beyond the established paradigms of Austrian, feminist, institutional-evolutionary, Marxian, post-Keynesian, radical, social, and Sraffian economics – opening up new lines of analysis, criticism, and dialogue among dissenting schools of thought. This crossfertilization of ideas is creating a new generation of scholarship in which novel combinations of heterodox ideas are being brought to bear on important contemporary and historical problems.

Routledge advances in heterodox economics aims to promote this new scholarship by publishing innovative books in heterodox economic theory, policy, philosophy, intellectual history, institutional history, and pedagogy. Syntheses or critical engagement of two or more heterodox traditions are especially encouraged.

1 **Ontology and Economics**
Tony Lawson and his critics
Edited by Edward Fullbrook

2 **Currencies, Capital Flows and Crises**
A post Keynesian analysis of exchange rate determination
John T. Harvey

3 **Radical Economics and Labor**
Frederic Lee and Jon Bekken

4 **A History of Heterodox Economics**
Challenging the mainstream in the twentieth century
Frederic Lee

5 **Heterodox Macroeconomics**
Edited by Jonathan P. Goldstein and Michael G. Hillard

6 **The Marginal Productivity Theory of Distribution**
A critical history
John Pullen

7 **Informal Work in Developed Nations**
Edited by Enrico A. Marcelli, Colin C. Williams and Pascale Jossart

8 **The Foundations of Non-Equilibrium Economics**
The principle of circular and cumulative causation
Edited by Sebastian Berger

9 **The Handbook of Pluralist Economics Education**
Edited by Jack Reardon

10 **The Coming of Age of Information Technologies and the Path of Transformational Growth**
A long run perspective on the 2000s recession
Davide Gualerzi

11 **Cultural Economics and Theory**
The evolutionary economics of David Hamilton.
William M. Dugger, William Waller, David Hamilton, and Glen Atkinson

12 **The Cultural and Political Economy of Recovery**
Social learning in a post-disaster environment
Emily Chamlee-Wright

13 **The Foundations of Institutional Economics**
By K. William Kapp
Edited by Sebastian Berger and Rolf Steppacher

14 **Alternative Theories of Competition**
Edited by Jamee K. Moudud, Cyrus Bina and Patrick L. Mason

15 **In Defense of Post-Keynesian and Heterodox Economics**
Responses to their critics
Edited by Frederic S. Lee and Marc Lavoie

16 **The US Economy and Neoliberalism**
Alternative strategies and policies
Edited by Nikolaos Karagiannis, Zagros Madjd-Sadjadi and Swapan Sen

17 **Technological Change and Network Effects in Growth Regimes**
Exploring the microfoundations of economic growth
Torsten Heinrich

18 **The Foundations of Evolutionary Institutional Economics**
Generic institutionalism
Manuel Wäckerle

19 **Re-Thinking Economics**
Exploring the work of Pierre Bourdieu
Edited by Asimina Christoforou and Michael Lainé

20 **Networks of Institutions**
Institutional emergence, social structure and national systems of policies
Shuanping Dai

21 **An Ecosystem Approach to Economic Stabilization**
Escaping the neoliberal wilderness
Rodrick Wallace

22 **The Economic Crisis in Social and Institutional Context**
Theories, policies and exit strategies
Edited by Pasquale Tridico and Sebastiano Fadda

23 **Trust and Economics**
The co-evolution of trust and exchange systems
Yanlong Zhang

24 **The Heterodox Theory of Social Costs**
By K. William Kapp
Edited by Sebastian Berger

25 **Advancing the Frontiers of Heterodox Economics**
Essays in honor of Frederic S. Lee
Edited by Tae-Hee Jo and Zdravka Todorova

26 **Marx, Veblen, and the Foundations of Heterodox Economics**
Essays in honor of John F. Henry
Edited by Tae-Hee Jo and Frederick S. Lee

27 **The Problem of Production**
A new theory of the firm
Per L. Bylund

28 **A New Economic Theory of Public Support for the Arts**
Evolution, Veblen and the predatory arts
Arnaldo Barone

This series was previously published by The University of Michigan Press and the following books are available (please contact UMP for more information):

Economics in Real Time
A Theoretical Reconstruction
John McDermott

Liberating Economics
Feminist Perspectives on Families, Work, and Globalization
Drucilla K. Barker and Susan F. Feiner

Socialism After Hayek
Theodore A. Burczak

Future Directions for Heterodox Economics
Edited by John T. Harvey and Robert F. Garnett, Jr.

Are Worker Rights Human Rights?
Richard P. McIntyre

A New Economic Theory of Public Support for the Arts

Evolution, Veblen and the predatory arts

Arnaldo Barone

Routledge
Taylor & Francis Group
LONDON AND NEW YORK

First published 2016 by Routledge

2 Park Square, Milton Park, Abingdon, Oxfordshire OX14 4RN
52 Vanderbilt Avenue, New York, NY 10017

Routledge is an imprint of the Taylor & Francis Group, an informa business

First issued in paperback 2020

British Library Cataloguing in Publication Data

A catalogue record for this book is available from the British Library

Library of Congress Cataloging-in-Publication Data
Barone, Arnaldo, author.
A new economic theory of public support for the arts : evolution, Veblen and the predatory arts / Arnaldo Barone.
pages cm
Includes bibliographical references and index.
1. Art and state. 2. Arts—Economic aspects. I. Title.
NX720.B37 2016
700.1'03—dc23
2015027668

ISBN: 978-1-138-91419-3 (hbk)
ISBN: 978-0-367-59740-5 (pbk)

Typeset in Times New Roman
by Apex CoVantage, LLC

Contents

Figures

Tables

1 Introduction

The Victorian era English art critic John Ruskin wrote: "Great nations write their autobiographies in three manuscripts, the book of their deeds, the book of their words and the book of their art" (Ruskin 1890: iii). This work is concerned with the last of these books, the book of art, and in particular with the way in which government and public resources are used to assist with and support in its writing and whether this can be justified.

The inspiration for this book came to me in a dream. The dream concerned a programme I had watched on the Australian Broadcasting Corporation many years ago. Appearing on this programme was an American trade official who lambasted Australia for its television local content requirements and regulations. At the base of his complaint was the idea that these regulations unfairly protected Australia's arts and cultural industries and disadvantaged US producers. The Australian interviewer sheepishly responded that this was merely an attempt to protect and support Australia's art and culture, to which the American official replied, "That's what the French say when they protect their farmers".

This exchange got me to thinking of the broader question of public support for the arts. Having received a music education from the Victorian College of the Arts (VCA) in Melbourne, my automatic response was "of course the arts should be supported". To be sure, this attitude was prevalent among both staff and students at that esteemed institution, for art produced in a profit-oriented capitalist economy could be none other than 'second-rate', and to think otherwise was heresy and simply not countenanced.

But while my colleagues at the VCA took their positions comfortably and for granted, the economist in me forced me to question this. Why should it be the case that the arts should receive public support? Is it necessarily so that the arts cannot survive in any 'serious' form in a modern capitalist society? Can economics shed any light on the nature of public support and whether there is a rationale for public intervention?

But how to approach this subject? My knowledge of neoclassical approaches left me unconvinced by many of the arguments presented in favour of public support. It led me to seek out an alternative approach, one that might shed new light on the phenomenon, both regarding its nature and potential rationales.

As an undergraduate student I had come across Thorstein Veblen, ironically as part of my instruction in neoclassical economics. My knowledge of Veblen was limited to the idea of a 'Veblen good' (which, we were informed, was otherwise known as a 'snob' good) and to how this might be appropriated for use in understanding the consumption of opera, so often associated with the 'opera snob'. This simple and admittedly trivial familiarity with Veblen caused me to turn in his direction to obtain answers regarding public support for the arts. But while my initial interest was limited by the notion of the snob good, closer examination of Veblen's ideas showed me that this would be an injustice and that his approach, whatever one thinks of it, is far more ambitious and has so much more to offer than the 'tit-bit' that is the Veblen good.

It is the intention of this work to apply this rich Veblenian approach to understanding economic development to investigate public support for the arts. Further, the aim will be to determine whether this approach can give us some ideas regarding plausible economic rationales for public support. As will be seen in the chapters that follow, Veblen developed an approach built on a Darwinian platform. The socio-economic manifestation of Darwinian natural selection is conceived through a duality between what Veblen called 'workmanship' and 'predation', with the former being community-regarding activities and the latter self-regarding. The interplay of these forces, shaped by technology, causes institutional change and with it economic and social evolution. It is this duality that will be the basis of the analysis of public support.

The work is divided into three parts. Part one comprises Chapter 2, designed to provide the reader with basic information on public support for the arts. It does this by surveying public support for the arts in two nations: the United States and Australia. Both nations represent somewhat different methods of providing public support for the arts, with one giving a direct role to the state and the other preferring an indirect, facilitatory role. The chapter also provides information on the models or approaches adopted by various governments across the world to provide public support and details the policy intent and the strengths and weaknesses of each.

Part two includes Chapters 3 and 4. It would be fair to say that both Chapters 3 and 4 present the neoclassical version of events. Chapter 3 is a survey of the economics of the arts. As Chapter 3 shows, the economics of the arts, otherwise known as cultural economics, is broad and touches upon many aspects of the arts and cultural policy. This subdiscipline of economics is sometimes accused of lacking coherence, leading some to question its status as a subdiscipline. However, its practitioners suggest that it does indeed warrant this title, and they point to three overarching 'strands' that bind together what is seemingly incoherent. One of these strands is the quest for a rationale for public support.

Chapter 4 is a survey of rationales given for public support for the arts. In essence, it is a detailed survey of one of the three strands of the economics of the arts. As will be seen, the work undertaken by 'economists of the arts' is overwhelmingly neoclassical, so rationales for public support tend to be built on this foundation. Among the rationales that are discussed in this chapter are externalities, the application of the Coase theorem, and the famed Baumol's disease. Its purpose is to give the reader an idea of where things stand with respect to obtaining a rationale for public support for the arts.

Chapter 5 commences the third and final part. Here begins the discussion and presentation of Veblen's ideas on economic development. Chapter 5 provides a brief biographical introduction before going on to discuss five key influences on Veblen's thinking. The chosen five include Darwinism, the pragmatist school of philosophy, the German historical school of economics, instinct theory and habit, and the salient aspects of the works of Karl Marx.

Chapter 6 presents the basic building blocks of Veblen's theory of economic and social development. As is shown, Veblen developed a model of economic development using the idea of natural selection. Just as genes are the source of variation in biological evolution, institutions are the source of variation in economic and social evolution. It is here that I outline how the interplay between workmanship and predation acts out and leads to economic and social evolution. The chapter outlines Veblen's four broad periods of social and economic development, which he dubbed the 'savage', 'barbarian', 'handicraft', and 'machine' ages.

In Chapter 7, I apply the foundations presented in Chapter 6 to provide an understanding of production and consumption from the Veblenian perspective. As is shown, workmanship and predation are pivotal to understanding production and consumption. Importantly, unlike neoclassical economics, Veblen's approach gives an explicit role to social factors in determining both consumption *and* production decisions.

Chapter 8 is where the ideas presented in Chapters 6 and 7 are applied to the case of the arts. The chapter considers public support through the prism of the famed Veblenian duality. The chapter has two aims. One is to consider public support in an institutional sense. This involves examining public support and its historical trajectory and the idea that public support is an institution that has undergone an evolution from an ancient system of patronage. The suggestion is that modern public support could be conceived as the most recent iteration of this institution. Secondly, I attempt to determine whether rationales can be obtained for public support for the arts. Again, it is the famed duality that is the basis of this analysis. The discussion considers the possibility that public support enables workmanship to be the dominant force in the production of art. However, the chapter also shows that it is possible that public support comes to be captured by predatory inclinations, thereby numbing or muting any intended workmanship aims of public support.

Chapter 9 is the conclusion. It is here that I draw together the analysis presented from Chapter 2 onwards and make my statement regarding the nature of public support and possible and plausible rationales for its existence.

Before proceeding to the book proper, one last piece of business requires attention, namely, what is meant by 'art' and 'the arts'? To be sure, this could prove the subject of a book in itself, and there has long been debate on how to define the arts. I have chosen to adopt the definition employed by the prominent arts economist David Throsby, who has defined the arts as "literature (including creative writing of nonfiction); the visual arts and crafts; the performing arts, comprising theatre, music, dance, opera and music theatre; film and video (including both drama and documentary); and multimedia arts" (Throsby 2001a: paragraph 3). This definition also fits well with those adopted by the purveyors of public support, as evidenced by the *Australia Council Act* (1975). That Act defines the arts as "creative and interpretative expression through theatre, literature, music, visual arts, film and crafts" (*Australia Council Act* 1975: section 1(3)). The adoption of the Throsby and Australian Council Act terminology might risk the trivialisation of philosophical debates on the matter of definition, but for the purposes of this work, the definition serves well.[1]

Note

1 The *Australia Council Act* definition is also in keeping with definitions used in similar acts to establish Australia Council analogues. For example, the *Canada Council Act* (1985) defines the arts as "architecture, the arts of the theatre, literature, music, painting, sculpture, the graphic arts and other similar creative and interpretative activities", while the US act to establish the National Endowment for the Arts defines the arts as "music (instrumental and vocal), dance, drama, folk art, creative writing, architecture and allied fields, painting, sculpture, photography, graphic and craft arts, industrial design, costume and fashion design, motion pictures, television, radio, film, video, tape and sound recording, the arts related to the presentation, performance, execution, and exhibition of such major art forms, all those traditional arts practiced by the diverse peoples of this country, and the study and application of the arts to the human environment" (*Canada Council for the Arts Act* 1985: section 2; United States *National Foundation on the Arts and the Humanities Act* 1965).

2 Understanding public support for the arts

2.1 Introduction

In early 1975, Australia's commonwealth parliament passed a bill to establish the Australia Council for the Arts. In the bill's second reading speech, the then-minister for the arts, Edward Gough Whitlam, who also concurrently held the prime ministerial position, stated that the purpose of the Australia Council would be to "administer Australian Government assistance to the arts" (Whitlam in Commonwealth of Australia, House of Representatives 1974: paragraph 1). The same speech outlined the motivation for the establishment of such a body and the provision of said assistance or support, which amounted to the belief that:

> Artists have an essential role to play in society. No one can imagine a mature civilisation without their contribution. . . . The Government believes they should be able to work in their own country secure in the knowledge that the community and the Government place a high value on their contribution to our way of life. . . . We want to ensure that our greatest artists remain in Australia and prosper in Australia, and that the whole Australian community is the richer for their presence. . . . I believe that, through the measures in this Bill, we will create greater artistic opportunities for all talented Australians. We shall be offering to all who by birth or choice have made this country their home the prospect of enriching their lives through participation in or appreciation of the arts.
>
> (Whitlam in Commonwealth of Australia, House of Representatives 1974: final paragraph)

The 1975 formation of the Australia Council followed decades of commonwealth government programmes to support the arts that "developed fitfully" (Whitlam in Commonwealth of Australia, House of Representatives 1974: paragraph 3). The earliest programmes can be traced to the first decade of Australian federation, when in 1908 the Commonwealth Literary Fund was established to provide pensions to Australian writers and their families (Seares and Gardiner-Garden 2011: 8). This was followed in 1912 with the formation of the Commonwealth Art Advisory Board and the Historic Memorials Committee, the former of which was founded to commission portraits of important Australians and government officials (Craik 2006: 4; Seares and Gardiner-Garden 2011: 8). An earlier version of the Australia Council arose as early as 1968 in the Gorton government, seven years before the passing of the 1975 Act. But unlike the 1975 version developed by the Whitlam government, this earlier incarnation did not carry parliamentary blessing and was less substantial in terms of both funding and activities. Its primary role was to manage public funding and support for opera, ballet and drama (Commonwealth of Australia, House of Representatives 1974). From this earliest guise into its more formalised 1975 form, the Australia Council enjoyed and was shaped by the counsel and direction of the economics profession. Two of Australia's most esteemed economists, H. C. 'Nugget' Coombs and Peter Karmel, served as the council's debut and second chairman (Commonwealth of Australia, House of Representatives 1974: paragraph 4).[1]

The Australia Council's establishment is in many respects a relatively late occurrence by international standards. Its creation follows similar moves by other nations to establish 'arts bodies' to manage and provide government assistance to the arts. As an example, Australia's Commonwealth 'sister' nation, Canada, created the Canada Council for the Arts in 1957. According to its foundation act, the Canada Council's function is to "foster and promote the study and enjoyment of, and the production of works in, the arts" (*Canada Council for the Arts Act* 1985: section 8).[2] In 1965, the United States followed its northern neighbour by passing the *National Foundation on the Arts and the Humanities Act*, thereby establishing the National Endowment for the Arts (NEA). Section 2(7) of the US act states that "the practice of art . . . require[s] constant dedication and devotion" and that because of this "it is necessary and appropriate for the Federal Government to help create and sustain not only a climate encouraging freedom of thought, imagination, and inquiry but also the material conditions facilitating the release of this creative talent". Indeed, US efforts to establish the NEA can be traced back to at least the 1950s and the administration of President Dwight Eisenhower, who, like Whitlam, couched the establishment of such a body in 'civilisational' terms:

> In the advancement of the various activities which would make our civilization endure and flourish, the Federal Government should do more to give official recognition to the importance of the Arts and other cultural activities.
>
> (Eisenhower in NEA 1965: 7)

The Australian, Canadian and US bodies followed in the pioneering[3] footsteps of the 'mother country', which in 1946 created the Arts Council of Great Britain by royal charter. Like the Australia Council, the ranks of the UK Council enjoyed strong representation from the economics profession, with its first chairman none other than John Maynard Keynes (Goodwin 2005: 558). Keynes considered that the Arts Council of Great Britain would "correct the market" and avoid the friction he considered unavoidable in the interaction between art and commerce, namely that the arts "cannot be successfully carried on if they depend on the motive of profit and financial success" (Keynes in Upchurch 2005: 532). In 1994, the Arts Council of Great Britain was split. In its place now is the Arts Council of England, with similar bodies created to administer government support in Scotland, Wales and Northern Ireland.

The eloquent language cited earlier by Whitlam and others to provide rationales for public assistance can be recast in more prosaic terms and reduced to two broad propositions. The first of these amounts to the simple assertion that in a modern capitalist economy the arts simply cannot exist without government support or, at the very least, that art produced without public support is of a dubious character. Following from this, the second proposition is that government support will result in art that is of a beneficial and superior nature, both artistically and socially. However, despite the representation of the economics profession (in the form of Keynes, Coombs and Karmel) among the rank of proponents of support, these propositions contain at least two implications that would cause immediate scepticism among many economists.

First, many economists question whether it is at all true to say that the arts would perish or decline without public support. Second, supposing for a moment that this first proposition is true, then the arguments made in favour of support rest on the notion that the activities supported by government will invariably be of a beneficial character, including the ability for Australia, the United States, Canada or indeed any nation providing support to claim a place as a mature and civilised nation with a rich artistic tradition.

As will be shown in the chapters that follow, many economists do not readily accept either of these two propositions, and even those who are sympathetic to the notion of public support ask that they be subjected to scrutiny and analysis. Indeed, it would be fair to say that the difficulty in accepting these propositions is not limited to economists and that many outside the discipline also question the validity of the claims made by the authors and standard-bearers of public support.[4] It is the friction between these viewpoints that is the motivation for this book, with the ultimate aim to determine whether rigorous and plausible economic rationales for public support for the arts can be obtained. In particular, from Chapter 5 onwards, an attempt will be made to understand the very nature and origin of public support and consider possible rationales using the tools of Veblen.

However, before entering into such an analysis, it is worth pausing to reflect on the 'basic facts' of public support for the arts. It is here that the purpose of this chapter lies, and its function is to present a 'state of play' of public support, for want of a better term, and to enable the reader to gain a richer understanding of the phenomenon at hand. To begin with, there will be a brief survey of public support in selected nations. Following this, the chapter will present information on the models used to provide public support for the arts. In total there are five generally recognised models, and the Australia Council represents just one of these.

2.2 Public support in select countries

From the discussion thus far, one could be forgiven for thinking that public support for the arts is limited to the 'Anglosphere' nations of Australia, Canada, the United States and the United Kingdom. [5] However, public support of one form or another is present in many nations and regions across the globe. Evidence of this is available in a number of ways. First, a number of reports make intercountry comparisons of public support for the arts, including in nations such as Singapore and Germany (Arts Council of Ireland 2000; NEA 2000; McCaughey 2005). The purpose of these reports is to make comparisons between nations and regions on the level of 'cultural spending'. [6] Importantly, that such reports have been developed at all is evidence that public support has a wide international presence. Second, a number of online resources exist that provide information on public support policies for the arts in various nations. As an example, the website of the International Federation of Arts Councils and Culture Agencies (IFACCA) contains cursory information and links on public support for the arts and culture in over 60 nations.[7] Again, like the previously mentioned intercountry reports, that such a federation exists at all is *prima facie* evidence of a widespread phenomenon of public support.

A survey of public support in each of these nations and regions would surely prove a daunting prospect. To give an indication of how public support operates, I will instead present a brief survey of public support for the arts in two nations: Australia and the United States. Australia was chosen for obvious reasons, namely that it is the author's home, providing a clear familiarity with it and its public support policies. But, in addition, Australia was chosen because it is a good representation of an attitude to public support that gives the state a prominent role in terms of direct support and funding. The United States was chosen because it represents a quite different attitude towards public support and funding for the arts. Unlike Australia, the United States shies away from providing direct support and funding in relative terms and prefers to support and fund the arts through indirect measures.

2.2.1 Australia

The nature of Australian public support for the arts is reflective of Australia's federal political structure. Public support for the arts is provided by each of Australia's three levels of government, with a number of agencies and organisations at the federal and state level established to provide funding and support for the arts, while local level support is generally provided through arts departments, divisions or sections of local governments.[8]

At the federal level, the key body responsible for public support for the arts is the already mentioned Australia Council for the Arts, which is responsible for funding and support to Australia's visual, performing and literary arts. As previously mentioned, the Australia Council was instituted in 1975, and its entry marked a consolidation of previously disparate commonwealth government support and assistance programmes. Many of these disparate programmes came into being in the 1950s and early 1960s, which is ironic considering that this period is often characterised as an 'ice age' for the arts in Australia. These Australia Council precursors included, *inter alia*, the Australian Elizabethan Theatre Trust, the National Institute of Dramatic Art, the Elizabethan Opera Company, the Australian Ballet, the Union Theatre Company and the Old Tote Company (Craik 2007: 10; Seares and Gardiner-Garden 2011: 9).

The other main provider of support at the federal level is Screen Australia. This body is responsible for providing government support to Australia's screen sector, more commonly understood to include the film and television sectors although increasingly moving into digital media. Screen Australia's object is to enable the telling of 'Australian stories', to "support the development of Australian programs that deal with matters of national interest or importance to Australians, or that illustrate or interpret aspects of Australia or the life and activities of Australian people" (*Screen Australia Act* 2008: section 6(3)). Screen Australia was founded in 2008 with the merger of three organisations that previously held responsibility for administering commonwealth government support to the screen sector,[9] although direct commonwealth government funding and support to the screen sector can be traced back at least 40 years to the 1970 establishment of the Australian Film Development Corporation by the Gorton government (Australian Film Commission 2006: 12).

Commonwealth funding to these two organisations is not inconsequential. As can be seen in Table 2.1, the commonwealth government provides in the order of $280 million *per annum* to these two premier arts funding agencies, breaking $300 million in 2014.

In addition to commonwealth support, each of Australia's six states and two territories has established agencies with responsibility for providing public support to the arts. Most states and territories have demarcated responsibility for support programmes along lines to similar those adopted by the commonwealth, with separate arms for the screen industries and for the more traditional performing, visual and literary arts. As an example, the premier body responsible for arts policy and funding in the state of Victoria was, until very recently, Arts Victoria, a body brought into existence through the passage of the *Arts Victoria Act* 1972.[10] The Victorian screen sector receives support through Film Victoria. Film Victoria was established as an independent authority under the auspices of the *Film Act* 2001, although its history can be traced back to the 1970s, firstly through the 1976 creation of the Victorian Film Corporation, which in 1982 morphed into Film Victoria with the passage of the now superseded *Film Victoria Act* 1981 (Film Victoria 2008: 4).

Table 2.1 Australian government funding provided to the Australia Council and Screen Australia (Australian $m)

	2009	*2010*	*2011*	*2012*	*2013*	*2014*
Australia Council	173.6	179.5	181.5	182.9	191.4	220.7
Screen Australia	102.9	93.6	89.4	91.8	98.1	101.1
Total Funding Combined	276.5	273.1	270.9	274.7	289.5	321.8

Source: Australia Council for the Arts Annual Reports 2009–10, 2010–11, 2012–13, 2013–14, and Screen Australia Annual Reports 2009–10, 2010–11, 2012–13, 2013–14 (http://www.australiacouncil.gov.au/news/media-centre/reports and http://www.screenaustralia.gov.au/about_us/Corporate-Information.aspx, both accessed 8 March 2015).

Australian government support for the arts is not limited to that provided through arts agencies. Considerable funding and support is provided in other, indirect ways, through the funding of government activities that have arts and cultural elements. Funding and resources provided to public television, public radio and the national and state libraries are examples of this kind of support. While support for the arts is not the primary or sole objective of these government activities, the funding and resources at the disposal of such public bodies is, nonetheless, often used in ways that support the arts. For example, Australia's national public broadcaster, the Australian Broadcasting Corporation (ABC), supports the arts by commissioning Australian-made movies, television series and drama to be broadcast on Australian public television.

The quantum of funding support provided to the arts by Australian governments is highlighted in Table 2.2. The table is broken down according to each of Australia's three levels of government, and in the case of the commonwealth and state and territory governments, according to 'heritage' and 'arts' activities. The heritage component in Table 2.2 includes such arts-related matters as funding for galleries, libraries and museums. The arts funding component in Table 2.2 includes Australian government support for activities such as opera, drama, dance, film, literature, music and music composition and publishing, as well as funding for other areas which are arts related (such as radio and television services and design).

From the table it is clear that the total support and funding provided by governments to the arts in Australia is not inconsiderable. Reflecting its financial power, the commonwealth is the biggest investor in Australian arts and culture, followed by the states and territories. Local government support is also significant, growing by about 60 per cent since 2004–05.

An appreciation of the importance and size of public support for the arts in Australia is strengthened by comparing it to support received by the arts from the private sector. Table 2.3 provides information compiled by the Australian Business Arts Foundation (ABAF) on the level of funding received by the arts from the private sector between 2001–02 and 2009–10. The data are also split between 'sponsorships' and 'giving', the latter being contributions made by private individuals and families. According to ABAF, total support provided by the private sector was until 2009–10 consistently less than ten per cent of that provided by the public, although there has been growth during this period. Clearly, the Australian arts sector relies far more heavily on the public purse for its activities. The significance of Table 2.3 will become clear in the discussion on the United States in section 2.2.2.

The forms of support discussed thus far are of a direct funding type, but Australian governments also provide support in other, more subtle ways. One way Australian governments have been known to do this is through the use of regulations and law. In television, for example, local content regulations require commercial Australian television networks to achieve a quota of locally sourced and made programmes (see *Broadcasting Services (Australian Content) Standard*

Table 2.2 Public spending on cultural activities in Australia Commonwealth, state and local government combined by financial year (Australian $ millions)

	2004–05	*2005–06*	*2006–07*	*2007–08*	*2008–09*	*2009–10*	*2010–11*	*2011–12*	*2012–13*
Commonwealth Government									
*Heritage**	349.2	388.6	386.5	476.1	536.7	564.3	507.2	487.4	517.9
Arts	1761.6	1896.6	1901.0	1639.3	1563.4	1654.6	1678.7	1744.5	1756.2
Commonwealth Total	2,110.80	2,287.50	2,115.40	2,100.10	2,218.90	2,185.90	2,231.90	2,274.10	2,285.20
State and Territory Governments									
*Heritage**	846.4	933.5	883.9	868.2	880.2	1049.3	1045	1120.4	1166
Arts	439.3	471.6	516.7	607.5	681.8	646.1	767.3	864.5	843.8
State and Territory Total	1,285.70	1,405.10	1,400.60	1,475.70	1,562.00	1,695.40	1,812.30	1,984.90	2,009.80
Local Government									
Local Government Total	897.7	1004.2	1083.7	1038.7	1148.6	1197.7	1259.9	1342.3	1397.6
Total All Governments	4,294.2	4,696.80	4,599.70	4,614.50	4,929.50	5,079.00	5,304.10	5,601.30	5,692.60

Source: Australian Bureau of Statistics, Cultural Funding by Government, Cat no. 4183.0

* Funding for 'environmental heritage', which includes "nature parks and reserves, zoological parks and aquariums and botanic gardens" (ABS Cat no. 4172.0) has been removed from the 'Heritage' figures in this table to give a better indication of funding towards arts-related activities as they are commonly conceived.

Table 2.3 Australian private sector support to the arts by financial year (Australian $ million)

Year	*Giving ($)*	*Sponsorships ($)*	*Total Private Sector Funding (Giving + Sponsorships) ($)*	*Share of Total Income to Arts Organisations (%)*
2001–02	64	47	112	6.7
2002–03	64	51	121	6.7
2003–04	75	57	127	6.8
2004–05	76	63	138	7.3
2005–06	82	87	169	8.3
2006–07	87	92	179	8.5
2007–08	105	99	204	9.2
2008–09	111	101	212	9.3
2009–10	123	98	221	10.4

Source: Australian Business Arts Foundation (ABAF) Survey of Private Sector Support, Measuring private sector support for the arts in 2008–09, http://www.abaf.org.au/Media/docs/AbaF-Survey-of-Private-Sector-Support-2010-Summary-b87493a2-cc2e-4c9f-b232-da5a066d0134–0.pdf accessed 2 June 2012, and ABAF Submission to the Mitchell Review of Private Sector Support for the Arts, http://arts.gov.au/sites/default/files/submissions/private-sector/pdf/AbaF-submission.pdf accessed 8 March 2015

2005).[11] In the absence of such a regulation, Australian networks may have chosen to use imported programming, or perhaps to produce less local programming than the government set quota. The result is that government regulation ostensibly supports local arts production. The trade implications of support through such regulatory schemes could be the topic of a book in and of itself. Such a detailed analysis is, however, beyond the scope of this work and has only been presented to highlight nonfunding measures used by the Australian government to support the arts.[12]

In 2011, the commonwealth government announced a review of Australia's cultural policies, which followed a similar review of the Australia Council for the Arts. The aim was to release a new national cultural strategy, the first such strategy since the *Creative Nation* strategy instituted by the Keating government in 1994 (National Cultural Policy Discussion Paper 2011; Craik 2006: 5–6). The revised strategy, *Creative Australia*, was released in 2013. At the time of its release, then Prime Minister Julia Gillard hailed the document as a "fresh expression of the values and priorities that will sustain Australia as a richly creative society in the 21st century" that "continues the spirit of engagement with the arts" (in Australian Government 2013: 2). The development and release of this strategy shows that, in government circles at least, the need for public involvement and support for the arts in Australia is well and truly beyond question.

2.2.2 United States

Like Australia, public support for the arts in the United States reflects its federal political structure. At the federal level, the US government has established an authority with responsibility for providing public assistance to the arts. The already-mentioned NEA was created in 1965 to be the lead federal agency to provide federal support to the arts. The NEA is complemented by its sister agency, the National Endowment for the Humanities (NEH), which was established by the same 1965 Act of Congress that created the NEA. The NEH is responsible for providing funding to the humanities, which includes funding for a number of arts-related activities, such as museums, libraries, public television and public radio. Again, as in the Australian case, funding provided for NEH activities is not specifically designed to support the arts. Nonetheless, this kind of funding is often used to support arts activities, for example, through the development of television programmes and documentaries for broadcast on the Public Broadcasting Service (PBS).

US federal support is complemented by support provided by state and local governments. Each of the 50 states has an agency responsible for managing state level public support to the arts, as do each of the six US jurisdictions.[13] Most states brought their agencies into being following the formation of the NEA in 1965. However, some states, like New York and Utah, established state agencies prior to this, in Utah's case more than a century ago (in 1899).[14]

Table 2.4 gives detail on the level of support provided by each tier of government in the United States since 2009. Interestingly, local government appears to be a far bigger funder of the arts in the United States than either the state or the federal governments. This perhaps reflects the larger role given to local government in the United States in the management and provision of goods and services that would be the responsibility of higher-level governments in other nations.[15]

In absolute terms, total government support for the arts in the United States is markedly less than is provided in Australia,[16] with the total absolute support provided to the arts and related activities by all levels of US government combined less than that provided by Australia's state and territory governments alone. Indeed, all levels of Australian government provide support that either surpasses or comes close to equalling the US levels. The smaller direct role played by government in

Table 2.4 United States public expenditure on the arts by federal (NEA), state and local government (US $ millions)

	2009	*2010*	*2011*	*2012*	*2013*	*2014*
Federal						
NEA	155.0	167.5	154.7	146.0	139.0	146.0
NEH	155.0	167.5	154.7	146.0	139.0	146.0
Total Federal	310.0	335.0	309.4	292.0	278.0	292.0
State	329.7	307.1	276.0	260.0	279	307.0
Local	823.3	765.0	688.5	706.0	727	777.0
Total All Governments	1,463.0	1,407.1	1,273.9	1258.0	1284.0	1376.0

Source: NEA, state and local figures obtained from Grantmakers in the Arts, Public Funding to the Arts Annual Update (see Han 2009 and 2010 and Stubbs 2012, 2013 and 2014); NEH figures obtained from National Humanities Alliance, http://www.nhalliance.org/advocacy/funding-priorities/national-endowment-for-the-humanities-fy2013.shtml, accessed 8 March 2015.

the United States is made more apparent by a comparison of funding to the NEA with that given to the Australia Council. While in absolute terms the level of funding provided to the NEA has often been similar to that given to the Australia Council, on a *per capita* basis the premier US agency receives far less than its Australian counterpart.[17] This *per capita* comparison could be extended from a comparison of funding to premier arts agencies and used to compare total direct funding to the arts across all programmes. Such a *per capita* analysis reinforces the greater role that direct government support plays in Australia, a nation with a population of about 20 million, to the United States, a nation with over 300 million inhabitants.

It should be noted that, unlike the Australian figures in Table 2.2, the figures in Table 2.4 do not include support for 'ancillary' areas,[18] such as funding for museums and institutions like the Smithsonian, which could be said to have an arts support aspect. That said, even taking such activities into account, US federal government appropriation to the arts and humanities totalled US$1.7 billion in 2013,[19] which is markedly less than that provided by Australia's commonwealth government.

The purpose of this discussion is not to compare the levels of funding in the United States and Australia for their own sake (which, as mentioned early in the chapter, is fraught with difficulty) but to highlight a different point. It would be easy to conclude from the comparison made earlier that public support for the arts in the United States is at best a token gesture and that as a phenomenon it has a negligible presence. However, the figures in Table 2.4 mask the role played by US governments in supporting the arts through other, indirect measures. The United States differs from Australia and many other Western nations in this regard, in that many of its support mechanisms give a larger role to private benefaction, encouraged and supported by government incentives, particularly through the tax code (NEA 2007: v; Osborne 2004).

Table 2.5 provides details compiled as part of *Giving USA: The Annual Report on Philanthropy*[20] on the total contribution made by the private sector to the arts, culture and humanities in the United States between 2007 and 2013. As can be seen, private contributions far outstrip direct funding provided by

Table 2.5 Private giving to the arts, culture and humanities in the United States (US$ billions current dollars)

Year	*Amount ($)*
2007	14.92
2008	12.29
2009	12.59
2010	13.38
2011	14.34
2012	15.45
2013	16.66

Source: Giving USA Data Tables (2014).

the three levels of US government. Comparison of Tables 2.4 and 2.5 shows that private subvention was about eight and a half times the level of public funding in 2009, while in 2013 it was twelve times larger. When compared with the Australian case shown in Table 2.3, it becomes clear that private sector support has a far larger role in supporting and funding the arts in the United States.

What a simple glance at the figures in Table 2.5 does not show is the considerable role the US government plays in providing incentives through the tax code in the form of charitable deduction provisions. These provisions date back to 1917 and allow income tax deductions to be claimed for contributions made to charities, including arts and cultural organisations (JCT 2011a: 4). The lost tax revenue associated with deductions for giving to the arts amounts to an indirect injection of federal funds to the arts. Thus, much US government support to the arts could be said to be hidden. The United States is not unique in providing such incentive mechanisms,[21] but despite deduction measures in other countries, it seems that the United States is unique in the far greater role played by charitable donations, not only in the arts but in many aspects of its society. Consider as a comparison that, in 2010–11, Australians claimed Australian $2.2 billion in deductions for charitable gifts (ATO 2015), while in the United States the 2010 figure was US$170.2 billion (JCT 2013: 46). Casting these figures on a *per capita* basis reinforces the far greater role for private sector charitable donation in the United States, a point reinforced by Philanthropy Australia (2011). The reasons for this could be as much cultural as they are financial and would warrant future investigation in subsequent work.

Exact figures on taxpayer expenditure associated with this indirect form of support to the arts are not available, but the US Congress Joint Committee on Taxation has developed figures for the tax expenditures associated with deduction for charitable contributions *in toto* (excluding education and health). These figures are reproduced in Table 2.6.

In nominal terms, between 1980 and 2009, the US government has forgone approximately $588 billion in revenue through the provision of the charitable deduction incentive.

Table 2.6 Tax expenditures associated with deductions for charitable contributions, other than for education and health (US$ billions)

Years	*Individual*	*Corporate*	*Total*
1980–1984	39.4	8.0	47.4
1985–1989	62.4	15.0	77.4
1990–1994	55.8	8.1	63.9
1995–1999	77.0	9.7	86.7
2000–2004	124.3	15.6	139.9
2005–2009	159.2	12.8	172.0

Source: Background Information on Tax Expenditure Analysis and Historical Survey of Tax Expenditure Estimates, *US Congress Joint Committee on Taxation (JCT 2011a).*

Alas, the figures in Table 2.6 are for tax expenditures across all charitable contributions, and so it is not possible calculate the cost to the taxpayer in terms of lost revenue associated with private support for the arts. But, from Table 2.5, it is clear that private funding plays a far larger role in funding the arts in the United States, and comparing this with Table 2.6, it also seems clear that the taxpayer provides far greater incentives in terms of lost revenue in order to maintain private subvention than is the case in Australia.

The larger point, however, is that while at first glance direct funding figures suggest that public support plays a small role, closer scrutiny reveals that even in the United States there is a view that government should play a role in supporting the arts. The difference is merely one of approach. True, the charitable donations provisions are not specific to the arts, but that the arts have been included as eligible beneficiaries of such a scheme represents at the very least tacit acceptance of the idea of public support.

2.3 Models of support

As the cliché goes, there's more than one way to skin a cat, and so it is that the method used to provide public support for the arts can be provided in more than one way. In section 2.2 it was shown that governments can use both direct and indirect methods to fund the arts. As was shown, the indirect method is favoured by the United States, while the direct method is that favoured in most other Western nations, including the example of Australia. While the United States and Australia use different methods to fund the arts, they share the same approach in terms of the government agencies (the Australia Council and the NEA) established to lead, guide and provide government support to the arts. The difference in funding methods represents one approach, while the types of body both have established is another. In general, there are five recognised models or approaches, each with different strengths and weakness and policy objectives, including (Craik 2007: 1–5, 81; Chartrand and McCaughey 1989):[22]

1. Patron
2. Facilitator
3. Architect
4. Engineer
5. Elite nurturer

2.3.1 Patron

The patron model sees governments take on the role of patron of the arts. Governments using the patron model provide direct support to the arts, whether in terms of funding or other resources. However, patron model countries and regions do not eliminate the private sector, and often government support is supplemented by some measure of private philanthropy. There may also be some requirement for box office receipts as a source of complementary funding.

Often, governments utilising this model establish independent bodies to make decisions on which artistic endeavours to support. This so-called 'arm's length' patron model originated in the United Kingdom with the establishment of the Arts Council of Great Britain in 1946 (Upchurch 2004: 203; Chartrand and McCaughey 1989). Its establishment has been described as "the great precedent" in arts funding (Straight in Upchurch 2004: 203) that led to the establishment of similar 'arm's length' bodies like the NEA, the Australia Council and the Canada Council for the Arts.

In patron model countries and regions, the determination of which arts activities to support is made by artistic peers and professionals through the auspices of independent bodies. The model, in essence, represents a form of peer review in the arts, which is said to align with best artistic practice and excellence. It is also suggested that since support is provided through independent bodies, art production is less susceptible to political influence and interference (Chartrand and McCaughey 1989).

The downside to such an approach is the risk that the art that is produced is simply that which marries with the tastes and views of the elite. In other words, the government patron model merely makes real and reinforces the world-view of the ruling classes, and not artistic excellence.[23] With respect to artistic excellence, this approach could simply support art that is dead or that is well matured and not art that is innovative or at the 'frontiers': as William Morris would say, it "make[s] art grow when it has no longer any root" (William Morris in Upchurch 2005: 532).

By definition, this model places control over what is supported in the hands of a few appointed government patrons. The smaller pool diminishes the diversity of views on art, with an accompanying limited manifestation in the types and forms of art that are supported. The limited tastes and views that shape artistic support choices could lead to the blunting of innovation and stunting of the growth and future development of art.

2.3.2 Facilitator

The facilitator model occurs when governments fund the arts through measures designed to encourage support from donors and private benefactors. The government adopts measures that *facilitate* private sector philanthropy, such as tax code incentives. This is the model most commonly associated with the United States, which, as was shown earlier in the chapter, has an arts sector that relies far more heavily on private sector funding. An advantage of this approach is that governments do not have direct control over the art that is produced, so the dangers of the arts becoming a tool for government propaganda or the play-thing of a ruling elite is markedly diminished, if not eliminated. The large number of potential private patrons also means that it is possible for greater diversity in the art that is produced.

Alas, while this approach mitigates the possibility that artists become slave to the whims of arts bureaucrats, it may replace one master with another. The artist instead becomes the 'slave' of the private patron, responding to and producing art that aligns with such a patron's tastes. Unlike the arm's length patron model, art that is supported is not chosen on the basis of peer review. Herein lies the drawback, in that this model may produce art that reflects not artistic canons or excellence but rather the unsophisticated tastes of the private patron. In addition, this model does not afford the public a means to change policy or permit it to have a say in what art is produced with its indirect support. It means that society subsidises the artistic whims of a private benefactor, but without any control or ability to change or influence art production, and, importantly, with potentially no societal benefit accruing from the public's indirect 'investment' in the arts. By contrast, in the patron model it is possible, at least in theory, to affect changes in policy and in the art that is supported through the ballot box or ministerial directive.

2.3.3 Architect

The architect model is similar to the patron model in that governments provide direct funding to the arts. However, support in this model is usually provided through a dedicated government ministry or department, giving greater control over arts production to the bureaucracy and potentially to politicians. As such, while this model shares the direct funding approach of the patron, it bypasses its arm's length principles and is "more interventionist" (Craik 2007: 1). Architect model nations or regions tend to support arts that achieve national arts and cultural objectives or that align with social welfare objectives. Unlike the peer review process of the patron approach, the supported arts often reflect not professional but community standards. The architect model is also far more formalised with respect to support eligibility requirements, often requiring artists to be members of the official artist unions.

While the patron model includes the possibility of some private sector funding, in architect nations and regions funding is almost entirely determined by government, leaving the "economic status of artistic enterprise" at the hands of the government bureaucrat (Chartrand and McCaughey 1989: "Architect", paragraph 1). Herein lies a strength, in that artists, comfortable in the knowledge of government support, can devote their efforts entirely to artistic pursuits. Efforts expended on other fundraising efforts, common in patron nations, can be discarded. However, the great control given over to such a government bureaucracy also has its dangers, in that "such a Ministry might grow into a sort of octopus, binding all creative activity with the chilly tentacles of the Civil Service" (Kenneth Clark in Goodwin 2005: 585).[24] And while the almost exclusive role of government could give some comfort and security to artists, the undiversified funding also means that the artist is far more susceptible to the whims and fancy of the government for his or her livelihood.

2.3.4 Engineer

The fourth method is the engineer model. This model sees the government casting a far more controlling influence over art that is produced within its jurisdiction. The art that is produced is often the property of the state, and public support is used to produce art that conforms with the ideology of the ruling regime, that aligns with its objectives or supports its propaganda. The decision on which artists to support is in the direct control of political apparatchiks who base their arts funding decisions on the ability to educate about the received ruling class perspective, not on the ability to advance art. Generally, supported artists come from within the ranks of the ruling party elite.

The engineer model appeals to regimes that wish to strictly control cultural and artistic output so as to ensure it aligns with and advances the regime's political, cultural and/or commercial objectives. It is not surprising, then, that the model is generally associated with totalitarian governments, like those of the former Soviet Union, Cuba and North Korea. However, democratic nations have also been known to use it, an example being South Korea (Craik 2007: 1).

An obvious weakness with this approach is that supported art is chosen not for artistic merit but for its ability to achieve the regime's objectives. Great art or artists who do not meet with the regime's aims will not be supported or will need to acquiesce and cast their work in a manner that is congruent with its aims in order to garner support.[25] In the case of totalitarian regimes, a further weakness is that the goals of cultural policy are likely to be "revisionary" and ever-changing, reflecting the whims of a capricious ruler or ruling elite (Chartrand and McCaughey 1989: "Engineer", paragraph 1). The artist who is supported in engineer countries or regions thus struggles to ensure that his or her work is properly reflective of the accepted cultural view.

No regime, democratic or otherwise, can ever hope to completely control artistic output. Herein lies another weakness of the engineer model, from the regime's perspective. In the attempt to tightly control artistic output, engineer nations may unintentionally encourage the development of artistic 'undergrounds' that are either hostile to the regime's goals or at the very least do nothing to advance them (Chartrand and McCaughey 1989). While this might be advantageous for the purposes of art, it may serve to counter the political, social and economic imperatives of the nations and regions that employ this model.

2.3.5 Elite nurturer

The final model is the elite nurturer. Under this model, governments 'nurture' by giving direct funding to a select group of arts organisations, enabling them to bypass agencies such as the Australia Council. The elite nurturer model appears to encompass elements of both the architect and the patron model. The bypassing of agencies such as the Australia Council aligns with the architect approach, where funding is directly provided to the arts and artists by a bureaucracy. On the other hand, the choices as to which organisations to nurture are supposedly based on artistic merit and excellence, which is more in keeping with the objectives of the patron model. The creation and management of the National Portrait Gallery in Australia is an example of support that follows this approach (see Craik 2007:18).

One advantage of this approach is that the certainty and consistency of funding enables nurtured organisations to invest confidently in the art that they produce and enables greater dedication of resources and effort to artistic pursuit. The result is that nations or regions using the elite nurturer model can develop arts

Table 2.7 Models of government/public support for the arts*

Model	*Where Used*	*Policy Objective*	*Funding Mechanism*	*Strengths*	*Weaknesses*
Facilitator	United States	Diversity	Tax expenditures and incentives	Diversity of funding sources	Excellence not necessarily supported; valuation of tax costs; benefits for benefactors; calculation of tax cost
Patron	United Kingdom, Australia	Excellence and international standards	Arm's length peer evaluation	Support for excellence	Favours traditional elite art forms
Architect	France	Social welfare, industry assistance	Department and Ministry of Culture	Relief from box office dependence; secures training and career structure	Creative directives lead to stagnation and resistance
Engineer	Former Soviet countries, Cuba, Korea	Political education, national culture	Government ownership of artistic production	Focus creative energy to attain political goals	Subservience; underground; counter-intuitive outcomes
Elite Nurturer	Australia	Selective elite development	Direct government ongoing funding of cultural organisations	Encourage excellence, financial stability	Insulates organisations from external influences/forces

*Based on Craik (2007: 81)

companies and organisations to the highest artistic standards. On the other hand, it restricts public resources and support to a select group of organisations and people and can reinforce and support existing art forms at the expense of newer and more innovative activities.

2.4 Conclusion

The purpose of this chapter is to give an overview of the phenomenon of public support for the arts. From the presentation in this chapter, it is clear that governments of different political forms across the globe have undertaken measures to provide support to the arts. As was shown, there are many ways in which this is achieved, and there may also be differences with respect to policy objectives. It is often the case that governments use a combination of these approaches. For example, while the United States favours the facilitator approach, through the establishment of the NEA and other similar bodies at the state level, there is evidence of the patron model. Australia, on the other, hand has adopted what is essentially a patron model, but like its American cousin, it uses some facilitator policy levers to support the arts.

However, the presentation earlier in this chapter does not give any indication of whether there is, from an economic perspective, a rigorous rationale for the provision of public support. In the chapters that follow, the objective will be to undertake a thorough analysis of public support for the arts. Importantly, there will be an attempt to determine if rationales for support exist.

Notes

1 H. C 'Nugget' Coombs was the first Governor of the Reserve Bank of Australia, Australia's central bank. Peter Karmel was an economics professor who held positions at a number of Australian universities, including as vice-chancellor (president) of Flinders University and the Australian National University.

2 The 'History of the Canada Council', available on the Canada Council of the Arts website, shows that the original 1957 statute and the 1985 update shared the same object. (http://www.canadacouncil.ca/aboutus/Background/kd127229037949843750.htm#45, accessed 31 May 2012).

3 The aspect that makes its establishment pioneering will be discussed in section 2.3.1.

4 On this point and as an example, President Ronald Reagan notoriously sought to undo the work of his Republican predecessor and planned to abolish the NEA upon assuming office in 1981 (Honan 1988). See also Craik (2007: 12) for Australian examples.

5 A notable absence in this list is New Zealand. For completion, it should be noted that New Zealand too established an arts advisory and funding body in 1974, known as the Queen Elizabeth II Arts Council. That council was replaced with what is now known as Creative New Zealand, or by its more formal name, the Arts Council of New Zealand Toi Aotearoa. Creative New Zealand came into being with the passage of the *Arts Council of New Zealand Toi Aotearoa Act* 1994.

6 International comparisons of this type are notoriously fraught with difficulty, a point recognised by each of the report authors and by the Australia Council (2004). However, it is not the goal of this book to solve the riddle of intercountry comparison. For further information on the difficulties associated with intercountry comparison and suggested solutions, see Australia Council (2004).

7 See http://www.ifacca.org/membership/current_members/ for the complete list. See also http://www.culturalpolicies.net, a website of cultural policies and information developed by the Council of Europe, which lists 42 nations with public support policies and mechanisms (both accessed 30 May 2012).

8 For example, the city of Moreland in Melbourne's northern suburbs has a 'Social Development' area that is responsible for administering and managing the city's art and cultural activities (Moreland 2011: 29). A similar division exists in the city of Melbourne (Melbourne 2011: 26).

9 These three organisations include the Australian Film Commission, the Film Finance Corporation Australia and Film Australia Limited (Screen Australia 2009: 4).

10 In 2015, machinery of government changes from the newly elected Andrews Labor government in Victoria resulted in the replacement of Arts Victoria with a new body known as Creative Victoria. At the time of writing, it was not entirely clear what the exact function and responsibilities of this new organisation would be nor how they differ from Arts Victoria, but some clue can be gleaned from the Labor Party manifesto, which outlined a 'vision' for Creative Victoria to lead "investment activity in the creative sectors" (ALP Platform 2014: 79). This suggests that Creative Victoria will, in essence, provide an organisational 'umbrella' to coordinate and support not only the traditional arts but the so-called 'creative industries' more broadly (see Chapter 3, section 3.3.8 for more on the creative industries).

11 Local content requirements are common in many locations and have been used by many governments across the world. See Bhattacharjee and Mendel (2001).

12 The Australian commonwealth government also has laws that require Australian-funded films to employ a quota of Australian actors, thereby providing support to local artists. Recently, the commonwealth government considered the relaxation of such requirements. In response, the Australian actor Simon Burke claimed that such a relaxation would come at the expense of local talent. In essence, these laws are a form of public support for local actors and the arts (see http://www.nationaltimes.com.au/opinion/society-and-culture/australian-stories-need-to-be-told-by-our-people-20110630–1gsn9.html, accessed 29 March 2012)

13 The six jurisdictions are American Samoa, District of Columbia, Guam, Northern Marianas, Puerto Rico, and the US Virgin Islands. See National Assembly of State Arts Agencies, http://www.nasaa-arts.org/About/About-State-Arts-Agencies.php accessed 2 June 2012.

14 See National Assembly of State Arts Agencies, "About State Arts Agencies" page and Utah Arts Council "What We Do" page (http://www.nasaa-arts.org/About/About-State-Arts-Agencies.php and http://arts.utah.gov/about_us/what.html both accessed 2 June 2012).

15 To be sure, local government in the United States is sometimes responsible for the delivery of goods and services that in Australia would likely be the province of state and territory governments. For example, while Australian state governments are responsible for providing a police force, for building sports and arts facilities, for education funding and for public transport, in the United States much of this is given over to the local and municipal authorities. As an example, consider that the police force in New York, the famed NYPD, is provided and managed by the government of the city of New York.

16 Such a direct comparison is possible because the US-Australian dollar exchange rate operated at or near parity for much of this period.

17 Many of the intercountry comparison reports show that US direct funding to the arts is far lower on a *per capita* basis than Australia and other Western nations. Research conducted by the Canada Council in 2005 found that, on a *per capita* basis, funding to the Australia Council for the Arts was 14 times higher than funding provided to the National Endowment for the Arts. A 1998 survey by the Arts Council of England found

that *per capita* spending on the arts and museums in total was 4.3 times higher in Australia than in the United States (McCaughey 2005: 2, 5). These figures should be taken with the proverbial grain of salt, given the already-mentioned difficulty in undertaking intercountry comparisons.

18 That is, other than those provided by the NEH.

19 The Congressional Budget Office obtained this figure by summing funding for the arts and humanities, including (among others) to the Smithsonian (US$776 million), the Corporation for Public Broadcasting (US$422 million), the National Endowment for the Humanities (US$139 million), the National Endowment for the Arts (US$139 million), the National Gallery of Art (US$122 million), the John F. Kennedy Center for the Performing Arts (US$35 million) and the National Capital Arts and Cultural Affairs programme (CB0 2013: 88).

20 *Giving USA* reports are produced jointly by the Centre on Philanthropy at Indiana University and the Giving Institute, a body established in 1935 and formerly known the American Association of Fundraising Counsel, which promotes ethical and high standards in American philanthropy. For further information, see http://www.givingusareports.org/about.aspx and https://givinginstitute.org/about/, both accessed 5 January 2013.

21 Australia has film-specific tax incentive mechanisms. The Producer Offset, which replaced the 10A and 10BA tax incentive schemes in 2007, is a refundable tax offset accessible to Australian screen industry producers (see http://www.screenaustralia.gov.au/producer_offset/ and http://www.arts.gov.au/film-tv/tax-incentives accessed 4 June 2012).

22 Craik (2007) has presented the salient points of each of these models in tabular form, highlighting the strengths and weakness associated with each model as well as the policy objectives. See Table 2.7.

23 See Chapter 9 for more on this from a Veblenian perspective.

24 Kenneth Clark was speaking of public support in a general sense, but his fear would probably be increased markedly in architect model nations, where support and control is given directly to such a bureaucracy.

25 As an example of this point, take the Russian composer Dmitri Shostakovich, who as a result of political interference and duress amended his form of musical composition in order to meet the accepted forms set by Stalin's Soviet regime. Shostakovich is said to have written his *Symphony Number 5* in a manner that fitted within the 'proper' Soviet musical forms and to 'atone' for his earlier 'heretical' 1934 opera *Lady Macbeth*, which was accused of corrupting the Soviet spirit and not following the accepted Soviet line. That Shostakovich acquiesced to the Soviet regime is best understood through the clearly subservient "A Soviet Artist's Response to Just Criticism" subtitle that his Fifth Symphony carried, which, it seems, was designed to placate the regime and ensure that the composer avoided further duress or future purge (from *Shostakovich's Symphony No. 5*, Public Broadcasting Corporation, http://www.pbs.org/keepingscore/shostakovich-symphony-5.html, accessed 10 August 2012).

3 The economics of the arts

3.1 Introduction

Economists have 'meddled' in matters of the arts since at least the time of Adam Smith (Towse 1997b: xiii; De Marchi and Greene 2005; De Marchi 1999). Many years later and closer to our own times, Lord Keynes, a famous member of the Bloomsbury Group and first head of the Arts Council of Great Britain, displayed a keen interest in the arts. Keynes considered:

> that these things [the arts] cannot be successfully carried on if they depend on the motive of profit and financial success. The exploitation and incidental destruction of the divine gift of the public entertainer by prostituting it to the purpose of financial gain is one of the worser [*sic*] crimes of present-day capitalism. How the state could best play its proper part is hard to say. We must learn by trial and error. But anything would be better than the present system. The position today of artists of all sorts is disastrous.
>
> (Keynes 1936: 344)

As manager of what was then the 'temporary' Council for the Encouragement of Music and the Arts in 1942, Keynes helped turn that now forgotten body into the recognisable Arts Council of Great Britain. Keynes ensured that funding and support for the Arts Council came directly from the senior, central and powerful Treasury agency of the UK government, reflecting his understanding of the methods and machinery of government (Moggridge 2005: 538).

While these two examples demonstrate that economists have shown an interest in matters of the arts since at least the time of 'Adam' (Smith), it was not until the middle of the twentieth century that the arts would undergo what could be seriously termed rigorous economic analysis and that a separate strand of the economic discipline would be created. Keynes's views on the arts, as encapsulated in the quote in the previous paragraph, are indicative of the general thrust of economic inquiry into matters around the arts: namely, it is inquiry that is driven by the notion that the arts do not fare well if left to the devices of the market and by the desire to discover a case (or cases) for intervention.

The starting point for the 'economics of the arts', what is now sometimes termed 'cultural economics', is generally traced to the 1960s (Throsby and Withers 1979: 1), with Galbraith's 1960 article 'Economics and Art' (Galbraith 1960). However, the touchstone and wellspring, the 'big bang' that the discipline looks to as its theoretical progenitor, is found in the seminal 1966 work of Baumol and Bowen, *Performing Arts: The Economic Dilemma.*[1]

Since these beginnings in the 1960s, the economics of the arts has grown to become a distinct stream in economics. In 1973, the discipline grouped itself, and the Association of Cultural Economics was founded, and since 1977, the discipline has had a separate outlet for its voices in the *Journal of Cultural Economics* (Towse 1997b: xvi). Recognition has also come from the American Economic Association's *Journal of Economic Literature*, where the Economics of the Arts is listed under its category Z ("Other Special Topics", placing it in the company of other subcategories like religion!), as Z11, a subcategory of cultural economics (Z1) (Throsby 2001: xii).

The purpose of this chapter is to begin to outline some of the major theoretical developments that have occurred in economics of the arts. This task, while potentially daunting, has been lightened by the publication of two major anthologies of the economics of the arts (Towse 1997 and Towse 2007);[2] two surveys of the major literature (Throsby 1994 and Blaug 2001); the production of 'handbooks' with contributions from the field's major researchers (Towse 2003 and 2011; Ginsburgh and Throsby 2006 and 2014) that follow a similar volume edited by Klamer (1996); and the release of textbooks specifically written for the field (such as Heilbrun and Gray 2001; Throsby 2001; and Towse 2010).

The chapter commences by outlining what makes the economics of the arts 'the economics of the arts', including the 'economic' approach to the arts. From there, the chapter outlines some of the major research themes, setting the scene for the principle concern of this work in the next chapter, which is public support, its consideration and treatment within the field.

3.2 What makes the economics of the arts "the economics of the arts"?

A subdiscipline would, in general, be driven by or founded on an overarching theme or paradigm. Trade theorists, for example, are driven by comparative advantage, and their models and inquiries are built upon this premise. Can the same be said of the economics of the arts? Does it have "an intellectual core akin, say, to the concept of human capital in the economics of education and health economics"? (Towse 1997b: xvi) According to Towse (1997b) and Blaug (2001), if we base our thoughts on this definition, then probably no. The economics of the arts is not underpinned by a single major paradigm. In the absence of such a foundation, what is it that has enabled the field to develop its own journal and gain distinct recognition from the American Economic Association?

While it may not have an 'all-conquering' paradigm upon which to build its theoretical edifices, the economics of the arts is said to possess a number of 'strands' that are woven through the field and that help to turn what seem divergent inquiries into a distinctive and coherent subdiscipline (Towse 1997b: xvi).

The first of these strands (or characteristics) is said to be the nature of the product in question. Specifically, inquiries in the economics of the arts are said to concern themselves with goods and services (products) that have both a public good aspect (to differing degrees) and an 'experience' aspect. The first of these characteristics (public goods) is recognisable to any economist and needs little definition,[3] but what is meant by experience goods? In essence, this refers to the idea that taste for the arts is developed only by actual arts consumption, that the arts must be 'experienced' (Towse 1997b: xvii).

Baumol's disease is said to be the second strand that glues the subdiscipline together (Towse 1997b: xvii). More on this later, but in short, it refers to the rising costs faced by the performing arts relative to other industries. These rising costs are traced to the fixed labour requirements necessary to produce output. These fixed labour requirements lead to relatively lagging or nonexistent productivity gains. Thus, without productivity gains, the costs associated with the performing arts rise relative to other industries.

The final strand surrounds the economic case for public support for the arts and related policy recommendations (Towse 1997b: xvii). The discipline is replete with investigations that aim to determine whether a rigorous economic case can be made to support subvention for the arts. Inquiries regarding subvention also deliberate on the best way to provide such support and on the level or amount of support that leads to optimal outcomes.

These three strands aside, ultimately, the economics of the arts is a consideration of the arts from the perspective and interest of the economist. Generally, the economic approach is the neoclassical one, built on rational choice theory and the binary architecture of individual consumers and individual firms (Frey and Pommerehne 1989; Frey 1994).

The neoclassical economic perspective has two basic elements, the first of which is economic scarcity. The arts and those involved in their production and consumption are just as prey to this reality as those involved in the production of other goods and services. For example, to produce art or mount a performing arts production, an artist or performing arts firm must compete for scarce resources.

The second element of the neoclassical economic perspective is that of individual reductionism, or methodological individualism (Frey and Pommerehne 1989). The key features of this approach are as follows (Frey 1994: 38):

1. The analysis is based on the individual, and not the state, groups or society. This does not mean that societal- or group-based outcomes are not considered, or that there is no interaction between individual agents. On the contrary, the idea is that whole economy outcomes can be understood by examining the actions of individuals.
2. Individuals will act according to their individual preferences. These preferences are subject to the usual resource and budgetary constraints. Frey (1994: 38) adds a further constraint, namely the social and other 'norms' that individuals face and are subject to.

3. The third relates to self-interest. Individuals aim to optimise and will respond to incentives.
4. Finally, a change in the actions of an individual is traced by some to a change in his/her constraints and not a change in tastes or preferences. More on this in section 3.3.1, but, briefly, this is based on the new consumer theory approach that assumes preferences or tastes that are stable and the same (or similar) across individuals (Frey 1994: 38; Becker 1998; Stigler and Becker 1977; Throsby 1994: 53).[4]

3.3 Areas of investigation in the economics of the arts

The aim of this section is to provide an outline of some of the areas of research that have occurred in the economics of the arts since the publication of Baumol's and Bowen's ground-breaking work. Word limitations do not permit an account of each and every one of the research programmes in cultural economics. Such a pursuit is likely to take up many books, let alone a chapter section! Therefore, in the interests of editorial 'parsimony', I have opted not for 'completeness' but to build a chapter section that gives some sense regarding the breadth of the field's work and the issues that inspire it. More importantly, coupled with Chapter 4, this chapter section should furnish the reader with ample information to allow clear differentiation with the new Veblenian approach developed from Chapter 5 onwards.

With this in mind, I have chosen to provide information on 12 research areas, including taste formation; demand, supply and understanding the market; ticket pricing; the art market (meaning the market for paintings and the other visual arts); economic history and the arts; arts labour markets; Baumol's cost disease; the 'creative industries'; the role of the arts and culture in economic and regional development; digitisation, the Internet and the arts; copyright in the arts; and work to understand festivals and cultural events.

A notable absence is public support. This omission is more apparent than real, with public support given a brief introduction later in the chapter in preparation for a fuller presentation in Chapter 4.

3.3.1 Taste formation

Taste, or preference, is central to neoclassical consumer theory. In the economics of the arts, interest centres on understanding how an individual's taste for arts consumption is developed. How does one go from being a loather of Mozart to an aficionado? Why do some people choose to 'consume' a production of *Hamlet*, while for others such an experience is akin to undergoing root canal treatment without pain-numbing anaesthesia?

The neoclassical approach is built on a utilitarian architecture, the so-called pleasure-pain calculus, where consumer choices are driven by a desire to minimise pains and maximise pleasure. One of the earliest considerations of the utilitarian 'creed' was made by the classical economist John Stuart Mill. In *Utilitarianism*

(1863), Mill posited two possibilities for why some things provide greater pleasure than others. The first rationale is one of *quantum*, where the pleasure associated with a thing is directly attributable to its being in greater quantity. The more we consume of a good, the greater our pleasure. But to this, Mill added a *quality* dimension. A thing may provide greater pleasure not because of its amount but because of its quality: the higher the quality, the greater the pleasure (Mill 1863: 119).

Mill's introduction of a quality measure inevitably leads to a hierarchy of pleasures, where some are deemed high quality while others are low. But how is it that some pleasures are high while others are low? What is the provenance of this hierarchy?

Mill considered that man is endowed with "faculties more elevated" than his cousins in the animal kingdom (Mill 1863: 119). "Once made conscious" of his higher faculties, men do "not regard anything as happiness, which does not include their gratification" (Mill 1863: 119). Thus, the higher pleasures are those that appeal to man's higher faculties. The pleasures associated with these higher faculties may be "attended with a greater amount of discontent" and may be "capable . . . of [producing] more acute suffering" (Mills 1863: 120). But despite the potential for suffering, few men would forfeit the higher faculties and the pleasures associated with them to "sink into . . . a lower grade of existence" (Mill 1863: 120). No man who has been made aware of the pleasures associated with his higher faculties would be "changed into any of the lower animals", even if this was accompanied by a "full allowance of a beast's [lower] pleasures" (Mill 1863: 120).

It is not difficult to see how Mill's high and low pleasure calculus might be used to provide an account for taste in the arts. For example, a taste for Mozart might be explained as a thing that appeals to man's higher faculties. A person who loathes Hamlet might be considered a "fool" or "ignoramus" (Mill 1863: 120) who is bereft of the necessary intellectual faculties required to enable enjoyment of high quality things.

Mill's ideas imply that we can objectively differentiate pleasures, so that we can identify some as high quality and others as low. But such objective notions are fraught with difficulty: Who is to determine what is high and what is low, and on what basis? Perhaps because of this, such notions are no longer in vogue, and instead modern neoclassical approaches prefer to base their analyses on notions of consumer sovereignty. In such a perspective, there is no pretence to objectivity: We no longer say that one pleasure is high and another is low, since one individual's preferences are considered just as valid as another's. That a person loathes Hamlet is not explained as evidence of possession of lower faculties that make him unable to appreciate higher pleasures, but merely as a reflection of the person's own, valid preference structure.

Thus, returning to the questions posed at the beginning of this section, how do tastes change, and how do we explain differences in tastes between individuals? Traditional neoclassical approaches would answer the first question by suggesting that the sovereign individual's preference structure had changed, while the second would be explained as the result of different preference structures between individuals. Importantly, traditional neoclassical approaches consider these preferences as given, as *data*, outside the scope of economics. Understanding how these preferences or tastes are formed is not the job of economists, and instead this task is generally exogenised and delegated to other disciplines such as psychology, anthropology and sociology (Becker 1998: 25).

For some economists, the traditional neoclassical approach is undesirable (Stigler and Becker 1977). First, the exogenisation of taste, a central tenet and building block of consumer theory, represents an 'abrogation' of the responsibility of economists to understand and explain all facets of consumer behaviour (Stigler and Becker 1977: 112). But, a second problem with the traditional approach is that tastes or preferences cannot be observed. Being unobservable means that they cannot be measured (at least not directly), so that traditional hypotheses of consumer behaviour built on a platform of unstable and/or different tastes and preferences are difficult, if not impossible, to test (Stigler and Becker 1977: 112).

In their 1977 work, Stigler and Becker proposed an alternative approach that they claimed could be traced to Alfred Marshall.[5] The Becker-Stigler approach holds that tastes do not "change capriciously nor differ importantly between people" (Stigler and Becker 1977: 112); in other words, tastes are said to be stable and essentially the same between different individuals. The assumption of a 'constancy' and 'equivalence' of preferences between individuals removes the need to consider changes or differences in *unobservable* individual tastes or preference structures to explain consumer behaviour. The assertion is that this assumption allows consumer choices to be explained through changes in directly *observable* phenomena such as "prices and income" (Stigler and Becker 1977: 112).[6]

Becker and Stigler built their approach on 'Z' theory (Stigler and Becker 1977: 113; Cowen 1989: 139), which can be summarised in the following three propositions (Cowen 1989: 140):

1. A utility function is dependent on Z goods, and not actual physical commodities X, and consumers maximise this utility function.
2. X commodities are used to produce Z goods, as represented by a household production function.
3. The taste for Z goods is constant and stable among all people and at all times.

In the Becker-Stigler approach, consumers gain utility not from the actual commodities they purchase but rather from the way in which these commodities are transformed into Z goods through the household production function.[7] In other words, Z goods are the source of utility. The household production function takes the X physical commodities and transforms them into Z goods with the aid of the consumer's time and skill.[8]

Given that Z goods are not exchanged or sold in markets, what do Becker and Stigler mean when they talk of observable prices for Z commodities? While Z goods do not have actual prices, they are said to have 'shadow prices' which are determined by the costs associated with their production (Stigler and Becker 1977: 113). It is to changes in these shadow prices that consumers respond and which determine their consumption choices. With unobservable preferences assumed to be stable, equivalent and fixed, Becker and Stigler claim that economists can concentrate on understanding consumer behaviour by focusing on observable factors such as the prices of X goods and, from this, derivable shadow prices.[9]

The potential application of the Becker and Stigler approach for understanding taste for the arts is apparent. As an example, consider the case of addiction. Traditional consumer theory would explain addiction as a change in consumer tastes or preference structure. So, for example, a consumer who previously loathed Mozart and who now finds himself 'addicted' has become so because his taste or preference structure has changed. On the other hand, in the new consumer theory, the consumer listens to Mozart, the X good, to produce a Z good, such as relaxation (Cowen 1989: 140). Exposure to Mozart leads the consumer to gain a stock of knowledge, or (personal) human capital. This increased knowledge means that the next time the consumer listens to Mozart to gain relaxation he will be facing lower shadow prices, since his increased stock of knowledge lowers the costs related to the production of the Z good, relaxation. Each time he listens to Mozart, his human capital increases, lowering the costs associated with the production of relaxation. In this way, the cycle continues, and further exposure to Mozart leads to even lower shadow prices, manifesting itself as Mozart addiction (Throsby 1994: 53).

As one would expect, not all have shown enthusiasm for the newer approach. Cowen has argued that the assumption of constant taste merely shifts the emphasis back onto the constraints that individuals face and argues that Z goods essentially amount to what we usually think of as tastes (Cowen 1989: 145–146). The model does nothing to explain a taste for relaxation, its origin or how it comes to be. The problem is again, essentially, exogenised.

Blaug (2001) has questioned the plausibility of the Stigler and Becker approach by pointing to studies in the economics of the arts that have 'profiled' arts audiences. These profiles invariably show that arts audiences tend to be "skewed to the right in income, age, occupation, and levels of education and indeed differ more markedly in years of schooling achieved than in any other personal characteristic" (Blaug 2001: 125). The results from these audience profiles suggest that tastes do differ between groups and people. Other studies (O'Hagan 1996; Morrison and West 1986) have also shown that those with an early arts education will generally have a participation in the arts later in life. If tastes were indeed constant and stable among consumers, this is not an outcome one would expect. It suggests instead that tastes are unstable (and perhaps also explains my own continued interest in the arts).

Finally, the so-called benefits provided by new consumer theory, in particular to limiting our analyses to only those elements that are observable, have been questioned:

> Imagine someone suggesting that the best way to gain understanding of literature is by focusing only on observable phenomena. We could watch lots of people reading, follow them around in bookstores, study the chemical composition of the books themselves, and so on. But we would never explore

what these books meant to anyone – including ourselves – because this is "unobservable".

(Callahan 2001: paragraph 20)

Despite these criticisms of the new consumer theory, Throsby considers that "the endogenization of tastes in economic models is likely to be essential if any progress is to be made in explaining demand for the arts" (Throsby 1994: 53).

Throsby's affirmations aside, I am sympathetic to the dismissals from Cowen and Callahan. Contrary to their assertions, Becker and Stigler offer no explanation for the development of taste. In the relaxation example, our desire for this so-called Z good is simply taken as given. Presumably, an explanation for its origins would thus yet again be farmed out to other disciplines. Further, while the suggestion is that shadow prices are derivable from directly observable factors like the prices of X goods, the household production function, pivotal to understanding how the Z good is produced, may not be so easily understood or observable. We have replaced one set of unobservable phenomena, namely tastes, with another nebulous concept, the household production function, suggesting that the so-called advantages of this approach are more apparent than real.

3.3.2 Understanding the arts market

A number of works in the field of the economics of the arts have centred on understanding the nature of the market for the arts based on the usual supply and demand dichotomy.

On the demand side, research has ranged from Withers' (1980) econometric analysis of demand for the performing arts in the presence of unbalanced growth (Baumol's disease) to studies of the demand for cinema (Cameron 1990), examinations of museum visitors (Dickenson 1992) and Lévy-Garboua's and Montmarquette's (1996) econometric work analysing theatre demand. Lévy-Garboua's and Montmarquette's analysis considers the usual factors of income and price but also analyses demand through variables such as the quality of the production and the effects of previous experience and knowledge of the arts. While Lévy-Garboua's and Monmarquette's analysis makes no reference, it should be noted that quality factors were considered by economists such as Carl Christian von Weizsäcker many years earlier.[10]

Towse (1997: Volume 1) categorises supply-side analysis into three broad themes: the performing arts, museums and the heritage industries, and the media industries. The analysis tends to focus on firms involved in the supply of the arts and consideration of the output decisions and the impacts of such decisions.

Some analysis of performing arts firms has sought to determine cost functions. So, for example, Gapinski (1980: 285) poses the question "Are there laws of production?" for the production of culture. His analysis posits an analysis of a production function for a nonprofit firm and provides econometric analysis.

Peacock (1976) considers the output of London orchestras between 1966 and 1975. Peacock finds that these orchestras were not driven by the profit or commercial motive but instead measured their 'success' using 'social indicators' (which cannot be expressed in terms of money) (Peacock 1976: 298). Still in London, Blaug (1978) considers the question of opera seat prices at Covent Garden and considers how output choices (such as which productions to mount) affect the seat prices that are charged. Blaug concludes that high seat prices are linked to the opera house's artistic policy (1978: 318).

Studies into museums and heritage are of a similar style. The ubiquitous Peacock works with Godfrey to consider the economics of museums and galleries in the United Kingdom (Peacock and Godfrey 1974). Their work begins with a survey of the finances of national museums and galleries in the United Kingdom, moving to a consideration of rationales for public support and subsidy and of the then-government's policy towards charging for entry. Other examples of museum studies include Paulus (2003), who considers museums in the United States and France and the evaluation measures used in the two countries to determine their performance and an interesting article by Frey (1994a), who "applies economic thinking to the arts", by which he means the neoclassical economic model, to "enlighten the social aspects of art" (Frey 1994a: 376). Frey notes that many museums have large stocks of art that are not displayed, meaning that the benefits in terms of, say, enjoyment by viewers are not realised. This practice represents an opportunity cost to the museum and presumably to viewers. Frey outlines a case where museum managers could sell works that are not displayed and apply the funds from such sales towards other museum endeavours. He proposes that museums be made more independent bodies that are freely able to buy and sell their stock of art and that government support and subsidy be determined by consideration of the social value produced by the museum (Frey 1994a: 381).

Heritage refers to preserving the past. The economic questions posed by this are immediately apparent. Examples include how to determine what should be preserved, how heritage should be supplied and the best way to preserve heritage. Examples of work in this area include Peacock (1994), Throsby (1997) and Benhamou (1996, 2003a and 2004).

The media industries include film, video, broadcasting and publishing (Towse 1997b: xvi). In 1966, at the time of Baumol and Bowen's influential work, Ronald Coase, the Nobel Prize-winning economist famous for the Coase theorem, published an analysis of the role that the economics of broadcasting had in the development of government policy (Coase 1966: 427). Withers (1983) examined the provision of broadcasting, in particular public broadcasting and the economic rationale for its provision. A ground for intervention noted by Withers is "the persuasive and pervasive role of broadcasting in our society . . . and the [lack] of incentive by commercial producers to take account of the social and political effects" of their broadcasting activity (Withers 1983: 449). The intervention manifests itself in what he terms public enterprise broadcasting, and he gives the Australian example, which includes a mix of public and commercial broadcasting.

3.3.3 Ticket pricing

Towse (2007) recognises ticket pricing as an area of research, updating its omission in the 1997 publication by allocating a separate section in the 2007 compilation.[11] Two works serve to give an idea of the avenues of research being followed here.

To begin with, much of the work in ticket pricing has centred on price discrimination in tickets. In traditional undergraduate microeconomic courses, price discrimination is presented as part of the study of the monopolist, in particular to show that such an approach would render the monopolist at least as efficient as perfect competition. Rosen and Rosenfield (1997) note, however, that price discrimination is not limited to the case of monopolists. Rather, price discrimination is visible in many monopolistically competitive industries, including airlines and hotels (1997: 127).[12] In terms of the arts, the problem presented by Rosen and Rosenfield is that of a "facility" that has two categories of seats, high quality and low quality. They also consider the price of complementary goods (such as food or drinks) that are sold at the venue and the interplay between these prices and those of the tickets.

Pascale Courty (2003) considers the case of ticket brokers who are involved in ticket reselling, such as can be readily found in places like London's Leicester Square. Courty presents an analysis of a primary market for tickets where an act or promoter advertises and sells tickets though the box office to the public and a secondary market where tickets are sold either through brokers at a physical location (such as Leicester Square) or, increasingly, through platforms such as *eBay* (Courty 2003: 153–154). Courty develops a model with two kinds of consumers: those who wish to wait until the last minute to obtain a ticket and those who wish to purchase the ticket in advance. These differences are used to explain the presence of brokers (Courty 2003: 158).

The research undertaken in this area is of special interest given that many firms operating in the arts act as nonprofit organisations. Indeed, in the performing arts, 'for-profit' firms, at least as 'permanent fixtures', seem mostly limited to New York's Broadway and London's West End. Presumably, the choices made in their ticketing policy would reflect their profit status. As such, analysis of ticket pricing can perhaps shed light on the choices made by both for-profit and nonprofit firms in their artistic output decisions and present opportunities for future research (see Hansmann 1981).

3.3.4 Art markets

The economics of arts would be incomplete without an investigation into the nature of the market for art. By 'art' here I mean what is often termed the 'fine arts'. These include the visual arts, such as painting and sculpture.

Economists working in the discipline have adopted tools developed to understand financial markets to shed some light on prices in the art market. Baumol (1986) uses the efficient market hypothesis to determine prices for art works. Art markets, like financial markets, are characterised as following a 'random walk' (Baumol 1986: 550). Here, markets use all available information at any point in time, eliminating profit opportunities and making prices unpredictable. In Baumol's analysis, art market unpredictability is due to the ephemeral and capricious nature of taste in art markets, which are characterised as ever chasing the latest fads (Baumol 1986: 553). These ever-changing fads and their ephemeral nature make price predictability difficult; hence the random walk.[13]

Ekelund, Ressler and Watson (2000) produced a seemingly 'macabre' paper (at least for artists!) that considers the "death-effect" on the prices paid for art. They considered the economic aspects of the cliché that the prices for an artist's works increase after his death. This cliché is often reduced to a very simple supply-demand analysis where, *prima facie*, the now fixed supply should lead to a rise in price. While the limited supply will no doubt be a factor, a complete picture will only develop after considering demand-side features. The demand feature of interest to these researchers is the inability of living artists to convince those who demand their work that it will not be " 'spoiled' in the future by 'overproduction' " (Ekelund, Ressler and Watson 2000: 367). Dead artists, being dead, of course do not have such problems in convincing potential clients of overproduction!

Art market analysis has also considered art as an investment. An example includes Mei and Moses (2002), who developed an index of art prices, with sub-indices for American, Old Master, Impressionist and Modern paintings and then used these to compare art investment to financial investment. Their analysis found that art provides returns that are below those associated with stocks (Mei and Moses 2002: 363), echoing previous work in this area (Frey and Eichenberger 1995, see also Baumol 1986: 552). Another example is Mandel (2014), who uses international trade flow data to determine whether art purchases would more properly be characterised not as investment but as consumption activity. Mandel finds the demand for art does not appear to move "in tandem with other investment flows", which points to a "relatively weak" investment motive, suggesting that "the average art buyer" would on the whole be best characterised not as an investor but as a consumer (Mandel 2014: 255–256).

3.3.5 Economic history

To plan for the future one must look to the past, so the saying goes. And so, too, economists working to understand the workings of the arts have turned to economic history, the study of the arts from a past perspective, in order to gain some insight into how such activities were organised by peoples long ago (or sometimes not so long ago) and to see if we might learn something from them that we can apply today. A few examples will serve to illustrate the nature of such output.

Baumol can again lay some claim to parentage for this line of investigation. His 1972 work with Oates (Baumol and Oates 1972) on the London theatre during Elizabethan and Jacobean times has been credited as the starting point (Blaug 2001: 129). Right up to its closure by Cromwell's Protectorate forces in 1642, the London theatre of the time had little subsidy and was characterised by theatrical productions that could prove profitable with only a two-week run (Baumol and Oates 1972: 3). Baumol and Oates relied on inference gained from surviving plays for much of their data (Baumol and Oates 1972: 4). From this they concluded that the flurry of theatrical activity during this period could be explained by low real wages arising from high levels of inflation at the time. The so-called 'Tudor inflation' had a high impact on prices, but one price that was not readily affected was wages, which changed rather more slowly (Baumol and Oates 1972: 16–18). Thus, for labour-intensive theatre production, low wages meant lower relative production costs, helping to keep admission prices and the costs of a 'night at the theatre' down (Baumol and Oates 1972: 21).

Rosselli (1989) outlines the evolution of Italian opera singers from being paid servants reliant on a princely or ducal patron to becoming full-fledged professionals able to obtain a price for their services on an "open market" (Rosselli 1989: 37). Rosselli considers three periods, the first, commencing circa 1600, where singers were dependent on a patron (usually an aristocrat of some sort) for funds and 'protection'; the second occurred between 1685 and 1715 and is a transition period where singers begin to display greater independence; and the third is characterised as the "coming of a market for the services of an opera singer" (Rosselli 1989: 58). McGuiness (2004) does for music what Rosselli did for opera, tracing the development of music in London during the eighteenth century from being a status symbol to its transformation into a commodity.

Not all research into the economic history of the arts concerns the performing arts. Examples include Montias's (1979 and 2004) record of art activity during the seventeenth century in Holland and De Marchi's (2004) analysis of the rules attached to auctions for paintings in London during the same century, which follows similar work he developed jointly with Van Miegroet (De Marchi and Van Miegroet 2000). Montias's work provides background to the art industry and market in seventeenth-century Delft, in particular the Guild of St Lucas in Delft, which "encompassed painters, glassmakers, book printers and sellers, art dealers, embroiders, faienciers and sculptors" (Montias 1979: 70).[14] Montias's work gives an idea of the earning power of an artisan at the time and compares it to the cost of staple goods such as housing and bread, the cost to train a boy to become a master painter or embroiderer, and the taxes paid by artists and artisans (Montias 1979: 70, 76 and 80).

3.3.6 Labour

Towse (1997: Volume 2) includes nine publications on the subject of labour, and her 2007 volume updates this with a further four. When one thinks of the starting point for the field, the development of Baumol's disease, laying as it does much of the blame for the financial ills (crises) plaguing the performing arts on its labour-intensity and concomitant productivity issues, it is understandable that the nature of labour markets for the arts would be examined.

The traditional, perhaps romantic, view of artists is to see them as struggling, starving, noble beings who find it difficult to make a subsistence level of income and receive little if any recognition during their lifetime. How does this view square with the superstar, one who is, to borrow a term from economics, at the 'commanding heights' of his field of artistic endeavour? It is too easy to dismiss the superstar as less than an artist, as one who 'sells out' or has little artistic integrity, but examples from history can challenge this. Mozart may have died a poor man, but at the risk of anachronism, for his era, he represents in many respects what could be termed a superstar. His poverty seems to owe more to a gambling addiction than a lack of income or recognition. In more modern times, Picasso represents a superstar in the fine arts who achieved artistic respect, was a leader of an artistic movement and was remunerated handsomely for his efforts. It would be a brave (and in my opinion, foolish) person to consider these two as examples of artistic 'sell-outs'.

This mythology has been tested and researched using the tools of economic inquiry. Rosen (1981) and MacDonald (1988) have both sought to understand the economic features of superstardom, while Filer (1986) has questioned the verisimilitude and mythology surrounding the notion of the starving artist – and concludes it to be a myth (Filer 1986: 244; see also Benhamou 2003: 71). Using 1980 census data, Filer concluded that, on average, artist earnings are in step with those of other workers, and, importantly, they align with workers who possess similar training and personal characteristics, such as age.

When undertaking my music degree studies at the Victorian College of the Arts, I often heard it said that the arts world is representative of the sexism present in wider society; indeed, some would claim that sexism was more prevalent in the 'arts world'. As 'proof' of this, many of my contemporaries would point to the lack of female composers. Cowen (1996) considered gender issues in arts labour markets and outcomes for women and men, testing whether differences in the outcomes for men and women in the arts can be attributed to, *inter alia*, genetics, training opportunities or discrimination. He concludes that historical evidence supports the sexism or discrimination hypothesis (Cowen 1996: 463). The findings in the arts are certainly consistent with the ideas developed by the Australian feminist scholar Germaine Greer, who, in an interview to discuss her seminal work *The Female Eunuch*, expressed the subjugation of women in husbandry terms, stating that "Like beasts . . . who are castrated . . . in order to serve their masters, . . . women have been cut off from their capacity for action" (in Weintraub 1971: paragraph 12). Based on Cowen's work, it seems, sadly, that this castrated female capacity applies all too well in the case of the arts.

Some arts economists (Throsby 1994a; Caserta and Cuccia 2001) have considered labour markets in the arts in a more general sense than the special cases or curiosities mentioned. In standard or general models, labour supply is assumed to be a source of disutility: It is sold merely to earn an income and enable a living. But sometimes this assumption is amended, so that some labour activities are assumed not to provide disutility but to give satisfaction. In these cases, workers receive pleasure not just from the income associated with the sale of their labour but also from the process of labour itself. This recognises that man (and indeed woman) has a "need for creative work" and his (and her) "well-being" is linked to the "achievement of intrinsically rewarding work" (Spencer 2009: xviii). Thus, work is not "merely as a means to consumption", or a source of disutility, "but also as an end in itself" (Spencer 2009: xvii).[15]

Suppose that this assumption was carried to the arts, so that artists derive satisfaction from the provision of their artistic labour. It is not difficult to see that, even in the face of falling wages, artists would choose not to decrease their supply of labour. Throsby (1994a) has explained this by suggesting that artistic labour is supplied for two reasons. The first reason is consistent with that present in standard models of labour supply: Namely, artists sell labour in order to make a living. But in addition to this, artists supply labour because of an unyielding desire and need to produce art. Thus, the supply of artist labour is determined by the interaction between these two forces.

This kind of modelling enables temporal elements to be introduced, so that at different points in the artist's life either one of these forces may prove more dominant. This is a point recognised by Caserta and Cuccia (2001), who follow Throsby by proposing three possible routes by which this might occur. The first is a human capital approach, the second is based on a consideration of household production, while the third they term 'evolutionary'. In short, the first two approaches assume that artist labour supply decisions are based on a desire to maximise utility over the artist's lifetime, so that at some points one or the other of the two forces proves more beneficial in ensuring optimum lifetime utility. The so-called evolutionary approach assumes an open-ended system, meaning that the final outcome cannot be determined. Using this approach, an artist does not seek to maximise utility over a lifetime but instead continually searches for 'local maxima', that is, for maxima at different points of their lives.

3.3.7 Baumol's cost disease

'Baumol's Disease', also known as the 'Cost Disease', 'Baumol's Cost Disease', 'Baumol's Law' and the 'Baumol Effect', was first developed by both Baumol and Bowen (but, perhaps unfairly, has lost the second investigator's name in the 'ailment's' title) (Baumol and Bowen 1965). In Baumol's words, the disease can be envisaged as follows:

> Any economic activity affected by it will tend to rise in cost persistently and at a rate faster than the economy's rate of inflation, obviously leading to financial pressures for anyone who supplies the product. Orchestral music is a prime example. The reason the problem arises is that orchestras experience little or no labor-saving innovation – no growth in productivity. A Haydn symphony written to be performed by 30 musicians and lasting one-half an hour will require 15 person-hours of human labor for an "authentic" performance, no less than it did at the end of the 18th century. But elsewhere in the economy it takes less and less labor every year to produce a product. The amount of labor needed to produce an automobile declines more than three percent each year, on the average.
>
> (Baumol 1996: 52–53)

From this, we can see that performing arts firms are beset by rising unit costs resulting from productivity lags in labour, meaning that "costs per performance have risen more rapidly than costs of other activities in the economy as a whole" (Baumol and Bowen 1966: 104). In contrast, in the general economy, productivity improvements would be expected to lead to lower unit costs.

What causes this labour productivity lag? Let us answer this by first considering labour productivity and the factors that contribute to it. Labour productivity is defined as output per worker in some defined unit of work time (usually an hour). In most industries, labour productivity has shown a steady increase over time. Increases in productivity have arisen (and still do) from a number of sources, including improvements in the state of technology; increases in the ratio of capital to labour; improvements in labour skill, such as those that accrue from improvements in the general level of education; improvements in production and management techniques; and economies of scale. The oft-cited comparison and example (apart from automobiles) is the production of watches, which has seen considerable improvement in labour productivity (Snowball 2007: 16).

Many industries facing rising labour unit costs can mitigate this by increasing labour productivity, by, for example substituting other factors of production in their production processes or adopting newer technologies. Thus the level of labour required for a given level of output generally declines over time. But the performing arts have little recourse to such measures to improve labour productivity. Take, as an example, a string quartet. To perform such a piece in 1800 took four musicians. To perform it today still takes four musicians. In other words, there has been no labour productivity improvement, and the nature of the good means that there is little or no scope to realise such gains.

The 'problem' for the performing arts, however, is that they operate in the economy as a whole and as such must compete with other firms for the resources used in production. Thus, without the productivity benefits experienced by other firms, their costs will increase relative to costs in other industries. Turning to Baumol again:

> This means that if wages rise at more or less the same rate in car production and in orchestras, then clearly, the cost per performance must rise faster than the cost per car, because in car production rising wages are offset by the reduced use of labor per car, while in orchestras there are few such offsets. Thus, orchestra costs are condemned to rise every year, cumulatively, at a rate faster than the average of the economy's prices; in other words, faster than the rate of inflation.
>
> (Baumol 1996: 53)

Performing arts firms must offer wages to artists at rates that enable them to compete with other industries, meaning that wages in the performing arts labour market must rise "by the same proportion as wages in the general economy to enable the arts industry to hire the workers it needs to carry on" (Heilbrun 2003: 92). The rub, however, is that because there is no avenue for productivity gain, we witness the previously mentioned rising unit costs in the performing arts sector, with the implication being an 'earnings gap'. The earnings gap refers to the situation where costs continue to rise as against revenues, which have "no in built growth mechanism" (Heilbrun 2003: 95). Because the performing arts cannot – both by definition and in reality – mitigate costs by, for example, adopting new production techniques (it will always take four players to perform a quartet, now and forever, amen!), the 'earnings gap' grows continuously. "As wages go up, there is no productivity offset to rising costs. So the costs and the prices of these things go up far faster than the average good or service in any industrialised country" (Baumol 1995: 53). This is used to explain the level of financial crisis that besets and is so often associated with so many performing arts firms.

The importance of Baumol's disease to the economics of the arts has already been stated not only as the theoretical starting point for the economics of the arts but also as one of the three strands that ties the field together (Towse 1997a: xviii). Since 1966, the scope and use of Baumol's disease has broadened from the performing arts to other industries. The ever-resourceful Towse has compiled a tome containing major works in the study of Baumol's disease (Towse 1997a) that have been penned by Baumol, both as a single author or jointly with other researchers. A glance at works in the compilation shows that Baumol's own analysis of the disease grew from his original concern with the performing arts to other areas such as health care and education (Towse 1997a; Baumol 1993). It is easy to see that it could also be readily applied to understand the rising costs of childcare.

As an argument for support and subsidy, the effectiveness of Baumol's disease is left to later analysis in Chapter 4. For now, it suffices to reiterate that Baumol's disease is clearly an important area of research in the economics of the arts.

3.3.8 The creative industries

In 2014, the Andrews Labor government in the Australian state of Victoria swore in Victoria's first minister for creative industries (Creative Victoria 2015). The announcement of the new portfolio almost overshadowed the absence of another, namely, that of the arts. While ostensibly an absence, the minister expressed otherwise, characterising his portfolio in 'Venn' terms, with the arts a subset of a creative industries[16] 'universal set'.

In many ways, the transformation of the arts portfolio into one with a larger creative industries remit corresponds with a similar growth in cultural economics, which has expanded its gaze from a desire to understand the economics pertaining to the operation and function of the traditional arts to a consideration of the so-called creative industries. This shift forms part of a larger trend in cultural economics away from the traditional confines of public support for the traditional arts towards a broader agenda where creativity is seen as a source of innovation, growth and prosperity. Implicit in this is the recognition that good policy will be best achieved only once the function and corresponding economic and cultural value of the creative industries is properly understood (Throsby 2010: i).

Few would disagree that many, if not all, human endeavour has a creative element attached to it, opening the possibility for all industries to be deemed 'creative'. An all-encompassing approach like this is likely to be too broad to provide useful or nuanced insights, making it unlikely that this is the intention behind the creative industries term. Governments and officialdoms seem instead to define the creative industries by identification of discrete industry sectors that are 'quintessentially' creative, such as and including the arts, screen industries, digital games, design, advertising, crafts and architecture (Foley 2015; see also DCMS 2001 and UNCTAD 2008). This approach does not capture or consider the entirety of human creative endeavour but rather limits it to industries closely related to what are traditionally known as the arts.

While governments and officialdoms seem to prefer definition through industry listing, [17] the economics of the arts appears to adopt an approach that relies not upon a 'register' but upon identifying the presence of particular characteristics or activities. That is, the creative industries are those with firms that "mass-produce goods and services with sufficient artistic content to be considered creative" or "contain a substantial element of artistic or creative endeavour" (Towse 2011: 125; Caves 2000: vii, 2; Towse 2010: 376; Towse 2010a: 462; see also Towse 2014: Chapter 6 and Potts *et al* 2008). Towse (2011) highlights two further identifying characteristics, including high fixed costs and negligible (or even zero) marginal costs[18] coupled with a highly uncertain and risky future regarding output. [19]

The 'identification' approach of cultural economics certainly permits the analysis to encompass a large number of sectors, from medicine to music recording, each with its own version of the creative element. But a glance through the works of cultural economics shows that, in practice, it too focuses on industries like "television, the film and cinematic industries, music and sound recordings, book and magazine publishing, fashion, advertising, design and video games" whose output has "cultural artistic or . . . entertainment value" (Caves 2000: viii, 1; Towse 2011: 125). Indeed, Throsby has characterised the creative industries as a series of concentric circles, with the traditional arts forming a creative core surrounded by outer circles whose constituent industries include such things as advertising, architecture and design. These 'outer' industries are said to employ creative inputs in the production of goods that, while not 'wholly' cultural, have some artistic or creative content (Throsby 2001: 112–113).

Cultural economics' interest in the workings of the creative industries can be traced to at least 1981 and the article *Policy and the Arts: the Forgotten Cultural Industries* by the late Augustin Girard, the person widely regarded as the father of France's Cultural Ministry (Gordon 2009). Despite this early interest, Richard Caves's *Creative Industries: Contracts Between Art and Commerce* (2000) is generally considered the first major work to attempt to understand and explain the machinations of the creative sectors (Moeran and Pedersen 2012: 1). Caves begins his analysis by noting that to produce and market their wares, artists and creators must avail themselves of the skills and input of 'ordinary' workers:

> Artists of all types are engaged in creative processes and tasks that come to completion only with the collaboration of "humdrum" (or "ordinary") partners. The painter needs an art dealer, the novelist a publisher. The cinema film requires a number of actors, a director, screenwriter . . . and many others.
>
> (Caves 2000: 1)

The support of the 'humdrum' worker – whose efforts are not 'directly' creative, but allow the artist to avoid the 'mundane' and focus on creative action – enables the creative artisan to function and produce output. In essence, the creative industries are made up of the relationships and processes between these two entities.

Perhaps the most important of the 'humdrum' workers is the 'gatekeeper', the person upon whose shoulders sits the burden for selecting which artists to 'take to market' and which to reject (Caves 2000: 21; Towse 2011: 129). Examples include the gallery owner, the film studio executive, the book publisher and the music producer. The gatekeepers' motivations vary. Some are driven by a yearning to advance the cause of art, while others brutally focus on a desire for profit above all other considerations. Whatever the case, it is the gatekeepers' privilege to decide which artistic endeavours to produce and which to discard.

The questions for economics include: How have the relationships between the humdrum and the artisan come about? What forces direct their interactions? *How* do they interact? And how have firm and industry structures developed? These questions enjoin cultural economists to look more broadly than public support for the arts and to instead identify the forces and processes that shape the relationships, structure and organisation of the industry sectors within which artists operate.

Caves begins by making the observation that interactions between humdrum workers and artists (or indeed between artist and artist or humdrum and humdrum) are made manifest through 'deals'. Deals can be formal, written instruments or take the form of a 'handshake' agreement. Whatever their form, they lend themselves to consideration and analysis through *contract theory*. Contract theory helps to explain *why* deals are struck the way they are, as well as providing some insight into their form and structure.[20] It can help to explain simple two party deals (such as that between an artist and a gallery owner) or more complex deals with multiple players (such as occurs in film production). But while contract theory serves to explain contracts and deals, it cannot on its own explain *how* the parties to these contracts find and interact with one another; nor can it help explain why some industries enjoy the presence of multiple firms while others are dominated by a monopolist. Further, it cannot explain why some deals take place within a single firm while others take place between discrete, independent entities. To answer these sorts of questions, Caves turns to *industrial organisation theory*.

Caves innovation was the marrying of these two ideas "that have seen little application" in the creative industries to shed light on why "some deals and contracts are structured the way they are; why some creative activities occur in ongoing organizations ('firms'), and others in one-off deals ('the market')" (Caves 2000: 1–2). He shows their usefulness through increasingly complex settings, beginning with the production and supply of creative goods involving two players to increasingly complex production processes like those in the film sector.

While Caves's work is indeed seminal, it is not alone, and since 2000, many others have made efforts to understand the nature and operation of the creative industries. Examples include Hesmondhalgh (2002) and Hesmondhalgh and Pratt (2005), who approach the subject from the vantage of sociology; Throsby (2010), who is concerned with issues around policy development and the benefits deriving from a thorough understanding of the creative sector; Moeran and Pedersen (2012), who look at the role of festivals in the operation of the creative sector; Potts (2011), who presents an "evolutionary economics of [the] creative industries" approach (Potts 2011: 1); and Hartley, Potts *et al* (2013), who take an interdisciplinary approach. Finally, Richard Florida's highly influential *The Rise of the Creative Class* (2002) considers an eponymous creative class, a "fast-growing, highly educated, and well-paid segment of the work force", and its pivotal role in the economic, social and cultural development and wellbeing of society (Florida 2002a).

3.3.9 The arts and culture in economic and regional development

Richard Florida, whose work ended the preceding section, once dubbed Canada's move to allow same-sex marriage "one of the great talent attraction packages of the last hundred years" (in Louv 2003: paragraph 3). To Florida's thinking, the expansion of the marriage franchise was not merely the extension of civil and human rights to a long-oppressed minority but a case of government policy to promote economic development. Its power as an economic development tool lay in its ability to herald Canada's social tolerance, this act supposedly making Canada attractive to the creative class. Since this class plays a central role in economic and social development, any policy that creates the circumstances for its attraction is one that will result in Canada's (or any other region's) economic growth and prosperity.

Some may quibble with Florida's assessment, and personally, I find the association of civil and human rights with economic development cynical, dangerous and offensive. But the core of Florida's statement, the notion that the arts and creative industries are or can be vehicles for urban and regional economic development, is one that has piqued the minds of many within the economics of the arts.

In some ways, the role and impact of the arts in urban and regional development has been a feature of the economics of the arts since the beginning, albeit mostly conceived as a positive externality resulting from the provision of public support (see Chapter 4). But as previously noted in the case of the creative industries, the economics of the arts has moved beyond the limited case of public support to consider the role of the arts and culture in urban and regional development and regeneration more broadly.

An important work in this area is Throsby (2001), who begins with a 'generous' definition of culture constrained not by traditional notions of the arts but instead viewed as a "set of values beliefs, traditions [and] customs" that "serve to identify and bind a group together" (Throsby 2001: 63). Throsby makes the not unreasonable proposition that culture acts upon the way individuals and groups act and think, and, as a consequence, on economic activities and outcomes. He then presents three broad ways by which culture might direct economic activity and development. First, culture can affect *efficiency*, by, for example, shaping the way decisions are made or influencing the organisation of production. Second, culture directs social views on *equity*, appearing in the way that society's spoils are shared and distributed. Finally, culture determines a group's "economic and social objectives", such as the quest for profit (Throsby 2001: 63).

Casson (2006) and Tubadji *et al* (2014) adopt a similar 'Throsbian' analysis, the first work by defining culture as the "shared values and beliefs relating to fundamental issues" (Casson 2006: 363), while the latter looks at the effect of culture on economic development and social wellbeing in the United States. Similarly, Santagata (2007) adopts a 'broad' approach that envisages a nation's "tangible . . . intangible . . . and material" culture as a "resource for economic development" (Santagata 2010: 7). In many ways, and as will be seen from Chapters 5 onwards, the emphasis on the role of cultural and social traditions and customs in economic development by Throsby, Casson, Santagata and Tubadji *et al* bears some similarity to Veblen's approach, and indeed Tubadji *et al* (2014) make explicit recognition of Veblen's contribution to developing this kind of broad cultural analysis (Tubadji *et al* 2014).

Others, such as Rushton (2013) and Phillips (2004), consider not culture in a broad 'Throsbian' sense but focus instead on the more limited notion of the arts. Two examples from Ruston (2013) include Maloney and Wassall (2013) and Markusen *et al* (2013). Maloney and Wassall (2013) examine arts-based development activities in three Massachusetts communities funded by the Adams Arts Program, an initiative of the Massachusetts Cultural Council designed to "revitalize communities, create jobs, grow creative industries, and increase engagement in cultural activities" (MCC 2015: paragraph 1). Among their findings is the presence in each of these communities of "vibrant sustained" partnerships between cultural leaders, community organisations and local government, which they note were instrumental in ensuring "sustained and purposeful" action towards the achievement of the programme's economic development goals (Maloney and Wassall 2013: 66).

Markusen *et al* (2013) apply a consumption-based theory to understand how investments in art and cultural activities have contributed to California's urban and regional development. There are four ways by which these investments generate consumption, including by offering "residents opportunities to spend more . . . discretionary income on new locally produced goods and services"; supporting "organizations that re-spend more of their earnings locally than others"; providing support to innovations that go on to develop export markets; or attracting innovative and highly skilled "firms and workers" (Markusen *et al* 2013: 37).[21] They attribute the levels of economic development enjoyed by particular Californian communities not to typical factors such as social and economic demographics or population size but to long-term investments in the arts and cultural capacity. As a consequence, they conclude that the arts are worthy vehicles for economic development, recommending "judicious investment in local-serving art and cultural capacity" (Markusen *et al* 2013: 56).

Phillips (2004) outlines four approaches by which the arts are used to rebuild "all aspects of community, not only the economic sphere" (Phillips 2004: 114). These include 'arts business incubators' "designed to foster . . . business development efforts" (Phillips 2004: 115) and enable artists to obtain the skills necessary to carry on a successful business; 'art cooperatives' where a "group of local or regional artisans" come together to pool their resources in an organisation that enables them to more effectively "market and promote their works" (Phillips 2004: 116); and investment in arts-related activities to attract tourists, such as by building a museum. These three approaches treat the arts as but one component in a larger suite of economic development initiatives. The fourth and final approach is more 'comprehensive' in that it places the arts not as one plank among many but as the very foundation upon which community and economic development is achieved (Phillips 2004: 118). Phillips posits that whichever approach is used is not without consequence, for while "arts-based community development" is feasible, alternate, non-arts-based strategies may produce a more "desirable type of economic development outcome" (Phillips 2004: 118, 120).

In recent years, municipalities across the globe have sought to preserve, restore and regenerate urban areas of cultural heritage in the hopes that urban renewal will make their cities more attractive and yield economic growth arising from activities such as greater tourism and visitor numbers (see Bille and Schulze 2006: 1069). Van Loon *et al* (2014) attempt to determine the effect of cultural heritage on city attractiveness and economic activity through the consideration of cultural heritage and preservation initiatives in the Netherlands. The impact of cultural heritage on city attractiveness is gauged through a willingness-to-travel model that looks at the number and type of "urban recreation day trips", including "recreational shopping", visits to "bars and . . . eating out" (van Loon *et all* 2014: 255). Van Loon *et al* conclude that cultural heritage makes a "significant impact on destination choice" and is "important for making a municipality attractive to visitors" (van Loon *et al* 2014: 272–273). While not testing the proposition themselves, they suggest that there may also be multiplier effects from cultural preservation strategies.

The American economist Tyler Cowen briefly notes the role that the arts and culture can play as an "engine of development" in less wealthy nations (Cowen 2011: 122). The argument centres on the inimitable cultural characteristics that poorer nations possess and their manifestation in cultural outputs. Importantly, these cultural characteristics and resulting outputs cannot be easily replicated, being completely unique and idiosyncratic to these nations (see Santagata 2011). Their role in regional development stems from the fact that cultural outputs cannot be judged in the way that one judges most other goods. To use Cowen's example, one *can* judge a "stereo system" made in the United States to be "unambiguously better" than one produced in Senegal", but one *cannot* apply such an 'empirical' approach to cultural output (Cowen 2011: 122). The latter is a matter of taste. As a consequence, a cultural producer from a poorer nation stands a chance to sell his wares in external markets. Importantly for economic development, it means that poorer nations could achieve economic development by developing strategies that focus on and highlight the richness and distinctiveness of their unique history and cultural heritage (see also Streeten 2006).

Bille and Schulze (2006) consider the relationship between culture and urban and regional development, looking at three approaches to culture that possess elements of both the 'Throsbian' and traditional arts definitions. These include "culture as aspect", by which they mean society's "ideas, values, norms and habits";

"culture as sector", which in essence comprises the creative industries, as outlined in the previous section; and "culture as art", which includes a quality element whereby, for example, only paintings that meet some putative quality requirement would be classified as art (Bille and Schulze 2006: 1054). Interestingly, Bille and Schulze's extensive and thorough paper looks not only to the impact of culture on economic and regional development but reverses this to consider the impact of economic and regional development on cultural output and demand. The arts and culture affect regional and urban development by (among other things) attracting industries, firms, highly skilled workers and tourists. On the other hand, economic and regional development affects culture by, for example, impacting upon the demand for cultural output, which would be expected to increase when wealth rises and decrease when economic activity slows down.

3.3.10 The Internet and the digital revolution

I will never forget how, as a young man, I ventured into the local pizza parlour to find the mechanical pinball machine had been replaced by electronic digital video games like 'Space Invaders' and 'Pac Man'. My friends and I marvelled at these (now quaint) digital machines and all their colours, movement and sounds. Little could I, nor indeed many others, realise that decades later, these digital pastimes and their 'ultimate' expression, the Internet, would produce a stream of research in psychology into a new, unforeseen and controversial 'disease' known as video game addiction (Lubman and Loton 2015; Ng and Weimer-Hastings 2005).

Like video game addiction in the case of psychology, the digital revolution has similarly resulted in new phenomena in matters relating to the operation, production and consumption of the arts. And, like video game addiction, the economics of the arts has increasingly turned to consider how the digital revolution has impacted upon the arts and creative sectors (see, for example, Towse and Handke 2013).

Cowen (2008) looks at the way digitisation and the Internet have affected the *kinds* of connections held between people and the implications for cultural economics. It is common to think of culture in tangible terms, as a painting on a wall or the music played by a symphony orchestra, but for Cowen, culture is about the bonds and ties we have with "other human beings" (Cowen 2008: 263). When one views (consumes) a painting (or indeed any other art form), one is actually consuming culture, which by Cowen's reckoning is ultimately a socially motivated act to bond with one's fellow human beings. While human beings have always sought out and enjoyed these bonds, the Internet, social media and mobile devices have put them "on steroids", strengthening and widening the number, kinds and ways to make connections (Cowen 2008: 263). The Internet has also rendered obsolete 'old-time' definitions of cultural consumption that differentiate between a state of 'cultural engagement' or 'cultural disengagement', based on whether one has or has not consumed a painting, the "theatre, . . . museums [or] . . . classical music"(Cowen 2008: 264). Cultural consumption is no longer limited to these sorts of 'tangible' and 'consciously active' pursuits but occurs through the very act of using the Internet and social media to access all manner of cultural content.

Therefore to think of cultural consumption as an 'on' or 'off' state, where 'on' corresponds to "now I am doing some culture" and 'off' refers to "now I have stopped my culture", is anachronistic (Cowen 2008: 265). The less 'differentiated' and more implied nature of contemporary cultural consumption has consequences for the economics of the art, which has typically adopted a more 'segregated' approach drawn in terms of participation (or not) in discrete cultural activities like theatre attendance or museum visits. It is not difficult to see that this has implications for many of the motivations and policy questions that have driven cultural economics research, including, and perhaps most importantly, those around public support for the arts and culture.

Arora and Vermeylen (2013) consider the effects of digitisation upon the visual arts. A key manifestation of digitisation has been the facilitation and sharing of knowledge through the creation of large digital art databases that have improved market transparency, enabled buyers and sellers to find one another more easily and lessened the need for specialist consultants (Arora and Vermeylen 2013: 2). The impact on galleries and museums has been mixed. Private galleries appear to use the Internet to advertise the artists in their inventory but have been slow to embrace it as a platform to sell said inventory (a practice that is actually frowned upon and avoided in the case of high-end galleries). Similarly, major private auctions houses like Sotheby's and Christie's have rudimentary digital strategies, using the Internet as little more than an extension of existing marketing strategies. The public museums and galleries, on the other hand, have embraced the digital possibilities with gusto, using digitisation and the Internet to engage with new audiences and transform their role from "custodian[s] of cultural heritage to . . . educator[s]" who engage and entertain (Aroro and Vermeylen 2013: 3).

Nguyen *et al* (2013) turn their attention to the effects of online streaming services like Spotify or YouTube on CD sales. Do streaming services denude sales of CDs, like illegal peer-to-peer file sharing is said to do (see Liebowitz 2014), or does the opposite occur, with CD sales actually bolstered by file sharing? Using a survey of more than 2,000 individuals in France, Nguyen *et al* found streaming services had no impact on CD sales. Further, online streaming was found to actually bolster attendance at live concerts, a feature it shares with illegal file sharing (Nguyen *et al 2013*: 323). The authors conclude that streaming services could be the "missing link between the music industry and the digital revolution", allowing record companies to counter or stem the negative revenue effects of illegal peer-to-peer file sharing while benefiting from increased attendance at live concerts (Nguyen *et al* 2013: 328).

Borreau *et al* (2013) also acknowledge the link between falling official music sales and illegal peer-to-peer music downloads (see Liebowitz 2014). But they point out digitisation has also markedly reduced music production and distribution costs, enabling digitally "adapted" record companies to increase their catalogues of titles and more easily cater to niche music markets (Borreau *et al* 2012: 330). Therefore it should be possible for 'digitally adapted' companies to counter the negative effects of illegal file sharing by increasing their music title numbers and selling these to niche markets through digitally assisted marketing techniques. Using data from a 2006 survey of the French music market, Borreau *et al* test whether 'digitally adapted' record companies have indeed been able to increase titles and, *ergo*, sales. They find that while digitisation has resulted in an expansion of titles in record company catalogues, the increase has not manifested itself in an increase in overall record company sales (Borreau *et al* 2012: 341).

File sharing has implications not only for music but for film too. McKenzie and Walls (2013) looked at the effect of pirating on box office revenues. An important factor contributing to pirating activities is the 'release gap', a reference to the different film release dates faced by consumers in different countries and regions. As a consequence, film studios have sought to remove this incentive to pirate by making increasing use of a single and coordinated worldwide release. Despite the impact of the release gap, McKenzie and Walls (2013) discovered that piracy had a small impact on box office revenues.

The apparently negligible impact on box office revenues found by McKenzie and Walls (2013) has not dampened the efforts of film studios to lobby governments heavily for the introduction of anti-piracy legislation. Orme (2014) studied the effectiveness of these legislative regimes, focusing on their ability to reverse downward revenue trends. He found their passage had little impact on long-run film studio revenues, with some policies actually harming short-run revenues. While their effect appears benign at best and 'pyrrhic' at worst (at least in the short-run), this seeming ineffectiveness may actually amount to a form of 'Ricardian equivalence', where alert studios and consumers factor in and respond to pending legislation ahead of its official promulgation (Orme 2014: 366).

Gornostaeva and Pratt (2006) use a London case study to look not at pirating but the impact of digitisation on the very act of film production. They look at four phases in the production process, including development, shooting, postproduction (including editing) and distribution and exhibition. After outlining the process in each phase under an 'analogue' production regime, they sketch out the impact and changes resulting from the new, digital tools. Among the benefits from digitisation are improved electronic means of communication, ease of file sharing and distribution, and advances in special effects. Despite these improvements, the authors found the digital impacts to be 'bounded' by 'social' factors, with face-to-face contact still an important part of the film-making process.[22]

Liebowitz and Zentner (2012 and 2015) consider the impact of the Internet on television viewing patterns. Their 2012 article looked at the effect of Internet usage on television viewing, finding that Internet usage resulted in slightly lower television viewing for the youngest, with no change in viewing patterns for the eldest among us. Their 2015 work looks to the expansion in channels and content that accompanied cable and satellite television to discern the likely impact of similar expansions made possible by digital distribution platforms like Netflix. Data from cable and satellite television usage and penetration for the period 1996–2008 in 52 countries revealed that increased content did not result in greater time spent viewing television programmes. However, the authors highlight a difference between the two platforms that requires caution in applying these results to digital distribution. Cable and satellite television is, in essence, an old broadcasting paradigm that, while increased in number, still 'locks' viewing to a predetermined transmission time (or times) (Liebowitz and Zentner 2015). Digital distribution, on the other hand, represents a 'quantum leap' that "entirely sever[s] the synchronization limitation . . . [and] considerably improve[s] the set of viewing options" (Liebowitz and Zentner 2015; see also Tadayoni and Henten 2013).

Farchy *et al* (2013) and Benhamou (2015) look at the effect of the electronic book (eBook) market on the publishing sector. Farchy *et al* (2013) consider how the advent of eBooks has affected the kinds of works on offer, its bearing on consumer use and the implications for cultural diversity. Benhamou describes a publishing market where eBooks have increased their share at the expense of traditional formats. Despite their increased sales and lower production costs, eBook sales have not enabled publishing houses to recoup losses from falling sales of traditional books (Benhamou 2015: 125). Benhamou suggests that publisher incomes are also affected by the oligopolistic nature of the eBook market, which is dominated by online retail giant Amazon and Internet company Google. Both Google and Amazon confront traditional publishing in their own way: Google, through the creation of its Google Library Project, which challenges traditional notions of 'fair use' (Benhamou 2015: 126), and Amazon by using 'punitive' measures to 'strong-arm' publishers into offering favourable rates (Benhamou 2015: 129). Benhamou characterises Amazon and Google as free-riders, Google for benefiting from works that it does little to develop or create and Amazon for gaining from traditional bookstores that bear the cost of holding products in 'physical' stores that Amazon customers attend to inspect before buying online.

The opening to this section referred to the impact of 'Space Invaders' upon this author's imagination. While once considered a frivolous pastime for children, video games and gaming technology have gained wide application and endorsement, including for use in 'serious' activities like solving the structure of retroviruses (Gray 2011). Thanks to the Internet, they have evolved beyond the confines of the pizza parlour and video arcade into socially connected global networks as well as gaining recognition as a serious art medium (see Antonelli 2012). It is a sector that has not been lost on those operating within cultural economics.

For example, Banks and Cunningham (2013) look at a "games and entertainment software" market that is "increasingly distributed and networked" and call for an analysis drawn in 'organisational studies' terms that recognises the economic, "social, cultural and technical" aspects of video games markets (Banks and Cunningham 2013: 422). Borowiecki and Prieto-Rodriguez (2014) profile video game consumers using data from a *Survey of Cultural Habits and Practices* in Spain. Among their findings is that video game playing is predominantly a male pastime that decreases as one ages. Interestingly, Borowiecki and Prieto-Rodriguez find that video games are consumed at greater levels by the less educated than those with higher levels of education. This is at odds with findings in the traditional arts, where consumption is positively correlated with higher levels of education (see Blaug 2001; Snowball 2005).

3.3.11 Copyright

In 2015, the Federal Court of Australia ruled in a case between Dallas Buyers Club LLC, the owners of the 2013 film *Dallas Buyers Club*, and a number of

Australian Internet providers. The case centred on whether the Internet providers had an obligation to provide Dallas Buyers Club LLC with the details of clients who used their Internet connection to pirate a copy of the Oscar-winning movie. The judgement was made against the Internet providers, requiring each to provide the contact details of the almost 5,000 customers who used their web connections to illegally download this film (Francis and Grubb 2015).

In essence, the Dallas Buyers Club case is one of copyright, more specifically, one of copyright infringement and the attempt by the owners of an artistic output to recoup losses in income from the illegal use of their work. It highlights the importance of this form of ownership to the arts and creative industries and serves as a good segue to a discussion on copyright in the arts.

Copyright is an extension of property rights over original works. It provides its owner(s) with rights around copying, production and distribution of said work. Copyright confers two types of rights, including economic rights and moral rights (Towse 2010a). Economic rights provide the copyright holder with the right to claim revenues associated with the sale or use of the protected work, while moral rights give some control over such things as how it will be used or to ensure appropriate attribution.[23] However, copyright has limited application. It does not, for example, provide ownership over an idea, only the original work. It merely acts to stop others from replicating or using the work without approval but does not bar others from taking the ideas inherent in the work and adopting them in their own, original creation (Landes 2011: 100; Landes and Levine 2006; see also Chapter 4, section 4.2.1 on 'artistic innovation').

The earliest economics-related research into copyright can be traced to the 1960s to what would today be called the 'economics of copying' (Towse, Handke and Stepan 2008), but the first major work in this area is said to be Landes and Posner (1989). In general, economists are said to approach copyright in one of four ways (Towse, Handke and Stepan 2008). To begin with, there is the "political economy approach to monopoly", where copyright is considered a "grant of monopoly" that is "anti-competitive" and produces a "deadweight loss" (Towse, Handke and Stepan 2008: 2). The second approach is that of "public goods and property rights". Since the good protected by copyright is in essence an 'information good', and since information goods are, like public goods, nonrival in consumption, copyright is seen as the extension of property rights over a public good (Towse, Hanke and Stepan 2008: 5). The third approach is "law and economics". In this case, copyright law is analysed through the prism of economic theory, including "price theory, welfare economics, public choice theory . . . and Coasean economics" (Towse, Handke and Stepan 2008: 6). Finally, there is "alternatives to copyright and rejection of copyright law". This fourth approach is followed by economists who reject notions of copyright and any rationale constructed in its defence (Towse, Handke and Stepan 2008: 5).

It is not too much of a stretch to see that copyright could have a major impact upon income streams and hence upon incentives to create and artistic output. Yet despite this, in relative terms, the economics of the arts is said to have largely ignored copyright and done comparatively little to consider its bearing upon creativity and the outputs of the arts and creative industries (Towse 2008).[24]

One of those seeking to address this apparent shortcoming is the leading arts economist, Ruth Towse. Examples of her efforts to increase the focus on copyright include Towse and Handke (2013), which provides a number of works that analyse the role of copyright in the arts, including eight that focus on copyright within the new digital paradigm; and Towse (2010a), which looks at the role that copyright plays as an incentive for creation.

In Towse (2006), she notes that copyright is often likened to the patent system and is frequently presented as a veritable *sine qua non* of creative output. But she argues that there is little basis upon which to make such an assertion.[25] Towse (2006) also calls for a decrease in the period of protection offered by copyright from 70 years to something like 20 years, which would be renewable at completion, presumably in a type of copyright renewal market. Towse argues that this change would result in accurate, market-determined valuations of the copyright-protected good and would certainly bring the protected period closer to the earliest forms of copyright protection, which set the protective term at 14 years with a further 14 possible at expiration (Towse 2006: 88).

Landes (2001) looks at the impact of moral rights provided to visual artists in the United States by the *Visual Artists Rights Act* 1990. The act enables artists to ensure that their work is safe from "distortion, mutilation, or other modification" (US Code in Boyle *et al* 2010: 28), and gives buyers and art lovers the confidence of a work's continued integrity and safety. On the other hand, the application of moral rights is likely to result in increased administrative and transaction costs. These costs, as well as the increased difficulty associated with current or future changes to an artistic work, would probably also result in a diminution in demand for public art, since building owners and developers, unsure of their ability or the costs related to such a change, opt not to commission or purchase art. Landes (2001) suggests that these increased costs should result in falling demand and, as a consequence, falling artists earnings, a finding confirmed by Boyle *et al* (2010).[26]

Alcalá and Gonzalez-Meastre (2012) consider the relationship between copyright and artistic creation using a life-cycle model that includes *young* and *senior* artists. Until recently, copyright protection only applied 50 years after the creator's death, but in recent times this been extended to 70 years. The authors claim that the extension results in reduced incentives to produce new works and falling levels of artistic creation. This is because it enables artists, specifically senior artists, to reap rewards from existing works for longer periods of time. The result is a change in incentives that causes artists (especially senior artists) to produce less output and instead work on strategies to increase income generation from existing works. As a consequence, young artists struggle to compete to have their voices heard, and the pool of young artists who grow to become senior artists is diminished. The overall effect is a reduction in artistic creation and a concentration of activity towards senior, established artists (Alcalá and Gonzalez-Meastre 2012: 652–653).

3.3.12 Understanding festivals and cultural events

A feature of the September calendar for the ancient Romans were the *Ludi Romani*, or Roman Games, a religious festival held in honour of the god Jupiter that would consume Roman passions and mirth for 15 or so days. The Roman event highlights the important role that festivals have long held in human affairs. Yet despite their longevity, festivals and cultural events were until relatively recently moderately rare occurrences on the annual calendar. I say *were* because in the twentieth century, a shift occurred. Suddenly, festivals and cultural events went from comparatively rare happenings to frequent occurrences, so frequent that on any given day, week or month, one is likely to find a festival or cultural event occurring in many towns, cities, villages and hamlets across the globe (Frey 1994b). How to explain this rise?

The Swiss cultural economist Bruno Frey (1994b) has explored this increase and provides an explanation based on four broad factors. To begin with, real disposable incomes rose markedly in the twentieth century, enabling greater expenditures on recreation activities and decreasing the share of income required for life's staples. Second, social changes have resulted in increased time for leisure activities. Third, festivals are said to have an edge over permanent arts companies that face rising labour costs and increasingly onerous regulations. In short, festivals are a means to circumvent the high costs and regulations that their permanent counterparts cannot avoid. Flexible labour regulations can also be appreciated through the prism of the 'cost disease', where festivals are an attempt to lower the wage costs associated with labour-intensive music and performing arts production (Frey 2011: 218). Finally, festivals benefit from low marginal costs while avoiding the high fixed costs (such as those associated with maintaining buildings) of permanent arts companies. The lessons from festivals apply to the visual arts too, where the festival equivalent, the 'blockbuster' exhibition, can be appreciated as a way to benefit from such things as low marginal costs resulting from preferential rates for exhibition spaces that permanent exhibitions might not be able to obtain (Frey 1994b: 37 and 2012: 218).

Some economists look not to festival 'origins' but instead seek to determine their impact. An example is Snowball (2005), which considers the economic impact of two South African arts festivals as well as testing the proposition that the arts are primarily enjoyed by a wealthy elite. Using a 'willingness to pay' method, Snowball analyses impacts on high- and low-income groups and concludes that the two festivals provide current and future financial gains, along with positive externalities such as civic pride and education. Further, the lower-income group enjoys these benefits at levels greater than those of the high-income group, challenging the idea that the arts (at least in the form of these festivals) are mostly consumed and enjoyed by South Africa's wealthy and educated elite. The closure of local arts festivals following the removal of public support would thus be felt disproportionately by the poor, since the rich have the resources to travel elsewhere for artistic experiences while the poor do not. Snowball concludes that this provides a justification for public support.

Others have turned their attention to determining influences on festival attendance and commercial success. Palma *et al* (2012) consider attendance at the Spring Fiestas in Seville, an important cultural event in the Spanish city centred around the city's "material and immaterial" culture, while Hiller (2015) looks at 'mammoth' annual music festivals like Coachella and considers how the 'quality' of the festival line-up and the use of big name bands and artists can help determine commercial success. The Spanish festival's attendance is found to depend on factors such as institutional and cultural links and notions of community benefit (Palma *et al* 2012). Hiller (2013) finds that commercial success is highly dependent on the ability of festival organisers to construct the right kind of line-up, and specifically on organisers' ability to minimise the costs of hiring big name bands while ensuring such bands are sufficient in number to draw large crowds and complementing these big names with unknown artists whose quality they recognise "ahead of the wider base of music customers" (Hiller 2015: 2).

Moeran and Pedersen (2011) is a compilation of works that considers the role of fairs and festivals in the creative industries. The work looks at various manifestations of the festival format such as art fairs, biennales, country music festivals and fashion weeks. The aim of this work is to highlight a point the authors claim is often overlooked in other analyses of the creative industries, namely the significant and important role played by festivals in the function and operation of the creative industries. This makes Moeran and Pedersen (2011) helpful to the understanding of festivals but also as a contribution to research in the creative industries.

3.4 Public support: A brief prologue

From early works such as the oft-mentioned Baumol and Bowen (1965 and 1966) through conference documents such as UNESCO (1969) to more current works such as Heilbrun and Gray (2001), it is clear that the question of subsidy and support to the arts has been both the well-spring of modern economic analysis of the arts and one of its perennial inspirations. The consideration by economists of public support has concerned justifications or rationales for support and subsidy to the arts, to determine how and how much should be given to the arts, and to understand how support and subsidy affect decisions made by firms.

Can rigorous economic justifications be discovered to justify government interventions into the arts? Can economists really provide answers to how and how much support? In the neoclassical tradition, justifications are based on notions of market failure: the idea that markets, if left unchecked, lead to less than optimal outcomes, meaning the arts economy cannot operate on the production possibility frontier.

Given that public support for the arts is the motivation for this book, the consideration of public support, including justification for such subvention, is given its own chapter and is left to Chapter 4. Suffice it to say for the moment that a major plank of research in the economics of the arts has been driven by the pursuit of rationales for support, and to a lesser extent, to the determination of transmission mechanisms for support and to how much the level of such support should be.

3.5 Conclusion

Since its fledgling beginnings, the economics of the arts has grown considerably. The arts have grown from being a 'side curiosity' for some economists, based on personal interest in the arts, to become a serious and recognised topic of inquiry, with thoughtful and rigorous research that has brought the arts firmly into the discipline's scope.

While, admittedly, the subdiscipline that is the economics of the arts appears at first glance to be motley, disparate and lacking a central paradigm by which to anchor its activities, it does possess three strands, or themes, that bind it together into a recognisable whole. As a result, practitioners of the economics of the arts have, since the 1960s, developed a field of inquiry that has been recognised as a rich and legitimate stream of economic investigation.

The growing maturity and confidence of this relatively new stream of economics is visible in the diversity of topics that it now dares to consider. Its *raison d'être* is not constrained to public support for the arts, but extends to areas such as taste formation in the arts, the nature of art prices, understanding the shape of artist labour markets, the creative industries and the role of the arts and culture in economic development. Practitioners in the economics of the arts have readily drawn from other fields of economic inquiry in order to solve economic riddles relating to the arts. But, equally, the findings developed in this stream of economics have proven valuable in shedding light on other questions in economics, as evidenced through the application of Baumol's disease to understand rising costs in industries such as health, education and childcare.

While the scope of the economics of the arts has increased, the importance of understanding public support is still very much a significant feature and inspiration in the research that is undertaken. The analysis of public support in this chapter was purposefully cursory, but given the importance of the topic to this work, a fuller discussion is warranted. In recognition of this, Chapter 4 will provide a more detailed analysis of the thinking that has been developed regarding public support for the arts.

Notes

1. Which was itself preceded by an earlier article 'On the Performing Arts: An Anatomy of their Problems' that helped to set the scene (Baumol and Bowen 1965).
2. Towse differentiates between the two publications. She considers the 1997 publication a collection of the 'classic' works in the field, whereas the 2007 publications is, among other things, a collection that displays the theoretical developments that have occurred since the mid-1990s (2007: xiii-xiv).
3. That said, more development of public good and related arguments will be presented in Chapter 4.
4. This admittedly seems counter to what one would expect in the case of the arts, where different tastes would logically seem to explain different arts consumption patterns. However, the adherents of this new approach claim that it enables one to make empirically testable hypotheses, since changes in constraints can be measured, whereas changes in tastes or preferences cannot (see section 3.3.1).
5. Specifically, the notion outlined by Alfred Marshall in his *Principles* that "the more good music a man hears, the stronger his taste for it [is] likely to become" (Marshall in Stigler and Becker 1977: 114).
6. Becker has claimed that treating taste in this way and explaining changes in behaviour as a response to changes in observable constraints results in superior economic explanation (Becker 1998: 4). That these constraints are observable, as opposed to unobservable preferences, is considered applicable *par excellence* to the study of consumer

activity, since consumer choices are now testable, making this approach preferable (no pun intended).

7 It is easy to see that the new approach, with its household production function, treats households as both consuming agents and production units (Ekelund and Ritenour 1999: 887), thereby creating a type of symmetry between consumer theory and theories of firm behaviour.

8 A simple example will help illustrate how X goods are used to produce Z goods. Consider the baking of a cake (the Z good). A consumer obtains eggs, flour, sugar, milk, baking powder (the X goods), which he transforms using his time and skill to produce a cake. He does not gain utility from these individual products but from the baked cake that the combined X goods produce.

9 The Z shadow prices are, at least in theory, derivable, since the prices of the X goods and other factors such as income are directly observable and obtainable.

10 See, for example, Thomas Von Ungern-Sternberg and Carl Christian Von Weizsäcker (1985), who consider the market for 'experience goods'. Experience goods are those for which "consumers are imperfectly informed about . . . quality" (Von Ungern-Sternberg and Von Weizsäcker 1985: 531). Von Ungern-Sternberg and Von Weizsäcker note that while consumers may not be able to "directly observe a product's quality at the time of purchase", they try to make up for this by "draw[ing] inferences about . . . quality from the past experience they (or others) have had" (Von Ungern-Sternberg and Von Weizsäcker 1985: 531). They also consider the incentives for suppliers to produce goods of a high or low quality. A supplier who has provided low quality products in the past would be looked at 'warily' by consumers. However, consumers would be more willing to purchase the wares of a supplier who consistently provides high quality goods.

11 Towse (1997) does not include a separate section on the area of ticket pricing research, perhaps suggesting that research in this area has grown since that time.

12 In the neoclassical paradigm, firms operating in perfectly competitive industries cannot price discriminate. That these industries can discriminate means that they would be characterised as monopolistically competitive. Monopolistic competition implies some measure of market power, and it is this that enables such firms to price discriminate. Hence, even Rosen and Rosenfield's 'competitive industries' can be thought of as containing some monopoly elements. It is worth noting that Rosen and Rosenfield make no mention of the idea of monopolistic competition in their 1997 publication.

13 Baumol's analysis adopts an approach that contravenes the Becker idea of constant taste, relying instead on the idea that changing tastes reflect changing preference structures. Becker might argue that it is not preference structures that are changing, but art prices and consumer income, and that changes in art consumption reflect changes in these two observable phenomena.

14 The guild included such notable figures as Vermeer (Montias 1979: 70).

15 However, Spencer argues that nonmainstream methods and ideas from the likes of Marx and Veblen suggest that the current capitalist structure erects "acute barriers to securing 'good work'" for many (Spencer 2009: xviii).

16 Or cultural industries, as some prefer (see Throsby 2010: 89).

17 Although one officialdom, UNESCO, adopts a more inclusive approach, defining the creative industries as those that "combine the creation, production and commercialisation of contents which are intangible and cultural in nature" (UNESCO 2006: 'Introduction' paragraph 4).

18 This suggests the creative industries possess the characteristics of natural monopolies, which in policy terms could make them appropriate targets for government intervention.

19 While many industries face such uncertainties and risks, it is suggested that they are heightened in the creative sectors. By way of example, consider an automotive company that produces a car that is not well received. For such a company, all is not lost, not for it can mitigate its losses by transferring some of the inputs used in the car's

production (such as engines) for use in other vehicles. The same cannot readily be said for the production of, say, a film. The film studio, faced with the high fixed costs associated with the production of a movie, is uncertain of its reception until these costs have been sunk, the film is produced and it is released. Only once these costs have been borne and the film exposed will it know whether its efforts will be well received or rejected. If rejected, there is limited (if any) scope to recoup or minimise losses by applying this film in other filmic outputs.

20 The importance of deals to the creative industries can be appreciated by Caves's 'admission' that his research was made possible not through use of structured and formal creative industry data sets (which are severely lacking) but through access to large amounts of information on the deals taking place between firms and individuals (Caves 2000: vii).

21 For example, an investment in a theatre company allows locals to view plays and musicals locally and reduces or even eliminates the need to travel to 'theatre capitals' such as New York City. In time, the theatre company becomes significant enough to attract not just locals but theatre lovers from outside and abroad, proving export earnings. As a beacon of cultural life, the theatre company also serves to attract highly skilled and talented workers, not only from the arts but from other industries too (see Bille and Schulze 2006).

22 However, advances in technology since the publication of Gornostaeva and Pratt (2006), in particular the ease of communication made possible through increasingly cost-effective video communication platforms such as 'Skype', may have reduced the need for 'in-person' face-to-face interaction.

23 The earliest attempts to extend moral rights right can be traced to France as early as the nineteenth century, but its codification in international law first occurred in 1928 with the development of the Berne Convention (Boyle 2010: 29).

24 As will be seen in Chapter 4, it has not been completely ignored, though what thought has been given to copyright has often been within the constructs of finding justification for public support for the arts, specifically in analysis of the role of copyright in artistic innovation.

25 Boyle *et al* (2010) also consider the link between artist incomes and creativity and conclude that artist incomes are not a good indicator of creative output.

26 However, Boyle *et al* note that some artists may "sufficiently value the non-pecuniary benefits associated with these laws", giving them a net increase in utility despite falling incomes (Boyle *et al* 2010: 43).

4 Public support for the arts

4.1 Introduction

In 2010, the Australian Broadcasting Corporation's *Q&A* television programme broadcast a programme from the Adelaide Festival in Australia that was concerned with the arts and their role and power in Australian Society (ABC 2010). Among the topics that were discussed was the role of government in providing support for the arts. The general consensus from the discussion was that public support is an essential requirement for a thriving and healthy arts sector, and this consensus was reached with little disagreement or controversy.

The sentiments of the *Q&A* panel and audience are not unusual, and, indeed, it would be fair to say that in many or most discussions on the arts, the need and desirability for government support is generally unquestioned. For economists, however, such expectations cannot be couched or supported without some analysis, and the analysis is generally around whether rationales for support can be provided. By rationales, it is meant 'rigorous' rationales rooted in economic theory that can withstand scrutiny and analysis, and by economic theory it is generally meant neoclassical theory.

Indeed, much of the economics of the arts has been concerned with the support and subsidy question and, as pointed out in Chapter 3, it is one of the three strands that bind together what is otherwise a disparate subdiscipline of economics.

In this chapter, I elaborate on the activities within the economics of the arts concerning public support for the arts. Much of the discussion will be around economic, and indeed 'noneconomic',[1] justifications for support (why). However, some brief discussion will also be around the means used to levy such support (how), how to determine the quantum or level of support (how much) and finally on positive models to assess the behaviour of economic agents to the presence of support. The discussion of the how, how much, and the positive models will be brief in comparison to that of justifications, perhaps reflecting that these kinds of analyses have been small in number compared to those motivated by questions of justification.

4.2 Justifications for support: The "why" factor

In the neoclassical competitive paradigm, otherwise known as the Walrasian model, government interventions, such as those in the form of a subsidy, are generally said to lead to market distortion. Government action to support the arts through the use of subsidies affects price signals and income, leading resources to be allocated in ways that may be or are at variance with those that would occur under 'natural', market-driven circumstances. The general presumption is that the outcome is less efficient, Pareto optimality is compromised, and the economy is unable to operate on the production possibility frontier. Thus, *a priori*, neoclassical economics commences with the premise that public support and subsidy is generally not desirable.

However, it would be folly to consider those who practice the discipline of economics and who operate under the general principles of the neoclassical school in monolithic terms. To be sure, within the neoclassical school there are those who are strictly and always against any form of intervention; but there are also those in the Marshallian and Pigovian tradition who consider that, on occasions and under certain circumstances, government interventions into the operation of the market are justifiable.

Generally, those who operate in the economics of the arts would be classified in the latter group: namely, those who are sympathetic to the notion that public support for the arts may be desirable.[2] Given this, how have those identifying themselves as 'economists of the arts' justified public support for the arts?

In the neoclassical tradition, justification is generally rooted in the presence of some form of market failure, and market failure is generally considered a situation whereby, left to its own devices, the market delivers an outcome that is less than Pareto-optimal. With the market failing to deliver an optimal outcome, intervention and subvention might be justified. What follows are the justifications found in the literature for the provision of support and subsidy to the arts.[3]

4.2.1 Externalities

Externalities arise when the activities of one agent have impacts upon other agents, some or all of which are not accounted for in the market process and the resulting price signal. In the case of a *positive* externality, an agent's activities produce benefits for other agents for which other agents are not charged. One good example of such is the benefit an apiarist receives from one who cultivates cut flowers in a nearby area. On the other hand, in the case of a *negative* externality, an agent is undertaking activities that produce costs to other agents. The producer is not charged the costs associated with the negative externality, and the affected agents are paid no compensation. The usual example is the effects of pollutants released by one factory on nearby producers (such as in the form of associated clean-up costs or lost production).

The market mechanism does not capture the costs (in the case of a negative externality) or benefits (in the case of a positive externality) arising from externalities. Thus, the price signals in the market do not convey or include all relevant information, the costs of external activities are not properly compensated for and the benefits are not paid for, meaning that price signals are askew and resource allocation is not Pareto-optimal.

In the case of the arts, the focus tends towards the first of these cases, the positive externality. The production of the arts is said to produce indirect beneficial outcomes and collective benefits that are not properly reflected in the market mechanism. Indeed, the arts are generally thought to be a source of positive externalities but of negligible negative externalities (if any) (Heilbrun and Gray 2001: 223).

A large part of the economics of the arts literature is concerned with externalities arising from the provision of the arts with the view to using these as a rationale for support and subvention. Presumably, the difficulties associated with defining and conferring property rights as the Coase theorem prescribes are such as to make Pigovian 'subvention' and support the preferable route to addressing the positive externality (see section 4.2.2). The task assumed by many arts economists has been to identify the positive externalities arising from the presence of the arts (Fullerton 1991: 566).[4] Beginning with Baumol and Bowen (1966: 369–386), the discipline has identified a number of positive externalities arising from the arts, some of which will now be outlined.

National identity, pride and prestige

In essence, the 'national identity, pride and prestige' argument states that the nation benefits from being the home of great artistic activities, such as art companies and galleries that are the pinnacles in their fields, performers who are the envy of other nations and so on (Fullerton 1991: 566; Heilbrun and Gray 2001: 227; Cwi 1980: 516; Towse 1994: 147; Moore 1968: 27). A strong arts sector dispels any thought of barbarism or philistinism, and the citizenry can instead be proud to be part of a sophisticated and civilised society.

The national pride and prestige argument is akin to that used to rationalise funding for elite sports, whereby gold medal success at the Olympic Games leads to a sense of national achievement. Indeed, it is not essential for the citizens of a nation to personally consume arts output for some gain to be apparent. For such citizens, the gain arises, to paraphrase Sir Humphrey Appleby, from the knowledge that the arts are 'there' and that they belong to a nation that is capable of ensuring that they are there (Peacock 1969: 508).[5]

A difficulty faced by proponents of national pride arguments is the presence of many other activities that provide national pride, such as the already mentioned sport (Towse 1994: 147). On a more martial level, war and success on the battlefield has also been known to inculcate pride in a nation's citizens, though one hopes few would argue for the pursuit of war for national pride motives. It should be noted that sources of national pride need not be limited to sport, the arts or war; indeed, being the locus of 'prestigious' industries at the so-called commanding heights, such as the auto or biotechnology sectors, may also lead to a sense of national pride – think of the impact that Silicon Valley has on the inhabitants of San Jose. Why the arts should warrant support at the expense of competing activities is uncertain. As Alan Peacock put it, "How do we compare, say, subsidizing the Arts with the subsidizing of Concorde, or . . . Leeds United to play Milan?" (Peacock 1969: 508)

National pride motivations can also have unintended consequences. Under the guise of national pride, some nations have 'protected' their 'culture' and imposed limitations on the export of their 'national treasures'. However, curbing access and imposing limitations to supposedly benefit the home country comes at the expense of the wider humanity (Fullerton 1991: 566). It seems that while mercantilist arguments are generally considered exercises in casuistry for much government policy, for policy relating to the arts, it still has its defenders.

On the other hand, some nations have used the arts as a means of 'national defence' and actively 'exported' their artistic wares. The following quotes in Kauffman (1990) from two members of the US Congress help to illustrate the importance of such considerations, at least during the Cold War:

> Do you not agree that . . . the sooner we can implement a program of selling our culture to the uncommitted people of the world as a weapon, the better off we are?
>
> (Representative Frank Thompson in 1954 in Kauffman 1990: paragraph 16)

> The new look in the policy of the Soviet Union might be said to be a shift in the continuing cold war from the arena of armaments and potential armed aggression to penetration into lands by economic and cultural campaigns accompanied by propaganda against the United States for its *laissez faire* attitude toward the arts.
>
> (Senator Herbert Lehman in 1956 in Kauffman 1990: paragraph 16)

Governments recognised the potential power of the arts and culture in promoting their international and military objectives. Thus governments have subsidised and used the arts to promote their cultural mores and win the hearts and minds of those abroad, sometimes in enemy lands (Moore 1968: 27). Such activities suggest that:

> Music, verse, fiction, the theater: the cold war was opening an aesthetic front. Books and symphonies and plays were sent . . . to contend with the Russians. As though a department of culture was going to vanquish Tolstoy.
>
> (Kauffman 1990: paragraph 17)!

Local economic benefits

The 'local economic benefits' argument refers to the direct and indirect economic activities associated with the arts and the benefits that accrue to a 'local' area from supporting such activities. 'Local' could assume many definitions, depending on preference and, presumably, policy, such as a nation, state, province, region or city. Cwi (1980: 516) considers four such local economic benefits.

The first of these includes the 'attraction' role. The arts are said to attract tourists, businesses and consumers; they are "people magnets" (Cwi 1980: 516).

Tourists and consumers are attracted by the presence of the arts themselves, but businesses are induced to settle in centres or locations because the presence of the arts implies an 'evolved' and attractive city life and cultural heart. Certainly, in the Australian context, the attraction of musical productions, festivals and art exhibitions has been justified on grounds such as these.[6]

The second benefit is associated with labour. In short, the arts, probably more specifically the performing arts, are said to be labour intensive industries, providing ample employment opportunities. But further, the diversity of tasks involved in arts production means that they provide employment opportunities for a "full range of job skills" (Cwi 1980: 516). Since the benefit arising from the provision of public support is the creation of employment, it is claimed that it should be quantifiable (Towse 1994: 147).[7]

The third benefit is the 'multiplier'. People employed in the arts, those who consume the arts and the producers and owners of arts companies spend their incomes in the community. This expenditure is considered to have beneficial impacts, both in terms of the direct expenditures in the community and also through the multiplier effects of said expenditure.

Cwi's fourth benefit is built on a 'sustainable industries' argument. Unlike many other industries, arts production does not rely heavily on the use of nonrenewable or "irreplaceable physical resources" (Cwi 1980: 516). As such, the arts do not have a major environmental impact, what in modern parlance would be referred to as a negligible 'footprint'.

Cwi adds a further dimension to the sustainability argument by moulding it in terms of community sustainability. In essence, Cwi suggests that arts consumers are vital to the continued health of their local communities. While Cwi does not specify why this is the case, it is presumably because those who consume the arts possess skills or other attributes necessary for the long-term viability and functioning of the community. The location of the arts in a community acts as an attractant to these vital individuals and helps to ensure its long-term health and viability (Cwi 1980: 516–517; see also Cwi and Lyall 1978).[8]

Echoing Cwi, Heilbrun and Gray (2001: 228) also discuss the business and tourism benefits associated with the arts, but point out that local economic benefits are only 'real' if tourists or businesses come from abroad and not from within the nation.[9] In the Australian context at least, local economic benefits, as manifested in state government competition for artistic productions, seem more about appeasing local constituencies. Much of what appears to be economic benefit amounts to mercantilist 'theft'. If a locality's artistic wares only serve to attract tourists and industries from areas within the nation, then we simply witness a shift of economic activity from one area of the nation at the expense of another. In Australian terms, Victoria wins, but New South Wales loses. (Heilbrun and Gray 2001: 228).[10]

As with national pride arguments, it is unclear whether public support to the arts is the best or most appropriate way to promote local economic activity (see Netzer 1978: 24–25; Heilbrun and Gray 2001: 228).

Educational and educative effects

Receiving an education provides not only private benefits but also social benefits. The presence of social benefits has been used to justify universal access to education, at least for access to a minimum level of education. It is argued that the arts possess similar educative effects, and implicit in such notions is that the arts, and indeed a liberal arts education, have an 'elevating influence' and promote particular sets of desirable outcomes in a better way than other activities (Fullerton 1991: 567). As Baumol and Bowen (1966: 385) put it:

> a liberal education confers indirect and non-priceable benefits upon the community, the same must be true of the arts. If the teaching of the humanities makes for a finer civilization, for a richer community, for a better life for everyone, this is necessarily so with the arts as well; for without the arts a vital element is taken from the humanities. . . . If the arts are reduced to an atrophied relic of ancient history, a critical component of our education system must concurrently be lost.

It is not simply that the arts make us aesthetically more aware or that they produce human beings with more 'cultivated' sensibilities. An arts education is not a matter of "cultural polish", but one of producing "full human sensibility – perceptual awareness, sensitivity to people, and understanding of personal meanings, and the capacity for feeling", for only the "arts have a singular ability to help us discover and extend" (Berleant 1980: 71). The production of human beings with full sensibilities is not achieved through the introduction of 'token' courses with an arts-related bent, as some sort of "addendum to the curriculum" to be slotted between 'serious' subjects like mathematics and grammar, but would be a process of "assimilating the arts into the very fabric of the subjects that are . . . taught" (Berleant 1980: 71).

Scitovsky (1983) considers the educational aspects of the arts from a different perspective. He begins by positing that human beings crave stimulation and excitement. Such stimulants come in many forms, including "literature and gambling, art and violence, sports and crime" (1983: 7). Scitovsky contends that the arts present external benefits (or positive externalities), while the alternatives, such as gambling, have external costs (negative externalities). The arts thus provide a less costly, more productive way to achieve human excitement, certainly less costly and more productive than crime, violence or gambling:

> "the arts and competitive sports are the main sources of stimulation that create sizable external economies (i.e. negative external costs), and at the same time create no external costs or diseconomies" (Scitovsky 1983: 11).

Support for the arts is thus justifiable because it allows humanity to be 'educated' in more productive and, importantly, less destructive methods and outlets to achieve thrill and pleasure. The benefits accruing from this would, presumably, outweigh the costs of support. Presumably, in the absence of support, there would be a reduced exposure to the arts, meaning that the human quest for thrill and pleasure would lead a less 'arts familiar' populace towards less desirable and more socially costly activities.

The future generations thing

Public support is sometimes justified on the grounds that the current generation has a responsibility to preserve an adequate supply of the arts for future generations (Baumol and Bowen 1966: 385; Netzer 1978: 23; Sawers 1993: 29; Heilbrun and Gray 2001: 226; Towse 1994: 146; Cwi 1980: 517; Frey 2003: 112). Future generations have no means of conveying their preferences for support or consumption of the arts. Thus it falls to the current generation to ensure that the arts are adequately funded so that future generations may enjoy them. Baumol and Bowen contend that a "program to preserve the arts for the nation's posterity is a case of indiscriminate benefits *par excellence*" (1966: 385).

Under this rationale, all art forms should be preserved, not just those that are in vogue. However, given the reality of economic scarcity, preserving all current art forms for future generations would be difficult. The arts are a broad church, with many and varied forms, many of which would face 'extinction' without some sort of government effort at preservation. It would be difficult to impossible to preserve all art forms, and choices would need to be made as to which of these to preserve for future generations. While these choices are notionally feasible and straightforward, in reality, such decisions would be riddled with political interference and be based on less than rigorous investigation. As Towse more soberly puts it, "what is defined as 'heritage' and what is not depends to a large extent on an arbitrary list at the relevant government department but also on the *ad hoc* demands of pressure groups" (Towse 1994: 146–147). A further issue is that the resources devoted to the preservation of existing arts forms would probably come at the expense of support for newer, innovative types (Towse 1994: 147).

The 'future generations' argument can only be supported in the absence of the private market providing an appropriate level of arts output. However, in some cases, the private market may already be providing an appropriate level. If the private market is adequately supplying such output, it would be difficult to see how public support can be justified (Sawers 1993: 29). Instead, the private market may instead decide to leave or abrogate responsibility for the production of the arts to government efforts.

Finally, a related idea to the 'future generation' argument is that of 'option demand'. In essence, option demand refers to the notion that while consumers may not participate in the arts now, they may wish to do so in the future. To keep this option open, they are willing to support and pay for the arts through their taxes. Whereas the 'future generations' argument is about preservation for descendants, the option demand argument is about preservation for the current generation (Towse 1994: 146; Frey 2003: 112).

Promoting social ideas and supporting democracy

Neoclassical economics is predicated on notions of an economy made up of free agents, each making consumption and production choices that maximise utility in the case of consumers and profit in the case of producers. In general, the ability of agents to operate freely is claimed to provide a nexus between the free enterprise capitalist system and a democratic system of government. Milton Friedman's *Capitalism and Freedom* (1962) and Hayek's *The Road to Serfdom* (1944) are examples of works that at the very least call for limited government intervention into the operation of free markets.

For a democracy to function, it requires an informed citizenry, one that can question the activities of its government to ensure that it is operating in an efficient manner and without reproach, free of corruption. It could be argued that the arts play a pivotal role in our democratic sustenance and in promoting social ideas (or social improvement) (Sawers 1993: 29; Heilbrun and Gray 2001: 229). The power of the arts is such that:

> [The] roots of the most lofty achievements in art penetrate deep into the soil of their entire civilization and are nourished by its cultural fertility and its social climate. An artistic culture, then, does not consist in a collection of objects; it is rather the very atmosphere of thought, interest, and activity from which those objects emerge. To put it more directly, the art works we value are but the more noticeable and identifiable features of a broad and inclusive cultural process. We should direct our efforts, therefore, to enriching such a process and not only to magnifying the signs of its success.
>
> (Berleant 1980 64–65)

For further evidence of the power of the arts, one need only look to the former Soviet bloc, where it was not uncommon for the state to imprison the poet, the writer, or the artist who spoke out against or questioned the activities of their government. Even in democracies the arts have faced the ire of governments. McCarthy's America chose citizens from its arts sectors to make an example of 'un-American' activity, reflecting the power of the arts in shaping public opinion.

Perhaps this is because the arts push the boundaries of thought, play a role in questioning government and continually challenge our paradigms of thought and the way we think of ourselves. Accepting for a moment that the arts do achieve these outcomes, it is still unclear whether such outcomes would be achieved in the absence of public support – in other words, whether public support is justified on these grounds. Support may increase the number of plays produced and books written, but this does not ensure that we will witness an increase in social discourse and democratic activity (Sawers 1993: 29).[11] Further, as Throsby and Withers ask, "What happens to citizens who see bad plays and bad operas?" (in Heilbrun and Gray 2001: 229).

It should be recognised that there is no guarantee that supported artists will produce works that challenge the government or hold it to account. On the contrary, an artist who is dependent on government funding may instead, in a wish to curry favour with his or her government patron, produce works that do the very opposite. Governments and rulers have long understood the status that many who operate in the arts have and the power they have to sway public opinion or to provoke fear in the hearts of its citizens. It is often a tool of government to use the arts and artists to promote its wares, to validate and legitimise its activities and to rally public support. Stalin used Shostakovich to promote his government. Similarly, Hitler used Albert Speer to promote Nazism through architecture. In essence, it is the opposite of regulatory capture. It is not the regulators who are captured, but the artists who are captured! [12]

A different but related issue is the notion that democratic government produces good art, whereas authoritarian government produces bad art. The idea is that dictators possess dubious tastes, and since they directly control the production of art within their societies, the artistic output will be unavoidably dubious. Frey challenges this argument and argues the reverse, namely, that it is authoritarian regimes that produce a "*greater diversity of quality of art*" than do democracies (Frey 2003: 144–145, his italics).

Frey's argument is premised on the idea that governments in democratic countries must be aware of and responsive to majority public sentiment. They need to be in order to be re-elected. Thus, in order to appease the public in matters of art, the government's art policy will tend to reflect the citizenry's tastes in art, good or bad. Authoritarian rulers, on the other hand, have no need to appease a public's desire, so the ruler's decisions and tastes are all that matter. If the ruler has 'good' taste, then the quality of the art will also tend to be 'good'.

Frey points to the pyramid and temple building of the Egyptian pharaohs as an example of an authoritarian system producing great art (2003: 145). Closer to our own time, the experience of the 'avant-garde' art sculpture *Vault* in Melbourne produced by Ron Robertson-Swann, and colloquially and disparagingly referred to as the 'Yellow Peril', could be seen as an example of a democratic public moving towards the 'low-brow' or philistine on matters of public art. While previous arguments suggest that the arts produce social benefits such as helping to preserve democracy, Frey's assertion suggests that democracy might, ironically, produce average or even bad art!

Of course, Frey's argument is premised on the possibility that the ruler will have good taste, but it may be the opposite, as the Australian art critic Robert Hughes noted in his television documentary *Visions of Space*. In one episode regarding the architecture of Nazi Germany, Hughes argued that Nazism resulted in:

> only . . . one way basically to make a building . . . only . . . one way to turn a corner, one way to make a window frame . . . the idea of a world covered from end to end with 'Speerian', 'Hitlerian' buildings in which you had your choice between . . . squared off pseudo classicism for official events and gemütlich kind of chalet architecture to keep the people happy and contented where they're living is just to me a nightmare. It was lucky, very lucky that it didn't last.
>
> (Robert Hughes in Griffiths and Hughes 2003: Episode 2)

Frey's argument seems to me to be a rather silly one. True, democracies may produce dubious art, but at least in democratic societies there is hope and an ability to change arts policy for the better. Further, there is nothing to bar the production of estimable art without government support. In totalitarian regimes, however, there is only the dim hope that the whims of the ruler will change for the better. And further, unlike democracies, such regimes may even enact policies to cruelly thwart the production of art that does not meet with their preferred canons, whether the art is produced with or without the regime's support.[13]

That said, despite my reservations regarding Frey's argument, it seems to me that the use of public support to promote democracy is not one that could be labelled a rigorous justification.

Artistic innovation

Innovation in science is protected through the patent system. While inventors, researchers and the like bear the costs of research and development undertaken, often over many years, they do this with the understanding that the patent system will enable them to claim potential benefits once a product is proven and put to market. Such innovation also occurs in the arts, an example of which is the development of the pentatonic scale in music. However, unlike the aforementioned scientific innovation, the arts have nothing akin to the patent system to protect the fruits of artistic innovation (Heilbrun and Gray 2001: 229–230).

Some may argue that copyright is such a system. However, copyright protects an individual work and is not extended to the "innovative principle . . . that is embodied in the specific work" (Heilbrun and Gray 2001: 230). Copyright does not protect ideas but merely protects the way that those ideas are presented within a particular work (Landes 2003: 135; see also US Code Title 17 Chapter 1, section 2(b)). While it might be theoretically possible to protect "original ideas", this "would involve substantial administrative and enforcement costs" (Landes 2003: 135). Thus copyright is generally used to determine if "B has copied A's original expression rather than A's original idea" (Landes 2003: 135). Copyright thus protects the sales of a pentatonic recording (such as a recording of Messiaen's *Quartet for the End of Time*) or sheet music of a pentatonic composition but does not bar others from adopting the pentatonic style of composition and producing original pentatonic works. The originator of this idea has no means to attract royalties for the fruits of his innovation.

The diminution or absence of innovation that might result from the lack of protection is considered by some as grounds for public support (Moore 1968: 31–32; Heilbrun and Gray 2001: 229–230; Netzer 1978: 24; Frey 2003: 113). In the absence of protections, it is argued, there is little encouragement for artistic innovation, since the costs associated with innovation (such as lost royalties) outweigh any potential benefits. But with the provision of public support to take account of these costs, artists would have an incentive to innovate.

This seems a plausible argument, and to have its desired effect, support would presumably need to be provided to 'avant-garde' artists, musicians and companies undertaking innovative and novel artistic activities. The reality, however, is that much public support is provided not to companies that produce new or innovative works but to those that produce safe works with little potential political flack, the so-called 'high-art' productions, many of which are centuries old (Heilbrun and Gray 2001: 230). This argument also overlooks other benefits that accrue to innovators. Being first carries prestige and gravitas, and this should not be underestimated as a motivation for artistic innovation. It might also prove difficult in practice to determine just who the innovators are and to ensure that support is not merely provided to artistic outputs that, while they may be new, are of a dubious nature.

Abbing notes that what may appear to be an innovation is in fact a "derivation from several other artists" (1980: 541), noting that the external effects here are felt by an individual artist but are internalised when we consider the industry, namely, the "company of artists" (Abbing 1980: 541). If one were churlish about it, it seems that artist is to the arts industry as man is to Hobbes's 'Leviathan'.

4.2.2 Externalities in the arts and the Coase theorem

Ronald Coase introduced his now famous theorem in 1960.[14] The Coase theorem essentially says that economic efficiency can be achieved through the market transaction process given properly defined property rights that are legally enforceable with zero transaction costs (Coase 1960; see also Hojman and Hiscock 2010: 241 and Polinsky 2003: 13). The Coase theorem means that under these conditions, markets can function efficiently, even in the presence of externalities (Zajac 1995: 38).

So, for example, in the case of a negative externality, which is the kind Coase is usually applied to, the perpetrator or producer of the negative externality would provide some compensation to the losers from the externality. They do this because we assume that the loser is the holder of property rights that enable him to seek such compensation from the perpetrator. Similarly, in the case of a positive externality, the beneficiary of the positive externality will pay the agent producing the positive externality. Again, the assumption is that the producer of the positive externality is conferred certain property rights that enable him to seek some form of payment for the production of the positive externality.

An important assumption here is that the victim of the negative externality has rights conferred upon him that he can then use to make claims against the producers of the externality. However, rights could also be conferred in the reverse order. In such a case, the producer would have rights that enable him to produce the negative externality. Given this, the victim would pay the producer to cease production of the externality.

One can see that a similar case can be made in the case of positive externalities. In our example, the producer of the positive externality is given the right to claim some form of payment for its production. The producer and beneficiary will, in such a scenario and through market processes, bargain until they find a mutually suitable outcome. However, it is just as possible to confer the rights upon the beneficiary of the positive externality. In such a case, the beneficiary has the right to demand the provision of the positive externalities and make a claim upon the producer. Again, it is through market interaction that the producer and beneficiary strike an agreement.

The beauty of Coase's analysis is that it provides another way of considering issues of externalities, including those arising from the arts. Prior to his now famous theorem, it was generally accepted that problems of externalities would require some form of government intervention (Tresch 2002: 167). Generally, this was in the form of a Pigovian tax in the case of a negative externality, or a Pigovian subsidy in the case of a positive externality. However, the theorem suggests that government intervention could be removed, or at the very least that government's role would be limited to the provision of a legal and administrative superstructure within which property rights can be defined and appropriately enforced.

Given the supposed externalities produced by the arts, the Coase theorem suggests that governments would (at least theoretically) have no need to provide public support. Instead, by properly defining property rights, the arts and their associated benefits would instead be provided by virtue of the Coase theorem and the market process. As mentioned earlier, the arts market would be able to function efficiently, even in the presence of positive externalities.

In reality, however, using Coase as a solution might prove problematic. First and foremost, while the zero transaction costs assumption is understandable in the case of stylised theoretical analysis, in reality such costs are unlikely to be zero. Thus, the feasibility depends very much on how high such costs are likely to be. The costs of enforcement, including, in many cases, associated court costs, would be part of such transaction costs. The extension from the stylised world into the actual world means that the assumptions and the so-called benefits of the Coase theorem quickly vanish in the face of high transaction costs.

Secondly, suppose that rights were conferred upon the producers of the externality, namely, artists and arts companies. In the case of easily identifiable large arts companies, such as a metropolitan opera company, this is an easy and straightforward task. However, if all artists produce positive externalities, then presumably the right to charge for externalities should be given to all artists. Thus, property rights would be conferred on a large opera company and the local poet. Suppose instead that rights are conferred not on artists but on beneficiaries so that they can demand the production of the positive externality. In this case, the problem would be to identify these beneficiaries. For example, the beneficiaries could cross national boundaries or might also include fellow artists, meaning that they are simultaneously producer and beneficiary of the positive externality. It is, essentially, a potential administrative and legal quagmire, and the high costs associated with defining beneficiaries would be prohibitively high.

My literature search has found no work on the use of the Coase theorem and the arts.[15] All that I have found that is remotely related to the arts is a work by Hojman and Hiscock (2010), which is concerned with the application of the Coase theorem to a local festival.[16] It may be that the dearth of literature is reflective of the difficulties that have been outlined, leading arts economists to ignore this as a line of arts-related research. Whatever the case, the use of the Coase theorem in this way could, at the very least, prove an interesting line of future research.

4.2.3 Public goods

Public goods are those that are said to be both nonexcludable and nonrival in consumption. They are nonexcludable since no single consumer can be barred from a public good's consumption and nonrival since one consumer's consumption of the public good does not negate another consumer from also consuming the public good (Baumol and Bowen 1966: 380; Fullerton 1991: 565). The quintessential example of a public good is national defence, and Grampp provides the further example of public order (Grampp 1989: 233). Public goods are also characterised by negligible, if not zero, marginal costs of production for each extra consumer.

Nonrivalry and nonexcludability means that there is little chance of private provision. Benefits from the provision of the good will flow to those who have paid for it but also to those who have not. In fact, barring factors such as moral compulsion,[17] it is unlikely that anyone will feel compelled to pay for the good, and the market will be characterised by 'free riders'. Given this reality, private producers will not be able to (nor would they want to!) produce the product at break-even point, let alone for profit (Baumol and Bowen 1966: 380).

Certainly, in the 'truest' sense, the arts are not public goods. As Fullerton notes, "art can be bought and sold, and admission to arts events can be charged" making the arts goods that are rival in consumption (Fullerton 1991: 565).[18] In addition, the physical architecture of places such as museums, theatres and performing spaces generally means that arts producers can readily exclude consumers who do not pay to consume their arts outputs.

These cases of exclusion aside, the arts are said to possess public good characteristics in other ways. For while a consumer may not wish to attend a concert or view an art exhibition, the consumer may value the fact that such things exist within his society. He benefits indirectly and "value[s] the continued preservation and availability of art, or the advancement of ideas, education, and culture" that arise from the continued production and provision of the arts (Fullerton 1991: 565; see also Heilbrun and Gray 2001: 231). It seems to me that this argument is highly reminiscent of those based on the idea of a positive externality.

Fullerton (1991: 565) has also suggested that rivalry matters only in cases where output is fully consumed. Consider a theatre that has not reached full capacity or a museum that is uncrowded. The addition of one more viewer or patron would add or impose limited marginal cost. If in these cases the producer of the arts decided to charge a price, the market would fail since there is already limited (or indeed little) demand for these artistic goods. Being unable to charge a price means that there would simply be no private provision of these artistic goods. In this sense, and in this kind of case, the theatre or museum has public good characteristics too.

4.2.4 Merit goods

The arts are said to possess beneficial qualities that render them a good that should be produced and consumed for the benefit of society; the so-called merit good (Fullerton 1991: 565; Heilbrun and Gray 2001: 241; Grampp 1989: 234; Cwi 1980: 514, 518; Frey 2003: 113). Merit goods are those judged by society, an individual or by the likes of Plato's philosopher kings and guardians to be goods that an individual or the whole society *should* have. They are, in short, "a class of goods and services with the unique quality of being better for people than they realize" (Heilbrun and Gray 2001: 242). This makes them different from goods that are generally provided on the basis of market outcomes and willingness to pay (see also West and McKee 1983 for more on merit goods).

To be sure, society has many circumstances where merit goods are manifest through laws that require the consumption of a particular good. For example, in most countries it is mandated through law that one obtains schooling/education up to a particular age. In this case, the education one receives is considered a merit good.

The arts are also assumed to be such goods. Turning again to Sir Humphrey Appleby, who perhaps best encapsulates the arts as merit goods argument, albeit from a cynical standpoint: subsidy is for art . . . for culture. It is not to be given to what the people want, it is for what the people don't want but ought to have.

While merit goods arguments provide some understanding (often political) for the existence of public support, some economists feel that they do little to provide a rationale or explanation for support (Sawers 1993: 25). For example, Frey notes that merit goods have little validity from an economic perspective since they contravene the notion of consumer sovereignty (Frey 2003: 113). However, as John Stuart Mill argued, goods can be divided between those that provide high and low quality pleasures. High quality pleasures are those that placate and serve man's higher faculties. Thus merit goods could be conceived as the extension of Mill's classification of pleasures, as those goods that satisfy man's higher faculties.

4.2.5 Baumol's disease

In Chapter 3, I described the phenomenon of Baumol's disease. Briefly, and without repeating points made in the previous chapter, Baumol's disease suggests that, due to productivity lags, performing arts production will face an earnings gap. The existence of Baumol's disease has been used by some as a justification for the provision of support (see Fullerton 1991: 561; Cwi 1980: 515; Peacock 1969).

While Baumol's and Bowen's treatment does provide an explanation for the financial stress faced by performing arts firms, on its own it does not provide a justification for public support. As stated in Chapter 3, many labour-intensive industries are susceptible to Baumol's disease; why the arts deserve special treatment while other industries facing cost disease pressures do not is unclear, other than a belief that the arts are 'intrinsically' beneficial and socially valuable (see

Fullerton 1991: 561). As such, it seems Baumol's disease is used to provide some form of theoretical 'cover' to bolster other arguments in favour of public support, such as those based on the presence of externalities or merit goods. Further, as Fullerton (1991) has noted, while the costs associated with arts production may be ever rising, it might also be the case that incomes are increasing too. If this is the case, it means that arts consumers are in a better position to bear the extra and rising costs associated with the production of the arts (Fullerton 1991: 561).

Baumol and Bowen's argument relies heavily on the notion that the performing arts have experienced little to no productivity growth, leading to the earnings gap. The string quartet still requires four musicians in order for it to be performed. Other industries have instead managed to increase their labour productivity. One would think, therefore, that there was a time that the performing arts were not in crisis, with levels of productivity that were once comparable to other industries. If this is the case, it suggests that the productivity lag and the plague of Baumol's disease is a feature of our modern age. However, far from being a modern ailment, financial crisis appears to have been a constant companion for the performing arts. Consider for example a £20,000 grant made in 1792 by Sir John Vanbrugh to the Royal Academy of Music to address the academy's financial crisis. The grant was offered in the hopes that "it would be sufficient to maintain opera 'til Musick takes such Root, as to subsist with less aid" (in Throsby and Withers 1979: 54).

Of course, the productivity argument rests heavily on the definition of output, with output being defined as the playing of the string quartet. Thus the four string players have an output of one performance. Using this output measure, then yes, no productivity gain has been experienced, since it still requires four musicians to produce one performance. But if, instead, the definition is the artistic experience achieved from the performance of the quartet, then it is possible to point to gains in productivity. For example, the creation of recording technology, both visual and audio, has enabled the quartet to reach larger numbers of listeners than was thought possible at the time of composing, say, a Mozart quartet. The advent of the Internet has increased these figures even further.

Baumol and Bowen point to the 'live performance' experience to bolster their arguments, saying the live performance output has not shown great productivity gain (1966: 13); but even here, architectural advances have made it possible to increase the size of live performance audiences. Where once a string quartet was chamber music, designed to be listened to in a smaller room,[19] acoustical advances have made it possible for this form of music to be heard in far larger auditoriums (Netzer 1978: 30). So even in terms of the live performance, the string quartet has experienced some productivity gain. To be fair, however, live performance productivity improvements appear to be less pronounced than those arising from recording (see DeBoer 1985).

A final word needs to be made regarding Baumol's disease. Consider the oft-cited string quartet and watch making. The suggestion is that the string quartet written in 1800 is still essentially unchanged, whereas watch production has, in response to technological advances, changed markedly. In my view, a problem with this analysis is that it compares apples with oranges. Is it right to compare a piece of music written in 1800, using the musical techniques of the time, to the production of a good using technological processes developed in the twentieth or twenty-first century? It seems to me that this analysis treats music as unaffected by 'technological' advance and that the musical techniques that informed the production of the quartet have remained unchanged. But on the contrary, music has advances of its own, and the tools that are used in its production change and advance along with much of human effort – from the sonata form to tone-row music; from traditional orchestral musical instruments to rock and roll; from Gregorian chants to complex harmonies; to the fusion of African and Western musical traditions to form jazz. All are examples of artistic change and growth, each of which could be considered 'technological' advancements in music. Beethoven's Ninth simply could not have been written in 1500 for the simple reason that the 'technological' tools necessary to write such music did not exist at that time.[20]

Is it perhaps not more proper to compare watch production in 2015 to the production of rock and roll music CDs in 2015? Instead, the basis of Baumol and Bowen's analysis is akin to comparing the production of jam using 1800 production techniques to watch production using 2015 techniques.

I do not wish to suggest that the string quartet from the 1800s is not worthy of preservation or support. What is merely being pointed out is that one could argue that the initial premise of the Baumol and Bowen technique, to compare a dated technology with an advanced one, is questionable.

4.2.6 Taste formation

Public support for the arts is sometimes justified on the grounds of taste formation (Towse 1994: 148). The root of this rationale can be traced to Baumol and Bowen (1966). Their influential work includes the 'education of minors' as a rationale for support, and by this they mean:

> If children and adolescents are not exposed to artistic performance during their minority, by the time they become adults it will be too late. The arts must be made available early, while tastes are still being formed and behavior patterns developed.
>
> (Baumol and Bowen: 1966: 380)

In this case, taste formation refers to the idea that public support for the arts could be used to create demand for the arts. By educating minors, we have the potential to create a future market for the arts. This stands in contrast to the discussion on taste in Chapter 3, which sought to show how new consumer theory was being applied to develop an understanding of taste for the arts.

Baumol and Bowen admit that their argument is predicated on the notion that "some classes of people are not competent to make their own decisions" (1966: 379). As Austen-Smith (1994: 246) notes, taste formation arguments could, at their base, be considered a case of paternalism, and like all good 'parents', they act in the hope that their 'children', so exposed to the arts will eventually see and appreciate the good sense of the arts education they have received.

An assumption made here is the idea that early exposure to the arts creates future appreciation and consumers of the arts. Indeed, Peacock (1969) expressed hopes in "the possibility that such support may serve to alter the preference functions of future generations to create receptivity to the benefits of culture" (Peacock 1969: 513). As noted in Chapter 3, studies by O'Hagan (1996) and Morrison and West (1986) have given succour to those who argue that early exposure to the arts leads to arts participation later in life. To be sure, there are also links with this rationale to the idea of future generations. It merely serves to show the interconnected nature of many of the rationales used to justify support to the arts and performing arts.

As with merit goods, such thinking could be considered in breach of consumer sovereignty. As an older Peacock noted, consumer sovereignty requires that "even if the individual may not be a good judge of his own interests and may recognise this fact, this is not to say anyone else is a better judge" (Peacock 1992: 548). However, the neoclassical perspective could be countered by pointing out that most, if not all, societies view children not as 'sovereign' but rather point to the need to guide the inexperienced young in making life choices.

4.2.7 Lack of information

Assuming fully informed agents is a feature of neoclassical analysis. Indeed, for markets to function effectively and efficiently, agents are assumed to be operating with all the available information regarding goods and services. A lack of full information means that consumers and producers are unable to make fully informed decisions, meaning that markets cannot operate efficiently.

What does this mean for the arts? Well, to begin with, it suggests that the arts are a good requiring a level of acquaintance to be fully (or even partly) appreciated (Netzer 1978: 25). This was the argument behind the 'education of minors' rationale discussed in the previous section. The assumption is that the esoteric and specialised nature of the arts and the time it takes to gain an appreciation of an art form means that the usual methods employed by producers to overcome this problem in other industries are not feasible. Heterogeneous and diverse arts production means that general educative, advertising and knowledge-raising campaigns available to other industries would be prohibitively expensive or ineffective (Heilbrun and Gray 2001: 237; Netzer 1978: 25).

Under this argument, many consumers who reject consumption of the arts do so because they lack the required knowledge. The lack of product knowledge means that when they do 'consume' the arts, they do not gain fully from the experience. It is like one who does not know how to eat a banana who eats it with the peel still attached and, after doing so, proclaims that he loathes bananas! Lack of information or knowledge on how to properly eat a banana has effectively turned it into a noxious good. Similar arguments are made with respect to the arts.

To be sure, there is some plausibility in the lack of information argument. How much richer, for example, is a performance of a Tennessee Williams play when one has an understanding of the South at the time, of the political and social undertones, the homosexual undercurrents and the double entendres. Pre-armed with such knowledge, one is able to gain a richer reading of 'the Bird's' material.

While greater knowledge may lead to greater appreciation of an art form, the question arises as to whether public support is warranted as a means of overcoming lack of information. Public support will certainly enable the production of artistic output that might prove difficult to sell under normal market conditions. However, as a rationale for public support, the lack of information argument is dependent on the implicit notion that arts consumption is a good thing and that consumers will recognise this only after gaining an appropriate education in the arts. In this, it shares the currents that run through the merit good and education arguments.

Moore (1968: 31) considers another dimension and introduces the infant industry argument, the idea that fledgling industries be supported through government interventions until they are able to stand on their own. It is an argument with which those schooled in international trade theory would be familiar. In the case of the arts, it is argued that the arts, as the infant industry in question, will only flourish if the public is provided with greater and more frequent exposure and information. This in turn will lead to greater participation in the arts. Thus, lack of information has been intertwined with the so-called infant industry.[21] As with arguments for other forms of support long since rejected in international trade theory (such as tariffs), Moore rightly dismisses this argument, noting that it "does not have a great deal of validity, either empirically or theoretically" (Moore 1968: 31).

Accepting the lack of information argument for the moment, one wonders whether longer-term strategies, through, for example, programmes to increase the nation's appreciation through the general education system, would be a more effective solution (see Champarnaud *et al* 2008). This of course is the basis of arguments put forth with respect to taste formation in section 4.2.6.

4.2.8 Equity and accessibility

The arts should be made available to all. This egalitarianism is the crux of equity and accessibility arguments (Baumol and Bowen 1966: 378; Towse 1994: 149). Public support to the arts is justified on the basis that without it, the arts would not be accessible to much of the populace. The implied and recognised argument here is that if left to the market, the arts would not be available to all, since markets are not concerned with matters of fairness and income distribution (Baumol and Bowen 1966: 379; Fullerton 1991: 564).

Making art accessible is a feature in many organisations tasked by governments to manage arts policy. For example, both the Australia Council for the Arts and the former Arts Council of Great Britain have within their charters the requirement that they make art accessible (Australia Council Charter; Towse

1994: 149). While it is common to read broad-brush statements such as those relating to accessibility within government policy documents and charters (what in Australia and perhaps elsewhere is known as the 'motherhood' statement), a difficulty is determining what this means on a tangible, operational level. What is actually meant by accessibility? Are we concerned with economic accessibility, geographic accessibility or social accessibility (Towse 1994: 149)? Or does accessibility refer to physical or individual accessibility? Should support and subsidy be used to ensure that those who are disabled are able to partake in artistic experience?

At the base of many accessibility and equity arguments is the idea that the arts are too costly for many to enjoy or take part in (Moore 1968: 28–29; Towse 1994: 149, Baumol and Bowen 1966: 379). It is contended that public support can help alleviate the cost of attending the theatre and the like by lowering prices and enabling greater participation. Yet as Towse notes, the price of a ticket for many "arts events . . . is lower than one for a rock concert, [and] a football match", yet few would suggest that these should be subsidised (Towse 1994: 149).

The Australia Council charter speaks of geographical accessibility, noting that it will "increase the visibility of our activities in the sector to provide access to audiences in Australian suburbs, regions and rural areas" (Australia Council Charter). The idea behind such statements is that the lack of such cultural facilities or activities constitutes a "denial of opportunity" (Baumol and Bowen 1966: 379). However, what does geographic accessibility mean in practice? Does it mean that all centres should have access to a Shakespearean theatre company? How large must a centre be to warrant such an expense? On the reverse, how small must a centre be before it becomes ineligible for such an expense (see Towse 1994: 149)?

Finally, with respect to social accessibility, many might not attend artistic events like opera for fear that they might not fit in, seeing these art forms as elitist, the province of the so-called 'opera snob' (Towse 1994: 149). Public support has been justified to develop educational programmes aimed at removing social barriers to participation. By making arts education a universal thing, presumably, it will turn the arts into a universal matter, something that all can enjoy easily and comfortably. By becoming universal, presumably any notions of elitism that are associated with the arts will be vanquished.

4.3 Public support: How?

Up to this point, I have noted the grounds put forward for providing support to the arts. But if we accept for argument's sake that the arts are justified to receive support, the next question is *how* such support should be rendered.

West (1986) proposes removing support from the hands of the producers of the arts and instead giving funds directly to consumers. Consumers would receive vouchers which they could spend on the arts experience of their choice.[22] West's analysis, using language such as "taxes the poor to subsidise the better-off", borders on the 'polemical' (West 1986: 665). He points to two examples of voucher- or consumer-based schemes (the Northern Arts Council in Britain and the Theatre Development Fund in New York) that he suggests support the idea behind such a system. West claims that the advantage of this system is that it "would allow the beneficiaries [the arts consumer] to exert some degree of influence over theatre policy" (West 1986: 666).

Towse (1994) suggests that "the form [of support] must be one that works through market incentives" (Towse 1994: 150). However, she notes that problems arise because "most institutions are either directly funded as government organisations or they are non-profit organisations and so may have different objective functions" (Towse 1994: 150). These objective functions include factors (such as the desire to maximise audience reach or production quality) that do not conform to the neoclassical market objective to maximise profits. Hence, designing support programmes that use market incentives would be problematic. Market-design difficulties aside, Towse recommends that the form of support would depend on the rationale provided for the support. So, for example, in the case of national prestige, support would only be given to artistic pursuits and artists who raise national prestige.

Champarnaud *et al* (2008) propose support for the arts through the provision of public education. Studies such as O'Hagan (1996) and Morrison and West (1986) have shown that early exposure to the arts leads to participation later in life. Champarnaud *et al* develop a model whereby public education – which they admit may be a longer-term alternative or solution to support (Champarnaud *et al* 2008: 111) – manifests itself as a factor through its impact on a consumer's cultural capital (which is also influenced by family culture and art consumption) (Champarnaud *et al* 2008: 113).

Rushton (2008) makes a comparison between direct support and support through the tax system, either in the form of tax credits or the designation of donations as allowable tax deductions. As was shown in Chapter 2, the tax system method is generally associated with the United States, whereas direct support, often provided directly to firms, is more recognisable in European and Australian policy approaches.[23] Studies undertaken to measure the quantum of indirect support have calculated they amount to more than one-third of all government finding for art and culture (Frey 2003: 118; Feld, O'Hare and Schuster 1983). As Rushton notes, the American approach has been claimed to lead to a situation whereby only those organisations that appeal to the wealthier elements of society receive support (Rushton 2008: 294). As a result, output choices reflect the tastes of the wealthy benefactor, while others in society have little or no input into artistic production choices. However, it would be naive to consider that such 'capture' would be absent in the case of direct support or subsidy. The difference appears to lie in the manner in which this capture or pressure is levied. In the case of direct support, it is more likely for pressure to be of a political or social nature. In the end, like the case of indirect support, only certain forms of artistic activities are given support.[24]

An additional question is whether to provide public support in lump sum or per unit/attendee terms. Lump sum supports are independent of output. Thus, whether one person visits a theatre production or 400, the production company receives the same level of funding. In contrast, per attendee or per unit support means that the level of funding is determined by the numbers who attend the theatrical production (Frey 2003: 120). In section 4.5, I discuss models that have been developed to understand how firms respond and make their output choices under each scenario.

Frey (2003: 116) considers government support that is aimed at making art more marketable by improving the market environment for arts producers. The approach does not require government arts bodies to make assessments regarding the merits of artistic output, or to 'pick winners', as is the case under directly funded grant schemes. Instead, government bodies aim to improve the general economic settings of the arts sector and deliver policies that will heighten the 'capabilities' for arts production. Similarities exist with government policies in other areas, such as Victorian government policies designed to increase the level of innovation (Victorian Government Innovation Statement 2002).[25] Frey's argument amounts to a similar approach for the arts. As an example of how this might play out in the arts, governments could improve the market environment for the arts by providing more favourable measures to protect artistic copyright. Another market setting approach suggested by Frey is the internalisation of external effects through the conferral of property rights to artistic bodies, such as theatres. These rights would enable artistic bodies and theatres to "obtain payments from the recipients of beneficial externalities, where necessary under threat of exclusion" (Frey 2003: 117).

4.4 Public support: Just how much?

Whatever method is chosen to determine *how* support should be provided, the next question is *how much* support should be given to the arts. It appears that most analysis of public support is concerned with the question of *why* public support should be provided, with *how* to provide support a distant second with respect to research output. *How much* support or subsidy to provide is the very poor third cousin. Perhaps this is reflective of the fact that *how* and *how much* will always be on shaky ground if plausible and strong cases cannot be provided for *why*.

Schneider and Pommerehne (1983) sought to answer the 'quantum' question through the use of voting and public expenditure theory. Schneider and Pommerehne present a model of consumer demand for support under a voting situation. Demand for public support is dependent on variables such as the expected tax increase resulting from support and the average price of admission to a theatre. They apply their model to the case of the Swiss canton of Basle-City and in particular to a referendum held in 1973 to approve an increase in public funding to the municipal theatre (1983: 633). The work by Schneider and Pommerehne followed Throsby and Withers (1979). Throsby and Withers developed a positive model of assistance that sought to explain private demand for state intervention into the arts. In particular, the model sought to understand the factors that lead individuals to supply personal arts patronage (Throsby and Withers 1979: Chapter 5).

Some approaches have used contingent valuation to determine the level of public support to the arts. The contingent valuation method uses surveys to determine the willingness and desire of households or citizens to provide public support (Thompson *et al* 2002: 88). An early use of this approach was made by Throsby and Withers (1985), who measured Australian willingness to pay for the arts via a survey of attitudes towards arts funding from people aged 17 and over (Throsby and Withers 1985: 579). The factors included in the Throsby and Withers survey were population attendance, interest in the arts and participation in the arts. The contingent valuation method approach has since been adopted by other economists, including Hansen (1997), who used it to consider Danish willingness to pay for the Royal Danish Theatre, and Thompson *et al* (2002) who used the approach to understand the same problem in Kentucky. Martin (1994) applied the method to the case of museums but coupled it with the travel cost method (Martin 1994: 256). As Martin notes, the contingent valuation method enables an understanding of the benefits accruing to a person who is willing to pay to maintain the museum (even though he may never actually visit or use it), while the travel cost method enables measurement of the benefits to those who actually use or visit the museum.

Skinner, Ekelund and Jackson (2009) also explore the case of museums and suggest that public support move from a year-to-year basis to a business cycle approach based on income-elastic attendance figures for museums. The assumption here is that in times of business cycle slumps, with lower income, one would expect lower attendance and, hence, the need for more public support. The reverse would obtain in times of boom. Thus, it is the business cycle that determines the level of funding, not willingness to pay, although presumably the latter would be affected by the former.

4.5 Public support: Understanding firm behaviour

The final area to be outlined is work developed to understand how artistic firms respond to the presence of public support. Generally, works that have analysed this behaviour have structured the firms as nonprofit or noncommercial, with goals other than profit maximisation (Heilbrun and Gray 2001: 5; Throsby 2001: 116–117). Examples include Hansmann (1981) and Throsby and Withers (1979). I have chosen to concentrate on Throsby and Withers (1979), mainly because it has been influential.[26]

The Throsby and Withers model (1979: chapter 3) presents a noncommercial, monopolistically competitive performing arts firm that is driven not by the profit motive but by other factors. These other factors include the desire to maximise its art form's reach (or audience reach) and the desire to mount productions of the highest quality. Both quality and audience reach affect production decisions via the firm managers' utility functions. In line with all neoclassical theory, the managers of the performing arts firm act to maximise their utility, and their utility functions are positively dependent on both quality and audience reach variables.

That is, the higher the quality and greater the audience reach, the higher the utility enjoyed by the firm's managers.

The firm's cost function is dependent on two factors: the quality of the performance and the number of outputs. They are positively related, so that the higher the quality and outputs, the higher the cost. In the case of quality, costs might rise because the firm hires an actor of high calibre and esteem who has the ability to charge more for his services.[27] Output can be measured in a number of ways, including the number of performances given, the number of separate productions mounted, the number of tickets available for sale, and the number of tickets sold or seats filled. Greater output entails greater cost because each individual performance entails an additional cost, such as theatre rental and extra actor or musician payments.

Throsby and Withers then posit three operating scenarios which are based on the firm's ability to affect either output or quality variables. The first is the very short-run, which is defined as a single performance. In this case, the firm faces fixed inputs to production, and cannot by definition affect the output.[28] The second scenario is the short-run, where the firm has some choices regarding its output, such as whether to increase the number performances but is limited in its ability to affect quality. The final scenario is the long-run, where the firm can adjust all inputs to production, can affect output decisions and can adjust quality variables.

After outlining each scenario and determining very short-run, short-run, and long-run cost functions, Throsby and Withers consider how the firm will respond in the absence of support. Throsby and Withers then contemplate the effect of different types of subsidies, such as lump sum and per unit or attendee subsidies. Finally, they consider the impact of subsidies provided to consumers. They conclude that the effect is the same whatever form of support is provided.

4.6 Conclusion

A clear fascination for economists working to understand the arts has been the desire to determine whether there are sufficient, plausible and rigorous grounds for the provision of public support. To the question regarding rationales, two others have been added, including how to determine the optimal means to transmit support and the levels or quantities of support to provide. Despite the addition of these questions, it would be fair to say that the first, finding rationales, has consumed the bulk of the field's attention. Perhaps this is understandable, since in the absence of adequate and watertight justifications, it would be difficult to pursue the other two objectives.

Whichever question is posed, each shares a common feature; namely, the analysis of each has been rooted in the neoclassical tradition. With respect to questions around justification, the plausibly or desirability of public intervention is thus built on the idea that an optimal equilibrium is not obtained. In such cases, the answers are premised on the idea that the *presence* of some factor, such as an externality, has thwarted market efficiency from obtaining, or alternatively, that the *absence* of a factor, such as information, has not allowed the attainment of an optimal outcome.

However, another feature common in the analyses is one not of commission but of omission. In short, little or no thought has been given to the origin of public support. Instead, the existence of public support is taken as a given, with little or no regard devoted to understand why public support exists or how it came into being, or to gain an appreciation of its institutional or historical origins. Implied in this is a lack of consideration of how these historical and institutional factors might be important to our understanding of public support for the arts and of potential rationales. Yet it is possible, even likely, that an historical and institutional analysis would provide insights that current approaches do not. It is possible that historical and institutional factors are important to understanding the existence of public support. It was Thorstein Veblen who perhaps best and (as was his wont) sardonically encapsulated the importance of historical and institutional insight to economic analysis, albeit by lampooning the ahistorical and institutionally 'agnostic' neoclassical approach:

> A gang of Aleutian Islanders, slashing about in the wrack and surf with rakes and magical incantations for the capture of shell-fish are held, in point of taxonomic reality, to be engaged in a feat of hedonistical [*sic*] equilibration in rent, wages and interest.
>
> (Veblen 1908c: 160)

In the chapters that follow, an alternative approach to understanding public support for the arts will be introduced based on the tools developed by Veblen. As will be seen, Veblen's approach is based on the idea of an ever-changing and evolving economy and society. It is my intention to use this approach to determine if a new understanding can be gained of public support for the arts and whether justifications might be derived for its provision.

Notes

1 By noneconomic, I mean those not motivated by ideas of market failure: in particular, those arguments couched in terms of equity and accessibility.

2 Though exceptions exist, such as Grampp (1989) and Banfield (1984).

3 Of course, this assumes that the costs associated with the subvention and intervention are less than the cost of the so-called market failure.

4 Indeed, Fullerton (1991) suggests that many of the other arguments presented to justify public support and subsidy described in this chapter are at their root arguments based on the idea of the presence of a positive externality.

5 Towse notes that pride and prestige arguments are not limited to the national case and can also be found at the local and regional level (Towse 1994: 147).

6 See for, example, the following two media releases from the Victorian government. The first (Holding 2009), concerned with the attraction of the production of *Wicked*, claims economic benefits for Melbourne and Victoria, thereby justifying government efforts to bring this musical to Melbourne. The second hails the attraction of the production of *Mary Poppins* to Melbourne (Brumby 2009) and lauds the economic benefits to come.

7 Again, in this case, as with others, it must be shown that the employment created by support and subsidy to the arts is greater than that created by the placement of the

support in another area (or, indeed, in the absence of any support or subsidy). Towse (1994: 147) makes this very point.

8 Richard Florida has also presented similar arguments in terms of the so-called 'creative class' (see Florida 2002).

9 The loss from one sector of the nation to the other perhaps explains why in the Australian context the national or federal government does not generally get into such practices. It is a case of intranational mercantilism.

10 For further confirmation that mercantilist or 'beggar thy neighbour' thought motivates such policies, consider the March 2010 Media Release from the then Victorian minister for tourism, in which he extols the fact that more interstate visitors come to Melbourne than Sydney on the basis of events and productions held in Melbourne (Holding 2010).

11 Indeed, other fields of human inquiry, such as those in the so-called 'hard' sciences, many of which also enjoy public support and subsidy, also play a role in provoking thought. Subsidy and support to the arts would generally only be justified in cases where the social and democratic outcomes are greater from the arts than from other sources.

12 See Netzer (1978: 36), who presents similar arguments regarding government interference and the fears held by artists of a greater government role in the arts.

13 Admittedly, even democracies can enact laws to block or reduce the production of certain kinds of art, such as those surrounding censorship. For example, up to the mid-twentieth century, film production in the United States operated under the 'Hays Code'. The code was a self-imposed set of rules and moral codes that limited and barred certain themes, stories or actions from being presented on the screen. The film industry adopted the code to avoid the threat of legislative and regulatory censorial intervention by the US government (Maltby 2003: 275). However, in time, the code gave way, and a system of movie classifications was introduced that freed up the topics that could be presented on the screen. While this example shows how even in democratic nations artistic activity can be thwarted, it also serves to show that a change to the control of film production was possible in the democratic United States that would be difficult to fathom in a totalitarian state such as Hitler's Germany.

14 Or, to use Stiglitz's cheeky terminology, the Coase 'Conjecture'. (Stiglitz 1994: 11) Stiglitz considered that the famed theorem more correctly warranted the 'conjecture' tag because in his view it was "never stated in a precise enough form really to merit that [the theorem] appellation" (Stiglitz 1994: 11).

15 Both Towse (1997) and Towse (2007), which are said by Towse, a leading researcher in the field, to contain the leading and seminal thought in the economics of the arts, contain no such research.

16 Though Frey (2003) also speaks of the "assertion of property rights that make the internalisation of external effects possible", so, while not explicitly evoking the Coase theorem, its use is implied (2003: 117).

17 Agents motivated by factors such as moral compulsion are likely to constitute a small proportion of the total market. However, some have considered the impact of altruism and public goods to mitigate free-riding (such as Peters *et al* 2004) while others (Fehr and Gächter 2000) have considered the punishments a group imposes on free-riders and show that free-riding diminishes and cooperation increases when punishments are present.

18 However, it should be noted that while arts consumption is 'individual', there are social aspects of such consumption, such as attending the theatre with friends, or the camaraderie associated with such consumption.

19 Hence the name 'chamber music', or in the Italian, *musica da camera*, meaning music for a room.

20 The 'technological' musical tool I am particularly referring to in this case is the sonata form. The sonata form did not appear in a technically specified form until the advent of the Classical period in the 1700s. From then on, the sonata form directed and shaped

musical development for at least the next two centuries, including Beethoven's *Ninth Symphony*. Indeed, the sonata form continued to advance so that it still held sway into the twentieth century; however, it was not as wedded to or structured by the relationships dominant during the Classical and Romantic periods, such as those based on harmony, but was instead built on amended platforms such as the tone-row techniques developed by Schoenberg (See Leichentritt 1951: Chapter 17 for more on the sonata form).

21 It seems that opera, after many centuries of existence, must still be an infant industry.

22 The discussion surrounding support for the arts and the call for vouchers is not dissimilar to familiar policy debates concerning government support for education. Friedman's celebrated tome *Capitalism and Freedom* (1962) argued for such a system of educational vouchers that would be given to "parents" and "redeemable for a specified maximum sum per child per year if spent on 'approved' educational services" (Friedman 1962: 89).

23 Although there are examples of the use of both direct support and tax measures in all jurisdictions. For example, in Australia, support for Australian film includes direct grants but also tax-based schemes such as the former 10BA tax concession scheme (Hodsdon 1995: 163), and in the United States, the National Endowment for the Arts represents direct support.

24 Indeed, Grampp (1989a) contemplates such issues, in particular, that arts policy is often an elaborate exercise to earn 'rents', notably by arts organisations and their audiences.

25 In that case, the Victorian government limited its role to "creating an environment which fosters creativity and enterprise", "encouraging the right business environment" and "showing leadership in the uptake of new technologies, processes and systems" (Victorian Government Innovation Statement 2002: 13).

26 This influence is measured by, among other things, that after 30 years, the Throsby-Withers approach is a major part of the outline of a performing arts firm model contained in Heilbrun and Gray's undergraduate textbook on the economics of art and culture (2001). I make what I consider a plausible assumption here, that because it is being used in an undergraduate textbook, there exists a large scope for the transfer of the model's insights to a large body of undergraduate students.

27 Though presumably in a less stylised world it would be possible for quality to be raised without an increase in cost.

28 However, if the output in question is ticket sales, then, even in the very short-run, the firm may have some control over output. It may be possible, for example, to limit seating to the stalls, or in venues with multiple theatre spaces, to utilise a smaller theatre.

5 Veblen and his muses

5.1 Introduction

Up to this point, I have provided an outline of the key economic thought and areas of investigation in the economics of the arts generally, but also on specific areas of consideration with respect to public support for the arts. While the insights and research afforded as a result of these analyses have undoubtedly done much to shed light on the economics of the arts and the issue of public support, is there another way to conceive questions around public support for the arts that might proffer different or richer outlooks?

Enter our protagonist, Thorstein Veblen.

Thorstein Veblen was born in Cato, Wisconsin, on 30 July 1857. Named after his maternal grandfather, Thorstein was the fourth son and sixth child of Norwegian immigrant farmers Thomas and Kari Bunde Veblen (Heilbroner 1953: 221) and one of 12 Veblen children in total (Jorgensen and Jorgensen 1999: 11). The stage upon which he treaded was one of rapid change, 'bookended' by two major historical events: the Civil War and the abolition of slavery at one end and the October 1929 Wall Street Crash and the Great Depression at the other.

Thorstein's academic career began at the age of 17 when he was sent by his family to be a student at the newly formed Carleton Preparatory School and College in Northfield. Carleton was where he would be taught by the leading neoclassical economist, John Bates Clark, and it would also be the place he would meet Ellen Rolfe, the women who was to become his first wife and a relationship that would ultimately fail and prove to be a source of scandal (Dorfman 1934: 66; Tilman 1996: 1; see also Jorgensen and Jorgensen 1999, Edgell 2001).

Following graduation from Carleton, Veblen taught at the Lutheran Monona Academy. He left Monona after a year to pursue postgraduate study at the newly established Johns Hopkins University, where he received instruction for a semester by the leading pragmatist philosopher Charles Sanders Peirce (Hodgson 2004: 127). Unhappy with Johns Hopkins, he left to pursue a doctorate of philosophy at Yale under the supervision of the university's president, the Reverend Noah Porter (Dorfman 1934: 41). Veblen's dissertation, completed in 1884, has long since been lost, but it is said to have compared Immanuel Kant to the autodidact philosopher, sociologist, and classical political theorist Herbert Spencer, and with respect to the latter, the presentation is said to have been "in a spirit of the disciple" (Hodgson 2004: 128).

Life after Yale proved difficult for Thorstein. He was without employment for some seven years, at least partly attributable to his agnosticism and the then-practice to draw college instructors from those with Christian 'dispositions' (Jorgensen and Jorgensen 1999: 25). Eventually, he found employment in the form of a graduate position at Cornell University, where he met the economist James Laurence Laughlin, a "stalwart exponent of the English classical school" who for many years refused to join the American Economic Association for fear that it was "socialistically inclined" (Galbraith 1973: paragraph 17). Laughlin was so impressed with the 35-year-old Veblen that, in 1892, he asked him to join him at the newly formed University of Chicago.

Veblen's Chicago years were fertile. It was here that he produced his first major and most famous work, *The Theory of the Leisure Class* (1899), followed by *The Theory of Business Enterprise* (1904). Both these works were predated by the journal article 'Why is Economics Not an Evolutionary Science?' (1898), a work that is important in many respects, including for the challenge Veblen made to the economic discipline's assertions and methods and (as will be seen) his taunt for it to adopt the Darwinian approach. But despite the production of high-profile scholarly works like *Leisure Class*, Veblen's advancement at Chicago was meagre (Tilman 1992: 22), attributable to sins personal and professional.[1] Veblen was eventually forced to leave Chicago in 1906.

With the help of his friend Jacques Loeb, a fellow Chicago academic and a leading psychologist and biologist of the time, Veblen managed to obtain a better-salaried associate professor position at Stanford University, conditional on his bringing his wife Ellen with him to Palo Alto. Despite accepting these terms, shortly after assuming his post, Veblen separated from Ellen while simultaneously developing strong and 'inappropriate' relations with two women. One was Sarah Hardy, and the other was Ann Bradley Bevans (Hodgson 2004: 145). Both were former students. Veblen was dismissed from Palo Alto after only three years.

He managed to secure a post in the economics department at the University of Missouri in Columbia with the help of a friend and former doctoral student. It was here that he produced *The Instinct of Workmanship and the State of the Industrial Arts* (1914), the work he considered to be his finest and "only important book" (Dorfman 1934: 324). He followed this with *Imperial Germany and the Industrial Revolution* (1915) and *An Inquiry into the Nature of the Peace and the Terms of Its Perpetuation* (1917). The two latter works proved controversial and resulted in his being "attacked for being both anti-German and anti-American" (Edgell 2001: 26). Professional scandal was mirrored in 'personal peccadillo' when in 1914, divorcée Veblen married divorcée Bevans (Edgell 2001: 25; Tilman 1996: 14). He left Missouri in 1918.

Life after Missouri was mixed. He took a position at the Food Administration in Washington, D.C., that he held for only a few months (Edgell 2001: 26). Eventually, Veblen settled in New York City to assume editorship of the *Dial*, a publication founded by Ralph Waldo Emerson (Dorfman 1934: 411; Edgell

2001: 27). The position was to last only a year after the publication became "one of the casualties of 1919" post-war patriotism and hysteria (Jorgensen and Jorgensen in Edgell 2001: 27). Veblen then took what would become his final position at the New School for Social Research in New York City, which he held until 1926.

The aim of this chapter is to consider the ideas and intellectual movements that contributed to and shaped Veblen's thoughts, the person E.K. Hunt described as "the most significant, original and profound social theoretician in American history" (Hunt 1979: 300). Indeed, there is no more pertinent and opportune authority and supporter for the premise and aim of this chapter than Veblen himself, and his views on technology, or what he termed the "state of the industrial arts", can readily be applied to intellectual thought:

> The state of the industrial arts is a fact of group life, not of individual or private initiative or innovation. It is an affair of the collectivity, not a creative achievement of individuals working self-sufficiently in severalty or in isolation. In the main, the state of the industrial arts is always a heritage out of the past; it is always in process of change, perhaps, but the substantial body of it is knowledge that has come down from earlier generations.
>
> (Veblen 1914: 103)

Alas, while there are grounds for this approach, there is some divergence among scholars as to which influences are relevant to understanding Veblen's ideas. William Golding once famously said that "Marx, Darwin and Freud are the three most crashing bores of the Western World", and it seems that many considerations of Veblen's antecedents trace some influence to two members of Golding's triumvirate: Marx and Darwin. For example, Dugger (1979) discusses five distinct influences, including the German historical school, Darwinian evolution, pragmatism, Marxism and behaviourism. Mirowski (1987) considers the relationship between pragmatism and the thoughts of both Veblen and John R. Commons, the economist who along with Veblen is considered the founder of what is now known as old institutional economics (Mayhew 1987; Hodgson 2004: 3). Stephen Edgell and Rick Tilman (1989) summarise the lines of influence that have been presented in various works that analyse Veblen's thought and come up with 12 distinct sources, including British empiricism, Scottish political economy and Norwegian Lutheranism.[2] However, they ultimately focus their attention on two sources, evolution – in particular the works of Darwin and Spencer – and socialism, including that of Bellamy and Marxism.

One method out of this potential 'quagmire' would be to outline each and every one of the possible influences. This 'catholic' approach would require that, at the very least, I describe each of the 12 sources listed by Edgell and Tilman, and then some. The alternative would be to pare such a list back and describe what are considered the relevant few. This approach would require that I develop an 'algorithm' to determine which to cut and which to include.

The method I have chosen is the latter; that is, I will not consider each and every possible area that has been cited as a possible influence on Veblen and his work. Rather, I will reduce this number and concentrate on five areas that I consider give the reader a greater appreciation of and richer context regarding Veblen's ideas as they are presented in the chapters to follow. On this basis, I have decided to build this chapter by focusing on:

1. Darwinian evolution
2. Pragmatist philosophy
3. The German historical school
4. William James's instinct theory and habit
5. Karl Marx, the materialist dialectic and historical materialism

What follows is a description of each. Given space constraints, what is being offered are vignettes; and given these constraints, I have attempted to focus on the salient points within each.

5.2 Darwinian evolution

As will become clear in subsequent chapters, Veblen was heavily influenced by Darwinian ideas, but a work that explicitly discloses his embrace and adoption of the Darwinian approach is his 1898 article "Why is Economics not an Evolutionary Science?" The article contains what is arguably Veblen's most famous quote, where he lampoons the discipline's adherence to a simplistic, hedonistic conception of human behaviour:

> The hedonistic conception of man is that of a lightning calculator of pleasures and pains who oscillates like a homogeneous globule of desire of happiness under the impulse of stimuli that shift him about the area, but leave him intact. He has neither antecedent nor consequent. He is an isolated definitive human datum, in stable equilibrium except for the buffets of the impinging forces that displace him in one direction or another. Self-imposed in elemental space, he spins symmetrically about his own spiritual axis until the parallelogram of forces bears down upon him, whereupon he follows the line of the resultant. When the force of the impact is spent, he comes to rest, a self-contained globule of desire as before.
>
> (Veblen 1898: 389–390)

Importantly, the article questions the lack of a Darwinian method in the economics discipline and chastises it for being more concerned with taxonomy.

This section will begin by presenting a précis of the ideas prevalent before the publication of Darwin's great leap forward. I do so because the power of Darwin's ideas can only be fully grasped by first considering the notions that they came to shatter and supersede. I then also outline Lamarck's ideas on evolution before finally presenting Darwin's discoveries, in particular natural selection.[3]

5.2.1 The Great Chain of Being and the designed universe

In a UK Channel 4 television presentation of *The God Delusion*, the Oxford biologist Richard Dawkins expresses his frustration that there are still those who question and challenge Charles Darwin's insights more than 150 years after they first saw light. While Dawkins's frustration is understandable, the consternation and inability of many to accept Darwin's insights is explicable when one realises the great challenge they posed to 2,000 or more years of Western thinking regarding man and his place in the universe.

For much of Western history, man's biological (and indeed philosophical) conception was shaped by two ideas. The first was the story of creation in the Old Testament, which presented man as created both in God's image and at the pinnacle of creation, to have dominion over the Earth and all that lived upon it (Oldroyd 1980: 2). The second idea was the 'Great Chain of Being', otherwise known as the 'Ladder of Life', or '*Scala Naturae*'.

The Great Chain of Being drew upon Aristotle's taxonomy and his linear classification of the animal kingdom. Aristotle's linear taxonomy was chiefly concerned with ranking the animal kingdom and all living matter in an order that reflected a degree of perfection. Each animal and form of living matter was said to have its own *essence*, which for the purposes of biology meant that one animal could not change into another (Oldroyd 1980: 4–8).[4] At the peak of this order was, of course, man, and at the base we find nonliving matter such as metals, pure earth and air (Oldroyd 1980: 6–10). The Christian interpretation would place God at the summit, and indeed man was to be considered as not just an animal, but rather an anointed being made in the Creator's image.[5]

These two notions presented three inescapable implications about the biological world and man's self-appraisal. John Adams, who would later become the second president of the United States, summed them up thus (in Wilson 1967: 2):

1. "There is, from the highest species of animals upon this globe, which is generally thought to be man, a regular and uniform subordination of one tribe to another . . . and the same subordination continues through the vegetable kingdom." This aligns with the view that living matter is ranked and the higher the rank, the closer to perfection.
2. "If we consider a little of this our globe, we find an endless variety of substances, mutually connected and dependent on each other." The idea of a perfectly designed Providence is evident here.
3. "It is worth observing that each species regularly and uniformly preserves all their essential and peculiar properties. . . . Every species has its distinguishing properties, and every individual that is born has all those properties without any of the distinguishing properties of another species". This confirms adherence to Aristotle's notion of essence.

Adams's views were not uncommon in the pre-Darwinian era (Wilson 1967: 3). He and his contemporaries viewed the Earth as static, as a world forged by a benevolent Creator to be the best of possible worlds, in which each species is made to be co-dependent, and coupled with the biblical authority, to serve man's ends. It fell to a continual and vigilant God to ensure the creation's equilibrium. Or, in Adams's words, "What now can preserve this prodigious variety of species and this inflexible uniformity among the individuals, but this continual and vigilant providence of God?" (in Wilson 1967: 3).

While the notion of design has been present in Western thought for millennia, its seventeenth-century coupling with mechanical philosophy and the burgeoning scientific movement centred on pursuits such as astronomy and Newton's physics led to a shift in emphasis (Ruse 1979: 4). The world and the universe were still seen as designed, but it was now one designed to adhere to and follow mechanical laws. Enlightenment thinking meant that the universe was viewed as being more watch-like than organic and its "design was seen in the law-like motions of the parts of the mechanism" (Oldroyd 1980: 62). A consequence of the 'scientific' design argument was that the designer (or 'unmoved mover') was to be appreciated in the understanding of the laws of his design rather than through biblical revelation or interventions such as miracles. This 'deistic' conception was to prove a challenge to the accepted Christian wisdom (Oldroyd 1980: 62–63).

5.2.2 Design, extinction and Lamarck's solution

The deist and theist (which amounted to Christian) design arguments shared a common characteristic in that both conceived of an ordered world and universe. In time, this common theme was to come under increasing attack from the likes of David Hume. Hume questioned how one could hold 'Pollyanna' views of order given that there is as much disorder as there is order in the world, not to mention evil. How can one square this reality with the idea of design by a benevolent and loving God-father in the theist tradition and an all-knowing and masterly designer of the deist way of thinking (Oldroyd 1980: 63)?[6]

Design arguments also implied that outcomes such as mass species extinction would not be possible, since extinction contradicts the idea of a designed perfect Providence and bounty. The impossibility of extinction held as a truism until, among other things, the appearance of the fossil record, which had two disturbing effects (Ruse 1979: 4). First, the fossil record helped to falsify the biblical view, made famous by Bishop Ussher, that the Earth's age was in the order of thousands of years. Second, the fossil record appeared to nullify the idea of a static, perfectly designed creation. Rather, the fossil record suggested otherwise to both points: that the Earth was at least millions if not billions of years old; and that species had come and gone, that creation was not fixed, meaning that extinction (including, disturbingly, man's) was possible (Ruse 1979: 4).

Some had come to accept extinction and made attempts to explain it in a scientific manner. For example, Louis Agassiz would explain extinction as a product of catastrophes that wiped out all flora and fauna. Agassiz estimated that mass extinction had occurred some 50 times since the Earth's formation and postulated that extinct species were replaced by new, improved and more progressive types. For Charles Lyell, the catastrophist ideas of Agassiz were unfathomable; rather, Lyell posited a steady-state hypothesis whereby the number of species was constant. Rather than mass-species extinction due to catastrophe, species became individually extinct after falling prey to unfavourable conditions. As one species disappeared, another would appear to take its place. However, Lyell was unable to determine how species replacement might occur, other than through supernatural intervention (Mayr 1991: 16).

Despite these scientific attempts, many continued to object to the idea of species annihilation on religious grounds. Those with religious compunctions would soothe their anxieties by describing fossils as the remains of still extant but not yet known or discovered animals (Ruse 1979: 4).[7] In time, a number of factors, including the appearance of 'alien' dinosaur fossil remains, discredited the plausibility of these explanations, and the accepted view was beginning to lose authority, making the acceptance of extinction more and more irresistible, despite religious objections.

For the eighteenth-century naturalist Jean-Baptiste Lamarck, religious arguments mattered naught; rather, the possibility of entire species extinction was unfathomable on 'scientific' grounds.[8] Unlike Lyell's and Agassiz's attempts to use science to explain extinction, Lamarck would instead use science to explain *away* what appeared to be extinction by recourse to the idea of 'evolution'. For Lamarck, the fossil record pointed not to the disappearance of life forms but rather to the appearance of new life forms, and he built his explanation on the Great Chain of Being.

Unlike traditional static conceptions, Lamarck's Great Chain of Being was dynamic. Species could move up the chain (but not down) from one rung of the ladder up onto another, making "constant progression up the scale as they changed in the course of many generations from the simplest to the most complex" (Ruse 1979: 7). The dynamic nature of Lamarck's chain meant that the bottom of the scale would see the constant appearance of new primitive organisms that would spring forth in an 'abiogenic' manner from inorganic matter.[9] Thus, for Lamarck, unrecognisable fossil remains (such as presumably those of dinosaurs) were not evidence of extinction but actually the remains of existing organisms that had been transformed by such magnitudes as to be rendered unrecognisable (Mayr 1991: 16).

Lamarck avoided Lyell's recourse to supernatural intervention to explain evolutionary change, instead building his mechanism for evolution on materialist foundations. Lamarck's decision to build evolution on the foundations of the Great Chain of Being meant that the direction of evolution was one that saw organisms ascend up the chain. Lamarck posited that evolutionary changes would be triggered by an organism's *besoins*, or needs, which arose in response to environmental factors (Ruse: 1979: 7).[10] Lamarck's evolution operated according to two "Laws of Nature", which can be stated as:

1. More frequent use of an organ will eventuate in that organ becoming gradually strengthened, giving it a "power proportional to the length of time it has been so used" (Oldroyd 1980: 30). On the flip side, any organ that is used less

or even permanently disused will be weakened, "progressively diminishing its functional capacity, until it finally disappears" (Oldroyd 1980: 30).

2. Following from no. 1, all gains and/or losses in organs will be passed on to offspring, provided that they are present in both the mother and father.

So *besoins* would make an organism strengthen or lose an organ, which would be passed on to its offspring. But how did the organism ensure that its body actually transmitted this *besoin* into physiological outcomes and changes? Just how were organs created? Lamarck posited that a body would respond to *besoins* by "triggering various bodily fluids that create or enlarge organs" (Ruse: 1979: 7):

> These subtle fluids moving incessantly in the interior of their bodies soon carve out special routes which they always follow till new ones are open to them. . . . Hence . . . the appearance of an irresistible propensity to carry out movements which, when continued or repeated, give rise to habits.
>
> (Lamarck in Oldroyd 1980: 34)

Higher animals had, in addition to their *besoins* and fluids, an inner consciousness that Lamarck termed the *sentiment interieur*, which "acts as a causal link enabling the organism to respond physiologically to its needs" (Ruse 1979: 7). Lamarck's mechanism "supposed that organisms made 'efforts' to meet the exigencies of their environment . . . and their bodies were modified accordingly . . . [with] the modification . . . transmitted to subsequent generations, thereby producing evolutionary changes" (Oldroyd 1980: 32).

Lamarck's method of evolution meant that, for example, a blacksmith, who by virtue of his profession develops superior musculature in his arms, would have progeny who would similarly have muscular arms. Lamarck himself would point to the giraffe as evidence of his evolutionary process, stating that the giraffe:

> is known to live in the interior of Africa in places where the soil is nearly always arid and barren, so that it is obliged to browse on the leaves of trees and to make constant efforts to reach them. From this habit long maintained in all its race, it has resulted that the animal's fore-legs have become longer than its hind legs, and that its neck is lengthened to such a degree that the giraffe, without standing up on its hind legs, attains a height of six metres.
>
> (in Oldroyd 1980: 31)

The nineteenth-century American botanist Asa Gray, in an 1860 defence of Darwin, declared that Lamarck's evolutionary process explained the origin of darker-skinned races in what amounted to an inherited tan: "living in a sunny climate might make a man's skin darker, in which case his children would be born with dark skin, so that eventually a black-skinned race would evolve (Gray 1860: 21).

The dynamic edge present in Lamarck's evolution meant that his version of the Great Chain could be 'extended' *ad infinitum*. But to reiterate, while Lamarck introduced a new dynamic edge to the understanding of the natural world, his process maintained elements of predecessor constructs. In short, Lamarck's process maintained the hierarchical, end-driven characteristics of predecessors, and like his predecessors, the only possible direction was one of ascension up the chain through a process of 'complexification'. Man was still found at the summit, but Lamarck parted with cotemporaries and predecessors in that he viewed man as improvable. Indeed, Lamarck considered that evolutionary advances could extend the Great Chain of Being beyond man in his current form (Oldroyd 1980: 32).[11]

Unlike Lyell, Lamarck produced a theory that relied less on supernatural activity to explain changes and the appearance of new organisms. Despite this, his theory was teleological, with all the trappings that this entails. It was still very much a notion of a designed adaptation and the "order and economy of nature" (Oldroyd 1980: 35). That said, Lamarck's "escalator of being" doctrine began to erode the edges of the previously unchallenged static notions and perhaps helped to usher in the "break-up of the eighteenth century world of classical order and harmony" (Gillispie 1960: 272; Oldroyd 1980: 35).

5.2.3 Darwin and natural selection

By the nineteenth century, the idea of design in nature was still prevalent. William Paley, the English theologian with whose works Darwin was well versed (Oldroyd 1980: 65), had presented a Panglossian view of the world that was common in Enlightenment thought:

> It is a happy world after all. The air, the earth, the water teem with delighted existence. In a spring noon, or a summer evening, in whichever side I turn my eyes, myriads of happy beings crowd upon my view. . . . A bee amongst the flowers in spring is one of the cheerfullest objects that can be looked upon. . . . At this moment, in every given moment of time, how many myriads of animals are eating their food, gratifying their appetites, ruminating in their holes, accomplishing their wishes, pursuing their pleasure, taking their pastimes?
>
> (Paley in Oldroyd 1980: 66)

Such notions of design are:

> simultaneously a scientific interpretation of nature, a theological argument, and a comforting moral view of the world. . . [that] implied that, whatever shortcomings men might experience from day to day, their lives and deeds could gain moral meaning and value if they were in harmony with God's (or Nature's) intelligible and purposeful scheme of things.
>
> (Wilson 1967: 3)

Design made ethical judgement and behaviour possible, and, without design, there could be only chaos (Wilson 1967: 3). Importantly, by being in harmony with God's intended design and nature, man would be able to achieve a better world.[12]

It was in this world that, in 1859, Charles Darwin published his great work *On the Origin of Species*. Darwin would begin his theory with a fundamental question, that is, by asking how new species are formed; but unlike Charles Lyell, Darwin's work avoided recourse to God or "intermediate causes" (Mayr 1991: 17). From the political economist Robert Malthus' work *An Essay on the Principle of Population*,[13] Darwin obtained the idea of struggle for existence and the importance of variation, providing a further foundation to his thought (Ruse 1979: 175), a point noted by Darwin in his *Autobiography*:

> In October 1838 . . . I happened to read for amusement Malthus on *Population*, and being well prepared to appreciate the struggle for existence which everywhere goes on from long-continued observation of the habits of animals and plants, it at once struck me that under these circumstances favourable variations would tend be preserved, and unfavourable ones to be destroyed. The result of this would be the formation of new species. Here, then, I had at last got a theory by which to work.
>
> (Darwin in Oldroyd 1980: 66)

From Malthus, Darwin came to understand that population pressures on limited resources would bring about a struggle for existence:

> A struggle for existence inevitably follows from the high rate at which all organic beings tend to increase. Every being, which during its natural lifetime produced several eggs or seed, must suffer destruction during some period of its life, and during some season or occasional year, otherwise, on the principle of geometrical increase, its numbers would quickly become so inordinately great that no country could support the product. Hence, as more individuals are produced than can possibly survive, there must in every case be a struggle for existence, either one individual with another of the same species, or with individuals of distinct species, or with the physical conditions of life. It is the doctrine of Malthus applied with manifold force to the whole animal and vegetable kingdoms. For in this case there can be no artificial increase of food. . . . Although some species may be now increasing, more or less rapidly, in numbers, all cannot do so, for the world would not hold them.
>
> (Darwin 1859: 48)

Darwin would liken the struggle for existence and the competition for scarce resources to "ten thousand sharp wedges packed close together and driven inwards by incessant blows, sometimes one wedge being struck and then another with greater force" (Darwin in Oldroyd 1980: 67). The struggle for existence and the pressure placed on populations meant that some would wither and die while others would flourish and survive. The ones that survived were those that possessed characteristics or variations that were favourable to their survival. On the other hand, those that did not possess favourable variations would be outcompeted by those that did and would die out in the struggle.

Darwin developed his ideas by first describing variation under domestication, in short, how man manipulated variations in domestic animals to produce organisms favourable to a particular task. He examined a number of animals, including domestic pigeons, and concluded that "One of the most remarkable features in our domesticated races is that we see in them adaptation, not indeed to the animal's or plant's own good, but to man's use or fancy" (Darwin 1859: 21). He then moved to show that a similar mechanism occurred in nature. This mechanism for determining which would survive and which perish was *natural selection*:

> Can it, then, be thought improbable, seeing that variations useful to man have undoubtedly occurred, that other variations useful in some way to each being in the great and complex battle of life, should sometimes occur in the course of thousands of generations? If such do occur, can we doubt (remembering that many more individuals are born than can possibly survive) that individuals having any advantage, however slight, over others, would have the best chance of surviving and of procreating their kind? On the other hand, we may feel sure that any variation in the least degree injurious would be rigidly destroyed. This preservation of favourable variations and the rejections of injurious variations, I have called Natural Selection.
>
> (Darwin 1859: 59)

Natural selection would determine which species survived but also helped to ensure that variations favourable to survival would continue and be passed on. The constant pressure between population and available resources meant that natural selection would be always and everywhere present:

> It may metaphorically be said that natural selection is daily and hourly scrutinising, throughout the world, the slightest variations; rejecting those that are bad, preserving and adding up all that are good; silently and insensibly working, *whenever and wherever opportunity offers*, at the improvement of each organic being in relation to its organic and inorganic conditions of life. We see nothing of these slow changes in progress, until the hand of time has marked the lapse of ages, and then so imperfect is our view into the long-past geological ages, that we see only that the forms of life are now different from what they formerly were.
>
> (Darwin 1859: 62, his italics)

Importantly, unlike Lamarck, who argued that variation came about as the result of an effort by an organism responding to its *besoins* to adapt to the environment, for Darwin, the variation among individuals was present first and the "ordering activity of the environment" followed afterwards through the process of natural selection (Hodgson 2004: 90). Organisms that possess favourable variations would find their position in the struggle positively amplified, enabling them to succeed in the hunt for resources over those with less favourable attributes. Those organisms that possessed attributes that were beneficial to their survival would survive, and these attributes would be passed on to their progeny. Importantly, Darwin's idea that variation was always present ran counter to then-orthodox views that saw variations as aberrations and temporary (Wilson 1967: 5).

Darwin also made a major departure by abandoning notions of teleology and final causes, the idea that nature does nothing in vain. As was shown, earlier attempts to understand the natural world, including those of Lamarck, were constructed in end- or goal-driven terms, what can also be considered final causes (Mayr 1991: 50). Teleological arguments started with the idea of a designed world, usually by God, with creation moving according to some purposeful supernatural plan. But natural selection meant that:

> The old argument of design in nature . . . which formerly seemed to be so conclusive, fails, now that the law of natural selection has been discovered. We can no longer argue that, for instance, the beautiful hinge of a bivalve shell must have been made by an intelligent being, like the hinge of a door by man. There seems to be no more design in the variability of organic beings in the action of natural selection, than in the course which the wind blows.
>
> (Darwin in Mayr 1991: 57)

Unlike the idea of design and teleology and parallel notions that the order of change is necessarily progressive, Darwin's evolution through natural selection was a "haphazard and opportunistic process" (Mayr 1991: 66). With natural selection, there could be no way of knowing just where the process would go and in which direction life would be taken. The implications of this are related by Christopher Hitchens, who explains how in examining the Burgess shale in the Canadian Rockies, the palaeontologist:

> Stephen Jay Gould arrived at the most disquieting and unsettling conclusion of all. He examined the fossils and their development with minute care and realized that if this tree [of life] could be replanted . . . it would very probably not reproduce the same results that we now "know". . . . If the numberless evolution from the Cambrian period could be recorded and "rewound," as it were, and the tape then played again, he [Gould] established there was no certainty that it would come out the same way. Several branches of the tree (a better analogy would be with small twigs on an extremely dense bush) end up going nowhere, but given another "start" they might have blossomed and flourished, just as some that did blossom and flourish might equally well have withered and died.
>
> (Hitchens 2007: 92)

Gould highlights the 'accident' of current 'creation' by pointing to the fossil remains of the creature *Pikaia gracilens*, mistakenly thought to be a worm but later recognised as a vertebrate:

> Wind back the tape of time to Burgess times, and let it play again. If *Pikaia* does not survive in the replay, we are wiped out of the future history – all of us, from shark to robin to orangutan. . . . And so if you wish to ask the question of the ages – why do humans exists? – a major part of the answer, touching those aspects of the issue that science can treat at all, must be: because *Pikaia* survived the Burgess decimation. This response does not cite a single law of nature; it embodies no statement about predictable evolutionary pathways, no calculation of probabilities based on general rules of anatomy or ecology. The survival of *Pikaia* was a contingency of "just history". . . . We are the offspring of history.
>
> (in Hitchens 2007: 93)

Gould's work, the unavoidable consequence of Darwin's discovery, challenges the idea of man's special position within the structure of life. Rather, man is the product of some evolutionary chance and not the result of divine determination. Darwin showed that man came about as an accident, nullifying previous solipsistic notions about our own importance and special status. The elegant and ordered world was actually a hostile one in which the 'opportunist' flourished. "Man had been trapped by his own 'fabrication of illusions'", and Darwin forced him to admit to his "evolutionary origins" (Dugger 1979: 4)

Importantly, Darwin's process of evolution through natural selection introduced a commitment to science as the process of unravelling causal explanations, a marked departure from his predecessors and many contemporaries, who considered that understanding origin was a subject for theology and religious explanation and not the realm of science (Hodgson 2004: 87). Natural selection and its relinquishing of predetermined final causes would usher natural science away from classification and taxonomy, the idea that science involved classification of phenomena, to the discovery of root causes and processes. Since the process was no longer a given, its discovery would be the focus of science. This posed implications for other sciences and fields of inquiry, including economics, which were very much still influenced by teleology and notions of natural law.[14]

5.3 Pragmatism

Pragmatism is a philosophical movement that arose in the United States during the latter half of nineteenth century. It came out of a grouping known as the Metaphysical Club, which comprised among its members William James, Charles Sanders Peirce and Oliver Wendell Holmes Jr. Among the topics central to the club's formation was the discussion of the definition of belief provided by the Scottish philosopher Alexander Bain as being "that upon which a man is prepared to act" (De Waal 2005: 1).

The philosophy's commencement is often traced to William James's "Philosophical Conception and Practical Results" (1898). This beginning is implicitly recognised by Arthur Lovejoy in his 1908 essay *The Thirteen Pragmatisms*, a work in which he asks that the central tenets of pragmatism be settled now that it "celebrates its tenth birthday" and "enters upon a second decade" (Lovejoy 1908: 1). However, in *What Pragmatism Means* (1904), William James traces the origin to Charles Sanders Peirce, in particular to *How to Make Our Ideas Clear* (Peirce 1878). It is here that we first see the term 'pragmatism' used to describe the ideas of this philosophy. Peirce claims to have come upon his ideas for pragmatism from his reading of Kant, where he also obtained the name for his new philosophy (Oldroyd 1980: 266).

Whatever the origins, the three figures who appear most prominently with respect to pragmatism and its development are Peirce, James and the American philosopher and psychologist John Dewey. As with many scholars of the period, pragmatism's practitioners were heavily influenced by Darwin's theories. How this is so will become apparent in the explanation that follows.

Before continuing, it should be pointed out that Dewey was a member of the Chicago University Academy at the same time as Veblen (Hodsgon 2004: 129). Charles Sanders Peirce, it should be recalled, was present at Johns Hopkins while Veblen was there as a student. Finally, recall that Veblen's doctoral dissertation was on the relationship between Kant and Spencer. These facts suggest that Veblen was well schooled or at the very least aware of the developments in this most American school of philosophy.

Given word limitations, it would not be possible to provide a recount of pragmatist philosophy *in toto*. As such, I will focus on two key ideas present in pragmatism which are most relevant to the study on Veblen. The first is the famous pragmatic maxim and its implications for meaning, and the second is pragmatism's 'teaching' with respect to inquiry.

5.3.1 The pragmatic maxim

As mentioned, while many trace the origins of pragmatism to William James, James gives the philosophy's genitor accolade to Charles Sanders Peirce. Like so many philosophers, Peirce was motivated into action by Descartes. In particular, Peirce wished to 'rebuke' Cartesian philosophy and its metaphysical underpinnings and present a new view of meaning rooted in science (Peirce 1878; West 1989: 44; Colapietro 2000: 44–48).

In *How to Make our Ideas Clear*, Peirce provides a view of meaning that he says is the foundation of pragmatist notions of meaning. In particular, a thought's meaning is to be determined by the habits it invokes, and a habit is a course of action to be undertaken in response to specific conditions. In Peirce's words: "To develop its [a thought's] meaning, we have simply to determine what habits it produces, for what a thing means is similar to what habit it involves" (Peirce 1878: 81). Thus, in order to grasp the full meaning of a thought, one must simply consider what habits it will produce. If we are able to determine the habits or course of action, then we can grasp a thought's significance. This conception of meaning has been dubbed the *pragmatic maxim*. Peirce famously stated the pragmatic maxim in the following manner: "Consider what effects, that might conceivably have practical bearing, we conceive the object of our conception to have. Then our conception of these effects is the whole of our conception of the object" (Peirce 1878: 82).

Peirce illustrates his maxim through the example of a hard object (Peirce 1878: 82). Here, our thought is 'hard', and we wish to determine what we mean when we say something is hard. Our understating of this meaning is to be determined by what effects the object has or produces. Thus to say that something is hard is to mean that it is unlikely to be scratched by many other objects. Accordingly, our understanding of the thought 'hard' is understood by the practical outcome that an object would not be scratched.[15]

Peirce's pragmatic maxim requires that meaning be connected to "what is tangible and conceivably practical" (Peirce 1878: 82). Meaning is to be understood in terms of how a proposal functions within our experience. So in this example, the object not being scratched enables us to see that it is hard. But importantly, the pragmatic maxim also serves to help determine meaningless. It is easy to see that by virtue of the pragmatic maxim, a meaningless proposition is one that does not have observable outcomes. To illustrate this point, consider Peirce's own example, that of transubstantiation (Peirce 1878: 82).

Transubstantiation, a notion dear to many a Catholic, states that though the bread and wine used in a mass do not change in any physical or observable way into flesh or blood, they do in fact actually turn into flesh and blood! According to Peirce's pragmatic maxim, this is nonsense. Peirce sought to show that many metaphysical questions that so plagued philosophy (such as transubstantiation) were meaningless and futile exercises, the province, to paraphrase Bishop Berkeley, of a mind debauched by learning. Indeed, Peirce claimed that the pragmatic method "serve[d] to show that almost every proposition of ontological metaphysics is either meaningless gibberish . . . or else downright absurd" (Peirce in Gallie 1946: 20).

If Peirce was the first person to develop the pragmatic maxim, it was William James who loudly announced it to the world, a feat recognised by Arthur Lovejoy in his 1908 essay *The Thirteen Pragmatisms*. While paying homage to Peirce for being the inventor of the pragmatic method, James presented the pragmatic maxim in slightly different terms from Peirce:

> If there were any part of a thought that made no difference in the thought's practical consequences, then that part would be no proper element of the thought's significance.
>
> The effective meaning of any philosophical proposition can always be brought down to some particular consequence of our future practical experience.
>
> (in Talisse and Aikin 2008: 11)

While outside the scope of this book (this is not, after all, a work on pragmatism), it is interesting to note that Talisse and Akin (2008: 11) show that while James's pragmatic maxim appears at first blush to be strikingly similar to that presented by

Peirce, his application and development of the maxim saw it go off into directions that troubled Peirce. Briefly, James is said to have 'psychologised' the pragmatic maxim. Whereas Peirce sought to develop a method that would enable philosophy to dispense with metaphysical arguments that led it into futile discourse and pointless dead-ends, James considered the pragmatic method a means to settle philosophical disputes. Talisse and Aikin describe the differences as follows:

> Peirce held that in order to grasp the meaning of a proposition, one must understand what experiences to expect were that proposition true. By contrast, James held that part of the meaning of a proposition (and the full meaning of certain propositions) is constituted by the psychological effects of *believing* it to be true.
>
> (Talisse and Aikin 2008: 13, their italics)

Indeed, Peirce was so troubled by such propositions and developments that in 1905 he rebaptised his philosophy "pragmaticism", a term he considered ugly enough to avoid kidnapping or capture by those not familiar with or in agreeance with his method (Talisse and Aikin 2008: 9).

5.3.2 Pragmatism and inquiry

If *How to Make Our Ideas Clear* sought to clarify meaning and thought, then Peirce's *The Fixation of Belief* (1877) provided the mechanism by which *belief* is achieved.

Peirce defined belief in a manner that would appeal to economists. For Peirce, belief is a "calm and satisfactory state which we do not wish to avoid" (Peirce 1877: 70). This 'equilibrium' state helps to "guide our desire and shape our actions" (Peirce 1877: 70). It is a state that provides "a more or less sure indication of there being established in our nature some habit which will determine our actions" (Peirce 1877: 70).

The polar-opposite of belief is *doubt*. Whereas belief enables us to develop habits to guide how we will act, doubt does not. Doubt is characterised as providing a disturbance, where current habits are no longer capable of providing a calm state of belief and are no longer appropriate as a course of action (Wiggins 1999: 12).

The desired state is one of belief, not doubt (Murphy 1990: 22). The unsatisfactory nature of doubt is such that we strive to change it into a state of belief. The method by which we strive to re-establish belief is through *inquiry*; it is the process by which the state of doubt is exchanged for one of belief. Indeed, doubt is such an annoying state that it "stimulates us to inquiry until it is destroyed" (Peirce 1877: 70).

A successful strategy for attaining belief would be to use a method of inquiry that produces a state of belief that is stable and unlikely to be subject to disturbance. In all, Peirce considered four mechanisms for inquiry and outlined their ability to achieve a stable state of belief.

The first such mechanism is that of *tenacity* (Peirce 1877: 72). Here, belief is maintained by ignoring the source of the doubt. In order to maintain such a position, one must ensure that one is surrounded by people with like views, since confrontation with divergent views would be to expose oneself to a possible state of doubt. The sustainability of tenacity is unlikely to hold, since through interaction one is bound to be exposed to those with views that challenge the state of belief. As Peirce says,

> the man who adopts it [tenacity] will find that other men think differently from him, and it will be apt to occur to him, in some saner moment, that their opinions are quite as good as his own, and this will shake his confidence in his belief.
>
> (Peirce 1877: 71)

The second way in which we may inquire is similar to tenacity, and is known as the method of *authority* (Peirce 1877: 72–73). Whereas tenacity requires the individual to purposefully exclude disturbing causes, authority gives the task of exclusion to social institutions and authorities. An example would be the church, which 'shielded' its flock from ideas contrary to accepted Church teaching. As a means of maintaining belief, authority might work for a limited period, but as Galileo and Copernicus showed, even the authority of a mighty institution such as the church will, in the long run, be shaken and tested. As Peirce noted, "no institution can undertake to regulate opinions upon every subject. Only the most important ones can be attended to", making authority a method leading to unstable beliefs (Peirce 1877: 73).

Peirce's third method of inquiry is known as the *a priori* method. This method requires that belief be attained by seeking out beliefs that are "agreeable to reason" (Peirce 1877: 73). The beliefs we have are attained because they sound good. Peirce considered this an unstable platform upon which to build belief, since the "opinions which today seem most unshakable are found tomorrow to be out of fashion" (Peirce in De Waal: 2005: 13).

The final method of inquiry is that of science (Peirce 1877: 74). The previous three methods require that we avoid disturbing influences; but as a long-run proposition, they are unlikely to be successful. Science, on the other hand, purposefully seeks out alternative views in the hope that any beliefs that it creates will prove to be stable, calm and able to withstand any disturbing effects. Indeed, Peirce considers science superior to the other three methods of inquiry in that the other three methods are purely human endeavours, since the beliefs that are struck by tenacity, authority and *a priori* inquiry commence with notions that we wish or choose to believe. Science, on the other hand, enables us to develop beliefs "determined by nothing human, but by some external permanency – by something upon which our thinking has no effect" (Peirce 1877: 74). Compared to the other three methods, science:

> is the only one . . . which presents any distinction of a right and a wrong way. If I adopt the method of tenacity, and shut myself out from all influences, whatever I think necessary to doing this, is necessary according to that method. So with the method of authority: the state may try to put down heresy

> by means which, from a scientific point of view, seem very ill-calculated to accomplish its purposes; but the only test *on that method* is what the state thinks; so that it cannot pursue the method wrongly. So with the *a priori* method. The very essence of it is to think as one is inclined to think.
>
> (Peirce 1877: 75)

With the scientific method, Peirce notes that:

> there are real things, whose characters are entirely independent of our opinion about them; those realities affect our senses according to regular laws, and though our sensations are as different as our relations to the objects, yet by taking advantage of the laws of perception, we can ascertain by reasoning how things really are: and any man, if he have sufficient experience and he reason enough about it, will be led to the one true conclusion.
>
> (Peirce 1877: 74)

Thus, whereas the previous three methods saw a willingness and a need for man to set the terms, to create beliefs that would bend nature to his needs, the scientific method recognises that nature sets the terms of human understanding. Our beliefs must accord with nature and with the world and universe around us. Science "is the most reasonable way of arriving at warranted and valid beliefs; [it] is a self correcting social and communal process promoted by smoothly functioning habits . . . and whose sole end is this settlement of opinion" (West 1989: 43).

Thus, Peirce and his ideas on inquiry link to the pragmatic maxim, the idea that if one was to perform A, then B would be observed. Only the scientific method provides this link, since the other forms of inquiry require us to ignore reality, to wilfully or implicitly refute beliefs or ideas that do not accord with our own, and that challenge the pragmatic maxim. For Peirce, the scientific method does not do this; rather, it embraces alternative beliefs and ensures that our belief accords with the pragmatic maxim. The link between belief and the pragmatic maxim means that "beliefs are identical if and only if they give rise to the same habit of action", and that "beliefs give rise to the same habit of action if and only if they appease the same doubt by producing the same rule of action" (Murphy 1990: 25).

5.3.3 Pragmatism and Darwinism

Pragmatism drew inspiration from the works of Darwin (De Waal 2005: 12; Oldroyd 1980: 266). As mentioned in section 5.2, previous considerations of man painted him as a god-like creature, anointed by the Almighty with the ability to reason. But Darwinism meant that thought itself could be considered an outcome of natural selection. Indeed, for Darwin, thought is to be considered as a secretion of the brain in the same way that gravity is a property of matter, no more, no less (Hodgson 2004: 87).

Pragmatism embraces this Darwinian finding, and the dualistic doubt-belief model suggests that the ability to inquire is merely a mechanism whereby humans adapt to the environment around them. It is natural selection at work in the realm of thought (De Waal 2005: 12).

The doubt-belief model itself has Darwinian overtones. The interplay between belief and doubt and the struggle to move from doubt to belief could be said to be akin to the struggle for existence. Just as limited resources and the struggle for existence lead to natural selection, so too does the irritation of doubt and the desire to attain a state of belief lead us to inquire (Murphy 1990: 22). And as Peirce suggests, only by means of the process of inquiry through the method of science do we attain such a stable state. Thus there is "a kind of natural selection process acting on ideas. The various ideas or concepts that a person may come up with are tested in the external world. Those that are true survive, those that are false are eliminated" (Oldroyd 1980: 266).

This model also has implications for notions of absolute truth. The schoolmen or scholastic philosophers would claim that such truth was provided by God. Later, the church itself would play such a role, being the vessel through which God's truth was revealed. After Descartes, the church and God no longer provided access to absolute truth. Instead, metaphysical exercises to determine an absolute truth upon which all knowledge would be hinged began to take hold, culminating with Descartes's famous *cogito ergo sum*. However, the pragmatists, in Darwinian fashion, moved to a view that did not see truth as absolute or perennial. Rather, it is a product of inquiry, and the doubt-belief dualism suggests that there is always a struggle in attaining a state of belief and that truth itself, in the metaphysical sense, does not exist, but is itself an ever-changing and evolving thing.

5.4 The German historical school

The German historical school, also known as the historical school of economics, was the dominant paradigm in the study of economics in Germany for much of the nineteenth century and into the early- to mid-twentieth century (Hodgson 2001: 57). The school was very much a response to the direction in which economic analysis was being taken by British economists: in short, the British pursuit of universal economic laws that would be applicable to all societies and periods and derived using a deductive method.

In contrast to British economics of the time, the historical school adhered to an empirical/inductive approach to understanding economic phenomena and a belief that different explanations are required for different periods and different societies: in others words, an economic construct built on historical specificity that followed from "a tendency to doubt whether the conception of laws could be applied to social science at all" (Schumpeter 1912: 168).

The German historical school's economics demanded a move away from pure theory to an economics that adopted ethical and cultural dimensions (Koslowski 1995: 9). For the historical school, this "put historical and . . . descriptive work on details into the forefront as the most important . . . task" in economics (Schumpeter 1912: 154). In contrast to British deductive methods, the historical school argued that "it was hardly possible any longer to talk of 'laws' in the field of social science and that at best it might be possible to talk of such regularities as can be discovered by detailed historical and statistical research . . . [that] might possibly be termed 'empirical laws'" (Schumpeter 1912: 170). In addition, the school was increasingly influenced by Darwinism and new and powerful arguments of evolutionary theory (Krabbe 1996: 63; Schumpeter 1912: 159).

However, the German historical school was not merely a reaction to British classicism. It was not driven solely by contrarianism and nationalist 'intellectual petulance', but was ultimately concerned with the development of German society and the desire to see it progress. That the German historical school was able to become so influential is attributable to the rise in social problems in Germany arising from industrialisation in the nineteenth century. Calls were beginning to be heard for government intervention to allay the negative consequences of the increasing machine age and concomitant social changes. The *laissez faire* perspective, a core doctrine of deductive classical economics, was seen to be ineffective or unacceptable in the face of such problems, causing it to lose much of its lustre (Grimmer-Solem 2003: 2).

The school is generally broken into three distinct periods. The first is known as the older historical school; the second period is that of the younger historical school; the final is that of the youngest historical school. This outline will focus on the older and younger schools, since the purpose is to elaborate those elements that would have contributed to the development of Thorstein Veblen's thought and, chronologically, these schools fit neatly within the period of Veblen's life. The leading figures in the German historical school include Wilhelm Roscher, Karl Knies and Bruno Hildebrand for the older school and Gustav Schmoller for the younger school (Blaug 1992: i).

While some, such as Pearson (1999), suggest that there is little to unify the thought of those who are said to make up the German historical school, a sentiment highlighted by Grimmer-Solem (2003: 25) when he says that "no single method, research project, or political orientation united the scholarship of the so-called 'German Historical School'",[16] others (Hodgson 2001: 59; Schumpeter 1912: 176–180) have argued that common themes do exist, with Schumpeter identifying six themes running through this school.[17] Veblen himself refers to a "historical school" (Veblen 1901: 70), meaning that whatever contemporary commentators and academics might think, at least to Veblen such a school did exist, warranting this outline.

The school's influence went beyond Germany, its tentacles spreading to the United States, other parts of Europe and Japan. In the United States, its methods are visible in institutional economics and, as will become apparent in the chapters that follow, in Veblen's economics. That it had such an influence can be at least partially explained by the prestige of German universities at the time (Grimmer-Solem 2003: 3; Hodgson 2001: 57).[18] Indeed, Germany's was the system of choice for many Americans wishing to undertake postgraduate studies, and among these American graduands was John Bates Clark, Veblen's teacher at Carleton College.[19]

With respect to Dr Veblen, it should be noted that his works suggest a direct understanding of and familiarity with the older and younger school, validating this approach. His familiarity with this economic school of thought is explicitly evident in at least two works, including his 1901 article "Gustav Schmoller's Economics" where he reviews Schmoller's work of historical economics *Grundriss;* and the hitherto mentioned "Why is Economics not An Evolutionary Science", where the historical school is discussed. In addition, as will be seen, the importance of institutions to Veblen's understanding of economics as well as Veblen's consideration of historical development, which he did through consideration of four distinct periods of human development, is testament to the influence of this school.

5.4.1 The older school

The historical school is said to have commenced with the publication of Wilhelm Roscher's work *Grundriss* (*Outline*) in 1843. The work's influence is evident by its being reprinted some 26 times, and in many respects it was considered the older school's manifesto (Hodgson 2001: 57). However, some trace the school's beginning to Friedrich List and his 1841 publication *National System of Political Economy* (Krabbe 1996: 12–14; Hodgson 2001: 58). That the former is considered the touchstone for this school is perhaps attributable to List's never having held an academic post, resulting in his not being considered a member of the historical school by his contemporaries (Hodgson 2001: 58).

Whatever its origins, the school's founders spoke explicitly of a "historical method" of research, and political economy was considered "the science of the law of development of the economy and of economic life" (Roscher in Hodgson 2001: 57–58). Their approach was built on a strong statistical and empirical basis in a desire to develop a system of economic thought that would enable German economic advancement (Grimmer-Solem 2003: 3). But while advancement since Adam Smith was generally couched in terms of wealth, for Roscher:

> The problem of how to best promote the wealth of nations is an important problem . . . but it is not our point. Political Economics is not merely an art of acquiring wealth; it is a political science based on evaluating and governing people. It is our goal to describe what the people of a nation have (economically) thought, felt, desired, striven for and reached; why they strived for it and why they reached it. Such a description is only possible in close connection with the other ethnological sciences, in particular legal, political and cultural history.
>
> (in Priddat 1995: 17)

The adherence to history as the method of analysis, in preference to other approaches, is understandable given "the extremely flourishing state of historical research in Germany" at the time and its "dominant role in Germany's intellectual life" (Schumpeter 1912: 160). The school's strong 'history' strains were patent in its desire for classical economic thought to be supplanted by an approach to economics that was historically oriented (Krabbe 1996: 18).

The older school's establishment of traditions that adhered to empirical analysis in preference to the development of deductively derived universal laws was to become the hallmark for it and its intellectual descendants. Whereas the classical approach was one of an:

> elaboration of ideas . . . we [the older German historical economists] try our hand at simple description, first of the nature and needs of a people, secondly of the law and institutions of the latter, and finally of the greater or smaller success enjoyed through these laws and institutions.
>
> (Roscher in Hodgson 2001: 59)

Roscher's "simple description" was to be obtained through "the facts of historical life" (Knies in Hodgson 2001: 60). Only by understanding "the history of economic culture in connection with the history of all political and judicial development of nations" can "a successful development of economic science" be undertaken (Knies and Hildebrand in Hodgson 2001: 60).

Economic theory itself was to be considered in epochal terms. For the historical school, averse as it was to the pursuit of axiomatic absolutes, this meant that:

> In contrast to the absolutism of theory, the historical conception of political economy is based on the following principle. The theory of political economics is also a result of historical development just as the economic conditions of life are.
>
> (Knies in Hodgson 2001: 60–61)

Related to this point, the German historical school did not view economic 'laws' as applicable to all societies at all times. Thus, the ideas emanating from British economists may have been applicable to an advanced economy but may be inappropriate in other nations, eras or places. British economic ideas arose in economically advanced Britain; and they made sense in and for Britain. For Germany, however, which had yet to attain a similar state of industrial development, British insights were of lesser value (Hodgson 2001: 61). Implicit in this is the idea of historical specificity and the need for cultural reflection and recognition in economics.

The older historical school was also united by another strand of thinking, the notion of society as an organism (Hodgson 2001: 63–64; Krabbe 1996: 22). In contrast to classical and later neoclassical constructs built on atomistic or individual foundations, the older historical school viewed the national economy as an organism "which can age and die" (Schumpeter 1912: 156). Schumpeter suggests that the presence of 'nonhistorical' factors in the development of the old school's economics accounts for such thinking.[20]

The school's embrace of the 'organism' idea and objection to individualist approaches stemmed in part from notions of 'free will'. Either man had free will, or he operated according to laws that predetermined his responses. For economists like Knies, the answer was resoundingly in favour of the presence of free will.

Knies considered that the eventual outcome of individualist approaches would be to conceive of man as operating according to laws, such as the pleasure-pain hedonism that was the hallmark of much classical analysis. But free will meant that the personification of human nature according to such fixed laws was not possible, negating individualistic approaches (Hodgson 2001: 62). As a consequence, the older historical school preferred to view society as an organism in and of itself. Much as the human body is made up of different organs, each working together to support the body as a whole, so too the national economic system was to be viewed (Hodgson 2001: 63).

5.4.2 The younger school

While Roscher wrote the original historical school manifesto, Schumpeter argued that it was the younger school under Gustav Schmoller's leadership that became the " 'historical school' par excellence" (Schumpeter 1912: 156). For Schumpeter, the use of "non-historical sources" by the older historical school, such as "ideas in the field of the philosophy of history", rendered this a less than historical tradition. In contrast, the younger school proscribed such "non-historical" sources "in the interests of unbiased and detailed historical study", making it a truly historical school (Schumpeter 1912: 157).

Schmoller characterised his method of economics as "historico-ethical" (Shionoya 2005: 14). It was a "historical and ethical conception of a nation and society contrary to rationalism and materialism" (in Shionoya 2005: 18). This conception led Schmoller's research into areas that were broader than economics, often including social and political dimensions (Grimmer-Solem 2003: 9).

While Schmoller's economics sought to update the older school by purging the method of nonhistorical sources, it held fast to another key facet of the approach, specifically the opposition to the axiomatic approach. The school's continued opposition to axiomatic approaches is perhaps attributable to the 'rebirth' and boost provided to classical economics with the advances of 'marginalism' arising from the British neoclassical, Walrasian and Austrian schools (Grimmer-Solem 2003: 2). The rise of these 'updated' versions of classical doctrine meant that the historical school would need to be vigilant and defend its approach.

Perhaps this vigilance informed Schmoller's decision to seize on Darwin's insights to consider social life in terms analogous to biological life. The biological analogy led Schmoller to base his research on three fundamental steps (Krabbe 1996: 63; Shionoya 2005: 18):

1. The first step is the idea that analysis of economic phenomena should take into consideration matters of time and space. This reflects the idea of historical specificity and also suggests an understanding of the need for cultural sensitivity and difference as relevant factors to understanding the development of economic phenomena.
2. Schmoller's second step is the requirement that economic phenomena be classified and defined according to a coordinated system.

3. The final step was the requirement that phenomena undergo causal explanation and that this causal explanation should recognise that economic phenomena have an interrelated nature.

The third step indicates recognition of the need for theoretical foundations; but as with his predecessors, Schmoller considered that such a theoretical construct could only be built by first undertaking empirical research. Indeed, the strain of empiricism and its importance was such that "when laws don't exist, we must be content with the broad observation of reality, the classification of these materials, and the inquiry of causes" (Schmoller in Shionoya 2005: 18). Schmoller's steps also point to the inheritance of a notion of society as a unified whole, the idea that each part of the economy is inseparable, rejecting ideas that economic systems are understandable by reducing their examination to the level of the individual.

In *Grundriss der allgemeinen Volkswirtschaftslehre* (*Outline of General Economics*) (1900), Schmoller adopted a dualistic approach to understanding economic development and outlined a theoretical foundation for economics that was 'teased out' of and built on a programme of empirical/historical research. The two pillars upon which he based his theory were, first, physical and biological causes (natural forces), and second, psychogenic and moral causes (moral forces) (Krabbe 1996: 63). Schmoller combined the two to consider the economic development of society as a whole (Krabbe 1996: 63):

> National economy can be seen as a system of moral as well as natural forces. It is both, at the same time, according to the point of view considered (Schmoller in Krabbe 1996: 63).

Schmoller's analysis divided economic systems into a 'mental', or decision, sphere, and a technological sphere. The decision sphere is that in which economic decisions are made. The technological sphere is that where nature is rendered "subservient" and suitable for the uses of "mankind" (Krabbe 1996: 67).

5.4.3 Empirical and a priori *constructs*

As can be seen, the German historical school held fervently that one must begin first with the data, the statistics, the historical facts, and only after this point can one begin to develop theories or identify laws, if any, to explain economic phenomena. A problem with the German historical school's favoured approach is that it fails to recognise that investigation generally begins with ideas or constructs first. Our *a priori* ideas or constructs can be explicit, such as a pre-stated hypothesis to be tested, or indeed implicit. Only when we are armed with these constructs do we move to test and determine whether they can be validated or whether they need to be rejected.

While the historical school practitioners did not recognise it, their approach was embedded with *a priori* conceptions. Classification of historical and statistical data itself involves implicit judgments on how to classify, and these judgements are built on *a priori* ideas of how to classify and of how the matter or matters in question fit together.

Take, for example, the classification of species. In this example, we wish to classify species such as birds, dogs, beetles and so on. Implicit in this is an *a priori* idea or conception of each of these organisms that includes how they are structured and also a relationship between them. Thus we have a predetermined idea of a thing we call a bird, another that we call a dog, another that we call a beetle and so on. Indeed, the notion of species is itself an *a priori* construct. This suggests that the German historical school's belief that science can be built on purely empirical foundations is flawed since it fails to recognise the important fact that investigation commences, whether explicitly or implicitly, with concepts and theories first (Hodgson 2001: 75).

5.5 Instinct theory and habit

Charles Darwin's *On the Origin of Species* and the theory of natural selection had removed the idea that man was an anointed being moulded by the hands of God. Rather, natural selection suggested that man's appearance was but a chance, a product of natural selection, and that man was no more special than a worm or fly. The application of natural selection to explain physiological changes of organisms was one thing, but could it be used to explain the origin of man's psychology?

It was inevitable that the new theoretical tool of natural selection would be extended in an attempt to explain the origin of man's psychological being and, in particular, whether man operated according to instinct. Prior to Darwin, instincts were seen as the hand of God at play in the functioning of animals. Thus:

> instinct in animals . . . is a feeling which compels them to perform certain acts without thought or reflection; . . . is in full force at the moment of their birth; . . . is the guidance of the Almighty's hand unseen; . . . was therefore perfect at the beginning, and has never varied.
>
> (Marryat in Boakes 1984: 29–30)[21]

While instinct was seen as driving animal behaviour, this was less so for more intelligent animals. The Almighty, in his wisdom, ensured that "the reasoning powers are chiefly, if not wholly, given to those animals which man subjects to his service and for his use" (Marryat in Boakes 1984: 29–30). Man, on the other hand, did not operate according to instinct at all (other than in the case of infants and small children), but rather free will. Darwin's grandfather, Erasmus Darwin, provides an example of such a view. Erasmus Darwin "tried to explain away patterns that appeared to be instinct as due to early learning, and thus affirm the role of volition as opposed to instinct" (Dewsbury 1993: 265).

But Darwin's theory of natural selection led to questions regarding how mental processes, the psychology of man, evolved, and implicit in this were questions as to whether natural selection could explain their development (Dewsbury 1993: 268). In particular, does man also function according to instinctive behaviour akin to that which drives behaviour in animals? It is clear that this notion of instinctive action would challenge the idea that man operates according to free will to one that instead envisaged man as a 'slave' to instinctive proclivities inherited through the process of natural selection: in essence, to a determinist conception of man.

For Charles Darwin, it was natural selection that would explain how man's instincts evolved, acting to ensure the preservation of those instincts that ensured the continuance of the species. However, while Darwin believed that instinctive behaviour was present in man, he also believed that man had fewer instincts than other similar species. That said, Darwin opposed views such as Marryat's that equated higher intelligence with less reliance on instincts (Dewsbury 1993: 267, see also Beer 1983).

Others would continue with the work commenced by Darwin on instincts, chief among these being George Romanes. Romanes first met Darwin three years after the publication of *The Descent of Man* (1871) and explained the origin of instincts via two forms or routes (Boakes 1984: 24). *Primary* instincts are those that arise via the process of natural selection. Here, natural selection uses reflexes to produce increasingly complex habits with no basis in intelligence (Boakes 1984: 30–31). In contrast, *secondary* instincts "originate as habits, which originally were performed intelligently, but which become stereotyped into permanent instincts" (Dewsbury 1993: 268). Learned behaviour is more important to the development of secondary instincts, and repeated learned behaviour becomes automated to the point that the animal no longer distinguishes it as learned behaviour, transforming it into instinctive behaviour (Boakes 194: 30–31). Thus, for Romanes, primary instincts appear to require no consciousness, whereas secondary instincts require consciousness. In addition, while primary instincts are Darwinian and follow natural selection, secondary instincts appear to be Lamarckian.

Of course, it is the basis of this chapter that we are considering those factors that played a part in shaping Veblen's thought, and the quote in the introduction to this chapter regarding 'the state of the industrial arts', drawn as it is from the work that makes explicit reference to the idea of instinct, gives currency to the notion that Veblen was indeed influenced by then-contemporary instinct theory. It is my assertion that the main contributor to Veblen's understanding here is William James, an assertion shared by Hodgson (1998: 417; 2004: 163). Thus, in what follows, I will lay out the major features of William James's instinct theory after first tackling some preliminary issues concerning the definition of instinct.

5.5.1. Problems of definition

Charles Darwin had himself introduced the idea of instinct in his *Origin of Species*, devoting a whole chapter to the topic (Darwin 1859: 194). In that chapter, Darwin described instinct as:

> an action, which we ourselves require experience to enable us to perform, when performed by an animal, more especially by a very young one, without experience, and when performed by many individuals in the same way,

> without their knowing for what purpose it is performed, is usually said to be instinctive.
>
> (Darwin 1859: 194)

Darwin provides what appears to be a definition of instinct, but only after making the contradictory pronouncement that "I will not attempt any definition of instinct", perhaps recognising the difficulty of such a task (Darwin 1859: 194).

A major consideration with respect to instinct is the difference between an instinct and a tropism and the relation between the two. A tropism can be described as a reflex action. The raising of a knee after being struck with a rubber mallet, or the drawing away of a hand from a fire, would be considered tropistic responses. Veblen was well aware of the difference since his friend and University of Chicago colleague, Jacques Loeb, was at the forefront of research into tropisms, developing theories of tropism by examining changes to animals in their reaction to light (Boakes 1984: 138; see Veblen 1914: Introductory).

This distinction between tropism and instinct would lead Herbert Spencer to define an instinct as a "compound reflex action" (Spencer in Hamlin 1897: 61). Spencer considered instincts an "invariable sequence, or chain, of simple reflexes" that are "automatically triggered by appropriate events in the animal's surrounding" (Boakes 1984: 30). Spencer appears to be equating instinct with a more advanced tropism. Spencer's definition removes, or at the very least mitigates, any idea of conscious action in instinct. Indeed, "no instinct need ever have been intelligent. In its higher forms, it is probably accompanied by a rudimentary consciousness, but this is an effect of the growing complexity of the instinct" (Spencer in Hamlin 1897: 61)

Darwin's disciple George Romanes took aim at Spencer's definition, and in particular the lack of conscious action. He would instead define instinct as "reflex action into which there is imported an element of consciousness" (Romanes in Hamlin 1897: 61). Romanes was not alone in arguing for the importance of consciousness, and his contemporary Wilhelm Wundt made similar claims (including the strange claim that "man shares with the birds the instinct to live in wedlock" (in Dewsbury 1993: 266)). Both Romanes and Wundt supported the presence of consciousness in instinct, which they did by recourse to three underpinning ideas (Hamlin 1897: 61):

1. Instinctive responses are generally due to an external change.
2. Instinctive responses do not automatically follow in the presence of some stimuli. Indeed, the response to external stimuli may "also depend upon the disposition of the animal". Take our example of the knee struck by the mallet. Upon being struck, it must raise. It can do no other. It is tropism through and through. However, according to Romanes and Wundt, there may be such cases where the animal may at one moment respond to an external stimulus, and at others not. This difference in reaction suggests the presence of consciousness in the choice made by the animal.

3. In more advanced animals, instincts are "accompanied by an unmistakeable expression of emotion".

These are but two examples of the differences in approach to instinct and the 'Gordian' nature of the task of adequately defining the concept. The lack of clarity around the topic was highlighted by British psychologist Conwy Lloyd Morgan in an 1895 article for *Natural Science* that attempted to define instinct:[22]

> Instinctive activities are unconscious (Claus), non-mental (Calderwood), incipiently conscious (Spencer), distinguished by the presence of consciousness (Romanes), accompanied by emotions in the mind (Wundt), involve connate ideas and inherited knowledge (Spalding); synonymous with impulsive activities (James), to be distinguished from those involving impulse proper (Hoffding, Marshall); not yet voluntary (Spencer), no longer voluntary (Lewes), never involuntary (Wundt); due to natural selection only (Weismann),to lapsed intelligence (Lewes, Schneider, Wundt), to both (Darwin, Romanes); to be distinguished from individually acquired habits (Darwin, Romanes, Sully and others), inclusive thereof (Wundt); at a minimum in man (Darwin, Romanes), at a maximum in man (James); essentially congenital (Romanes), inclusive of individually acquired modifications through intelligence (Darwin, Romanes, Wallace).
>
> (in Dewsbury 1993: 266)

5.5.2 William James and instinct

William James introduces his ideas on instinct in Chapter 24 of his *Principles of Psychology* (1890). James commences the chapter by offering the following definition of instinct: "Instinct is usually defined as the faculty of acting in such a way as to produce certain ends, without foresight of the ends, and without previous education in the performance" (James 1890: 383).

As with Darwin, James rejected the idea that instincts present in animals are provided by benevolent Providence, going so far as to dismiss such conceptions of instincts as "ineffectual wastes of words, because their authors . . . smothered everything in vague wonder at the clairvoyant and prophetic power of the animals – so superior to anything in man – and at the beneficence of God in endowing them with such a gift" (James 1890: 384–385). James argued that what appears to be beneficence on the part of the Almighty is a product of an *ad hominem* conception of the actions of animals. So-called strange animal action arises because as humans we anthropomorphise their actions, and using human conceptions, mundane animal reactions become wondrous, "clairvoyant" and "prophetic" (James 1890: 386).

Drawing on the work of contemporaries, James thought that the structure of an animal's nervous system dictates its instincts. The "actions we call instinct all conform to the general reflex type", which are "called forth by determinate sensory stimuli in contact with the animal's body, or at a distance in his environment" (James 1890: 384). Thus, says James, the cat chases the mouse, not because he has "notions either of life or death, or of self, or of preservation . . . [rather] He acts in each case separately and simply because he cannot help it" (James 1890: 384). The cat's nervous system is a "preorganized bundle of reactions" that makes it chase when confronted by that which we call a mouse (James 1890: 384). The same could be said for all animals, each compelled by a nervous system structured in such a way as to make it react in a particular way in the presence of a particular stimulus.

James equated instincts with *impulses* and divided impulses into three distinct types, "sensation-impulses, perception-impulses and idea-impulses" (James 1890: 385). When we draw our hand away from a hot flame, we are experiencing a sensation impulse. If we see others running and we turn to follow, then we are experiencing a perception impulse. An idea impulse, which James also calls an imagination impulse, is present when we seek out shelter in the presence of rain. These three types of impulse can work independently, but more likely they will be present concurrently, working together to achieve a particular end (James 1890: 385).

James's "reflexes grade into instincts, with reflexes generally affecting our own bodies and instincts affecting the outside world" (Dewsbury 1993: 273). His conception of instincts appears to be better aligned with Spencerian notions than with those of Romanes or Wundt. Consciousness does not appear in James's analysis of instincts, and, indeed, his explicit mention of a "lack of notions of life or death" in the example of a cat chasing a mouse suggests that James was closer to Spencer in viewing instincts as complex tropisms than to Romanes's conscious-laden approach.

5.5.3 James and the variability of instincts

It appears difficult to reconcile notions of reason with James's ideas of instinct. If instincts are reflex-like, albeit complex reflexes, how to explain reason? The exercise of reason would seem difficult, or indeed impossible, in the presence of such instincts.

James commenced by opining that reason is "not the mere[ly the] power of 'inferring' but also the *tendency to obey impulses* of a certain lofty sort, such as duty, or universal ends" (James 1890: 389, his italics). Recall that James equated impulse with instinct. Thus it seems that James considered that instinct "covers all impulses whatever, even the impulses to act from the idea of a distant fact" (James 1890: 389). Here James is introducing a nexus between the idea of reason and instinctive behaviour. But still, what of reason, and how can it exist if we are driven by instinct? James proposed two mechanisms that would ensure that, while behaviour may be driven by instincts, it is nonetheless variable and thus suggestive of what we call reason.

The first mechanism through which instincts are rendered variable is that associated with *experience*. James contends that man possesses a breadth of impulses greater in number than any animal. These human impulses are on their own blind and fulfil the Spencerian notion of instinct. However, man is endowed with a memory (as are some animals to a lesser degree), and the ability to remember enables man to act in the presence of a stimulus with "a foresight of those results" (James 1890: 390). This foresight ensures that "every instinctive act, in an animal with memory, must cease to be 'blind' after being once repeated" (James 1890: 390). Instinct, when combined with experience and memory of that experience, means that any subsequent actions must be modified. So, for example, a young hen that keeps her brood warm for the first time will be surprised when confronted with a hatching egg; but on subsequent hatchings she will no longer be surprised. Her experience, coupled with her memory, has modified her behaviour accordingly.

The second mechanism by which instinctive behaviour can be made variable is *inhibition*. Recall that James's physiological foundation explained instinctive behaviours as the product of pre-organised reactions in an animal's nervous system. This meant that just like reflex actions, instinctive action could be inhibited (Dewsbury 1993: 275). James also considered that the presence of numerous instincts would be such that the actions of one instinct may act to counter that of another. James's postulation that man is endowed with a far greater number of instincts than any other animal means that variability in man would tend to be greater (as indeed it is for all 'higher' animals):

> *Nature implants contrary impulses to act on many classes of things*, and leaves it to slight alterations in the conditions of the individual case to decide which impulse shall carry the day. Thus, greediness and suspicions, curiosity and timidity, coyness and desire, bashfulness and vanity, sociability and pugnacity, seem to shoot over into each other as quickly, and to remain in as unstable equilibrium, in the higher birds and mammals as in man. . . . *Each one of them, then, is an instinct*. . . . But they contradict each other.
>
> (James 1890: 392, his italics)

The conflict between instincts means reflexive patterns that would otherwise suggest the absence of any form of reason instead lead to a loss in the " 'instinctive' demeanour" and enable the presence of reason (James 1890: 393). As a result, man appears to "lead a life of hesitation and choice, an intellectual life; not, however, because he has no instinct – rather he has so many they block each other's path" (James 1890: 393) In this way, James salvaged notions of reason from what would otherwise lead to an idea of man as one destined to operate according to instinctive endowment.

5.5.4 James and two principles of nonuniformity of instincts

The mechanisms of experience and inhibition render instincts variable and help to explain the appearance of free will and the ability to reason in man. Following from these ideas, James would go on to develop two principles or laws through which the nonuniformity of instincts would be explained:

1. Inhibition of instincts as a product of habits.
2. The transitory nature of instinct.

The first principle essentially says that "when objects of a certain class elicit from an animal a certain sort of reaction, it often happens that the animal becomes partial to the first species of the class on which it has reacted, and will not afterward react on another specimen" (James 1890: 394). James proposed an "energy model" whereby the original impulse to, say, choose a home "exhausts itself in its first achievements and . . . leave[s] no surplus energy for reacting on new cases". In this example, there is no energy left to choose a different home (James 1890: 395). The habit is formed since the initial use of the instinct leads to a "depletion of energy from the impulse" (James 1890: 395). But in addition to this, the habit now so formed is "grafted onto the instinct", so that the ability to extricate ourselves from our habitual form is restricted (Dewsbury 1993: 277).[23]

The second principle, transitoriness, states that "many instincts ripen at certain ages and then fade away" (James 1890: 398). James goes further and says that "most instincts are implanted for the sake of giving rise to habits, and that this purpose once accomplished, the instincts themselves, as such, have no *raison d'être* in the psychical economy, and consequently fade away" (James 1890: 402). While instincts are transitory and come and go, James himself considered that the character of a man is essentially fixed by the time he reaches the age of 30 (Boakes 1984: 66). Thus it seems that even transitoriness has its upper limits.

5.5.5. James and human instincts

After stating that "man has a far greater variety of impulses than any lower animal", James then moves to present a list of special human instincts (James 1890: 300). James begins by listing instincts present in infants, such as the instinct of sucking, and continues with what appear to be rudimentary instincts, such as biting, clasping and crying. He then goes on to describe locomotion and continues in this vein until we reach what appear to be less reflex-type instincts and move to the instincts of imitation, emulation or rivalry, and sympathy. Strangely, James also includes in this list of special human instincts the instinct of fear, and then moves on to add play, constructiveness, curiosity and parental love (James 1890: 403–441).

Many of these, such as the instinct of emulation and parental love, will become important in the subsequent chapter, since they, among others, formed the basis of the ideas of instinct employed by Veblen to explain the development of economic institutions.

5.5.6 James and habit

Before leaving discussion of James and instinct, it is worth considering his views on habit. As elaborated upon earlier in the chapter, James saw a link between habit and instinct. In particular, the first principle or law of nonuniformity provides a direct nexus between instinct and habit. But what of habit in society?

James described societal habit as:

> the enormous fly-wheel of society, its most precious conservative agent. It alone is what keeps us all within the bounds of ordinance, and saves the children of fortune from the envious uprising of the poor. It alone prevents the harshest and most repulsive walks of life from being deserted by those brought up to tread therein. . . . It dooms us all to fight out the battle of life upon the lines of our nurture or our early choice, and to make the best of a pursuit that disagrees, because there is no other for which we are fitted, and it is too late to begin again. It keeps different social strata from mixing. . . . You see the little lines of cleavage running in the character, the tricks of thought, the prejudices . . . from which the man can by-and-by no more escape than his coat-sleeve can suddenly fall into a new set of folds. On the whole, it is best he should not escape. It is well for the world that most of us, by the age of thirty, the character has set like plaster, and will never soften again.
>
> (James in Boakes 1984: 66)

As will be seen in Chapter 6, Veblen's ideas on habit, instinct and the institutions that guide and shape society are remarkably similar in timbre to those of James.

5.6 Karl Marx, the materialist dialectic and historical materialism

If Charles Darwin is considered among the most influential figures in history, then it is an accolade any fair-minded person would ensure he shares with Karl Marx. Marx's influence over the course of human history is firmly forged in the popular consciousness and needs no discussion. On this basis alone, it would be reasonable to assume that Veblen was at the very least familiar with Marx. This argument by conjecture is, however, strengthened by recourse to primary sources, including Veblen's discussion of Marx in *The Socialist Economics of Karl Marx and his Followers* (1906a). It was there that Veblen spoke of the "boldness" and "logical consistency" of Marx's system, noting that as "a whole" it "has an air of originality and initiative" that is "rarely met with among the sciences that deal with . . . human culture" (Veblen 1906a: 575).

Among Veblen scholars there is some debate over the nature of Marx's influence on Veblen. Some, like Hunt (1979a) and Dugger (1979; 2007), suggest that Veblen's approach is in essence an extension of the Marxist paradigm (see also O'Hara 2000: 8, Chapter 3).[24] Others, such as Edgell and Tilman (1989), characterise Marx's influence as "negative" (Edgell and Tilman 1989: 88). By this, they seem to mean that Veblen's thought was indeed influenced by Marx but as a 'cue' to determine what *not* to adopt for his own method of economics.

Whether positive or negative, the question that arises regarding any outline of the Marxist system is 'where to begin'? The breadth of Marx's work is such that a comprehensive outline could take up volumes, let alone a chapter section. To get around this quandary, and in keeping with the method used thus far, I will focus on the points considered to give the reader a greater appreciation of the Veblenian paradigm as it is presented in later chapters.

With this in mind, the elements that will be outlined are the *materialist dialectic* and its application by Marx to the development of a 'science of history'. These topics have chosen because they could be said to constitute the basic or fundamental building blocks of Marx's method.

5.6.1 The materialist dialectic

If one were given the opportunity to ask Karl Marx to explain the materialist dialectic, the result might be a fit of confusion. This is because what we refer to as the 'materialist dialectic' was actually never known as such by Marx. It was the nineteenth-century German philosopher Joseph Dietzgen who coined the term, also referred to by the shortened *diamat* (Collier 2008: 136). Both Dietzgen's terminology and the portmanteau betray the fact that the materialist dialectic is at its core the blending of two ideas. The first of these is the Hegelian dialectic, while the second refers to a materialist epistemology. Marx's materialist dialectic is best understood by explaining these component parts.

Hegel's dialectic is built on the idea that "all things are contradictory in themselves" (Hegel in Callinicos 2011: 114). The meaning of contradiction in Hegel's dialectic is of a thing being defined by the existence of another. For example, a master is defined by the existence of a servant. The servant is also defined by the presence of a master. The whole idea of servant and master is dependent upon the other. Another example is light and dark. We define the notion of light by the presence of darkness, and *vice versa*. Sometimes, the opposites are referred to as the *thesis* and *antithesis* (Collier 2008: 137).

Hegel posited that contradictions provide the impulse necessary for the development of knowledge and give an explanation for historical movement. This is because inherent in a contradiction is a tension that requires resolution. Consider the example of light and darkness. Suppose a person had only ever known darkness. Such a person would have no ability or cause to be familiar with light. Similarly, another has only been aware of light. Now for some reason, they become aware of one another's existence. The 'dark' person is now made aware of the existence of light, while the 'light' person is confronted with the possibility of darkness. We have a contradiction. Both are now aware that their knowledge is incomplete. The tension arising from this must be resolved. The resolution occurs by 'synthesising' their singularly held knowledge so that a new understanding is struck that combines both their knowledge. In this example, the *synthesis* is a spectrum between absolute darkness and absolute light.

The resolution in this example can be thought of as consisting of three distinct stages. To begin with we have a simple unity, the thesis. At this point, no change has occurred, and we see an object or state of being as itself. Then we are confronted with its 'negation', or antithesis. In the third and final stage, the two are "reconciled" to form a "greater unity", the so-called *synthesis* (Callinicos 2011: 116).

However, the resulting synthesis is transitory. This is because a synthesis is merely the resolution in the contradiction as it existed at a particular point. But as new knowledge appears, so too do new contradictions. When these occur, they will also require resolution, creating further movement and change. The dialectic is thus a process, "a state of continuous movement and change, of . . . . . . renewal and development, where something is always arising and developing, and something always disintegrating and dying away" (Stalin 1940: 7).

There is, however, an endpoint, a teleological finality. This is because while things appear disjoint or different and thus seem to give rise to a negation, they are actually part of the same, connected whole; where all "all phenomena are interconnected and interdependent" (Stalin 1940: 12). With each increase in knowledge that occurs after each synthesis, the whole becomes clearer. Once the whole has been understood, the dialectic process ceases. At this point, all tensions are extinguished, all negations resolved and knowledge of the whole is complete (Callinicos 2011: 116).[25]

Hegel conceived his dialectic on *idealist* foundations, the belief that thought comes first and reality follows. In the Hegelian construct, the most important mind and the crucible of all knowledge is that of the 'Absolute Spirit', or God. In Hegel's apprehension, man had become alienated from the Absolute Spirit. The consequence of 'divine disconnection' is that man's knowledge is incomplete; he is unable to conceive the unity or 'wholeness' of reality. Thus man sees contradictions in what are actually the connected thoughts of the Absolute Spirit's mind. It is this inability to see the unity of things that gives rise to contradictions. But as each contradiction is resolved into a new synthesis, man comes closer to understanding the true nature of God's mind and of the unity of creation. The dialectic is complete once man achieves unity with God (Callinicos 2011: 117–118).

For many, the Hegelian dialectic contained the seeds of understanding, but they could not countenance its idealist foundations and recourse to notions of an Absolute Spirit. Instead, they sought to keep the dialectic process but base it on materialist foundations. Unlike Hegel and the idealists who saw thought as the foundation of reality, the materialists considered the physical world as precedent to all thought. Among those who sought to place the dialectic on firm materialist footings was the German philosopher Ludwig Feuerbach, Hegel's student, who refused to consider the existence of anything other than the material (Shimp 2009: 39).

In Hegel's construct, man's abilities are not considered part of his very substance but a result of an 'alien' God's grace in endowing man with his skills. Man is thus 'alienated' from his own powers of thought and reason; his skills and abilities are considered not part of his own being but, instead, a godly gift (Callinicos 2011: 120; Wolff 2002: 17). A consequence is that man has cast man as an inferior being while the Absolute Spirit represents the paragon (Wolff 2002: 17). But worst, try as he might, man must exist in the knowledge that he will *never* achieve the greatness of the Absolute Spirit. Man must settle with his wretchedness, cast as a cheapened 'insect' in the scheme of creation.

For Feuerbach, man's abilities owe naught to a mythical deity but have a physical provenance. What good or skill that is falsely attributed to God is in reality a reflection of man's intrinsic physical substance, what Feuerbach called "species being" (Callinicos 2011: 121). Once made aware of this fact, man will be liberated, no longer wrongly casting himself as a wretched, wicked and weak being requiring salvation but instead finally realising that his ability to achieve good and perform worthy acts is part of his very physical substance (Wolff 2002: 17–18).

While Marx approved of Feuerbach's efforts to place the dialectic on materialist footings and debunk superstition, he was dismissive of his method. Marx agreed that the idealist "Hegel fell into the illusion of conceiving the real as the product of thought" (Marx 1973: 101). However, he considered that Feuerbach had merely supplanted one set of idealist notions with another by arguing that a change in thought or ideas (where humans recognise that their skills are physically innate and not divinely gifted) brings about a change in the material. Marx and his long-time friend and colleague Friedrich Engels famously lampooned this form of 'materialism' in a well-known passage from *The German Ideology*:

> Once upon a time a valiant fellow had the idea that men were drowned in water only because they were possessed with the idea of gravity. If they were to knock this notion out of their heads, say by stating it to be a superstition, a religious concept, they would be sublimely proof against any danger from water.
>
> (Marx and Engels 1976: 30)

Because what was prescribed was actually the replacement of one type of idealism with another, Marx and Engels accused Feuerbach and his fellow Young Hegelians of being the "staunchest conservatives" whose 'anti-religious' and " 'world-shattering' statements," were more apparent than real (Marx and Engels 1976: 36). Despite this, Feuerbach's attempts had shown that one could attempt a materialist reappraisal of Hegel's dialectic.

Marx considered that a dialectic built on materialist grounds should be one that salvaged the "rational kernel" within the "mystical shell" (Marx 1867: 13) that was Hegel's dialectic and improve upon Feuerbach's materialist 'first steps'. A materialist dialectic thus begins with the following reality: Man's thought does not create the world; rather, his thought is a reflection of the actual, physical world (Marx 1973: 101). In Marx's words, "it is not the consciousness of men that determines their being, but on the contrary, their social being which determines their consciousness" (Marx 1977: 21). The materialist dialectic thus "inverted" Hegel's order (Marx in Callinicos 2011: 119), suggesting that a change in man's physical conditions is brought about not by a change in ideas but by a change in the physical itself. And since the physical precedes and determines thought, amendments in thought can only be explained by changes in the material conditions of life.

5.6.2 Historical materialism

It is easy to see from the previous section what Marx's science of history, sometimes referred to as *historical materialism*, would look like. Historical development would be explained as the thrust and parry resulting from the interplay and resolution of contradicting forces, while adherence to a materialist foundation means that the contradictions are the consequence of physical phenomena. In other words, it is a dialectical process, but one where the contradictions arise not from thoughts, but from the physical. This materialist basis of history represented a marked departure in a period when ideas were still considered the primary force behind historical development.

Marx's analysis of history began by recognising that man is first and foremost a producer and transformer of nature. Like all animals, man must produce to survive. But unlike animals that rely upon instinct to satiate their needs, man has the ability and imagination to conceive and to bend his mind and his skills to new modes of production and methods of controlling nature:

> Labour is . . . a process in which both man and Nature participate, and in which man of his own accord starts, regulates, and controls the material reactions between himself and Nature. He opposes himself to Nature as one of her own forces, setting in motion arms and legs, head and hands, the natural forces of his body, in order to appropriate Nature's productions in a form adapted to his own wants. . . . A spider conducts operations that resemble those of a weaver, and a bee puts to shame many an architect in the construction of her cells. But what distinguishes the worst architect from the best of bees is . . . that the architect raises his structure in imagination before he erects it in reality. At the end of every labour-process, we get a result that already existed in the imagination of the labourer at its commencement.
>
> (Marx 1867: 124)

Human production has a dual basis. First, it is *physical* and involves the transformation of nature into the objects necessary to sustain life. This aspect is referred to as the 'forces of production' (Callinicos 2011: 155). The forces of production comprise two further elements. The first is 'labour power', the physical (and mental) contribution made by man's labour towards production, while the second is the 'means of production', which comprises the bounty of nature available for man to ply into the objects of his needs and the tools used to do this (Callinicos 2011: 156).

But while production is clearly physical, it is also *social*, and this forms the other half of the production 'duality'. Production is social in the common sense of the word, where people work together and participate in the creation of goods. But since the materialist conception is one where the physical shapes thought, production is also social in the way that it shapes social relations. The social relations reflect a given force of production, but as the forces of production develop and change, we also see a reordering of the social relations that underpin society (Callinicos 2011: 155, 159).

An example might help illustrate this. In rudimentary societies with little to no economic surplus, there is little call or ability for a small group to control the economic booty. However, as technology develops and the forces of production advance, a situation arises whereby a minority can and do seize control of production. At this point, we see the arrival of class, based on those who control and those who are controlled. The appearance of class has occurred because technological development reached the level necessary for a minority to lay claim to and control the output of society. Thus, the physical aspects of production have resulted in the social manifestation of a class that *controls* the means of production. And it is upon this physical economic 'base' that the social 'superstructure' is erected:[26]

> In the social production of their existence, men inevitably enter into definite relations . . . namely relations of production appropriate to a given stage in the development of their material forces of production. The totality of these relations of production constitutes the economic structure of society, the real foundation, on which arises a legal and political superstructure and to which correspond definite forms of consciousness. The mode of production of material life conditions the general process of social, political and intellectual life.
>
> (Marx 1977: 20–21)

The materialist base thus 'trickles *up*' to affect the very manner in which people think and their 'common ideologies'. It gives rise to society's institutions, political or otherwise. It is upon this physical grounding that the religious 'firmament' was erected, a social manifestation designed to give comfort to the large swathe of the populace for whom physical existence was harsh:

> The wretchedness of religion is at once an expression of and a protest against real wretchedness. Religion is the sigh of the oppressed creature, the heart of a heartless world, and the soul of soulless conditions. It is the opium of the people. The abolition of religion as the illusory happiness of the people is the demand for their true happiness. The call to abandon illusions about their condition is the call to abandon a condition which requires illusions. Thus, the critique of religion is the critique in embryo of the vale of tears of which religion is the halo.
>
> (Marx 1843: 131)

Materialist notions thus explain how the physical shapes thought as well as the appearance of social manifestations like religion. This was the part that Feuerbach and the Young Hegelians had failed to apprehend: that religious thought has a materialist basis, that it is physical reality (in this case physical suffering) that gives birth to such a social manifestation and that a change in this realm occurs only with a change in the physical.

That social institutions like religion have undergone marked change needs no discussion. But what accounts for this change? For this, we return to the dialectic.

Recall that the dialectic is a theory of a process fuelled by the appearance of contradictions 'yearning' for resolution. In the Marxist paradigm, the key contradiction is between those who control the means of production and those who do not. In other words, the contradiction manifests itself in the form of a class struggle that has been a feature throughout much of human society:

> The history of all hitherto existing societies is the history of class struggles. Freeman and slave, patrician and plebeian, lord and serf, guild-master and journeyman, in a word, oppressor and oppressed, stood in constant opposition to one another, carried on an uninterrupted, now hidden, now open fight, a fight that each time ended, either in a revolutionary re-constitution of society at large, or in the common ruin of the contending classes.
>
> (Marx and Engels 1888: 62)

The controlling class wishes things to stay as they are. Clearly, their position of power confers certain privileges upon them that they do not wish to relinquish. However, for those who are 'controlled', the situation is one that must be changed; they wish to improve their lot. But the status quo will only be affected by a change in the material conditions of life, such as technological advancement. Where such a change occurs, we see a change in the 'nonmaterial' aspects of life, and the relationship between the oppressor and the oppressed is affected. The ensuing struggle between these contradictory forces propels historical development.

This dialectical 'struggle' results in a new synthesis. The appearance of the new synthesis sees a change in the very fabric of society so that it squares with the methods and goals of the new ruling paradigm. To return to earlier language, the superstructure reflects the change in the base. But in the event that the new synthesis results in a new ruling class, then it will also necessarily mean the appearance of a new form of 'Untermenschen'. The result is a new contradiction requiring resolution, further propelling the dialectic process. As Engels put it:

> all successive historical systems are only transitory stages in the endless course of development of human society from the lower to the higher. Each stage is necessary, and therefore justified for the time and conditions to which it owes its origin. But in the face of new, higher conditions which develop in its own womb, it loses its validity and justification. It must give way to a higher stage which will also in its turn decay and perish.
>
> (in Callinicos 2011: 118)

In *The German Ideology* and *The Communist Manifesto*, Marx and Engels discuss various stages of development and epochs of history that correspond with "different forms of property" (Marx and Engels 1976: 38) and which have as their marker a historically specific form of the contradiction.[27] And like Hegel, Marx's dialectic has an end-term, the point where contradictions are exhausted. It is easy to see that this will be when there is no longer a ruling or oppressed class.

While Marx's contemporaries among the classical economists characterised capitalism in as an 'unimpeachable' form of society where the competitive struggle worked for the good of all, Marx viewed capitalism as merely a transitory step in a dialectic that would ultimately yield a society absent the forms of ownership and class that had beset human development. This could not be so with capitalism, since its class-based architecture ensured that it contained within its very essence the seeds that would lead to its demise and usher in a new synthesis. The modern capitalist society and ancient Rome may be markedly different in many respects, but they share a fundamental feature: They each consist of the controlled and controller.

Only a communist society is without this contradiction, and hence without the very forces or motions that have compelled historical transformation. Marx famously considered that communism would follow the capitalist form of society. This next communist step in history would occur once the oppressed proletariat rose up in revolution to set the existing capitalist order asunder.

5.7 Conclusion

The influences presented in this chapter suggest that Veblen was a polymath whose influences varied from those of a philosophical nature to the 'hard sciences', as represented by Darwin. Interestingly, the three movements or ideas that were presented subsequent to the section on Darwinian evolution did themselves draw from the insights of Darwin and the Darwinian method. Thus Veblen was in accord with many of his contemporaries in attempting to draw from the one major intellectual outcome of the period, Darwinian evolution. Key among the insights was the desire to move scientific process away from teleological straitjackets and for science to annexe responsibility for understanding root causes from the realm of theology.

The other influence was that of Karl Marx. While there may be some controversy regarding the nature of this influence, there is little disputing that Veblen held Marx's paradigm in esteem for the bold nature of its scope. Perhaps, as Dugger notes, Veblen's work was an attempt to excise the "taint of optimistic teleology" in Marx and update it with the 'blind chance' of Darwin (Dugger 1979: 7).[28] Indeed, Veblen's dualism (which will be discussed in the following chapters) has been said to essentially mirror the contradictions present in the materialist dialectic (Dugger 1979: 7). It is as though Veblen kept the basic foundations of Marx's ideas, stripped them of their teleological inevitabilities and notions of natural rights and updated them to accord with Darwinian principles (see Hill 1958: 139). Furthermore, Veblen's description of human development, through the interaction of these forces and in the development of societal institutions, appears to bear some similarity to Marx's 'theory of history' and human development.

In the next chapter, I will begin to outline Veblen's method as well as his objections to the neoclassical approach. The ultimate aim will be to see what his approach means for public support for the arts and whether it offers a conception of the issue that proffers new or better insights.

Notes

1 Veblen had a publicly 'strained' marriage with Ellen and a notorious reputation for philandering (see Jorgensen and Jorgensen 1999; Edgell 2001). He "offended" the Chicago university administration by 'failing' to adequately "advertise the University" (Tilman 1996: 1) and by producing a work that satirised the businesslike administration of universities. The offending work was eventually published in 1918, and we now know it as *The Higher Learning in America: A Memorandum on the Conduct of Universities by Business Men*. It seems University of Chicago President William Rainey Harper took the work as a slight and affront against his own administration (Tilman 1996: 14).

2 With respect to Lutheranism, Edgell (2001: 12) suggests that Veblen's agnosticism was 'tainted' by his Norwegian Lutheran roots, so much so that he credits Lutheranism as the root of Veblen's disdain for wastefulness.

3 The reader will note that this section outweighs elaboration on the other 'muses' to follow. This is partly because I consider Darwin's method and insights to be of such importance that they warrant greater explanation but also because Darwin's discoveries informed the development of three of the other areas chosen for outline, including pragmatism, the German historical school and instinct theory and habit.

4 So, for example, a dog could not turn into a cat. Importantly, while a dog could not turn into a cat or *vice versa*, essence did not entertain the possibility that they shared a common ancestor, which as will be seen is a fundamental plank of Darwinian evolution.

5 Arthur O. Lovejoy would say that the Great Chain of Being was made up of three intellectual underpinnings, 'plenitude', 'continuity', and 'gradation' (Lovejoy 1936). Plenitude is a Christian idea that suggests that God is showing his goodness by producing all possible species. In essence, this refers to the bounty of God's creation. Continuity means that there would be no gaps between creatures. The sage God created enough species so that each would be linked to another. So, for example, man was connected to apes, which were connected to monkeys. Gradation means that there is a rank, from lowest to highest forms.

6 Further, with respect to deists, Hume showed that the design argument appeals if we consider the world as a machine. However, it is plausible and possible for the world to be conceived as a vegetable or some other organic being that sprang forth almost as though from a seed. The second option means that the world may have come about without the need for divine providence or intervention. The "logical possibility that the world had caused itself" presented problems for the idea of design (Oldroyd 1980: 63). Perhaps, as Oldroyd says, the world was designed, but by a bungling designer, a committee of designers or perhaps an apprentice (Oldroyd 1980: 63)!

7 Others still would explain the fossil record not as the remains of once living but now extinct organisms but as manifestations of forms in the inorganic world (Ruse 1979: 4).

8 That is, extinction was impossible apart from the special circumstance where a species becomes a victim of man's destructive forces (Ruse 1979: 6).

9 Lamarck's chain differed also in that it was divided in two, with one chain for animals and another for plants. He would later amend the chain again by further dividing the animal chain in two (Ruse 1979: 7).

10 While Lamarck posited that *besoins* were a response to environmental factors, he was unclear as to whether movement up the Chain occurred regularly or as a response to changing environmental circumstances. When presented with evidence purporting to show a lack of change in organisms, Lamarck would respond that this was because

there had been no environmental shift to cause a change. Then, somewhat inconsistently, he suggested that movement up the chain would occur "no matter what happens or fails to happen", contradicting his earlier position (Ruse 1979: 8).

11 As an aside, Lamarck's adherence to the Chain of Being, albeit a dynamic one, implied a gradual continuity between organisms. Continuity precludes the existence of *species*, that is, "distinct organisms, unable to breed with other kinds" (Ruse 1979: 10). Within species there are organisms. To illustrate, consider the case of the dog. The species in this case is the dog, and within this species exist organisms such as wolves, dingos and the domestic Labrador. It is possible to interbreed these organisms. However, take another species, the deer. It is not possible to breed a dog with a deer. The Great Chain's implied continuity suggests that there would be organisms between species that would bridge the divide and enable interbreeding. Lamarck struggled to explain this, other than by turning to improvised solutions such as suggesting that the 'bridging organisms' were yet to be discovered, or that they may once have existed but now cease to after falling prey to man's destructive force (Ruse: 1979: 10). Lamarck's theory was thus an explanation for the origin of organisms and not the origin of species (Ruse 1979: 10; Oldroyd 1980: 33).

12 Proponents of this optimistic view included the Marquis of Condorcet and William Godwin (Rima 1991: 117). Both believed that human perfection and, as a result, happiness could be achieved. In Godwin's case, this was through the establishment of a "simple form of society, without government" (in Rima 1991: 117), whereas Condorcet appealed to reason gained through the "cumulative character of knowledge in the arts and sciences" (Rima 1991: 117)

13 Malthus was responding to Godwin and Condorcet, who considered that humanity and society could be perfected (Rima 1991: 118). Unlike their optimistic perceptions, Malthus presented a world that had inherent features that would act against the ability to achieve utopia. In short, these features were the tendency for population to grow exponentially, against a food supply that could only grow arithmetically. Food shortages would be the necessary result. Thus, mankind would always be the victim of "famine, poverty, disease and war unless some means of limiting population could be found" (Rima 1991: 118–124, Oldroyd 1980: 67). It has been suggested that Malthus's ideas were thus the "logical predecessor of the Darwinian theory of evolution" (Ambirajan1959: 200–201). By "shattering natural law . . . Malthus gave prominence to the idea of competitive struggle for existence and . . . survival of the fittest", which of course was later famously adopted by Darwin to explain the workings of the natural world (Ambirajan1959: 200–201).

14 This refers to the idea that things are the way that they are because that is the way the Creator intended them to be. Veblen would say that "Natural laws are corollaries under the arbitrary rules of status imposed on the natural universe by an all-powerful Providence with a view to the maintenance of his own prestige. The science that grows in such a spiritual environment is of the class represented by alchemy and astrology, in which the imputed degree of nobility and prepotency of the objects and the symbolic force of their names are looked to for an explanation of what takes place" (Veblen 1906: 594).

15 Peirce's conception of 'hard' here is no doubt rooted in the physical world, and no doubt he was thinking of an object such as a diamond, betraying his background as a chemist. However, this is but one meaning of 'hard', and there are many others. For example, hard can be used to describe a *hard* problem, or indeed, a *hard* worker. Murphy (1990) redeems Peirce's 'oversight' and shows that the Pragmatic maxim works effectively when our conception of hard is broadened to include these and other uses of 'hard', thereby showing the applicability of the Pragmatic maxim (Murphy 1990: 27–28).

16 Although earlier in the piece Grimmer-Solem says that "the 'Historical School', whatever it was, seems real enough, and attempts to dismiss it would appear to be both fruitless and unnecessary" (2003: 21)

17 These were:
   i. "The point of view of relativity", essentially the idea and importance of historical relativity and historical specificity
   ii. "The point of view of the unity of social life and of the inseparable correlation between its elements"
   iii. "The anti-rationalist point of view"
   iv. The point of view of evolution
   v. The point of view of the interest in individual correlation
   vi. The organic point of view.

18 Consider, as a comparison, that early nineteenth-century Germany had about 20 academic chairs devoted to the study of economics, with the first of these founded at the University of Halle in 1727. Thus, when the German historical school appeared, a rich tradition in economic scholarship had already been formed. Against this, while some chairs in economics had been established in some British universities during said period, the number was far less. However, despite the lack of recognition through chairs, economic instruction occurred in some form in most British universities (Hodgson 2001: 57).

19 Clark had studied at the University of Zurich and the University of Heidelberg, where he received instruction from Karl Knies (Bateman 2004: 195).

20 As an example of these 'extra historical' inputs, Schumpeter speaks of the works of "Vico and Comte" and the idea of the "parallel development of the various nations and the idea of the nation as an organism which can age and die" (Schumpeter 1912: 156–157). It would later be the desire of the younger school to purge the historical approach of any such sources in their endeavour for an "unbiased and detailed historical study" of economics (Schumpeter 1912: 156–157)

21 Frederick Marryat was a well-known writer and Royal Navy officer who lived between 1792 and 1848. He is principally known for his novel *Mr Midshipman Easy*. The quote comes from his novel *Masterman Ready, or the Wreck of the Pacific* (1841).

22 The names in parentheses are of the contemporaries of Morgan who were associated with the particular view.

23 James demonstrates this principle through the example of a cow which gives birth to a calf while wandering off into the woods. In such a case, if the calf does not have human contact for a week or more, then when confronted by man it "is wild and almost as fleet as a deer" (James 1890: 396). Contrast this with a calf that has human contact from birth, which shows no such wild tendencies (James 1890: 396).

24 Dugger actually claims that Veblen was a "radical and a Marxist" (Dugger 2007: paragraph 2).

25 Another way to think of this is through the metaphor of the jigsaw puzzle. Suppose each resolved contradiction represented an additional piece of the puzzle. As we resolve and add a piece we begin to comprehend that each piece is part of a larger picture. Eventually the puzzle is complete, we see the complete picture and we have the whole.

26 The Russian philosopher and Marxist Georgi Plekhanov summarised the base-superstructure relationship in a five-tiered hierarchy. To begin with, we have the base that comprises the "state of productive forces". These productive forces then "condition the economic relations". It is upon this "economic 'basis'" that "the socio-political system" is "developed". Consequently, the "mentality of social man" is forged "in part by the economic conditions obtaining, and in part by the entire social-political system that has arisen on that foundation". Finally, we have the "various ideologies that reflect the properties of that mentality" (Plekhanov 1910: 166–167).

27 The first of these is *tribal*, sometimes known as *primitive communism*. During this period, technology is at a rude state, and the contradiction is present in a "latent" form of slavery that occurs within family structures. The second period is the *ancient communal*. Here, the division of labour is more pronounced, and the latent slavery of the predecessor period has given way to a full-blown version. The third period is *feudal*,

when the brute slavery and contradictions of civilisations such as Rome are transformed into a system of serfdom. The fourth system is *capitalism*, where the contradiction occurs between the profit-oriented goals of a capitalist class and a proletariat that is seemingly free but is forced to earn subsistence subject to the whims and coercive forces of the ruling capitalist class (Marx and Engels 1976: 38–41; Marx and Engels 1888: 62–63).

28 Indeed, at first blush it appears that Veblen adopted the basic ideas presented by Marx and updated them with the discoveries of Darwin, in particular by discarding the teleological inevitabilities that arise through reliance on the Hegelian dialectical system. This point is not germane to the analysis that follows in subsequent chapters. However, it is my view that the idea that Veblen's economic system is a Darwinian update of Marx would be a worthy subject for future research.

6 Veblen's economic edifice

6.1 Introduction

In 1921, H.L. Mencken rather colourfully recounted how he had set upon the task of reading the works of Thorstein Veblen:

> I managed to get through the whole infernal job. I read "The Theory of the Leisure Class", I read "The Theory of Business Enterprise", and then I read "The Instinct of Workmanship." An hiatus followed; I was racked by severe neuralgia, with delusions of persecution. On recovering I tackled "Imperial Germany and the Industrial Revolution." Malaria for a month, and then "The Nature of the Peace and the Terms of Its Perpetuation." What ensued was never diagnosed, probably it was some low infection of the mesentery or spleen. When it passed off, leaving only an asthmatic cough, I read "The Higher Learning in America." And then went to Mt Clemens to drink the Glauber's salts. Eureka! The business was done! It had strained me, but now it was over.
>
> (Mencken 1921: 64–65)

Those familiar with Veblen's works would readily identify the inspiration for Mencken's passage. Mencken is of course referring to Veblen's 'unique' style of writing, which he goes on to describe as "almost unbelievable tediousness and flatulence", leading him to dismiss Veblen's ideas as "quite simple, and often anything but revolutionary in essence" (Mencken 1921: 65–66). Indeed, Mencken goes further, claiming that "practically the whole system of Prof. Dr. Veblen was in his first book and his last. . . . Read these two, and you won't have to read the others" (Mencken 1921: 65).

Whether one subscribes to Mencken's dismissive view or holds an alternative, more 'generous' view, the passage illustrates a simple point that few would find objectionable: Understanding Veblen's work and his economic ideas can turn into quite a task given his use of prolix and dense language, and, as such, the power and significance of his ideas can be easily missed or lost, even to great minds like Mencken.

To be sure, in researching for this book, a difficulty I encountered was getting to the point of Veblen's ideas on economics: Just what was Veblen trying to say?

Veblen's verbal flourishes, excessive use of 'elegant variation' and ever-present pleonasms make distilling his thoughts into key salient points a difficult task. Despite this, in this chapter, I make an effort at just that and begin to outline the building blocks of Veblen's economic analysis. To put it in terms more befitting of Veblen's thoughts and intellectual geist, I will provide an outline of the genetic material that forms Veblen's economic body of work.

First and foremost, I begin by delineating Veblen's criticisms of neoclassical economics. Indeed, Veblen coined the hyphenated term 'neo-classical' a century or so ago as a means to refer to the intellectual heirs of the classical school (Veblen 1900; Colander 2000: 131; Fayazmanesh 1998).[1] From there, I lay the foundation of Veblen's economic scheme. I commence with instincts, moving on to habits and the formation of institutions and their appearance through periods of cultural development and the role played by technology. As will become clear, Veblen's work adopted a Darwinian approach, and the idea of natural selection was extrapolated by Veblen to understand and explain change in society, culture and economic organisation.

6.2 The pre-Darwinian nature of neoclassical economics

Veblen produced two works that arguably most clearly and completely expound his criticisms of neoclassical approaches to understanding economic phenomena. These were "Why is Economics not an Evolutionary Science?" (1898) and "The Preconceptions of Economic Science", with the latter being a set of three articles published in 1899 and 1900.[2] Veblen's criticisms amount to the following: that neoclassical economics (and, as will be shown, its classical forebears) was teleological, that it was taxonomic and that it was built on an out-dated hedonistic conception of human behaviour (Ghosh 1984: 475). What follows is a delineation of these objections.

6.2.1 An antiquated science

Veblen's criticisms of neoclassical economics[3] are built on the idea that the science was antiquated in its approach. In short, economics was not a 'modern' science. He commences his criticism in a manner that leaves no uncertainty on this point:

> the science stands in need of rehabilitation. . . . It may be taken as the consensus of those men who are doing the serious work of modern anthropology, ethnology, and psychology, as well of those in the biological sciences proper, that economics is helplessly behind the times, and unable to handle its subject matter in a way to entitle it to standing as a modern science.
>
> (Veblen 1898: 373)

An implication arising from the preceding passage is the need to answer the following questions: What makes a science, and what makes a science modern?; and why did economics not fulfil the criteria? Veblen considered three possibilities (Veblen 1898: 373–375).

Some critics claimed that economics was not a modern science because it failed to deal with facts; but, as Veblen showed, economics does indeed deal with facts, "often in the most painstaking way" (Veblen 1898: 375). To highlight the point, Veblen turned to the case of the German historical school, which as was shown in Chapter 5, had among its markers an almost 'fanatical' insistence on the collection and use of 'facts'. The use of facts was not limited to the historical school, and Alfred Marshall's claim that economics had "established . . . harmony between the study of facts and of ideas" suggests the use of facts was being applied more generally (Marshall 1897: 133).

Another argument was that economics failed to provide a "theory of a process, of an unfolding sequence" (Veblen 1898: 375). But as Veblen showed, many of the doctrines developed by economists of his day did indeed espouse theories of "certain economic processes" (Veblen 1898: 375). Pointing to John Stuart Mill's "doctrines of production, distribution and exchange" Veblen showed that economics had indeed developed theories of some economic processes (Veblen 1898: 375).[4] For Veblen, this charge seemed to hold little water, so it was not here that Veblen was to base his criticism.

In contrast to these two objections, Veblen built his criticisms on the failure of economic science to embrace the Darwinian revolution. Economic science was not modern because it was not evolutionary, in the Darwinian sense. "Modern sciences", on the other hand, "are evolutionary sciences", and:

> The difference between the evolutionary and pre-evolutionary sciences lies not in the insistence on facts . . . nor does the difference lie in the absence of any efforts to formulate and explain schemes of process, sequences, growth and development in the pre-evolutionary days. . . . The difference is a difference of spiritual attitude or point of view in the two contrasted generations of scientists.
>
> (Veblen 1898: 374)

Recall from Chapter 5 that pre-Darwinian generations adhered to notions of an unchanging, designed universe, held together and operating according to natural laws, generally conceived as serving human ends. A corollary of this is teleology, the idea that things move towards some purpose, that they are end or goal driven; another way of thinking of this is that they move to fulfil the design. Darwin helped uproot these preconceptions, leading to the casting of scientific questions in a different manner:

> The modern scientist is unwilling to depart from the test of causal relation or quantitative sequence. When he asks the question, Why? he insists on an answer in terms of cause and effect. . . . This is his last recourse.
>
> (Veblen 1898: 377)

Modern, post-Darwinian science examined processes in terms of matter-of-fact, sequential cause and effect. This was sufficient for the Darwinian scientist, who sought no higher purpose, no grand scheme to colour or give higher purpose to his explanations:

> The great deserts of the evolutionist leaders – if they have great deserts as leaders – lie, on the one hand, in their refusal to go back of the colorless sequence of phenomena and seek higher ground for their ultimate syntheses, and, on the other hand, in their having shown how this colorless impersonal sequence of cause and effect can be made use of for theory proper, by virtue of its cumulative character.
>
> (Veblen 1898: 378)

By contrast, pre-Darwinian scientists would colour their analyses in terms of a design operating with a tendency or goal; a 'grand scheme' that governed or directed the function of the universe and the phenomena within it. This is what Veblen means when he says that modern sciences refuse to "seek a higher ground for their ultimate syntheses". However, it is precisely this higher ground that imbues pre-Darwinian, 'antiquated' approaches to science. For pre-Darwinian scientists:

> this ground of cause and effect is not definitive. Their sense of truth and substantiality is not satisfied with a formulation of mechanical sequence. The ultimate term in their systematisation of knowledge is a "natural law." This natural law is felt to exercise some sort of a coercive surveillance over the sequence of events, and to give a spiritual stability and consistence to the causal relation at any given juncture. To meet the high classical requirement, a sequence . . . must be apprehended in terms of a consistent propensity tending to some spiritually legitimate end. When facts and events have been reduced to these terms of fundamental truth and have been made to square with the requirements of definitive normality, the investigator rests his case.
>
> (Veblen 1898: 378)[5]

At least two outcomes arise from the pre-Darwinian perspective and its 'quasi-spiritual' appreciation of phenomena. The first is the already mentioned idea that nature is conceived as being static and subject to natural laws that ensure that things tend to a particular end or design. But a preconceived end suggests that there is a right way of being and a wrong way of being, or in Veblen's terminology, a legitimate end and, presumably by contrast, an illegitimate end.[6] The right state is that which fits with the preconceived legitimate end; it is the state that fits with the natural order and 'obeys' natural law.

If the right or legitimate state or end is that where natural law prevails, then the opposite case must be where natural law has not been able to assert its beneficent authority. How does this come about? Pre-Darwinian thought conceived of this as being due to some disturbance that does not allow the natural order to obtain:

> Any causal sequence which is apprehended to traverse the imputed propensity in events is a "disturbing factor." . . . The objective point of the efforts of the scientists working under the guidance of this classical tradition, is to formulate knowledge in terms of absolute truth.
>
> (Veblen 1898: 378)

By contrast, Darwinian methods require that one relinquish preconceived notions of legitimate ends and disturbing causes. With Darwin, there is no way of knowing where things might end, meaning that one cannot commence with some view of the world as it should or ought to be. There is no predetermined right or wrong way; there is just the way it is, and this is "drawn in terms of cause and effect" (Veblen 1909a: 625). The modern scientist is content to leave things at that. Given no predetermined ends or ultimate design to be fulfilled, the modern scientist actually dares to discover the laws that drive the universe; he does not take them as predetermined givens – hence, Darwin and his 'daring' discovery of the mechanism of natural selection to account for the origin of species, thereby challenging the preconception of the Great Chain. Veblen used the example of chemistry to show how a science that had once been 'infected' by the old ways of thinking had managed to change, colouring and shaping its analysis so that it was now modern:

> the chemist's experimental inquiry into any substance is, What comes of the substance determined? What will it do? What will it lead to? . . . There is no ultimate term, and no definite solution except in terms of further action. The theory worked out is always a theory of a genetic succession of phenomena, and the relations determined and elaborated into a body of doctrine are always genetic relations. In modern chemistry no cognisance is taken of the honorific bearing of reactions or molecular formulae. The modern chemist, as contrasted with this ancient congener, knows nothing of the worth, elegance, or cogency of the relations that may subsist between the particles of matter with which he busies himself, for any other than the genetic purpose.
>
> (Veblen 1899a: 123–124)

The advances Veblen claims to have occurred in chemistry were also occurring in "modern anthropology, ethnology, . . . psychology, as well as . . . the biological sciences proper" (Veblen 1898: 373). By contrast, economics was "helplessly behind the times" and had not achieved what was being achieved in other disciplines (Veblen 1898: 373). However, it seemed the slow pace of economic science in relinquishing adherence to the older 'metaphysic' was not due to a lack of knowledge on the part of economists of Darwin's discoveries. Indeed, Veblen was aware that "Economists of the present day are commonly evolutionists, in a general way" (Veblen 1900: 265). Even Alfred Marshall, Veblen's 'anointed' spokesman for the discipline (Veblen 1898: 374) considered that "Darwin's development of the laws of struggle and survival gave perhaps a greater impetus to the careful and exact study of particular facts than any other event that has ever occurred" (Marshall 1897: 119). And like Veblen, Marshall considered that the science should draw more inspiration from the 'life' sciences than from mechanics, famously claiming in the preface to the eighth edition of his *Principles* that the "Mecca of the economist lies in economic biology rather than in economic dynamics" (Marshall 1920: xiv). Whereas Veblen chastised the science for being behind the times, Marshall showed less impatience, and he considered that the prevalence of pre-Darwinian notions and methodologies in economic science was due more to the difficulty of the task in absorbing the new paradigm rather than 'obstinance', ignorance or unwillingness on the part of economists to adopt modern approaches (Marshall 1920: xiv).[7]

Veblen credited Marshall for recognising the importance of Darwin and even considered that Marshall's work showed a direction toward evolutionary ways by "advance[ing] . . . the science outside the scope of taxonomy" (Veblen 1900: 265). But while economists may have ultimately accepted the truth of Darwin's insights and their application to the natural world, the application of "evolutionist methods [to] . . . their own science . . . made its way . . . to . . . a very uncertain degree" (Veblen 1900: 265).[8]

6.2.2 The origins of economics' preconceptions

Veblen's 1898 article outlined why economic science was not modern, but the three 'follow-up' articles that make up "The Preconceptions of Economic Science" trace the history and development of the science and the development of its preconceptions. Veblen begins with the physiocrats:[9]

> Physiocratic economics is a theory of the working-out of the Law of Nature (*loi naturelle*) in its economic bearing. . . . The settled course of material facts tending beneficently to the highest welfare of the human race, this is the final term in the Physiocratic speculations. . . . Conformity to these "immutable and unerring" laws of nature is the test of economic truth. . . . Economic theory is accordingly the theory (1) of how the efficient causes of the *ordre naturel* work in an orderly unfolding sequence, guided by the underlying natural law – the propensity immanent in nature to establish the highest well-being of mankind, and (2) of the conditions imposed upon human conduct by these natural laws in order to reach the ordained goal of supreme human welfare.
>
> (Veblen 1899a: 126–128)

The physiocrats conceived economic activities as being guided by a law of nature. The law of nature beneficently guides economic conduct so as to maximise human welfare, its ultimate purpose being to make possible an "ordained goal of supreme human welfare" (Veblen 1899a: 128). Like all laws, the law of nature may be broken, and as such the law of nature is not 'binding'.[10] Thus, while optimum human welfare is the aim of the law, man can "through infirmity or perversity, wilfully break over the beneficent trend of the laws of nature" (Veblen 1899a: 127).[11]

The physiocrats and their notions of an *ordre naturel* and *loi naturel* were succeeded by Adam Smith and his ideas of an 'invisible' or "unseen hand" (Smith 1776: 364; Veblen 1898: 381). Like the *loi naturelle*, the invisible hand worked to ensure a beneficent end arising from the disparate economic actions and choices of individuals. In essence, the invisible hand sought to vindicate the notion that the "Creator . . . established the natural order to serve the end of human welfare" (Veblen 1900: 397). As with physiocratic conceptions, the invisible hand is not binding in that optimum human welfare may not obtain. However, like the physiocratic *loi naturelle*, when things do go wrong, they are conceived in terms of an interference that bars the natural order of things from obtaining. Of course, it follows that when "things have gone wrong, they will right themselves if interference with the natural course ceases" (Veblen 1900: 398).

The traditions established by the physiocrats and carried on by Adam Smith continued in modified form by the later "neo-classical" economists (Veblen 1900: 261, 265, 268), including Alfred Marshall. Indeed, Alfred Marshall's inheritance of these ideas is visible in his statement that "the Laws of economics are statements of tendencies" (Marshall 1890: v–vi; Veblen 1898: 375). For Veblen's neoclassical contemporaries, including Marshall, tendencies manifested themselves in ideas of an optimum equilibrium, the notion that markets settle upon some efficient equilibrium outcome, and "an uncritical conviction that there is a meliorative trend in the course of events" (Veblen 1900a: 242). It would be true to say that such a view is visible in Marshall's modern neoclassical descendants, who still couch their models in such terms, ever striving for the market equilibrium, the natural outcome in the absence of any pesky market distortions.

6.2.3 Teleology and economic taxonomy

Veblen's objections with respect to the teleological nature of a pre-Darwinian economic science are that it showed "too many reminiscences of the 'natural' and the 'normal', of 'verities' and 'tendencies', of 'controlling principles' and 'disturbing causes'" (Veblen 1898: 381). But consider for a moment what is meant by teleology and the consequences of this thinking. Underlying it is a tacit sense or understanding that, since a legitimate direction and end is known, all that is left to do is decipher and explore the various movements and motions that work within and lead to the predestined end. For example, in the case of the Great Chain of Being and its fixed notions of creation, the scientist's role was not to discover underlying laws, since these were, by definition, given.[12] Rather, his role was to classify and list the creatures that inhabit the Earth and place them within the predetermined construct of the Great Chain.

Now, consider the outcome of such thinking for economics. The classical economist's 'equivalent' to the Great Chain of Being could be said to be 'natural law'. Classical notions of natural law were later 'transformed' by neoclassical economists into the notion of market equilibria, of "Laws of Equilibrium" (Jevons 1871: vii). Both the classical and neoclassical ideas intimate that there are economic actions that are 'natural' or legitimate, those that, as mentioned earlier, are in keeping with the natural state and lead to 'optimal' outcomes. By conceiving of economics in this fashion, the economist's role is to determine which actions or behaviour lead to the optimal and which do not; which actions concur with the natural state and which do not. It could be said that the economist's role amounts to the development of an 'economic moral code', or in slightly less effusive terms, a 'code of ideal economic conduct'. Veblen would call this the "canon of truth":

> [Economic theory] is a projection of the accepted ideal of conduct. This ideal of conduct is made to serve as a canon of truth, to the extent that the investigator contents himself with an appeal to its legitimation for premises that run back of the facts with which he is immediately dealing, for the "controlling principles" that are conceived intangibly to underlie the process discussed, and for the "tendencies" that run beyond the situation as it lies before him. . . . By this method the theory of an institution or a phase of life may be stated in conventionalised terms of the apparatus whereby life is carried on, the apparatus being invested with a tendency to an equilibrium at the normal, and the theory being a formulation of the conditions under which this putative equilibrium supervenes.
>
> (Veblen 1898: 382–383)

Predetermined ends, which in the economist's case are market equilibria, are "occupied with the adjustment of values to a given situation", reducing the economist's role to listing or categorising the behaviour and the activities that lead to or concur with the stylised optimal predetermined end; that is, those activities that lead to and correspond with an equilibrium (Veblen 1909a: 62). The economist's role is to discover and 'codify' the 'canon of truth' that legitimately guides economic activity to this end. So, for example in the case of the " 'natural' system of free competition", what economists today might refer to as perfect or pure competition, "economic theory consists in the definition and classification of the phenomena of economic life in terms of this hypothetical competitive system" (Veblen 1908c: 154).

It was this that Veblen was referring to when he said that economics was a system of "economic taxonomy", a science that was 'reduced' to classifying and categorising a scheme of activities that fulfil a predetermined, stylised and legitimate end:

> The agencies or forces causally at work in the economic life process are neatly avoided. The outcome of the method, at its best, is a body of logically consistent propositions concerning the normal relations of things – a system of economic taxonomy.
>
> (Veblen 1898: 384)

An implication of this thinking is that the results of this taxonomy can be used so that the stylised legitimate account can be 'mimicked'. If the world we live in does not match the model, then we should re-craft our economic world to make it congruent with the economic construct, or at the very least try as hard as possible to match it. How do we do this? Since failure to meet a construct-like perfect competition is explained in terms of disturbance, we merely excise the disturbance. In modern economics, we refer to the outcome of disturbances as market failures. By removing or addressing these barriers or disturbances, we can achieve or at least come closer to achieving the outcomes in the model, and natural law can be reasserted.[13]

6.2.4 Pre-Darwinian conceptions of human behaviour

Veblen's third objection is perhaps his most well known and relates to economics' account of human behaviour. The economics of Veblen's time utilised a hedonistic conception of man. This 'algorithm' of human behaviour was not limited in use to the neoclassical school but was prevalent among other economic traditions, most notably (and emphatically) the Austrians (Veblen 1898: 389):

> In the classical-Austrian scheme of theory the center and circumference of economic life is the production of what a writer on ethics has called "pleasant feeling." Pleasant feeling is produced only by tangible, physical objects (including persons), acting somehow upon the sensory.
>
> (Veblen 1908: 122)

The hedonistic conception is based on a Benthamite conception of human behaviour; it is a utilitarian manifestation. Under this model, man is conceived as a pleasure machine, passively responding to pleasures and pains (Hunt 2002: 320; see Schumpeter 1912: 22).

Veblen objected to this appraisal of human activity and behaviour on a number of grounds. To begin with, Veblen considered that its use was inappropriate given that conceptions of human behaviour had undergone update in light of new anthropological and psychological insights and discoveries that found that man's behaviour was more complex than the simple hedonistic framework (Ayres 1958: 25–26). In fact, these new discoveries showed that man's behaviour was the product of generations of adaptation and change that resulted in its current iteration. As a product of natural selection of both a physical and cultural nature,[14] man's current behavioural state is merely the most recent step in a cumulative process of adaptation and change that took place over generations and millennia. This process of change has not halted, either, and, indeed, human behaviour continues to evolve and change. In which direction it will change no one knows, but it will surely continue to evolve, to adapt and to change. By contrast, hedonism considered man's nature as given and immutable (Veblen 1898: 389–390). It could be said that economics' adherence to the older hedonistic framework is akin to using Ptolemaic astronomy to understand the movement of the stars even after the discoveries of Copernicus and Galileo.

While hedonism portrayed man as a passive pleasure machine, a 'behavioural blancmange', the new discoveries revealed that man is a creature who acts with a purpose. He is an active agent who seeks out answers and acts to achieve goals. In this sense, man's behaviour is teleological, in that man acts so as to achieve some end (Veblen 1899: 10; 1914: 3).

The adoption of a behavioural framework that presents man as 'teleological' seemingly conflicts with Veblen's aversion to teleological economic constructs. It seems that Veblen's aversion to "cosmological teleology" was contradicted by an enthusiastic embrace of "individual teleology", the idea that "human behaviour is purposively motivated" (Coats 1954: 529). I consider that this conflict is more apparent than real. First, I consider that Veblen was not arguing that the ends towards which men strive are known, just that man acts towards achieving goals, with a purpose. Man's individual teleology was unlike the teleology of neoclassical economics, where the predetermined legitimate ends *are* known. Second, rather than a basis for conflict, the discovery that man is motivated by an individual teleology actually serves to reinforce Veblen's aversion to and arguments against 'cosmological teleology'.

Recall that Veblen objected that the hedonistic conception 'reduced' man to a passive entity, waiting patiently to respond to stimuli. In this scheme, 'atomised' man lacks social interaction and waits in isolation for the next force of impact. As Veblen very famously (infamously?) put it:

> The hedonistic conception of man is that of a lightning calculator of pleasures and pains, who oscillates like a homogeneous globule of desire . . . under the impulse of stimuli that shift him about the area but leave him intact. . . . He is an isolated, definitive human datum, in stable equilibrium except for the buffets of the impinging forces that displace him in one direction or another. . . . When the force of the impact is spent, he comes to rest, a self-contained globule of desire as before.
>
> (Veblen 1898: 389–390)

Now contrast this with the discoveries made in anthropology and psychology. These discoveries could not be squared with an economics that would continue its adherence to a pre-Darwinian teleological framework. Why is this so? It is because, given a legitimate end:

> no discretion resides in the intermediate terms through which the end is worked out. Therefore, man being such an intermediate term, discretion cannot be imputed to him without violating the supposition. Therefore, given an indefeasible meliorative trend in events, man is but a mechanical intermediary in the sequence. It is as such a mechanical intermediate term that the stricter hedonism construes human nature.
>
> (Veblen 1900: 248)

In Veblen's mind, it was inconceivable to adopt the new anthropological and psychological insights into the existing economic paradigms. The new insights allowed for change and adaptation in human behaviour, which implied that human behaviour is open to discretion. But as Veblen argued, such discretion was not possible since the teleological apparatus conceived human behaviour in a fixed manner that squared with and ensured the fulfilment of the predetermined end. In addition, man is merely an intermediary in the process, a pawn if you will, and his entry into the neoclassical scheme was designed and formulated in a manner that would ensure the unfolding of the process towards the fated end. But man was no such passive intermediary; he conceives to act with a purpose. These tensions made the new psychology difficult for ready absorption into the existing pre-Darwinian economic paradigms.

Before proceeding to the next section, it is worth noting that some, like the economist Karl Anderson (1933), criticised Veblen's objections to the neoclassical paradigm. In Anderson's mind, the question is not one of the "adequacy of the concept of equilibrium, nor . . . the merits of pure description" but one of "establishing boundaries of scope" (Anderson 1933: 626). Anderson suggested that the so-called deficiencies of neoclassical economics arise because Veblen and his institutional school colleagues wished the discipline to be "enlarged into a theory of social evolution" (Anderson 1933: 626). Implicit in this argument is that the hedonistic calculus is fine if the scope of economics remains in its 'traditional' areas.

Anderson also considered that Veblen deserved criticism even if one accepts the need for a new account of human behaviour. Anderson's criticisms here are based on Veblen's decision to replace the hedonistic calculus with a model of human behaviour that draws on the "apparatus of instincts" (which will be the topic of discussion in Section 6.3.1) (1933: 622). Anderson considered that Veblen's decision merely exchanged one 'flawed' model of human behaviour with an instinct model that was also increasingly being discredited. As a consequence, Veblen's analysis was "not worth very much" (Anderson 1933: 622). The implication is that an economics built on discredited foundations could not possibly yield useful insights (Ayres 1958: 25, Diggins 1999: 68).

However, Veblen's heir apparent, Clarence Ayres, argued that in dismissing Veblen his critics:

> demonstrated their own lack of understanding not just of Veblen but of human behavior. For even after we have rid ourselves of the false simplicity of "inborn", or genetically determined, behavior patterns, the fact remains that human behavior differs very substantially from that of any other creature and that such differences must have their taproots somewhere.
>
> (Ayres 1958: 25; see also Hodgson 2004: 162)[15]

It is interesting to note that as he advanced in years, Veblen's teacher at Carleton, the neoclassical economist John Bates Clark, amended his views of economics, in part under the influence of Darwinism (Homan 1927: 44–45). Clark is said to have argued for a reappraisal of human nature so that economics would no longer be reliant upon a model that stresses self-interest. While hedonistic conceptions may be convenient for the purposes of analyses, they amount to "gross caricature"

(Homan 1927: 43). Instead the science should build a model of human behaviour that reflects the actual ways of human conduct. Despite the merits, Clark recognised that replacing hedonistic approaches and generating a "correct view of human nature" will "afford work enough for one generation" (Homan and Clark in Homan 1927: 43).

Clark also expressed concerns with the economic analysis of competition[16] and argued for society to be conceived as an organism and not as an "aggregation of individuals" (Homan 1927: 44). Interestingly, and as Homan noted, the criticisms of economics that Clark expressed in his 'dotage' bear "remarkable resemblance to some of those advanced by Veblen" (Homan 1927: 45).

6.3 Developing a modern economics

While there is no single *magnum opus* produced by Veblen that outlines his preferred 'modern' method, he nonetheless outlined his ideas regarding the shape of a modern economic science throughout his many published works, and his approach can be gleaned by piecing together information strewn throughout. As has been noted, Veblen's preferred approach is one that was inspired to follow the trail initiated by Darwin. His Darwinian evolutionary pedigree can be explicitly evinced by the omitted secondary title of the work that gave him widespread fame, *The Theory of the Leisure Class*, which was originally to have carried the subtitle "A Study in the Evolution of Economic Institutions" (Saram 1999: 226).

Veblen's modern approach is one that abandons any teleological preconceptions and notions of legitimacy. Capitalism is not to be afforded any special or high status as the putative product of a beneficent *deus ex machina*. On the contrary, capitalism should be appreciated as merely the most recent economic 'offspring' in a process of adaptation over many generations. The task for economic science is to answer how capitalism came into being and to describe the process and forces that shaped and enabled this institution to flourish ahead of others: in short, to determine why the 'species' of capitalism survived in the race for economic existence ahead of its 'competitors'. The explanation for such change should not be couched in terms of fated progress, as though in Lamarckian terms, where capitalism is but one move up a dynamic socio-structural chain. While "others saw progress, Veblen saw only change", and it is the process of change that was primary in Veblen's thought (Commager in Tilman 1996: 49). A modern economics is one that is motivated to answer such questions in such terms, to consider and provide an account for the presence, the rise and fall and the persistence of institutions (Veblen 1914: 2).

6.3.1 Instincts

Veblen's approach begins by rejecting the fixed hedonistic construct of human behaviour. Human behaviour is not immutable or given; there is no "original nature of man" and nor was there a "sudden appearance of reason" (Ayres 1958: 26; Hodgson 2004: 164–165). Veblen's knowledge of anthropology and psychology convinced him that man's behaviour, ability to reason and, indeed, consciousness itself, are the result of generations of slowly paced human evolution (Ayres 1958: 26; Hodgson 2004: 163–165). This process has produced a species of man who is a social creature with an intellectual capacity and power far beyond that of any other living being (Veblen 1914: 6; Veblen 1898a: 188; Edgell 2001: 78–79). Moreover, man's actions are guided by a set of "hereditary" instincts, the "irreducible traits of human nature" resulting from the same evolutionary process:

> For mankind . . . the life of the species is conditioned by the complement of instinctive proclivities and tropismatic[17] aptitudes with which the species is typically endowed. Not only is the continued life of the race dependent on the adequacy of its instinctive proclivities in this way, but the routine and details of its life are also, in the last resort, determined by these instincts. These are the prime movers in human behaviour, as in the behaviour of all those animals that show self-direction or discretion. Human activity, in so far as it can be spoken of as conduct, can never exceed the scope of these instinctive dispositions, by initiative of which man takes action. Nothing falls within the human scheme of things desirable to be done except what answers to these native proclivities of man. These native proclivities alone make anything worth while, and out of their working emerge not only the purpose and efficiency of life, but its substantial pleasures and pains as well.
>
> (Veblen 1914: 1, 3)

Man is possessed of both instincts and tropisms. Instincts involve "the conscious pursuit of an objective end" (Veblen 1914: 5). This conscious pursuit implies that instincts involve some purposeful action or actions; that they lead to actions that make men move toward achieving some purpose or goal. To adopt Coats's terminology, it implies individual teleology (Coats 1954: 529). This feature differentiates instinct from tropism, which is the proverbial 'knee-jerk' reaction. Unlike instincts, tropisms involve no thought but are uncontrollable, 'autonomic' impulses, such as pulling one's hand away from a fire.[18]

Like Darwin and his discovery that variation is always and everywhere present, so too in the case of instincts one finds that the "complement of instincts fluctuates from one individual to another" and between different peoples and cultures (Veblen 1914: 14–15).[19] The current cache of instincts is a product of natural selection that enables the human animal to successfully propagate and flourish under a particular set of circumstances. However, "a change in the situation . . . [means] the requirements of survival are likely to change", and so we would see a change in the species' endowment of instincts (Veblen 1914: 16). As a result, human behaviour is not fixed, but rather is dynamic and responsive to cultural and environmental factors, and so the instincts present in any given period are subject to amendment, addition and/or subtraction. However, due to the slow pace of biological evolution, the biological factors that contribute to human behaviour would remain "specifically the same" within any given generation (Veblen 1914: 18).[20]

Veblen's initial work revolved around two instincts, namely the instinct of workmanship and the predatory instinct. In his later work, he supplemented these with other instincts, such as parental bent and idle curiosity.[21] However, in essence, these additions do not stray too far from Veblen's initial thoughts, and, as such, man's dowry of instincts can generally be placed into a dual typology. The first type includes those that make us take stock of the interests of others and "promote human life" (McCormick 2006: 7; Edgell 2001: 80). These instincts make us act to advance the cause of the group and society ahead of our own individual gain. In short, they encourage cooperative behaviour and can be grouped under the head *group-regarding*, or in Veblen's language, 'workmanship'. Workmanship is an innate human desire to "turn things to human use" (Veblen 1898a: 191). Veblen's instinct of workmanship seemingly stands in contrast to a major tenet of neoclassical economics, which sees work as a good that produces disutility and which humans wish to exchange for leisure (Veblen 1914: 3, 31).[22] Neoclassical economics' portrayal of work as "irksome" means that:

> the perfect economic *affliction* [my italics] is unremunerated labor. Man instinctively revolts at effort that goes to supply the means of life. A consistent aversion to whatever activity goes to maintain the life of the species is assuredly found in no other species of animal. Under the selective process through which species are held to have emerged and gained their stability there is no chance for the survival of a species gifted with such an aversion to the furtherance of its own life process. If man alone is an exception from the selective norm, then the alien propensity in question must have been intruded into his make-up by some malevolent *deus ex machina*. . . . The instinct of workmanship . . . is a human trait necessary to the survival of the species.
>
> (Veblen 1898a: 187, 190)

A species that is slothful, lazy and keen to avoid work is one that ensures its own extinction. It is a species that will struggle to survive in the race for resources. Yet this is the construct of man developed and adhered to by neoclassical economics. On the contrary, said Veblen, man is, by virtue of the instinct of workmanship, compelled to undertake work "to develop and conserve" the species, and workmanship is "chief among . . . instinctive dispositions that conduce directly to the material well-being of the race, and . . . to its biological success" (Veblen 1898a: 194; 1914: 25).[23] Workmanship casts man as "an agent seeking in every act the accomplishment of some concrete, objective impersonal end . . . possessed of a taste for effective work and a distaste for futile effort" (Veblen 1899: 10).[24]

In diametric opposition to group-regarding instincts are those that cause us to act for our own benefit "at the expense of others" (McCormick 2006: 7, Edgell 2001: 80). These instincts can be grouped under the heading *self-regarding*, or what Veblen would interchangeably call 'invidious', 'predation', 'ceremonialism' or 'sportsmanship' (Veblen 1914: Chapter 1; Veblen 1898a; Ayres 1958: 26). Among these instincts is the desire for survival and self-preservation prevalent in all species, and, to be sure, a self-preservation instinct is necessary for the survival of any species. But this group of instincts also includes those responsible for the development of social ranks; for the creation of taboos and mystic rites that give a priestly class lone access to a god or gods and hence singular authority for the development of a moral code; for the reduction of women to chattel class and their subjugation. In other words, they inculcate behaviour that through theft, 'usufruct' or other means takes resources, power and control from others for one's own benefit (see Ayres 1958: 27).

What is evident from these two groupings is that the instincts are divided according to their objective aim, that is, their teleological nature and purpose. The "teleological scope and aim of each instinctive propensity differs characteristically from all the rest . . . and are . . . distinguished and classed on the ground of their teleological content" (Veblen 1914: 3–4). In the case of an instinct such as parental bent, its aim is to further the progress of the species, for the "life and comfort of the community at large" and "unselfish solicitude for the well-being of the incoming generation", and so by these intentions it can be placed in the group-regarding column (Veblen 1914: 27. 46). On the other hand, the predatory instinct enjoins us to act for our own good at the expense of others, to seek "one's own advantage at the cost of the enemy" through such means as " 'aggression' in a 'contest' in order to obtains goods and services by 'seizure or compulsion' " (Veblen 1914: 160; Edgell 2001: 80). This would make it easily locatable in the alternate grouping.

While these two examples serve to highlight the difference between group-regarding and self-regarding instincts, in reality the difference can be difficult to determine. Like the two-faced Janus, it is sometimes the case that instincts can be both group- and self-regarding, depending on the circumstance at hand. Consider the instinct of emulation, which Veblen judged to be one of the "strongest and most alert and persistent of the economic motives proper", bettered only by the instinct of self-preservation (Veblen 1899: 74). Emulation can cause us to jealously compare ourselves to our peers and, in extreme cases, to ensure that our station in society is at or above that of others, sometimes at all costs. On a group level, it can cause nations to go to war with other nations in an effort to improve their relative 'rank'. Consider the effect of this instinct in driving the European colonial expansions of the nineteenth century. Italy's Fascist expansion in northern Africa during the earlier part of twentieth century is another example of emulation commencing with self-regarding motives. On the other hand, emulation can cause us to mimic activities that have beneficial group-regarding outcomes. As an example, consider the practice of washing one's hands in order to avoid the spread of disease. This practice only took hold once society's elite adopted it. Once the elite were convinced, the 'lower' classes followed and unwittingly helped to reduce the spread of disease and improve public health outcomes (McCormick 2006: 13).

Equivocal cases such as the instinct of emulation with its multifarious ends perhaps coloured Veblen's view that the "several instincts spring from the common ground of sentient life" (Veblen 1914: 12). That they spring forth from this common ground perhaps also explains his belief in the crosscontamination of instincts. Veblen believed that the "concatenation of these ultimate psychological elements" meant that each instinct "contaminates or is contaminated by the working of other propensities", making it difficult to determine where one instinct begins and another ends (Veblen 1914: 3, 12):[25]

> The instincts, all and several, though perhaps in varying degrees, are so intimately engaged in a play of give and take that the work of any one has its consequences for all the rest, though presumably not for all equally. It is this endless complication and contamination of instinctive elements in human conduct, taken in conjunction with the pervading and cumulative effects of habit in this domain, that makes most of the difficulty and much of the interest attaching to this line of inquiry.
>
> (Veblen 1914: 29)

The various instincts may reinforce each other (Diggins 1999: 68; see also Veblen 1914: 48). On the other hand, they may also act contrary to one another. It is this interplay between instincts that is pivotal in Veblen's account of cultural change and institutional development. As will be shown in this chapter, the antithesis and interactions between the two rival forces was, in Veblen's thinking, the mechanism by which institutional development and social change occurs (Ayres 1958: 29).

6.3.2 Habits, institutions and social evolution

A behavioural construct based on the idea that man operates according to instinct poses a challenge. If human conduct operates according to slowly changing innate instincts, then, in essence, human behaviour should show very limited change over a given period. In such a scenario, with limited change in human instincts we might also expect very slow change in human society. Yet man has experienced social change and growth over the past five to ten thousand years of such a magnitude that would be difficult to explain through a change in the endowment of instincts. The question arises: How do we account for the marked growth in human ingenuity and civilisation given a relatively static complement of instincts (see Hodgson 2004: 106)?

The preceding question supposes that human behaviour is determined solely by the species endowment of instincts. To put this in popular terms, it implies that human behaviour is determined by nature alone. Indeed, Veblen himself considered that while "men take thought . . . the endowment of instinctive proclivities . . . decides what they shall take thought of and to what effect" (Veblen 1914: 13, 6). But Veblen also contended that human behaviour is shaped and guided by two concurrent forces; that human behaviour is simultaneously "wholly organic and wholly social", that is to say that all "human behavior is organically conditioned . . . and all human behavior is socially organized" (Ayres 1962: 93).[26] We are individually driven to act according to our instinct, but it is in the social realm, in human culture that we see their "concrete, actual expression" (Hunt 2002: 319). While it is true to say that instincts change slowly, "instinctive behavior is subject to development and hence modification by habit" (Veblen 1914: 38). Unlike instincts, instinctive behaviour in the form of habits changes more rapidly, being more responsive to changing circumstances.

As individuals, our instincts give us a clue as to how to respond to a particular situation, but over time and with experience, our responses solidify and become *habits*. These habits help us to deal with the complexity of the world around us and ensure that we know how to respond the next time we are confronted with the same or similar situation. By forming habits, we develop an efficient means to deal with the large and diverse set of situations and occurrences we confront in our everyday lives. Habits negate the need to recalculate our responses and decide what action or actions to take each time we are confronted by the same or similar scenario. Rather, we respond to them in a habitual manner.

Often, knowledge of how to respond to the various situations we are likely to confront, as encapsulated in habits, is passed on from person to person, parent to offspring, class to class, and from generation to generation. Such habits can be adopted by more than one person and may even be adopted by an entire group or society. When they take on such a generalised form, they become what I call generalised habits. Like habits in individuals, generalised habits give society the means to function. They manifest themselves as society's traditions, customs, norms, mores, conventions, laws and rules and provide order, guidance and structure, telling us how we should act under given circumstances. Veblen referred to these generalised habits as *institutions* (Veblen 1914: 7).

Institutions "are settled habits of thought common to the generality of men" that have been "handed on from one generation to the next, by tradition, training, education . . . by which the young acquire what the old have learned" (Veblen 1909a: 626; 1914: 38–39). Through continued and repeated use, institutions become the approved means of social conduct. So embedded do they become into the social consciousness that they take on the character of unquestionable "common sense . . . right and good", and hence are able to withstand rapid or marked change (Veblen 1899: 74):

> Under the discipline of habituation this logic and apparatus of ways and means falls into conventional lines, acquires the consistency, custom and prescription and so takes on an institutional character and form. The accustomed ways of doing and thinking not only become an habitual matter of course, easy and obvious, but they come likewise to be sanctioned by social convention, and so become right and proper and give rise to principles of conduct. By use and wont they are incorporated into the current scheme of common sense. As elements of the approved scheme of conduct and pursuit these conventional ways and means take the place as proximate ends of endeavour.
>
> (Veblen 1914: 7)

Thus human conduct can be appreciated as being driven concurrently by both innate instincts and extrinsic culture, by 'nature' and 'nurture'. As individuals, we act according to the dictates of our instincts, but our propensity to act, our desires, goals, proclivities, and sometimes even our very natures, are tempered or even thwarted, sometimes "under pain of disesteem and ostracism", by the social structure; that is, by the scheme of institutions (Veblen 1909a: 620). But society's institutions are formed by humanity itself, and similarly are moderated by human instincts.[27] Hence Veblen's approach is neither solely reductionist nor exclusively collectivist. We cannot understand the economic system by recourse to 'Robinson Crusoe-*esque*' models, or constructs based solely on the summation of the individual preferences and profit functions of consumers and firms. This won't do for Veblen, because such approaches neglect the social aspects of human development and conduct as manifested in institutions. Similarly, however, Veblen sees a pivotal role for individual human agency, so it is not possible to understand economic development without also gaining some idea of how the individual human agent functions, based on modern anthropological and psychological ideas as opposed to pre-Darwinian hedonistic paradigms.

Institutional development has occurred on terms not dissimilar to the development of individual human instincts; that is, through the "natural selection of institutions" (Veblen 1899: 125). Just as the complement of instincts present in any given period is that which has resulted from the selection of those best suited to ensure the species' survival, so too the "growth of culture is a cumulative sequence of habituation" and the current complement of institutions is made up of those suited to a given environment and state of affairs (Veblen 1909a: 628; Veblen 1899: 141). In essence, Veblen proposed that society itself evolves and changes along lines very similar to that which occurs in the biological sphere. It was not merely in terms of metaphor or allegory that Veblen adopted Darwinian principles, but rather, he held strongly that this is the actual manner in which society changes and evolves. The genetic material of society and the human culture that are handed from generation to generation and that are subject to the Darwinian principles of variation, inheritance and selection are its institutions (Hodgson 2004: 189). It is worth quoting Veblen at length on this:

> Like all human culture this material civilization is a scheme of institutions – institutional fabric and institutional growth. But institutions are an outgrowth of habit. The growth of culture is a cumulative sequence of habituation, and the ways and means of it are the habitual response of human nature to exigencies that vary incontinently, cumulatively, but with something of a consistent sequence in the cumulative variations that so go forward – incontinently, because each new move creates a new situation which induces a further new variation in the habitual manner of response; cumulatively, because each new situation is a variation of what has gone before it and embodies as causal factors all that has been effected by what went before; consistently, because the underlying traits of human nature (propensities, aptitudes, and what not) by force of which the response takes place, and on the ground of which the habituation takes effect, remain substantially unchanged.
>
> (Veblen 1909a: 628)

While society's institutions have evolved through a process of natural selection, it is important to understand that this does not mean that the current scheme of institutions is that which is optimal for human life and progress. Evolution "carries the baggage of its past", and while it is true to say that institutions provide the order and structure that "regulate the community's life", it is not true to say that society is ordered or regulated in the best or most efficient way (Hodgson 2004: 44; Veblen 1914: 35). On the contrary:

> Disserviceable institutions easily arise and continue to hold their place in spite of the disapproval of native common sense. . . . History records more frequent and more spectacular instances of the triumph of imbecile institutions over life and culture than of people who have by force of instinctive insight saved themselves alive out of a desperately precarious institutional situation.
>
> (Veblen 1914: 28, 49)

The suboptimal nature of social function and organisation is in part because the institutions we have today arose in response to a particular set of circumstances. But this response has a lag, or as Veblen put it, the "situation of today shapes the institutions of tomorrow" (Veblen 1899: 126). Repeated observation of institutions stereotypes them into the popular consciousness as right and proper, even though social development may render them no longer useful. Hence, today's imbecile institutions may in fact be yesterday's serviceable institutions, and indeed *vice versa* (McCormick 2006: 25–26). Thus, the institutions we operate under at any given point are "adapted to past circumstances, and are therefore never in full accord with the requirements of the present" (Veblen 1899: 126). Just like vestigial human organs such as the appendix, it seems that social evolution has its 'hang-ons'. But, in addition, human society is not organised in the most efficient possible manner because while man develops institutions to further the progress of the group, he also develops institutions that act against 'optimal' development. Unlike the humble appendix, which, apart from the acute case of appendicitis, causes no apparent harm, some of society's vestigial institutions, what Veblen calls its disserviceable or imbecile institutions, may actually serve to hinder or at worst harm human social potential.

How do such institutions come to be? Their entry is possible because man is "distinguished . . . by his amazing skill in manipulating physical objects and by an equally amazing capacity for self-deception and mutual exploitation" (Ayres 1958: 27). In other words, man is notable for both his drive for 'workmanship' and 'predation', and the duality that is present in the sphere of man's instincts is equally present in the institutional structures that he erects to order and direct society. Human culture is a product of an ongoing antithesis, a struggle, if you will, between two types of institutions, including those:

> of acquisition or of production; or to revert to terms already employed . . . pecuniary or industrial institutions; or in still other terms, they are institutions serving either the invidious or the non-invidious economic interest. The former category have to do with "business," the latter with industry, taking the latter word in the mechanical sense.
>
> (Veblen 1899: 137)

This dichotomy, antagonism, antithesis, what have you, is Veblen's 'Higgs boson', the very substance that drives cultural and societal change.[28] Human social and cultural development can be understood to be the result of an interplay between institutions of predation and institutions of workmanship. As in the case of instincts, the difference between the two is a case of the institutions that promote the welfare and success of the entire group and society versus those whose aim is self-regard and benefit for an individual, group, sex, caste or class at the expense of others. Thus, the traditionally exalted position of males through the subordination and subjugation of women in various cultures is an example of a predatory institution designed to serve men at the expense of women. The formerly accepted divine right of kings is yet another, as is Veblen's famed leisure class. On the other hand, universal education is an institution that displays workmanship characteristics, although as in the case of the instinct of emulation, the situation can be vague, with many institutions containing both workmanship and predatory aspects.[29]

At points in human development, one cluster attains supremacy over the other, but the antagonistic interaction between these two forces ultimately means that this supremacy is subject to 'capitulation', with the possibility that the converse becomes dominant. It should be noted that by 'supremacy' it is not meant that the alternate cluster completely vanishes. Indeed, it seems the two clusters of institutions are always simultaneously present, each tempering the other so that it does not take full control. However, their role in society and their ability to manifest themselves is suppressed, while the impact of the alternative group is inflated. Thus, at particular points human culture displays characteristics of predation more than workmanship, while during other periods the converse is true. At different periods in human history and development workmanship is more prevalent, while during others predatory characters come to the fore.[30]

This dichotomy can be applied to any number of areas. When concerned with social psychological phenomena, the interest is between individuals and classes dominated by self-regarding behaviour as against those who are community-regarding. In economic terms the dichotomy is a 'struggle' between 'business' and 'industry', with the latter represented by Veblen's famed engineers. From the perspective of sociology, frictions arise between ceremonialism, sportsmanship and superstition on the one hand and science and the matter-of-fact-nature of the 'machine process' on the other (Hunt 2003: 157). Marc Tool listed the various faces of this dichotomy, based on various descriptions used by Veblen, which I have reproduced in Table 6.1 (1977: 454). I have placed the two into a group-regarding column and a self-regarding column.

6.3.3 Technology and cultural development in 'four acts'

While the interplay between workmanship and predation is the mechanism for change, technology is the cause that sets this interplay in motion. It is the catalyst and the reactive agent that causes the shift and change in the make-up of institutions. Through the impact of technological change and development, existing institutions have their mettle tested, so that some whither and some are altered, while new ones may also appear. Ever the Darwinian, Veblen avoided "occult

Table 6.1 The many faces of Veblen's dichotomy

Self-regarding	*Group-regarding*
Salesmanship	Workmanship
Business	Industry
Ceremonial	Technological
Ownership	Production
Free income	Tangible performance
Vested interests	Common man
Sabotage	Community serviceability
Pecuniary employment	Industrial employment
Invidious emulation	Technological efficiency
Conscientious withdrawal of efficiency	Inordinately productive enterprise
Competitive advertising	Valuable information and guidance
Business prosperity	Industrial efficiency

Source: Tool (1977: 454)

agencies" such as "manifest destiny, national genius, [or] Providential guidance" to explain change. He insisted that any answer be couched in terms of "efficient cause" and not the "postulate of efficacious guidance" (Veblen 1915: 32):

> There are two lines of agency visibly at work shaping the habits of thought. . . . These are the received scheme of use and wont, and the new state of the industrial arts; and it is not difficult to see that it is the latter that makes for readjustment; nor should it be any more difficult to see that the readjustment is necessarily made under the surveillance of the received scheme of use and wont.
>
> (Veblen 1915: 32)

Veblen gave thought to how this duality manifested itself throughout human development by considering four periods of human social and cultural evolution. The four periods that Veblen outlined are *savagery*, *barbarism*, *handicraft* and the *machine age*. His analysis is often said to mirror the anthropology of Lewis Henry Morgan, and, as such, Morgan is often claimed to be an influence (Edgell 2001: 88; Tilman 1996: 59). However Edgell notes that there is no direct evidence that any of Morgan's works were in Veblen's possession, so claims of Morgan's influence can be said to take on the character of conjecture (Edgell 2001: 88). That said, Veblen did make references in his work to other leading sociologists, anthropologists and palaeontologists of his day, including Werner Sombart and Sophus Muller (see for example Veblen 1914: 232, 121). In addition, one cannot help but notice the similarity between the Veblenian epochs and those that are commonly outlined in Marxian analysis, as outlined in Chapter 5. As such, it seems plausible to suggest that Marx's influence is also visible here.

Veblen commences his survey with the period he calls *savagery*. Of the four periods, this is the one that sees man at his most vulnerable to the elements, having what can be termed a rude state of technological proficiency. So rude is this

state that what activity does take place is concerned solely with the production of goods necessary for the "subsistence for the group and the rearing of offspring" (Veblen 1914: 122). Such a 'hand-to-mouth' existence is not favourable to those who do not have a community-regarding disposition, since survival depends on qualities of cooperation and mutual assistance. As such, the savage period is characterised as being dominated by the workmanship cluster.

The state of technology does not allow for the creation of a surplus, meaning that all hands and resources must be devoted to the production of subsistence goods. Resources and hands that can be redirected towards production of nonsubsistence goods are in limited-to-no supply. In the absence of such goods, there is little motivation for "individual, or private gain" that would warrant the development of ownership (Veblen 1914: 142). Thus we find no "institution of ownership and property rights" during the savage era, and outshoots of ownership, such as "bartering or hiring" and "price" are also in abeyance (Veblen 1914: 142, 143). This is not to say that there are no goods that are privately owned, just nothing that would warrant the development of property rights and the institution of ownership. What "trinkets and personal belongings" one does have during the savage era are not of a calibre that would make them worthy of the development of trade, "belong[ing] to their owner or bearer in much the same sense as his name" (Veblen 1914: 144).[31]

Savage era communities possess technology that, using modern parlance, sees a marked advance in the level of productivity as compared to the earliest ever humans; however, the "rudimentary technological equipment" held and used by these communities still necessitates that the bulk of their time be devoted to producing the necessities for life and survival. These communities have an absence of "stores of portable wealth", what was referred to earlier as the surplus (Veblen 1914: 123). As a result, Veblen considered that savagery was a "peaceable" period (Veblen 1914: 120).

How is this so? It is because the lack of surplus reduced the group's enthusiasm for "annoying its neighbours" (Veblen 1914: 123). Internecine predatory activity was similarly a pointless exercise (Veblen 1914: 123). There is no point to such activity since there is little fruit to be harvested. On the contrary, given the precarious circumstances of savage era groups, the resources devoted to undertaking raids and the effects of harming those from within one's ranks reduces the resources available for the production of the goods necessary for life and survival and hence actually reduces the prospects for the group's survival.[32]

The drive of workmanship eventually leads to an increase in the community's stock of knowledge and an improvement in its technical abilities. The improvement means that, eventually, the savage communities can begin to produce a surplus. With the surplus and portable wealth now in hand, it becomes possible to divert some resources from the staples of life to other pursuits, including the production of goods that are not absolutely essential for survival. The surplus arising from the improvements in technology ushers in the next phase of human development, which Veblen called the *barbarian* era.

How does the surplus have this effect? Veblen's main thesis is that technology acts as the agent that causes a reappraisal of and amendment to the institutional scheme of life, and in the barbarian era, the effects of technological change were at least threefold. First, the surplus means that the group's existence does not require all to contribute. It is now possible for some members of the community to survive without contributing to production of life's necessities. Second, the improved technological conditions mean that the community can now produce objects that are not imperative to survival but take on a more 'frivolous', 'ceremonial' character. Thirdly, as a result of these two occurrences, we have the conditions suitable for the introduction of the institution of ownership.

Ownership has traditionally been explained as the "productive labor of the owner" (Veblen 1898b: 352). This traditional view traces these origins to the "putative savage hunter" who stored "valuables . . . as were enabled by efficiency, diligence or fortuitous gains" (Veblen 1898b: 352; 1914: 155). Veblen rejected this explanation, arguing instead that it was technology that provided the route for the institution of ownership. Technology served to alter the institutional make-up of the savage era communities through two key routes.

The first route was through fraud. The savage cultures were known to possess a "class of magicians, an inchoate priestly class, who get their living in part 'by their wits' . . . by some sort of tithe" (Veblen 1914: 155). As the community's material standing improves and with more at stake, the services of this priestly class gain appeal. The priests convince the community of the need to maintain good relations with the gods. Since the priests alone have access to the relevant gods, only they can ensure things such as a successful harvest. As time progresses, given the gravity and importance of this task, the priestly class can absolve itself from undertaking the menial tasks of the community, that is, those that directly contribute to the material wellbeing of the group. Instead, the priests devote their time to ecclesiastical and liturgical services. Eventually, their informal tithable claims are transformed into a formal entitlement that must be paid by the group. The 'lay' members of the group become "subject" to the "wealth and power" that now rest in the hands of the clerics (Veblen 1914: 156). Spiritual power is transformed into temporal power.

The second route is that of 'force'. While the priests come to power and ownership through 'wit', others take control through brute aggression. The changed technological circumstances and improved economic conditions mean that there are now goods worth obtaining through force. Some of this force is wielded by the more predatory persons in one's own group, whereas some aggression is in the form of raids on and pillages of adjacent communities. These occur because the marked accumulation of wealth now makes it worthwhile for individuals and communities to obtain wealth through aggression against one's fellows and neighbours. Indeed, in time, the fellows and neighbours themselves would come to be seen as worthwhile booty, and we see the emergence of the institution of slavery. Initially, slaves comprised the "female captives", but in time grew this institution grew to include "women and other slaves" (Veblen 1899: 16; 36).

Thus, technological gain has seen a shift in animus away from workmanship towards the predatory. Veblen considered that predation appeared only once the barbarian period took hold, as opposed to workmanship, which he considered was present in the species from the outset.[33] This view was probably tempered by his view that without workmanship the species might never have achieved the means to survive, let alone attain a surplus, but that only the achievement of a surplus would provide the reason for the appearance of predation (Ayres 1958: 29; Hunt 2002: 325). Ironically, then, this view sees workmanship itself as allowing for the introduction of a cluster of activities that serve to thwart it. It is by virtue of workmanship that technological advance occurs. Only through such technological advance can the group prosper and produce a surplus. Only after such a surplus does predation enter in the ledger of feasible or desirable activities, and only this surplus allows for the development of ownership. In Hegelian terms, one might say that the initial unity gave 'birth' to its negation.

Accordingly, in an analysis that is akin to those made by Marx, the classless society of the savage era gives way to the hierarchical barbarian society. This hierarchy is a corollary of the institution of ownership, which now causes differentiation based on those who own and those who do not. It is no surprise then to find that in a society where warlike aggression becomes acceptable and valued that we find at its peak: "the war chief, into whose hands authority and pecuniary emoluments gather somewhat in proportion as warlike exploits and ideals become habitual" (Veblen 1914: 157).

With ownership comes power and authority. Men (and the subjugation of women ensured that it was men) suddenly had a reason to envy their neighbour, for "invidious distinction" based on comparing what one owns to his neighbours' stock of ownership and with the authority and power that flows from it (Veblen 1899: 18). Inevitably, the new social ranks expressed themselves in the functions and occupations of the various members of the community. In the savage era, dominated as it was by workmanship, social ranks were absent, and there were a limited[34] number of occupations and activities in the community. But in the barbarian era, demarcation among employments arose, so that some activities or employments were now seen as honourable while others were seen to be unworthy or even unclean. Which were honourable and worthy was determined by the predatory element involved in its exercise:

> As the predatory culture reaches a fuller development, there comes a distinction between employments. The tradition of prowess, as the virtue *par excellence*, gains in scope and consistency until prowess comes near being recognized as the sole virtue. Those employments alone are then worthy and reputable which involve the exercise of this virtue. Other employments, in which men are occupied with tamely shaping inert materials to human use, become unworthy and end with becoming debasing. The honorable man must not only show capacity for predatory exploit, but he must also avoid entanglement with the occupations that do not involve exploit. The tame employments, those that involve no obvious destruction of life and no spectacular coercion of refractory antagonists, fall into disrepute and are relegated to

> those members of the community who are defective in predatory capacity; that is to say, those who are lacking in massiveness, agility, or ferocity. Occupation in these employments argues that the person so occupied falls short of that decent modicum of prowess which would entitle him to be graded as a man in good standing . . . the able-bodied barbarian of the predatory culture, who is at all mindful of his good name, severely leaves all uneventful drudgery to the women and minors of the group. He puts in his time in the manly arts of war and devotes his talents to devising ways and means of disturbing the peace. That way lies honor.
>
> (Veblen 1898a: 199–200)

In the first instance, the division in function "coincides with a difference between the sexes", so that some activities are viewed as suitable only for women while others, generally those involving predation, are considered the domain of the males of the community (Veblen 1899: 8). So, for example, women continued their savage era responsibility for such activities as farming and animal husbandry, but such activities came to be considered servile and drudgery; men, on the other hand, contributed through participation in predatory activities requiring 'guile' and exploit, such as through the bellicose arts (Veblen 1914: 93–94):

> The group divides itself conventionally into a fighting and a peace-keeping class, with a corresponding division of labor. Fighting, together with other work that involves a serious element of exploit, becomes the employment of the able-bodied men; the uneventful everyday work of the group falls to the women and the infirm. In such a community the standards of merit and propriety rest on an invidious distinction between those who are capable fighters and those who are not. Infirmity, that is to say incapacity for exploit, is looked down upon. One of the early consequences of this deprecation of infirmity is a tabu on women and on women's employments.
>
> (Veblen 1899c: 504)

Only women and men who are by misfortune not of a suitable physical stature, what Veblen calls "infirm", undertake the peaceable activities of the community. As a result, women become associated with the infirm, and in the "apprehension of the archaic, animistic barbarian, infirmity is infectious" (Veblen 1899c: 504). Any "able-bodied man who is mindful of his virility [will] shun all undue contact and conversation with the weaker sex and . . . avoid all contamination" (Veblen 1899c: 504). The idea of the 'unclean woman' and of institutions that relegate women to an inferior class can claim their origin during this period. In time, social classifications grew beyond gender lines, and we see the introduction of predatory institutions such as class and, in some societies, caste.

The division among employments is an unavoidable consequence of the institution of ownership and the social strata and stigmas that it initiates. Ownership is the means to differentiate between members of society. Recall that ownership during this period arose as the result of predation, whether through plunder and war, which Veblen considered "force", or through spiritual and religious subterfuge, which Veblen termed "fraud" (Veblen 1914: 159). Only ownership through predatory behaviour bestowed *dignitas*. Since ownership bestowed *dignitas*, and since the only 'acceptable' means of obtaining ownership was through the anointed predatory employments, then one can see that the institution of ownership and the social rank of employments are inextricably linked. This view held sway for much of the barbarian era, so that ownership through avenues involving exertion other than in the acceptable vocations was considered unclean, lacking honour or unworthy.

As the barbarian period continues into its "higher stages", the opportunities to obtain ownership through the preferred avenues diminish (Veblen 1899: 1, 19–20). With these means lessened, acquisition through nonpredatory activities – that is, through peaceable work – begin to take on an acceptable face. While work in the nonpredatory employments is still generally to be avoided and predatory employments and activities are still held in the highest regard, nonpredatory employments begin to carry some favour if the goal of these exertions is to increase one's ability to acquire; that is, if the object of the employment is to enable one to partake of the institution of ownership (Veblen 1914: 173, 183). Hence, ownership in and of itself becomes the important goal; how the 'title' to ownership is obtained becomes less important.

With the realisation that war has a tendency to destroy possessions and property, the institution of ownership increases its avenues for participation, from martial inclinations and priestly duties alone to now also include predatory behaviour that manifest itself within commercial institutions. This is a key feature of the *handicraft* era, the period that follows the barbarian. With predatory behaviour now finding outlet in commercial activities and a subsequent lessening of warlike pursuits, and with workmanship now in a "dominant position among the factors that made up the discipline of daily life", Veblen describes the handicraft era as "quasi-peaceable" (Veblen 1914: 234, 187).

The exact steps from the barbarian to the handicraft era are not overly clear, but we can see that it was possible because the predatory elements of the barbarian period were unable to completely vanquish the workmanship predilections of the race.[35] The state of savage era technology meant that all had access to the stock of knowledge, and this was also true for much of the barbarian era. But, in time, increasing technological advances allowed for the beginnings of some specialisation and with it the "growth of craftsmanship" (Veblen 1914: 232). In turn, the handicraft era 'muting' of warlike exploit and the transformation of aggression into pecuniary arrangements allowed for the freer hand of workmanship to make its presence, enabling even greater technological advance. With greater advance, we see "more elaborate technological processes", and in an echo of Adam Smith, even greater specialisation of employments (Veblen 1914: 275). Greater technology also expands the goods available for consumption, including "exotic luxuries" and "curious articles of great price", providing even greater motivation for ownership (Veblen 1914: 276). In time, we see even greater specialisation and the means to produce such goods becoming beyond "the industrial framework of the manor or its equivalent" (Veblen 1914: 276). Thus we see the traditional hold of the feudal lord becoming ever more tenuous, so that in time, these craftsmen "congregate in industrial towns and find a living by the work of their hands" (Veblen 1914: 276). They are free:

> "masterless men," who broke away (or were broken out) from the bonds of that organisation in which the arbitrary power of the landed interest held dominion. By tenacious assertion of the personal rights which they so arrogated to themselves, and at great cost and risk, they made good in time their claim to stand as a class apart, a class of ungraded free men among whom self-help and individual workmanlike efficiency were the accepted grounds of repute and of livelihood.
>
> (Veblen 1914: 276)

The initial reward for the craftsman's labour is that which "allowed a fair livelihood" (Veblen 1914: 233). But the means for these craftsmen to acquire and increase their power improved as the idea of "just price . . . passed over into the modern presumption that any article of value is worth what it will bring" (Veblen 1914: 233). As their wealth and stock of ownership increase, so too does their power. We see the emergence of a new class that is neither aristocrat nor serf. Society has been transformed to include three classes, with:

> the upper being typically that (aristocratic) class which is possessed of wealth without having worked or bargained for it; . . . the middle class [which] have come by their holdings through some form of commercial (business) traffic, and the lower class [which] gets what it has by workmanship. It is a gradation of (a) predation, (b) business, (c) industry; the former being disserviceable and gainful, the second gainful, and the third serviceable.
>
> (Veblen 1914: 184)

Veblen's distinction between the workmanship and predatory is evident in his characterisation of the three classes. [36] The aristocrats align with the older order of predatory warrior and priestly class, who obtained their wealth and power by the older predatory means. The new middle class is a 'mixed bag'. They have both predatory and workmanship elements, but, unlike the aristocrats, their predatory inclinations play out in commercial and pecuniary trade and activities. However, unlike the aristocrats, they are also driven to workmanship, and being masterless they are free to devote greater time to workmanship pursuits. This drive to workmanship is provided by two general incentives. First, since their livelihoods are dependent on their own skills and ability (and not on some ancient dowry), they aspire to produce goods in the most efficient manner. In addition, with the move away from 'just price' to one settled in the course of market interactions, we see price becoming the important factor in determining outputs; that is, outputs are determined more and more by markets. Thus, the improved methods of production and newfound freedom allowed for the expansion of markets and improved means for gaining wealth. Here we find the second driver, the desire for ownership, since improved wealth provides for greater acquisition and, ultimately, power (Edgell 2001: 95). Thus we see a reversal of fortunes: Whereas workmanship served to undermine itself in the savage era and usher in the barbarian period, the chief predatory institution arising from the barbarian period, namely, ownership, helps to weaken the predatory and sees a 'renaissance' in workmanship.

The penchant for ownership, the desire for increased markets and the technological gains that were used to achieve these aims eventually saw the introduction of production techniques that were beyond the scope of the individual craftsmen. The savage and, indeed, much of the barbarian era were characterised by a stock of knowledge that "had not grown so unwieldy as to require special pains to assimilate it" (Veblen 1914: 278). The era of the craftsmen had become more specialised, but the level of knowledge was such that it was still "accessible at the cost of some application" (Veblen 1914: 278). As time progressed, "work could no longer be carried on . . .in strict severalty" and instead required a "gang or corps of workman in cooperation, and . . . something in the way of a 'plant' suitable for the employment of such a corps" (Veblen 1914: 278). At this point we see the shift from the era of handicraft into the *machine* age.[37]

As production becomes more complex, a separation occurs. Whereas in the handicraft era the craftsman was both producer and owner, the machine process era sees a separation between those who own the premises where production takes place and those whose task it is to undertake production. Part of this is necessitated because, while the handicraft era technologies were within the reach of individual craftsmen, the technology of the machine age was of a magnitude that rendered it too difficult for the production methods of the handicraft era.[38]

An important outcome of the machine era is the separation between those who produce and those who own. In the handicraft era, the craftsman was producer and owner, analogous to what Engels referred to as "simple commodity production" (in Marx 1894: 617). In time, as production processes become more complex, requiring an 'army' of workers, the role of the owner is to direct. However, as the machine age proper sets in, we see an even greater separation, so that those who own have a more limited role in the day-to-day affairs of production, turning their minds instead to the "conjectures of business" (Veblen 1904: 24). Production processes are in turn in the hands of the engineers, those who have the technical ability needed to run the large-scale machine industry of capitalism but who more often do not own or control it (see Veblen 1921).

Here comes the crunch. Whereas the engineers are driven by workmanship and a desire to produce the most technically efficient and optimal output, the business owners are driven by pecuniary self-interest, and their chief concern is with profit. Veblen considered that the drive for profit drove business towards "sabotage", that is, to "retardation, restriction, withdrawal, unemployment of plant and workmen – whereby production is kept short of productive capacity" (Veblen 1921: 42). The engineer's predilection is for the most technically efficient and optimal output, in short, for workmanship, whereas the businessman is concerned with producing a "rate and volume of output . . . with a view as to what the traffic will bear . . . [so as to] yield the net returns in terms of price" (Veblen 1921: 42).

The resurgence in workmanship of the handicraft era gives way to the factory system of the machine age. This in turn leads to a separation between the owners and the producers, between business and industry. The machine age owners, that is, the businessmen, and their quest for profit curtail the needs of the community. Their desire for profit is the modern manifestation of the predatory, and in their desire for profit they are less concerned with producing optimal community outputs but instead those that produce a suitable profit.[39] Thus, with the machine age the shift between workmanship and predatory occurs again, and once again predatory cluster activities begin to gain the upper hand, appearing through the institutions of capitalism.

Veblen's Darwinian aversion to teleology means that the next step in human development is unknown. However, he considers that the machine age has within it the seeds to undermine the predatory 'afflictions'. First, the machine age requires educated workers, and as a result we see the beginnings of mass education. In addition, the machine process is a matter-of-fact process; any superfluous 'ceremonial' aspects of production are excised. These features could serve to affect the way in which people appraise the world around them:

> With due but not large exceptions, the effective body of the modern population has been growing more matter-of-fact in their thinking, less romantic, less idealistic in their aspirations, less bound by metaphysical considerations in their view of human relations, less mannerly, less devout. Taken generally . . . [they] have been moving in the direction of a more impersonal, more matter-of-fact, less conventional point of view. In this composite cultural growth the matter-of-fact habit of mind has on the whole been gaining at the expense of the conventional, and the conventional premises that have been retained have also come to bear more of a matter-of-fact character, – as, e.g., in the supersession of feudalistic or theocratic principles of law by natural rights. So that the position . . . is a more matter-of-fact position.
>
> (Veblen 1904: 345)

In Veblen's view, cultural development has been a 'see-saw' between predatory and workmanship proclivities. In the most recent machine stage of development, the predatory has taken on a greater part, but within this system there are elements that could possibly serve to weaken their hold on the future course of human development. Or to be Darwinian about it, possibly not.

6.4 Conclusion

In this chapter, I have presented the basic building blocks of Thorstein Veblen's proposed method for understanding economic phenomena. Veblen built an apparatus that was based on an antagonistic interaction between two main forces. On the one hand, we have community-regarding forces, what he called workmanship. On the alternate we see self-regarding forces, or predation. Veblen used instincts and the findings of anthropology and psychology to build his account, and, in doing so, he rejected the pre-Darwinian mind-set and preconceptions of many of his fellow economists. Instead, he built an account of human development based on the natural selection of institutions whose development is subject to blind chance as opposed to providential order.

Veblen used his insight to provide an account of cultural change over four periods of human development. The mechanism for cultural change was the interplay between workmanship and predation, but the trigger for change was the changing technological means of the species. Indeed, it was in technology that we find the root of ownership. It was technology that provided the main motivational force for change, and through technology we find the force that causes men – and increasingly, women – to re-evaluate the institutional ways and means and recast them in a form more suitable to the given technological circumstances.

In the next chapter, I will consider how the institutional apparatus appears in two traditional economic considerations, consumption and production. In turn, I will consider how these play out in an analysis of public support for the arts.

Notes

1 'Classical' was a term coined by Marx to refer to English and continental writers from Petty and Boisguillebert to Ricardo (see Keynes 1936a: 3).

2 These works are complemented by other works that outline key objections, including, *inter alia*, "Professor Clark's Economics" and "Fisher's Rate of Interest", written in 1908 and 1909, respectively.

3 Indeed, his objections were levelled against the economics of his time more broadly. For example, in "Why is Economics not an Evolutionary Science", Veblen shows dissatisfaction with the German historical school. Veblen accused the historical school of relying on "pre-Darwinian speculations" as opposed to "lines which modern science would recognize as evolutionary" (Veblen 1898: 388). The historical school's work amounted to a "narrative survey of phenomena, not a genetic account of an unfolding process" (Veblen 1898: 388).

4 J.S Mill's theories are outside the scope of this book, but for further information see *The Economics of John Stuart Mill* (1985) by Samuel Hollander.

5 One can see in Veblen's objections the influence of his schooling in the modern pragmatist philosophical injunctions that rejected religious or metaphysical pursuits of absolute truth in favour of truth based on practical outcomes and along Darwinian lines. See Chapter 5.

6 Although technically there are not illegitimate ends, only, as will be seen, disturbances to the natural order that prohibit the legitimate end from obtaining.

7 It should be noted that while Veblen was chastising economics in his 1898 work, he also seemed to recognise that even among modern sciences there was "no abrupt transition from pre-evolutionary to post-evolutionary" and that the "process of change in the point of view . . . is a gradual one", as a Darwinian might expect (Veblen 1898: 381)

8 It is interesting to note that the focus of Veblen's criticisms was Marshall, and yet, from what I have been able to determine, he expressed no thoughts, criticism or otherwise, of the neoclassical economist *par excellence* that was Lèon Walras.

9 This made sense, since the physiocrats are commonly ascribed 'first mover' status in economics, with physiocratic economics often considered to be the first detailed account of economic processes (Schumpeter 1912: 43; Veblen 1899a: 126).

10 It is not 'binding' in the sense that the law of gravity is always binding. One cannot escape the law of gravity, short of entering into the vacuum of space. But even in space its effects are unavoidable since it is felt in the motions of the stars and planets.

11 This idea is still prevalent in economic theory and discourse in terms of disturbing or distortionary effects or causes that create a barrier to the attainment of optimal outcomes.

12 Since creation is static, the scientist has no need to discover a mechanism such as natural selection to account for the appearance of species; and recall from Chapter 5 that species disappearance was generally not fathomable to pre-evolutionary science.

13 The point suggests that the problem is with the world, not with the model. We should make the world match our model, not the other way around. It makes me recall something I read some time ago, that what economists refer to as 'market failures' could instead be recast as 'market realities' (See Sheehan 1996; see also Szostak 1999). Moving from the former to the latter would mark a major change in *a priori* thinking for the discipline.

14 More on this in section 6.3.

15 Veblen himself recognised the flaws in the instinct model. Despite this, Veblen considered that the demands of his intellectual pursuits differed from those of the psychological and biological sciences. What may not be of use for one intellectual endeavour or inquiry may provide analytical fruit for another, so that for the "sciences that deal with the psychology of human conduct . . . the broad term 'instinct' is of too unprecise [*sic*] a character to serve the needs of an exhaustive psychological analysis. But the needs of an inquiry into the nature and causes of the growth of institutions are not precisely the same as those of such an exhaustive psychological analysis" (Veblen 1914: 2).

16 Clark considered that competition had degenerated into a form of "quasi-combat", where the "action of self-interest and unrestricted competition" had morphed into a form of "annihilating competition". The capitalist society in which Clark lived was one were competition was "self-destructive", a "dubious expedient" and "ought to disappear" (Homan and Clark in Homan 1927: 44)

17 *Tropismatic* is another way of saying 'tropistic', namely, something that operates in the way of a tropism.

18 Differences aside, Veblen considered that tropism and instinct share a physiological basis and that "there is enough of similarity in the working of the two to suggest that the two classes of phenomena must both be accounted for on somewhat similar physiological grounds" (Veblen 1914: 10).

19 So that, for example, the "civilised peoples" have a greater complement of instincts than those from "lower cultures" (Veblen 1914: 15). That said, Veblen considered that though the instincts may "vary appreciably from one race to another . . . the complement of instincts native to the several races is after all of much the same kind, comprising substantially the same ends" (Veblen 1914: 24).

20 Although as will be seen in Section 6.3.2, Veblen considered that human behaviour is only partly moulded by biological factors, with a large role also given to social elements. While biological factors are slow to change, social factors change with relative speed. Thus, changes in social factors provide a mechanism to explain changes in human behaviour over shorter periods that would not be possible were biological factors alone at play.

21 Veblen best summed idle curiosity when he said that "human curiosity is . . . 'idle' . . . in the sense that no utilitarian aim enters in its habitual exercise; but the material information which is by this means drawn into the agent's available knowledge may none the less come to serve the ends of workmanship" (Veblen 1914: 88).

22 Although as was shown in Chapter 3, there are examples within the neoclassical school where this does not hold. In section 3.3.6, one example that was given was of arts workers who derive reward not solely from income associated with the sale of their labour but from the process of labour itself. Similar moves away from the standard model include work by the English economist David A. Spencer, who considers the effects of work quality upon labour supply decisions. Standard labour supply models focus "solely upon the duration of work", but newer models consider the relationship

between labour supply, "*how* they [workers] spend their work time" and the "*quality* of work activities" (Spencer 2004: 442, his italics).

23 Hodgson (2004: 198–201) has suggested that Veblen's notion that this instinct negated the neoclassical assumption is flawed and overstated. Essentially, Hodgson noted that there may evolve in species an aversion to "energetic energy".

24 It interesting to note that the use of a 'group-regarding' concept was also being developed by the Russian biologist and polymath Peter Kropotkin. Kropotkin's use of group-regarding behavior was similar to Veblen's, in that he suggested that evolutionary models that include "standard competition for survival" urges also include complementary "cooperation for survival" forces (Dugger 1984: 973). The cooperative survival forces gain in importance as a mechanism for survival once we move from the individual level to the family and onto the social level (see Dugger 1984).

25 Recall from Chapter 5 that a desire of late nineteenth century and early twentieth century thinkers like William James was to show that man could be guided by instincts and still possess free will and the ability to reason. Recall that James considered that the overlap and crosscontamination of the vast number of human instincts that work with and against one another ensures that no single instinct can dominate human thought and action, thereby providing a plausible avenue to explain and enable free will. Note the similarity between Veblen and James here, and how Veblen took from James those aspects of this instinct theory that he believed to be useful in the pursuit of a modern economic science.

26 Ayres uses the metaphor of salt to make his point. Salt "may be said to be composed entirely of electrons, protons, neutrons, etc.; or it may be said to be composed entirely of atoms; or it may be said to be composed entirely of crystals. None of these propositions invalidates the other. None can be substitutes for any other" (Ayres 1962: 93).

27 The development of language provides a useful metaphor to understand this point. We are able to use language because of our physiology and the way our throats have evolved, but language itself is a social phenomenon, and the structure of that language, the rules, syntax, the manner of speech and the things we say to others, are socially determined. In a similar fashion, society's institutions and individual instincts are related, with each affecting the development of the other (Ayres 1962: 94). An explicit example of this is the case of the instinct of self-preservation and the effect of social norms on its manifestation. This instinct provokes us to eat to survive, to live. As humans, we are fortunate in that we can obtain sustenance from any number of sources, such as spiders and insects. Yet as far as I am aware, no Western nation has within its culinary tradition recipes involving insects and spiders (although these do admittedly exist in some Asian cultures). These food sources might prove nutritional, but Westerners have been inculcated with cultural norms that make them recoil at the prospect of spider and insect soup! However, the instinct of idle curiosity may cause Westerners to reconsider this practice, and so in time they may see their nutritional value and begin to eat spiders and insects, as famed chef Heston Blumenthal suggests (see Heston's Feasts, http://www.youtube.com/watch?v=XLW4CKIy6VY accessed 8 Feb 2012).

28 One might describe this as a Hegelian contradiction. Some have argued that it is in essence the extension of the Hegelian-Marxian dialectic process, although as noted in Chapter 5, there is some disagreement among economists on this point (see Dugger 1979 and Edgell and Tilman 1989). The argument against is built on the idea that Veblen's Darwinism and his desire to move the science away from teleological notions puts him at odds with the teleological Hegelian dialectic.

29 For example, the institution of dress that requires that we cover ourselves with garments probably started as a means to ensure that the species is protected from the elements. However, this positive aspect has been tempered by requirements to dress in particular ways depending on factors such as class or sex that add little to the welfare of the species. See Veblen (1899: Chapter 7)

30 Veblen applied this dichotomy to understanding four periods of human development, which will be the topic of discussion in section 6.3.3.
31 As Veblen points out, names were not considered a "pecuniary asset before the use of trade-marks and merchantable good-will" (Veblen 1914: 144).
32 Veblen points to the lack of weapons found in archaeological sites as evidence that predation did not dominate savage era communities. Material discoveries at these sites found that while "weapons are to be counted by the dozens the tools are to be counted by the hundreds" (Veblen 1914: 128).
33 Ayres notes that in this Veblen appears to be incorrect, using the example of ceremonial burials to show that while man was driven by workmanship, ceremonialism was also present during the savage era (1958: 29).
34 The number and type of employments were limited by the very crude state of technology.
35 This is not universally true, and Veblen talks of some barbarian era cultures that are "predatory in a peculiarly overt and accentuated degree, so that their institutions foster the invidious sentiments . . . beyond what commonly happens" (Veblen 1914: 169). In such communities, "the discipline of life . . . is consistently unfavourable to any technological gain", and the "instinct of workmanship is constantly dominated by prevalent habits of thought that are worse than useless for any technological purposes" (Veblen 1914: 169). However, in Europe, the handicraft era was able to take root probably because its "peculiar topography" meant that the "predatory culture . . . never fully developed or naturalised" (Veblen 1914: 231). The economic historian Eric Jones also points to Europe's "geological, climatic and topographical variety" (Jones 1987: 227) but in addition ascribes part of Europe's economic rise to its political structure. While other regions were made up of large empires, Europe was a collection of "relatively small . . . states" that learned that "they could attract and retain the most and best paying constituents" by "supplying the services of order and adjudication" (Jones 1987: 233). As a result, Europe experienced a "competition among states" to provide an advantageous environment that was not present elsewhere (Jones 1987: 233). Jones suggests that this latter political reality contributed to the success of Europe over its Asian and Mughal rivals.
36 One cannot help but notice the similarities between Veblen, Smith and Ricardo in the characterisation of the classes that make up society. Smith said society was made up of "three great, original, and constituent, orders" – "those who live by rent . . . those who live by wages . . . and to those who live by profit" (Smith 1776: 212). Ricardo too spoke of "three classes of the community": the "proprietor of the land . . . the owner of stock of capital, and the labourers by whose industry it is cultivated" (Ricardo 1817: 5). The similarities between Veblen and these two English economists reflects Veblen's familiarity with both their works and gives credence to the premise underpinning chapter 5, that no person can produce ideas without some base prepared by predecessors and upon which successors can erect new thoughts.
37 Although Veblen considered that the development of the two eras was such that while "Historically the machine age succeeds . . . [the] handicraft . . . the two overlap very extensively" (Veblen 1914: 278).
38 This point regarding the complexity of production technologies and the origins of capital will be expanded on in Chapter 7.
39 Note that I have purposefully used the term 'suitable' as opposed to maximum profit. This is because of a wish to distinguish between the neoclassical and Veblenian perspectives. In the neoclassical construct, at least in the case of perfect or pure competition, the businessman's quest for profit is assumed to coincide with the optimal outcome of the community. With Veblen the question for profit is not always consistent with optimum human welfare.

7 Production and consumption through the Veblenian prism

7.1 Introduction

When asked to define the focus or purpose of economics, most laypersons respond by saying that economics is the study of supply and demand. It is true that traditionally much of economics has considered the workings of the economy by crafting analysis in terms of demand and supply, what some refer to as the 'Marshallian scissors'. Generally, demand is equated with consumption, and supply with production. The dual distinction has led to the separation of much of economic theory into models of production and of consumption. Neoclassical economics, built as it is on a consumer and firm (producer) maximising calculus, is an example of this dichotomous approach.

This chapter will continue this traditional form of analysis and consider consumption and production from a Veblenian perspective. To do this, I have unequivocally 'cherry picked' those elements that I consider are germane to this work.[1]

The chapter is divided into three sections. The first section deals with consumption. It outlines Veblen's key ideas on consumption, including his well-known idea of conspicuous consumption. As will be seen, Veblen approached consumption as a socially influenced thing. Given the role of institutions, this section will outline the chief institutions of consumption, particularly the leisure class, as well as ancillary aspects, such as emulation, canons of taste, conspicuous consumption and conspicuous leisure, and vicarious consumption.

The second part of this chapter deals with production, or, in Veblen's language, business enterprise. I explore and outline the key components of Veblen's approach to business enterprise, including Veblen's explanations for the origin of capital, the nature of payments to capital, the characteristics of the machine age, and the effects of predatory ownership of the productive system.

The third part focuses on Veblen's 'solution', which is to 'hand control' of the productive forces of the economy to a group he referred to as the engineers. As will be seen, the engineers recast the productive forces of the economy away from a pecuniary predatory foundation towards production that is motivated by technical efficiency and workmanship.

The analysis in the chapter is presented with an overarching purpose in mind: to provide the means to understand what Veblen's economic approach might tell us about the specific question of public support for the arts. It is my intention to use the information in Chapter 6 and in this chapter to provide a Veblenian understanding of public support for the arts in Chapter 8.

7.2 Consumption

Veblen's reputation in modern economic analysis is assured by virtue of the neoclassical 'adoption' of his notion of conspicuous consumption and Veblen goods, where the consumer derives utility from the price paid for the good and not solely from its consumption. While the idea of conspicuous consumption seems to have been appropriated within the dominant neoclassical paradigm, some like Hamilton (1973; 1987) suggest that this is only 'nominal'. Neoclassical interpretations of conspicuous consumption treat the concept as an aberrant form of consumption behaviour, a special case, if you will (Hamilton 1987: 360). In addition, neoclassical economics has neglected the central idea in Veblen's theories of consumption, specifically that consumption has social determinants (Hamilton 1987: 366–368). The full colour and effect of Veblen's ideas on consumption have mostly been missed in orthodox expressions of economic science. However, there are notable exceptions, such as the economist Robert H. Frank, whose ideas regarding *expenditure cascades*, *positional goods* and *nonpositional goods* have an obvious Veblenian bent (Frank 2007, 2011; Challenge 2008).[2]

In the pages that follow, I will delineate Veblen's major ideas on consumption. The bulk of this is drawn from Veblen's first major work, *The Theory of the Leisure Class* (1899), although his ideas regarding consumption can be traced back further to his 1891 article 'Neglected Points of Socialism'. Hamilton describes *Leisure Class* as the "first major work of institutional economics" and one motivated to present a theory of consumption (Hamilton 1987: 359; 1973). One need not rely on Hamilton to establish the *Leisure Class's* consumption credentials, with verification easily attainable from a quick reading through its chapter titles. These include such headings as 'Conspicuous Consumption' and 'Pecuniary Canons of Taste', among others, each revealing that this is a work that has among its aims a desire to present an alternative institutional approach to the then still relatively new but increasingly dominant marginalist hedonistic felicific calculus.

7.2.1 The leisure class

When Thorstein Veblen published the *Theory of the Leisure Class* in 1899, the marginalist revolution had all but cast out the ghosts of the labour theory of value.[3] The marginalist revolution was a belated realisation of Bentham's hedonistic utilitarianism. In the case of consumption, its expression was seen through the desire by consumers to maximise pleasure and cast out pain (or at least to minimise it) (Hamilton 1987; Diggins 1999: 43–44).

The earliest forms of the marginal revolution adopted an explicitly 'vulgar' hedonism. In essence it was a pleasure-pain calculus, and it was explicitly articulated as such by William Stanley Jevons when he said that consumers actually seek to maximise pleasure and minimise pain (Jevons 1871: xxxiii). By the time the likes of Leon Walras, Alfred Marshall and John Bates Clark (who was also Veblen's teacher) got their hands on the doctrine, the pleasure-pain calculus had been amended so that discussion referred instead to the more innocuous nomenclature of utility and disutility. In essence, this change was camouflage, and pleasure-pain hedonism was still the core of neoclassical conceptions of consumer behaviour (Hamilton 1987: 358–359).[4]

The classical and neoclassical treatment of consumption was also affected by Adam Smith's famous declaration that "Consumption is the sole end and purpose of all production" (Smith 1776: 537). Implied in Smith's statement is that production is the area where economic analysis lies. Unlike consumption, which is by this definition consummatory and hence final, production is a process to be considered and accounted for. This suggests that economics should instead be devoted to understanding production.

A further consideration is that of the 'dire' reality of economic scarcity, always casting doubt on the ability to produce a level of output that meets the 'final needs' of consumption. Again, implied in this is that production is the part of the economy to be accounted for, while consumption can be taken as its conclusion. Cast in these 'dismal' terms, economists' theories of consumer behavior were built so as to determine the equilibrium between supply and demand, between the process of production and the *end-point* of consumption, and to determine how the price a consumer is willing to pay for good x coincides with the price of its production at equilibrium (Hamilton 1973: 200; Diggins 1999: 44).

Being an end-point, the analysis of consumer behavior is not concerned with why a consumer wishes to have good *x* in the first place (other than to yield utility). The classical economists and their neoclassical descendants did not seek to understand why a good produces utility, in other words, to determine the "origin of wants" (Hamilton 1987: 358). Nor did they explore why good *x* produced greater utility than good *y* (Hamilton 1987: 358). Instead, the source of utility was beyond their scope, taken as a given, and so, armed with hedonistic utility, the focus of their investigations shifted to why a consumer is willing to pay price *z* for good *x*. The actual process of consumption, its cultural determinants and drivers (if any) were cast aside.[5] All that need be known is that consumers wish to optimise utility by maximising pleasures and minimising pains (or maximising utility and minimising disutility) (Hamilton 1973: 198). Consumption is final, driven by the "inner yearnings of a pre-programmed [hedonistic] human heart" that are "made in heaven" (Hamilton 1987: 358).

It is worth pausing to make a related point made elsewhere in this book: An outcome of the neoclassical pleasure-pain, utility-disutility apparatus is the casting of man in passive terms, as a being who sits patiently in isolation in a state of inaction waiting for the impact of the next pleasure-pain stimuli. Consumption activity is thus seen as the result of some disturbing force, as set in motion not by the consumer but by forces outside him. The implication is that the natural state for the consumer is one of rest, or equilibrium. But as Veblen pointed out, man is a creature who does not sit idly at rest but actually seeks to achieve and take action, including in consumption.[6]

For Veblen, human nature and wants are not, to use an earlier term, made in heaven. Veblen did not disagree with neoclassical notions of utility; on the contrary, he considered that "whatever form of expenditure the consumer chooses, or whatever end he seeks in making his choice, has utility to him by virtue of his preference" (Veblen 1899: 65). Where he parted ways with his contemporaries is on the importance he placed on social determinants of utility. In other words, human wants are not made in heaven but are made right here on Earth.

In contrast to neoclassical economics, Veblen's analysis of consumption is one drawn in social and institutional terms. Consumption in a capitalist economy (and indeed in any economic system) is apprehended through the way in which it appears in institutions. As was shown in Chapter 6, these institutions are understood as being the product of natural selection. Institutional selection occurs because of the relationship and interplay between the concomitant predatory and workmanship bents of the human species. It is the state of technology that affects how institutions appear and which of these two forces has the upper hand at any given time.

There are two key institutions pivotal to an understanding of consumption. The first of these is the institution of ownership, while the second is the leisure class. Veblen contended that one could not emerge without the other. Ownership and the leisure class are twin institutions, essentially two sides of the same coin. Their simultaneous appearance is a result of their being born of the same set of economic motions, that is, the appearance of a surplus set in train by the advance of technology. The surplus enables ownership, but it is those who are victorious in the competition for these resources who are able to enjoy ownership. We call these victors the leisure class (Veblen 1899: 15).

Using Veblen's dichotomy, the leisure class and ownership are outcomes of the predatory traits in the species. Ironically, the appearance of these predatory institutions is made possible because of the workmanship drivers inherent in the race. Workmanship causes the species to improve its technological abilities, which leads to the production of a surplus of goods. The surplus creates the circumstances that encourage the introduction of predatory activities. This predatory bent manifests itself in a number of ways, including the institution of ownership; but the surplus created by increasing technological proficiency also means that some members of the group no longer need contribute towards the wellbeing of the community. Those who are exempt are those who by force or fraud have been able to advance their own position at the expense of others, the so-called leisure class. Thus, for the leisure class to appear:

> (1) the community must be of a predatory habit of life . . .; (2) subsistence must be obtainable on sufficiently easy terms to admit of the exemption of a considerable portion of the community from steady application to a routine of labour.
>
> (Veblen 1899: 5)

Veblen traces the earliest phase of the leisure class to the barbarian era (Veblen 1899: 1). It is here that we see the origins of distinctions based on ownership, employment and function, and with these of honour and dishonour. It is the goal of the leisure class to obtain and maintain honour. Honour is gained in two ways, one 'active' and the other 'passive'. The *active* means is by pursuing activities that are overtly predatory, such as the bellicose arts, hunting and clerical or priestly duties. Since honour is associated with the predatory, involvement and success in these explicitly predatory functions conveys honour (Veblen 1899: 1). The second route to achieve honour is via those things that one purposefully and actively avoids, and in this sense the route is *passive*. Honour is earned by avoiding any activities that are obviously nonpredatory. Since nonpredatory employments also imply "subjection to a master" there is a further incentive to avoid them (Veblen 1899: 25).

Leisure itself comes to be a sign of the predatory. Others in the group must contribute to the production of goods needed for the group's survival. But those who are able to absent themselves from these duties and instead enjoy leisure can only do so because of their 'superior' predatory skills (Veblen 1899: 62). They have been able to exploit the group's situation and demand a share of the group's production without actually contributing to it. On the contrary, they go out of their way to enjoy leisure, to actively *not* contribute to production.[7] In this way, the ability to enjoy leisure comes to yield honour. Avoidance of workmanship duties sends a signal; it tells others in the group that this man is one of such stature and power that he need not concern himself with nonpredatory activities. Instead he enjoys leisure and is able to foist these unworthy tasks onto others, and by virtue of their performing these tasks these people are deemed to be beneath him.

The nature of the earliest predatory activities lent themselves more readily to the stronger male physique. The result was that at this earliest phase, the leisure class was synonymous with men; it was a male institution (Veblen 1899: 5). However, as technological feats continue, this earliest patriarchal hegemony gives way to a differentiation based on factors other than gender, and we see the development of a full-fledged class system such as that of feudal Europe (Veblen 1899: 1). The role of technology is again probably responsible for this development. With the growth of technology comes an increase in the various functions necessary to ensure life. We see an increase in the number of roles associated with drudgery and nonpredation. Some of these come to be taken on by men, and with this we see the appearance of class.

The leisure class's institutional twin is the institution of ownership, and it arose as a result of the conflict for control of the newly derived surplus of goods. To win control one had to be in possession of superior force or have more savvy skills at fraud. In other words, one came to ownership through predation. If one had ownership over the group's production, it meant that one was the victor in this struggle and could claim all the honour pertaining to that victory. The more successful in predation one was, the more one owned, with a commensurate increase in honour. As a result, ownership and the amount one owned came to display one's predatory skills, with the level of honour corresponding with the level of ownership. The increasing honour arising from increased ownership provided an incentive for ever greater "accumulation of wealth" (Veblen 1899: 17).[8] It served to indicate the owner's rank in the group and position in the leisure class. Given the male dominance of barbarian era societies, and in particular of the leisure class, it is unsurprising to find that the "earliest form of ownership [was] ownership of the women by the able bodied men of the group" (Veblen 1899: 15).

With ownership and noble and ignoble differentiation in employment and function, we see an amendment to the emulatory bent of the species. During the savage era, emulation was a serviceable activity, working within the wider workmanship activities of the community. However, as the community moves into the barbarian era, the scope for emulation grows to include emulation of a predatory kind (Veblen 1899: 10–11). The appearance of both ownership and the leisure class, and the distinctions within the group based on gender and function (and membership or otherwise of the leisure class), introduce an invidious element. The honour associated with ownership and wealth and the desire to win esteem through a display of accumulated wealth create the conditions for an increased role for envy. One is envious of those who have greater accumulated wealth and ownership. Envy implies that there are those that we wish to be like, to copy or perhaps even to usurp. We wish to copy their methods, to be better at predation than they, and if possible, to be in their social position and to achieve their rank. We seek to *emulate* them and improve our position within the hierarchy, or perhaps even jealously guard our position against potential rivals. Hence, emulation operates in a two-pronged manner. First, it makes us strive to achieve the standards set by those above us, to copy them. But it also causes us to maintain our own rank at the risk of losing it to others. Through the twin institutions of ownership and the leisure class, we see a transformation of emulation so that it becomes contaminated by "ideals of self-aggrandisement" and predation (Veblen 1914: 217; 1899: 11).

In time, as society moves through the upper barbarian period and into the handicraft and the machine age industrial communities, the overtly martial and sacerdotal predatory exploits of the leisure class give way to predation of a pecuniary kind. Predatory prowess is displayed by pecuniary strength, and the respect of the community is dependent on the ability to display wealth arising from these pecuniary pursuits (Veblen 1899: 57). Workmanship is never fully banished, and men still seek to avoid "futile effort" (Veblen 1899: 22). But workmanship becomes 'infected' so that the desire to achieve and to act purposefully unfolds within predatory pursuits. In the case of the modern machine age industrial societies, these achievements manifest themselves within pecuniary pursuits:

> The propensity for achievement and the repugnance to futility remain the underlying economic motive. The propensity changes only in the form of its expression. . . . Under the regime of individual ownership the most available means of visibly achieving a purpose is that afforded by the acquisition and accumulation of goods; and as the self-regarding antithesis between man and man reaches fuller consciousness, the propensity for achievement – the instinct of workmanship – tends more and more to shape itself into a straining to excel others in pecuniary achievement.
>
> (Veblen 1899: 22)

The power of emulation and invidious comparison makes pecuniary pursuits the embodiment of purposeful action, and so, as Veblen says, "repugnance to futility to a good extent coalesces with the incentive of emulation" (Veblen 1899: 22). As will be seen, emulation is a key determinant in consumption. Invidious emulation is a key, if not the key factor in the development of what is known as conspicuous consumption and conspicuous leisure (elaborated upon in this chapter). The institution of the leisure class, coupled with invidious emulation, is essential to understanding how these patterns of behaviour play out in consumption decisions.

7.2.2 The leisure class: Arbiters of taste

When someone commits an act that others consider uncouth or in 'poor taste', an oft-heard denunciation is "very classy!" Implied in this statement is the idea that the behaviour of the person in question did not meet some acceptable standard. A further implication is that the acceptable standard or canon of behaviour is socially determined, associated with a particularly favourable class. In a hierarchical society, that class is likely to be the one at the apex, like Veblen's leisure class. Being at the apex, this class can, through its authority, set the norms of acceptable behaviour.

In a similar fashion, we may refer to objects as being 'classy', as in a classy car or watch. In these cases, we associate the goods in question with the class to be aspired to, and the suggestion is that a person of repute and good breeding, in other words, of that class, drives a classy car or sports a classy watch.

Whether the case at hand is behaviour or goods, the etymology of the term 'classy'[9] is similar, and these two examples serve to make an important point: that much if not all that we consider desirable or undesirable, whether behaviour or goods, has a social dimension. The implication is that our taste for what is good and what is bad is socially determined. Using this example, what is classy, and hence good, is a thing we learn from our interactions and immersions within society. [10]

Veblen's conception of society is one that operates under a superstructure of institutions that represent its conventions, traditions, mores and norms. The institutions we hand from generation to generation are used to instil the norms of behaviour of society, and some of these institutions give us guidance on taste. Hence, taste is institutionally inculcated.[11] Our wants and the tastes that shape them are not assumed to be stamped in the womb (the classical perspective), but are acquired after birth, from the interactions we have within the society in which we live. True, often our need to consume has an individual physiological dimension, but even in such cases, how and what we consume is tempered and moulded by the social construct. Through the scheme of institutions that direct societal function, our desires come to take on the shape of canons of (acceptable) taste:

> Canons of taste are . . . habits, acquired through a more or less protracted habituation to the approval or disapproval of the kind of things upon which

> a favorable or unfavorable judgment of taste is passed. Other things being equal, the longer and more unbroken the habituation, the more legitimate is the canon of taste in question.
>
> (Veblen 1899: 259)

What role does the leisure class play in shaping these canons of taste? As the group at the summit of society, the leisure class are the arbiters of taste, what in crude terms one might refer to as 'trendsetters'. How do they achieve this role? It is because of the drive for emulation, which Veblen considered to be bested in strength only by self-preservation (Veblen 1899: 74). A modern hierarchical society such as ours creates the circumstances for envy and social comparison. Social comparison provides the incentive to improve one's standing, or at the very least to jealously maintain and guard one's current social rank. The way to improve social standing is by adopting the practices of those who have managed to achieve high esteem, meaning one's social superiors. If we want to be part of the superior group, then we mimic their actions and behaviour, including by trying to adopt their modes of consumption; in other words, we emulate.

By virtue of their position at the peak at human society, the leisure class become the definitive group to aspire to and to emulate. They are the ultimate paragon so that, by their actions, they establish the acceptable and desirable patterns of both behaviour and consumption. In their choices, they determine what is honourable, what bestows gravitas and what is *tasteful*:

> The leisure class stands at the head of the social structure in point of reputability; and its manner of life and its standards of worth therefore afford the norm of reputability for the community. The observance of these standards . . . becomes incumbent upon all classes lower in the scale. . . . [T]he norm of reputability imposed by the upper class extends its coercive influence with but slight hindrance down through the social structure to the lowest strata.
>
> (Veblen 1899: 56)

Being at the social apex, the leisure class establish the acceptable parameters for consumption. Emulation causes us to strive to match the mores of our 'betters', and since leisure class mores are driven by ownership and wealth, society's canons of taste are of a pecuniary kind (Veblen 1899: Chapter 6).

While the leisure class are the final arbiters, the reality for many is that they look not to the leisure class for their cues on how to act or consume but to those immediately above them in the social hierarchy. As a result, while one aspires to emulate one's immediate 'betters', one must not look too far above one's current life station for the appropriate canons. Instead, the:

> members of each stratum accept as their ideal of decency the scheme of life in vogue in the next higher stratum, and bend their energies to live up to that

> ideal. On pain of forfeiting their good name and their self-respect in case of failure, they must conform to the accepted code, at least in appearance.
>
> (Veblen 1899: 56)

So, for instance, in a simple three-tiered society with a working, middle and upper (leisure) class, the middle class would aspire to the actions and consumption patterns of the upper class, and the working class to that of the middle class.[12] As the ultimate arbiters of taste, leisure class canons 'trickle down' and are interpreted by the lower classes into their own 'class specific' canons of taste:

> variation in matters of taste, from one class of society to another, is visible . . . as regards many . . . consumable goods. . . . This diversity of views as to what is beautiful in these various classes of goods is not a diversity of the norm according to which the unsophisticated sense of the beautiful works. It is not a constitutional difference of endowments in the aesthetic respect, but rather a difference in the code of reputability.
>
> (Veblen 1899: 88)

In other words, each class's canons of taste are accommodated to fit within the parameters established by the leisure class. One may aspire to be in the next stratum or social rank, but one must first ensure that one meets the acceptable canons of taste in one's own class. It is the class-specific canons of taste that one must strive to meet, lest one risk the disesteem of one's fellow class members and, indeed, the prospect of wider social opprobrium.

Sometimes our individual physiology drives us to consume, such as in the case of individual hunger, but even in such cases we arrive at our *tastes* to consume things like food (and indeed on what and how to eat it) from our interactions with our friends and family, and the wider society. Importantly though, sometimes our consumption decisions are not based on any biological imperative but have their origins purely within the social realm. This kind of consumption is most definitely not stamped in the womb and is unquestionably made right here on Earth. Whatever the case may be, the hierarchy means that those at the top act as the final judge of what is acceptable and tasteful and set the pattern for others to follow. However, the social stratification of society also creates grades of acceptable behaviour, so that while the leisure class modes of operation are at the pinnacle, they are not necessarily free to be followed by all. To be sure, there may be some activities that are exclusively prohibited for action or consumption of the lower classes.[13]

One final remark should be made regarding the origin of the activity or good that earns the esteem of the leisure class and hence enters the canons of taste. The discussion so far seems to imply that a good or activity that falls within the acceptable canons of taste must originate with the upper classes and cannot have its origins in the lower classes. Veblen's model seems to be one that explicitly moves in one direction, from on high to those below. However, history is replete with examples of goods or behaviour that were initially associated with the lower grades only to later be adopted by those at the upper echelons of society.[14] This direction seems counter to the 'top down' direction proposed by Veblen, and some have suggested that this is an important oversight (Slater 1997: 158). Indeed, as far as I can tell, Veblen does not explicitly entertain or introduce the possibility that taste may move in the other direction; that is, from the lower classes to those above. Is this an oversight, or is it possible to square the role of the leisure class with the possibility that goods that enter the canons of taste originate in the lower classes?

Perhaps one way to achieve this is to recall that the leisure class are, by their position and power, the final arbiters of taste. According to Veblen, an object or action becomes acceptable and receives absolute social approbation only once it has been accommodated within the leisure class's scheme of acceptable behaviour or consumption activity. Since the leisure class have the status, goods that were previously associated with lower classes become reputable only once the leisure class begin to consume them. Only then do they achieve honour, only then do they become acceptable. Thus, while the goods may originate in the lower classes, the canons of taste still move from those above to those below.

7.2.3 The need to be seen

As has been stated, a hierarchical society is one that fosters invidious behaviour and encourages emulation, in particular of one's social superiors. But how does one know what one's superiors do and, hence, what to emulate?

While the leisure class are the definitive arbiters of taste, the manner in which they adjudicate questions of taste is not through decree or statute (although there may be cases where this has occurred). Instead, they herald what is tasteful by enjoying both their consumption and their leisure in a manner that is visible to others. By consuming both leisure and consumption in a *conspicuous* manner, they give information to others regarding what is tasteful.

Of course, the leisure class are not motivated to consume or take leisure in an ostentatious manner by some noble desire to ensure that society is not riddled with persons whom they consider are fashionably challenged! Their desire is to ensure that their wealth and power are properly recognised and that they receive the esteem that they consider is owed them. Given a hierarchical society, their drive comes from their desire to earn the appropriate social respect and cement their position in the hierarchy:

> In order to gain and to hold the esteem of men it is not sufficient merely to possess wealth or power. The wealth or power must be put in evidence, for esteem is awarded only on evidence . . . the evidence of wealth serve[s] to impress one's importance on others and to keep their sense of his importance alive.
>
> (Veblen 1899: 26)

This is the origin of Veblen's famed *conspicuous consumption*[15] and *conspicuous leisure*, where conspicuous leisure: "connotes . . . non-productive consumption of time. Time is consumed non-productively (1) from a sense of the unworthiness of productive work, and (2) as an evidence of pecuniary ability to afford a life of idleness" (Veblen 1899: 30).

In a similar vein, conspicuous consumption implies consumption that is non-productive. That is not to say that this form of consumption (and indeed leisure) does not produce utility. Indeed, as has already been mentioned, Veblen considered that it would produce utility. The point is that is does not add to human welfare, since the source of the utility stems not from workmanship but from predation. Not only do conspicuous leisure and conspicuous consumption not add to human welfare, they actually produce 'waste':

> From the foregoing survey of the growth of conspicuous leisure and consumption, it appears that the utility of both alike for the purposes of reputability lies in the element of waste that is common to both. In the one case it is a waste of time and effort, in the other it is a waste of goods.
>
> (Veblen 1899: 57)

While Veblen considered waste an "unfortunate" term, he believed it to be apposite as a means to make clear that consumption of this nature "does not serve human life or human well-being on the whole" (Veblen 1899: 65). Veblen says his definition of waste was not used in an "odious sense, as implying an illegitimate expenditure", but was drawn from the "language of everyday life", which he says is an "outcropping of the instinct of workmanship" (Veblen 1899: 66). In order to qualify as serviceable and *not* wasteful, an "economic fact must approve itself under the test of impersonal usefulness" (Veblen 1899: 66). Impersonal usefulness differs from personal usefulness in that it is "usefulness as seen from the point of view of the generically human" (Veblen 1899: 66). Under this definition, it is not sufficient that an 'economic fact' be considered useful to an individual, for such a good or service may serve an individual but not the wider community. It must, however, serve to advance *total* human welfare. Impersonal usefulness is an appeal to man's sense of workmanship, one of the two constant travellers in the organisation of human society, which enables us to determine whether an 'economic fact' is not wasteful and leads to an increase in human welfare (Veblen 1899: 66).

Unfortunately, Veblen offered no method to enable one to determine or measure whether total human welfare is served. Another problem with Veblen's pronouncements regarding waste is that they are in keeping with his wont to claim to speak with the air of dispassionate and unbiased science but almost always adding a layer that has a hint of moral stricture. One can easily envisage a scenario where different individuals holding differing views come to diametrically opposed conclusions regarding what is impersonally useful, what is not wasteful and what advances total human welfare.

Despite such problems, one way to 'clear the air' on waste is to consider the related issue of efficiency. While a discussion of Veblen's views on efficiency pre-empts some of the analysis of production that will take place in section 7.3, it also aids an understanding of consumption.

Unlike neoclassical economics, which bases its definition on Paretian foundations, Veblen based his definition of efficiency on a technical engineering footing, drawing on the then-prominent industrial efficiency ideas of the American engineer Frederick Winslow Taylor (Knoedler 1997). As the Taylor disciple and engineer Henry Gantt noted, in terms that would not be out of place in a tract written by Veblen, an industrial system operated by business is one where the "production of goods" is "always secondary to the harvesting of dollars" (Gantt in Knoedler 1997: 1012). In such a system, it is the 'laws of business' (such as the imperative to reduce costs) that determine the level of output. Business 'laws' are, however, "dependent upon bargain and sale", while engineering principles are based on "mechanical laws" that are "invariable and immutable" (Trowbridge in Knoedler 1997: 1012). The constancy and absoluteness of the latter means that efficiency would be best defined in technical terms as the ability to minimise physical 'losses' (waste) in output from a given production process, as though some physical law for the conservation of energy applied to the productive forces of industrial society.

However, as the American sociologist Louis Schneider argued, a technical definition of efficiency might be able to tell us *how* something should be produced, but it offers little guidance on "*what* specifically should be produced" (Schneider in Tilman 1992: 182, his italics). By dismissing price as 'ceremonial artifice' and preferring efficiency to be measured in technical terms, Schneider argues that Veblen effectively exalted technology to the "locus of value" (Schneider in Tilman 1992: 183).[16]

Schneider's criticisms aside, how do Veblen's views on waste and efficiency relate to consumption, particularly since the latter seems to apply so much more to an analysis of production? It is clear that Veblen envisaged two broad heads or forms of consumption. The first is of a workmanship type, the other is predatory, although ceremonial might be the better descriptor here. Consumption that falls under the ceremonial head could be referred to as self-regarding; it produces waste and is undertaken at the group's expense. Hence conspicuous consumption and conspicuous leisure could be said to be synonymous with *conspicuous waste*. The ability to waste in a manner that can be witnessed by others is a means to earn status and esteem. However, it needs noting that, given the presence of workmanship, even this desire to produce waste is tempered by the human desire to minimise futile effort (Veblen 1914: 90). But despite this, the pursuit of ceremonial consumption comes at the expense of efficiency. Productive forces that could be used for the production of goods or services that would serve to elevate total human welfare are instead used in the production of goods that serve individual 'personal usefulness' at the community's expense.[17]

The personal usefulness or utility deriving from these conspicuous ceremonial acts can be brought back to the principle woven throughout the discussion: Such open displays of leisure and consumption provide a means to inform others of one's standing in the community. But how did a need for such overt displays commence? Again, technology plays a role.

The earliest incarnation of the leisure class was in tribal hamlets during the early barbarian period. In these circumstances, one's position and status is easily recognisable by one's peers. However, as technological advancements are made that enable the size of the community to grow, the ability to advise others of one's status becomes ever more difficult (Veblen 1908a: 524). In such larger impersonal communities, one cannot rely on the possibility that one is recognised or that one's position or importance is known. Instead, one must develop alternative means to convey power and earn esteem:

> As the population increases in density, and as human relations grow more complex and numerous, all the details of life undergo a process of elaboration and selection; and in this process of elaboration the use of trophies develops into a system of rank, titles, degrees and insignia, typical examples of which are heraldic devices, medals, and honorary decorations.
>
> (Veblen 1899: 30–31)

Status is therefore earned through conspicuous displays of wealth, stereotypical examples being such things as large country houses, ownership of expensive jewels and the like (Veblen 1899: 47). In addition to these kinds of physical 'trophies', wealth and power can be displayed by one's personal presentation and appearance, as for example in the form of dress one wears. Yet another way is to partake in such things as "knowledge of the dead languages and occult sciences" and other esoteric pursuits (Veblen 1899: 31). Time spent playing sports could also be a means to display wealth. The point of many of these exercises is that they take time to master or to pursue, and only the leisure class can devote time to such pastimes (Veblen 1899: 31). These actions send a signal that one can avoid drudgery, that this is a person of such power and esteem that he need not occupy his time undertaking ignoble pursuits. Veblen considered that even manners evolved from a useful activity into a means for the leisure class to indicate their superior position and rank in society:

> The knowledge and habit of good form come only by long-continued use. Refined tastes, manners, habits of life are a useful evidence of gentility, because good breeding requires time, application and expense, and can therefore not be compassed by those whose time and energy are taken up with work. A knowledge of good form is *prima facie* evidence that that portion of the well-bred person's life which is not spent under the observation of the spectator has been worthily spent in acquiring accomplishments that are of no lucrative effect. In the last analysis the value of manners lies in the fact that they are the voucher of a life of leisure.
>
> (Veblen 1899: 33)

While both leisure and consumption serve to indicate one's position, the role of leisure comes to take a lesser role. In a growing community, consumption becomes a more efficient means to earn status. Far more people can be made aware of one's importance through one's ownership of a mansion than from knowledge of occult languages. The latter requires personal contact, while the former requires no such interaction:

> So long as the community or social group is small enough and compact enough to be effectually reached by common notoriety alone . . . so long the one method is about as effective as the other. . . . But when the differentiation has gone farther and it becomes necessary to reach a wider human environment, consumption begins to hold over leisure as an ordinary means of decency. . . . The means of communication and the mobility of the population now expose the individual to the observation of many persons who have no other means of judging of his reputability than the display of goods.
>
> (Veblen 1899: 58)

The presumption in the discussion so far has been that the conspicuous act was an individual matter; in other words, that leisure has to be personally enjoyed, or a good personally consumed. This need not be the case, and honour can be obtained through vicarious modes of both conspicuous leisure and conspicuous consumption.

Take the former. Veblen suggested that the possession of servants amounts to a case of vicarious leisure. How is this vicarious leisure, given that the master of the household would undoubtedly consider the servants' work drudgery? It is because "these occupations are chiefly useful as a method of imputing pecuniary reputability to the master or to the household on the ground that a given amount of time and effort is conspicuously wasted" (Veblen 1899: 40).

Veblen considered that the function of such servants is mostly ceremonial. So, for example, a person of wealth might employ a butler to signal his status. The butler is essentially ceremonial and does not, in Veblen's mind, contribute to total human welfare, but rather represents lost effort in that the butler could have been diverted to activities that would service the community. That the butler is taken from such serviceable activity is possible only because the butler's 'lord' is of such wealth and means to enable it. Thus, taking the butler from serviceable activities to undertake ceremonial duties sends a signal that is similar in effect to the master's own avoidance of workmanship activities. In this way, it constitutes vicarious leisure. Veblen admitted that such a case might be better termed "wasted effort", in keeping with his definition of waste. However, he chose 'vicarious leisure', feeling that it had the "advantage of . . . neatly suggesting the substantial economic ground of . . . utility" (Veblen 1899: 40). The point is that the butler's wasted effort is for the benefit of his master's status and utility.[18]

Vicarious consumption is the cousin of vicarious leisure. The principle is the same, in that one obtains status through others. In this case, the status is obtained in the ability of others to consume conspicuously on one's behalf. Returning to our example of household servants, vicarious consumption occurs by, for example, providing servants with living arrangements or clothing that are beyond the means of the servant. Instead, the servants live in salubrious quarters and wear clothes of a quality designed to display the wealth of their master (Veblen 1899: 47). Similarly, a husband may display his wealth by providing his wife and family with the latest conveniences, with jewels and furs and other luxuries. Such vicarious consumption is ceremonial in character. A servant could wear clothes that are functional but instead wears clothes that are designed to display the wealth and power of his master. As in the case of vicarious leisure, the master earns status in a way that is similar in effect to his own conspicuous consumption of such goods; and as in that case, the servants' wearing of the ceremonial is for the benefit of the master's good name, status and utility.[19]

The idea of ceremonial and workmanship consumption raises the question of beauty. How does beauty fit into Veblen's ideas of consumption? Dividing consumption between ceremonial and workmanship types seems to deny the possibility that goods are desired simply for the sake of so-called beauty. Veblen's ideas on workmanship seem to suggest a 'practical' apprehension. In design terms, we might say that workmanship consumption is for goods that are all 'function' and little or no 'form'. On the other hand, 'ceremonial' suggests that form and aesthetic considerations overly dominate, leading to waste. Some have accused Veblen of "impoverishing aesthetic values by attributing them solely to a wasteful and parasitical leisure class" (Tilman 1996: 144). The suggestion is that Veblen equates beauty with predation and fraud; that beauty amounts to a 'sham' to conceal or provide an excuse for a ceremonial good or act designed to earn prestige. Thankfully, Veblen considered this possibility, perhaps pre-empting this charge:

> It frequently happens that an article which serves the honorific purpose of conspicuous waste is at the same time a beautiful object. . . . Many objects, as, for instance, the precious stones and the metals and some other materials used for adornment and decoration, owe their utility as items of conspicuous waste to an antecedent utility as objects of beauty. Gold, for instance, has a high degree of sensuous beauty; very many if not most of the highly prized works of art are intrinsically beautiful, though often with material qualification. . . . Except for this intrinsic beauty which they possess, these objects would scarcely have been coveted as they are, or have become monopolized objects of pride to their possessors and users. But the utility of these things to the possessor is commonly due less to their intrinsic beauty than to the honor which their possession and consumption confers, or to the obloquy which it wards off.
>
> (Veblen 1899: 85–86)

It seems that Veblen does not omit the possibility that an object or thing may be intrinsically beautiful. What he instead appears to be saying is that beauty and desire are not always simultaneously present. Gold may be intrinsically beautiful, and yet we covet it not because of its inherent beauty but because the canons of taste have rendered gold an object that conveys and earns status. On the other hand, pyrite, better known as fool's gold because of its look and lustre, has a similar intrinsic beauty to gold, and yet we do not covet it because social mores have not given it gold's prestige. A good may be inherently beautiful, but it is not beauty that determines whether it enters the ledger of the acceptable or reputable.[20]

Thus the means by which the canons of taste are communicated is through conspicuous acts of leisure and consumption, whether personal or vicarious. Changing technological circumstances, coupled with conspicuous means of conveyance, trigger constant amendment to the canons of taste and standards of reputability. In a society where the leisure class scheme of life dominates, where predatory influenced and pecuniary status emulation drive acts of consumption, we are also likely to see amendment to the level of ownership associated with a particular level of status.

Consider the implication for economic scarcity of conspicuous consumption, conspicuous leisure and status craving. Economic scarcity says that we are faced with unlimited claims on limited resources. What this statement does not make explicit is that these claims are likely to change in response to the dominant social paradigm. Now consider the duality in consumption. Workmanship consumption is that needed for survival, but ceremonial consumption is consumption we undertake to fit in, to ensure our status. Because of our need to ensure our status, and given the presence of technological advancement, perceptions of what is 'needed' for life are ever-changing:

> In any modern community, the proximate ground of expenditure in excess of what is required for physical comfort is not a conscious effort to excel in the expensiveness of their visible consumption, so much as it is a desire to live up to the conventional standard of decency in the amount and grade of goods consumed. . . . The standard is flexible; and especially it is indefinitely extensible. . . . It is much more difficult to recede from a scale of expenditure once adopted than it is to extend the accustomed scale in response to an accession of wealth. Many items of customary expenditure prove on analysis to be almost purely wasteful, and they are therefore honorific only, but after they have once been incorporated into the scale of decent consumption, and so have become an integral part of one's scheme of life, it is quite as hard to give up these as it is to give up many items that conduce directly to one's physical comfort, or even that may be necessary to life and health.
>
> (Veblen 1899: 69)

In a society characterised by a "protracted dominance of a predatory, leisure-class scheme of life", tastes are likely to evolve such that we see ever-growing claims on the Earth's limited resources (Veblen 1899: 259). This is inevitable in such a competitive society, where esteem is based on the level of wealth and ownership and the ability to flaunt this wealth. Since greater ownership provides a greater ability to flaunt, in turn equating to greater esteem, it suggests that the claims on these resources are unlikely to be satiated, with implications for economic scarcity.[21] The competitive nature of such societies means we see an ever-growing shift in the content and quantity of goods and leisure that convey status:

> So soon as the possession of property becomes the basis of popular esteem, therefore, it becomes also a requisite to the complacency which we call self-respect. In any community. . .an individual should possess as large a portion of goods as others with whom he is accustomed to class himself; and it is extremely gratifying to possess something more than others. But as fast as a person makes new acquisitions, and becomes accustomed to the resulting new standard of wealth, the new standard forthwith ceases to afford appreciably greater satisfaction than the earlier standard did. The tendency in any case is constantly to make the present pecuniary standard the point of departure for a fresh increase of wealth; and this in turn gives rise to a new standard of sufficiency and a new pecuniary classification of one's self as compared with one's neighbours.
>
> (Veblen 1899: 20–21)

The behaviour described by Veblen in this passage has found expression in works by modern economists, such as Robert Frank who has referred to this as an 'expenditure arms race' (Frank 2007: 3). In Veblenian terms, to maintain membership of the leisure class it is imperative that one keeps up. Again, given conspicuous consumption, the effect is to amend the canons of taste and respectability for all classes from the leisure class down, so that even the most "abjectly poor" would rather endure "squalor and discomfort. . .before the last trinket or the last pretense of pecuniary decency is put away" (Veblen 1899: 57). However, the presence of workmanship may serve to alter the dominant predatory paradigm. Through the inbuilt disdain for waste that Veblen claimed was innate in the species, the manifestation of workmanship may cause a reappraisal, so that in time, it is entirely possible that the current 'unquenchable' predatory scheme of consumption and invidious comparison is tempered by workmanship characters that lead to a lower claim on the Earth's resources.

7.3 Business enterprise and production

In the opening to this chapter it was stated that the analysis would be built by focusing on production and consumption. While this serves an analytical purpose, in some senses this is a false dichotomy. The dichotomy makes sense in classical terms, where consumption is considered a final term, the final destination of production. But reality can be much less rigid than this, making it much harder to determine what constitutes production and consumption. Particularly in Veblenian terms, where consumption is either ceremonial or shaped by workmanship, the distinction between what is consumption and what is production can be nebulous.[22]

This ambiguity serves as a nice segue into the next section, which will outline Veblen's pronouncements regarding production and business enterprise in a capitalist economy. This section is based on a number of sources, including various articles, but mostly it is drawn from Veblen's second major work, *The Theory of Business Enterprise* (1904), with input also from *Absentee Ownership and Business Enterprise* (1923), his final work, published six years before his death. As will be seen, Veblen's ideas are based on an industry-business dichotomy that follows the workmanship and predation duality.

7.3.1 A technological explanation for the origins of capital

Veblen's socially based theories of production stand in contrast to the neoclassical perspective dominant at the time. Neoclassical economics presented production in terms not dissimilar to those of consumption. Like the idea of a discrete consumer, production was conceived in terms of a discrete firm that, given a state of technology, acts to produce an output that maximises its profits. Such a firm is often conceived to use three factors in production, the first being land, the second labour and the third capital. Factor payments to each are based on its marginal product.

To say that factor payments are based on the marginal product of the factor seems a harmless idea. And yet built within this it is a hypothesis that says that capital as a factor is productive (Clark 1899: v), that it contributes to production and so can legitimately be rewarded with a payment. Just as wages go to the owners of the labour used in production, namely the workers, so too the payment arising from the contribution to output made by capital goes to the owners of capital, the capitalists. The marginalist view thus gives a justification for payments to the owners of capital. While a detailed analysis of Marxist views is beyond the scope of this book, it is worth pointing out that the neoclassical marginalist view of capital stands in diametrical contrast to Marxist views that considered payments to the owners of capital as an improper appropriation of 'fruits' that should go to labour. This Marxist view is predicated on the labour theory of value, which sees any capital that is used in production as simply the embodiment of past labour.

Veblen shared the Marxist objection to the neoclassical view, but his objection was based not on the labour theory of value but on the role of technology and the taxonomic nature of neoclassical analyses of production.[23] Veblen considered technology, or the state of the industrial arts, to be the stock of human knowledge. In his own words:

> The state of the industrial arts is a fact of group life, not of individual or private initiative or innovation. It is an affair of the collectivity, not a creative achievement of individuals. . . . In the main, the state of the industrial arts is always a heritage out of the past; it is always in process of change, perhaps, but the substantial body of it is knowledge that has come down from earlier generations.
>
> (Veblen 1914: 103)

Technology, or what Carl Sagan once referred to as "communal memory", is imperative to any consideration of production because it is the source of productivity. When we say that a factor is productive, what we mean is that some part of the community's experience and knowledge has been applied to render it useful. Consider a traditional factor of production such as land. Land is productive because humanity's accumulated stock of knowledge enables it to be used for things such as the growing of crops or as a site for the erection of a building. Without technology we would not be able to put land to these (or any other) uses. Land is not alone in being made productive through the application of knowledge, and the argument used in this example easily applies to all factors used in production, including labour:

> The workman . . . is a "productive agent" in the manner and degree determined by the state of the industrial arts. . . . He or she – or rather they – . . . are productive factors or industrial agents . . . only because and so far as the state of the industrial arts enables them to do so. . . . Apart from the common stock of knowledge and training, the individual members of the community have no industrial effect.
>
> (Veblen 1914: 144)

Thus it is technology that enables a man or woman to be productive. Just how productive he or she is depends on the state of technology. A farmer in the twenty-first century is far more productive than one from the tenth century. Why? Because he has access to knowledge and technology that makes his productivity supremely higher than that of his ancestors. Importantly, this passage also confirms Veblen's 'social' views on production. Neoclassical theories that present production as an output of discrete firms acting and making decisions in isolation may be convenient, but they ignore the significance of the social character of production.

Just like labour and land, capital is only productive because technological know-how enables it to be made and applied to some productive purpose. Without this knowledge, capital is just nuts and bolts (or wood and nails, whatever the case may be). That technology is the source of productivity is visible when we recognise that a capital good that is today considered 'productive' will tomorrow go " 'to the junk heap' " because some advance in technology renders it obsolete (Veblen 1908c: 165). What might not be recognised by such an example is that the obsolescence of the capital good is also an obsolescence of its underlying technology, so that the technology itself "ceases to be an immaterial asset" (Veblen 1908a: 540). Neoclassical explanations for payments to capital (and indeed all factors) bypass the pivotal role of technology. By 'exogenising' technology[24] and turning it into a given, neoclassical economists reduced its role to terms not dissimilar to the treatment of the origin of wants in consumer analysis. On the contrary, said Veblen, technology is not some pesky given but is pivotal to understanding the origins and existence of productivity and of payments to the owners of capital.[25]

For much of human development, the stock of knowledge used in production was such that it was readily accessible to all. In other words, there were no circumstances to provoke or enable the institution of ownership to extend its reach into the technology used in production. While individual workers may have owned the tools used in the production of goods, they did not own and could not prohibit others from utilising the technology that underlies and informs the construction and use of said tools:

> In . . . all but the late phases of culture and technology, this immaterial equipment at large is accessible to all members of the community as a matter of course through the unavoidable discipline that comes with the workday routine of getting along. . . . All have free access to this common stock of immaterial equipment.
>
> (Veblen 1914: 106)

As human development moved from the barbarian period into the handicraft era, the stock of knowledge accumulated so as to encourage greater specialisation. Despite this growth, even in this relatively recent period of human development, technology was "still a sufficiently simple and obvious matter" and was still readily "acquired in the routine of work" (Veblen 1914: 235).

Things change, however, when we move into the machine era. The machine era is characterised by the "factory system" and "large-scale industry" (Veblen 1914: 299). The tools of production grow markedly in magnitude, and so it becomes "impracticable for the individual craftsman [to] readily . . . acquire the material means for work" (Veblen 1914: 299). Those who do have the means are placed in an advantageous position. They can now ask for some payment for the use of the 'material means'. But since these tools are only productive because they use the community's stock of knowledge, they are in effect charging the community for the use of its technology; they can claim or 'coerce' some reward or payment for its use.[26]

The ability to ask for such a payment provokes the development of property rights over capital goods and their underlying technology. These property rights provide an incentive for the accumulation of ever more capital. Put another way, the level and scale of technology had grown so that it was finally feasible for the institution of ownership to extend its auspices over the technology used in production. It became a practical and desirable matter to 'partition' the community's stock of knowledge (or at least those parts in evidence in the capital goods) and claim exclusive ownership over it. Since the institution of ownership is an outcome of the predatory predilection of the species, payment to capital can be conceived as the extension of predation to technology itself. However, the process by which the predatory makes its presence felt has changed. While ownership was traditionally obtained through 'vulgar' predatory means such as armed combat or hereditary title, it is now also feasible to claim ownership through predatory pecuniary activities. Whichever means one uses to claim ownership of technology, the salient point is that the community's workmanship outlets have been 'corrupted' by predation:

> The usufruct of the handicraft community's technological proficiency . . . came to vest in the owners of the plant. . . . Under these circumstances, and

> in proportion as these technological exigencies take effect in one branch of industry and another, the usufruct of the industrial community's current productive efficiency comes to vest effectually in those who own the material means of industry. Their effectual exploitation of the community's industrial efficiency will extend to such industries, and with such a degree of thoroughness and security, as the state of the industrial arts may decide.
>
> (Veblen 1914: 151)

Thus, in contrast to the neoclassical theories that explain payments to capital as resulting from 'inherent' productivity, Veblen traced this payment to the advancement in the state of technology that enables a predatory few to take for their own gain and use that which was developed by the community (Veblen 1908: 527). The appearance of this 'Proudhon-*esque*' payment to capital has antecedents, in particular payments to another factor used in production:

> All land values and land productivity . . . are a function of the "state of the industrial arts." It is only within the given technological situation, the current scheme of ways and means, that any parcel of land has such productive powers as it has. It is, in other words, useful only because . . . men have learned to make use of it. This is what brings it into the category of "land", economically speaking. And the preferential position of the landlord as a claimant of the "net profit" consists in his legal right to decide where, how far, and on what terms men shall put this technological scheme into effect.
>
> (Veblen 1908a: 530)

The ability to partition and claim ownership over land has historically been a feasible matter and has enabled its owners to claim payment for its use. But as Veblen suggests, land's productivity and uses are dependent on the state of technology. Without technology, land has no use and no productivity. The rent payable to a landlord is predicated on a system of property rights, not to any contribution he makes to production. Since the landlord makes no contribution, his payment is considered an unearned increment.[27]

For much of human development, the ability to claim property rights over technology was not feasible. However, the increased growth and specialisation of knowledge and the resulting large-scale methods of production eventually made this possible. As in the case of land, men could now claim property rights for the use of technology, as evidenced in their ownership of capital goods. Hence, as in the case of land, payments made to the owners of capital are not based on the so-called productivity of capital goods but rather on the ability of capital owners to claim a payment deriving from their 'usufruct' and 'cornering' of the community's stock of knowledge.[28] Like rent payable to landlords, payments made to the owners of capital are unearned, so that the "argument concerning the unearned increment [in the case of land] may be carried over, with scarcely a change of phrase, to the case of 'capital goods'" (Veblen 1908a: 530).

7.3.2 On the nature of payments to capital

As has been shown, Veblen objected to the neoclassical account for the origin of capital ownership and of its explanations of payments to capital. By his account, the origin of capital ownership can be traced to technological advancement. His objections related not only to the origins of capital ownership and payment for its use but also on the nature of the payment.

As was stated earlier, the neoclassical view of the payment is that it is due to the marginal product of capital. John Bates Clark claimed that payments of income to capital and labour can be traced to their contribution to production:

> the distribution of the income of society is controlled by a natural law, and that this law, if it worked without friction, would give to every agent of production the amount of wealth which that agent creates. However wages may be adjusted by bargains freely made between individual men, the rates of pay that result from such transactions tend, it is here claimed, to equal that part of the product of industry which is traceable to the labor itself; and however interest may be adjusted by similarly free bargaining, it naturally tends to equal the fractional product that is separately traceable to capital.
>
> (Clark 1899: v)

Thus the payment to capital is based on its marginal product. Veblen considered the neoclassical view 'born' of a time when the "undertaker was the owner of the industrial equipment"; his role was to coordinate "industrial processes with a view to economies of production and heightened serviceability" (Veblen 1904: 23, 41). In such a world, the firm's capitalised value could be traced back to its stock of capital goods, and the expected income deriving to the firm was by virtue of the ownership of these goods. However, with the advent of the corporate structure, we see a change in the nature of capital:

> Capital has been spoken of as the capitalized (aggregated) cost of industrial equipment . . . but since corporation finance has come to pervade the management of business this view is no longer of particular use for a theoretical handling of the facts . . . the basis of capitalization was the cost of the material equipment owned by any given concern; and so far as the methods of partnership and private firms still prevails such may still be the current method of capitalization. . . . But in so far as business procedure and business conceptions have been shaped in the image of the modern corporation . . . the basis of capitalization has gradually shifted, until the basis is now no longer given by the cost of material equipment owned, but by the earning-capacity of the corporation as a going concern.
>
> (Veblen 1904: 137)

Modern corporate firms are capitalised on the basis of their earning capacity. In the neoclassical conception, earning capacity is traced back to the firm's stock of capital goods, and the payment received by virtue of their ownership of such productive machinery. In firms that still operate in the older 'entrepreneurial' way, this view may still have currency. But for those that have evolved into corporations, this conception no longer holds value. Veblen considered that corporate earning capacity was based on two sources. The first equated with the stock of capital goods, which Veblen referred to as the corporation's "tangible" assets (Veblen 1904: 138; 1908b: 105). The second source of earnings was the firm's stock of "intangible" assets, what he also referred to as "good will" (Veblen 1904: 138; 1908b: 105):

> The effective (business) capitalization . . . is . . . an ever recurring valuation of the company's properties, tangible and intangible, on the basis of their earning-capacity. Good will includes such things as "established customary business relations, reputation for upright dealing, franchises and privileges, trade-marks, brands, patent rights, copyrights, exclusive use of special processes guarded by law or by secrecy, exclusive control of particular sources of materials.
>
> (Veblen 1904: 138–139)

The corporate firm's capitalised value is the sum of these two assets and, importantly, of the earning capacity derived from their ownership. The earning capacity comprises the prospective stream of earnings of both tangible and intangible assets "rated on the basis of their income-yielding capacity to their owner" (Veblen 1908b: 115). Capital ownership is desired for its expected earnings, which Veblen claimed consists of two separate streams. One is related to capital goods and machinery and the other to the value of intangible assets.

> [Tangible assets] capitalize such fraction of the technological proficiency of the community as the ownership of the capital goods involved enables the owner to engross. [Intangible assets] capitalize such habits of life, of a non-technological character . . . as will effect a differential advantage to the concern to which the assets in question appertain. The former owe their existence and magnitude to the usufruct of technological expedients involved in the industrial process proper; while the latter . . . are of a pecuniary rather than a technological character.
>
> (Veblen 1908b: 116–117)

Capital thus has two income streams: one from the tangible assets, the other from the intangible. Income arising from tangible assets is, "on the aggregate",[29] assumed to be used for "materially productive work", and so can be related to the community's technology (Veblen 1908b: 115–116). True, the ownership of such goods is representative of the extension of the predatory bent of the species, since ownership is a predatory institution; but capital goods and the underlying technology that makes them possible derive from group-regarding behaviour. On the other hand, income from 'intangible' assets has no technological basis[30] and serves "no materially productive" function, and so arrives by virtue of man's ceremonial predilections (Veblen 1908b: 115).

The existence of the two income streams has implications for the behaviour, strategies and actions of firms. The neoclassical view ascribes all income deriving to the owners of capital to the productivity of capital goods, so that firms increase capitalisation by increasing their stock of capital goods. But the existence of intangibles means that there are other income streams available to them. These alternate means of income provide incentives for corporations to increase the value of their capitalisation by such acts as guarding trademarks or by improving brand recognition through advertising campaigns. It also means that they have an incentive to increase capitalisation by increasing their ownership of intangible assets. The capitalist's "constant endeavor [is] to create or gain for himself some peculiar degree of advantage in the market, in the way of monopoly, good-will, legalized privilege, and the like . . .in the way of intangible assets" (Veblen 1908b: 133).

Hence, a neoclassical explanation for a takeover would be limited to considering the stock of capital goods arising from this takeover and the resultant ability to raise production. But it might be the case that such a firm purchases another not for its tangible stock of capital goods but for an intangible asset such as reputation. In such a case, the firm might base its decision on a belief that improved reputation increases its ability to claim some reward or income from an enhanced reputation. Veblen would say that it is clear in such a case that the income deriving from the ownership of capital is not due to the ownership of tangible capital goods but from some other 'nonproductive' intangible source.[31]

7.3.3 Modern machine industry

Modern industry is that of the machine. The machines used in modern industry are also known as capital, and as was shown earlier in the chapter, Veblen considered capital ownership to be an extension of the institution of ownership into the realm of technology. While Veblen was not averse to referring to this period by the more common "capitalistic system" (Veblen 1904: 1), his use of the term "machine age" or "machine process" suggests that he wished to highlight something other than the ownership feature conjured by the term 'capitalism'.

While it is true to say that modern industry is that of the machine, Veblen considered that the "machine *process* [my italics]" meant "something more comprehensive . . . than a mere aggregate of mechanical appliances" (Veblen 1904: 5). It is not enough to identify the machine age by the tools or instruments that are used in production, nor by the nature of their ownership (although as will be seen, this has some impact on how effectively they are used). Instead, the machine age is identified by the nature of the methods that guide production. Just as the barbarian period was identified not by its instruments of production but by the exploitative and predatory ethos that drove it, so too the machine age was marked by its underlying spirit:

> The scope of the process is larger than the machine. . . . Wherever manual dexterity, the rule of thumb, and the fortuitous conjunctures of the seasons have been supplanted by a reasoned procedure on the basis of a systematic knowledge of the forces employed, there the mechanical industry is to be found, even in the absence of intricate mechanical contrivances. It is a question of the character of the process rather than a question of the complexity of the contrivances employed.
>
> (Veblen 1904: 5–6)

The spirit that guides the machine age is 'efficient cause'. Efficient cause and "reasoned principles" lead to production methods that are increasingly based on the "knowledge . . . [of] the material sciences" (Veblen 1904: 6–7). The machine age is the first period where production is directly and constantly informed by science. Even the relatively technologically advanced period of handicraft production did not stand in "close or consistent relation with the avowed science of the time" (Veblen 1904: 303). Using Veblen's dichotomy, the workmanship inclinations of the species led to scientific discoveries and technology that in turn led to the machine process industrial system (Veblen 1914: 302). Being coloured by workmanship, the machine process 'abhors' the entry or existence of futile actions in production. But unlike even the handicraft era, this time production comes under the *constant* surveillance of a workmanship-influenced *scientific* mind-set that excises production steps that are identified as 'ceremonial' and are thus unnecessary:

> The machine technology takes no cognizance of conventionally established rules of precedence; it knows neither manners nor breeding and makes no use of any of the attribute of worth. Its scheme of knowledge and of inference is based on the laws of material causation, not on those of immemorial custom, authenticity, or authoritative enactment. Its metaphysical basis is the law of cause and effect.
>
> (Veblen 1914: 311)

Just as the leisure class come to affect the canons of taste in a trickle-down motion to the lower classes, so too the machine process methodologies come to resonate throughout all processes of production. The resonance is so prevalent that even industries that do not have the convenience of modern tools or technologies adopt its *modus*. While these industries might have limited scope to change the tools or methods used in production, we find a marked change in the apprehension of the process so that "a determinate, reasoned routine replaces the rule of thumb" (Veblen 1904: 6–7). Even Veblen's famed Aleutian islanders[32] might have seen fit to discard the use of magical incantations for the capture of shellfish had they been exposed to the principles of efficient cause and the exigencies of the machine process.[33]

The machine age saw an increase in specialisation of function. Adam Smith famously used the example of a pin maker to show how specialisation through the division of labour leads to increases in production (Smith 1776: 11). Smith's example demonstrated the benefits of specialisation by showing how a handicraft era (to use Veblen's term) pin maker could increase production from one pin per day to about 12 pounds through specialisation and the division of labour. The growth in output deriving from this change is striking when we realise that each pound comprised "four thousand pins" (Smith 1776: 11).

Smith's pin-making firm was a "small manufactory . . . where ten men only were employed", with specialisation dividing production processes among the workers in the firm's employ (Smith 1776: 11). But suppose that the division of labour occurred not among the ten workers within Smith's 'manufactory' but between many different 'manufactories', each specialising in different aspects of the pin production process. One firm produces pinheads; another draws the wire; and so forth. They are then given to another firm that combines them to make pins. This simple example encapsulates Veblen's characterisation of the modern machine age industrial system as a "concatenation of industries" (Veblen 1904: 15).[34] The smaller production concerns that grew out of the handicraft era gave way by the time of the machine age to a large-scale industrial system of interlocking firms where "each follows some and precedes other[s] . . . in an endless sequence" (Veblen 1904: 7) of production:

> [The] Industrial process shows two well-marked general characteristics: (a) the running maintenance of interstitial adjustments between the several sub-processes or branches of industry, wherever in their working they touch one another in the sequence of industrial elaboration; and (b) an unremitting requirement of quantitative precision, accuracy in point of time and sequence. . . . Standard physical measurements are of the essence of the machine's regime.
>
> (Veblen 1904: 8)

The interlocking nature of modern production means that "each draws upon and presupposes the proper working of many other processes" (Veblen 1904: 7) and firms increasingly rely on other firms for inputs to their own production. Crucially, firms must be confident that inputs obtained from other firms can be seamlessly incorporated into their own production processes. The way reliability and confidence is achieved is by virtue of standardisation. Standardisation and "uniformity" of gauge, weight, length, and other "legally adopted weights and measures" is the feature that enables the development of increased specialisation and interlocking production (Veblen 1904: 8). Pin production that takes place over many individual firms can only be successful if firms are confident that the pinheads produced by one firm can be made to fit the wires produced by another.

Labour itself yields to standardisation, and the manner in which labour is bought and sold changes to suit the vagaries of industrial mechanisation and the standardisation of industry (Veblen 1904: 11). The production of services such as communication, rail transport and roads also takes its cue from the standards set by the machine (Veblen 1904: 13). Since "modern life goes by clockwork", we find, for example, that the rail companies standardise their output by providing their services according to clock time and scheduled timetables (Veblen 1914: 311).

The standardisation of services affects the manner in which consumers interact with service providers. Increasingly, homes relinquish habits based on solar time and instead base their movements and patterns of consumption on the timepiece (Veblen 1914: 311). In the case of a service such as rail transportation, it requires that consumers bend their patterns of behaviour to meet the provision of rail services based on standardised scheduled timetables.[35] This requirement to bend and adjust patterns of consumption is felt across the entire range of goods and services that comprise machine process output:

> Modern consumers in great part supply their wants with commodities that conform to certain staple specifications of size, weight, and grade. The consumer . . . furnishes his house, his table, and his person with supplies of standard weight and measure, and he can to an appreciable degree specify his needs and his consumption in the notation of the standard gauge. . . . [T] he idiosyncrasies of the individual consumers are required to conform to the uniform gradations imposed upon consumable goods by the comprehensive mechanical processes of industry.
>
> (Veblen 1904: 11)

Standardisation of industry cascades along the production process, so that final consumer goods also become standardised. The very products we can choose from as consumers are determined by the standardised methods of machine production. In the handicraft era, it might have been possible to satisfy individual wants. But the unavoidable standardisation of the machine process means that our wants must now adapt and meet standardised output. "Local color" and "craftsmanlike skill" capitulate to "mechanical standardisation" (Veblen 1904: 9, 11). Hence, the methods of production have a bearing on the development on the canons of taste (Veblen 1904: 12). Consumer wants, our needs and our desires, must conform to the standards of industry output. We may wish to have pins, but we must choose among the standard sizes and types of pins that industry is willing and able to provide. The increasingly pervasive nature of the machine process and its forces of standardisation come to direct our very apprehension and interaction with the wider world:

> The frequency, duration, intensity, grade, and sequence are not, in the main, matters for the free discretion of the individuals who participate. . . .There comes to prevail a degree of standardization and precise mechanical adjustment of the details of everyday life.
>
> (Veblen 1904: 14)

The idea that consumer wants bend to industry standards reinforces Veblen's idea that taste is socially determined, shaped by society's institutions, which are in turn shaped by technology. Technology has led to the machine age, and the methods underlying this period have ensured that production outputs become standardised.

However, in the so-called post-Fordist[36] era, production outputs are supposedly less dictated by notions of 'mass markets' and 'mass consumption' and are instead more flexible and able to serve more differentiated tastes and needs. However, even in this supposedly more flexible production environment, Veblen's contention regarding the role of social factors in deciding tastes holds. We may have more to choose from, and mass markets may have given way to 'niche' markets, but our consumption choices are still largely determined by social factors, including those in production.

7.3.4 The predatory control of modern industry

In the classical and neoclassical world, individual economic agents acting from self-interest are said to lead to harmonious and optimal allocations of resources. In such a view, the way and the uses to which the owners of the industrial system set it to work concur with the optimal welfare of the community. Adam Smith famously encapsulated this notion when he said that the "butcher, . . . brewer, or . . . baker" do not provide "our dinner" out of some sense of "benevolence" but from "regard to their own interest" (Smith 1776: 19). The provision of these necessities of life stems not from "their humanity, but . . . their self-love" (Smith 1776: 19). In some cases optimality is not achieved, but when this occurs, it is reckoned to be the result of some disturbance that has not allowed the optimal order to obtain. Once this disturbance is eliminated, the proper order can be re-established. In other words, the inability to obtain the optimal is a special case, while the unfettered optimal order is the natural case.

Veblen agreed that the businessmen who own the industrial system act from their own self-regard, but (as will be shown later) he disagreed that the outcome was inherently benevolent. The presence of predatory drivers, a fundamental trait in the human species, necessitated a rejection of the unavoidably benevolent classical and neoclassical characterisation.[37] Self-interest stems from these predatory drivers, so that contrary to orthodox assertions, the businessman's self-interested actions levy a cost on the community that reduces its welfare. What is more, this is not some special or aberrant case but is fundamental to the nature of the capitalist industrial system.

There was a time (particularly in the late handicraft and very early stages of the machine age) when production mostly took place in small firms. The businessman who owned such a firm was also responsible for directing it. His livelihood and fortune depended on his ability to ensure the efficient regulation of the productive processes under his control. He was familiar with the production processes in use, and he had an incentive to produce output in the most efficient manner possible. Veblen considered that the firms that form the core of the neoclassical and classical model of production are of just such a small-scale type (Veblen 1904: 23, 41).

But by Veblen's time, these smaller industrial concerns had evolved into a large-scale industrial system controlled by similarly large firms. It was the advent of the corporate system, and the capitalist at the helm of this modern industrial system has evolved into an absentee owner (Veblen 1923: 37). Unlike the director of the smaller handicraft firms, absentee owners are not dependent on a single firm's efficient production for their livelihood, nor is achieving technically efficient production their goal. Instead, their goal is to predatorily manipulate the industrial system for pecuniary gain, since their wealth, and hence their esteem, is based on their ability to successfully undertake financial deals. So we find that the machine process that grew out of the handicraft era, and which has as its driving ethos efficient cause and the tenets of science and industrial efficiency, comes to be owned, managed and dominated by the predatorily natured, who are driven by a different philosophy. Theirs is a philosophy shaped not by workmanship and efficient cause but by predation and pecuniary gain:

> The motive of business is pecuniary gain, the method is essentially purchase and sale. The aim and usual outcome is an accumulation of wealth. Men whose aim is not increase of possessions do not go into business, particularly not on an independent footing.
>
> (Veblen 1904: 20)

Ironically, the very same technological advance that brought the machine process also enabled ownership and control of production to fall into the hands of corporate businessmen. Under their control, industrial efficiency capitulates to pecuniary advantage. Since the system is under the businessman's control, his pecuniary priorities and desires override any other consideration. While it may have been desirable to organise and operate the industrial system in accord with a workmanship scheme where serviceability of output and community welfare is paramount, we instead find an industrial system that operates according to the tenets of a predatory pecuniary scheme. In this scheme, efficiency means not technical industrial efficiency but "pecuniary efficiency" (Veblen 1914: 354):

> The vital point of production . . . is the vendibility of the output, its convertibility into money values, not its serviceability for the needs of mankind. A modicum of serviceability, for some purpose or other, the output must have if it is to be salable. But it does not follow that the highest serviceability gives the largest gains to the business man in terms of money, nor does it follow that the output need in all cases have other than a factitious serviceability. There is, on the one hand, such a possibility as overstocking the market with any given line of goods, to the detriment of the business man concerned, but not necessarily to the immediate disadvantage of the body of consumers.
>
> (Veblen 1904: 51)

In making production decisions, the businessman's point of departure is financial gain, and so he deploys his productive resources so as to obtain profit. If his drive for financial gain necessitates a "conscientious withdrawal of efficiency", then so be it (Veblen 1921: 43). This makes sense in a paradigm where efficiency means not "technological mastery . . . but proficiency in pecuniary management and acquisition of wealth" (1914: 349).[38] To be sure, it is a feature of capitalist economies that reduced or zero profits will generally cause businessmen to partially or completely withdraw plant and machinery from use. Such a withdrawal may cause a reduction in the community's welfare, but since pecuniary advantage dominates the businessman's mind and since control and ownership of the industrial system falls into his hands, his desires trump all other considerations (Veblen 1914: 351). And so we find the 'shutdown' and 'start-up' rules for production determined not by community needs and industrial or technical efficiency but by pecuniary 'decree'.

In his quest for financial gain, Veblen's businessman adopts whatever strategies or means that enable him to achieve his goal. Sometimes this will cause him to view other businessman as "rivals" with whom he is in a "struggle" for pecuniary advantage; it becomes a case of "inflict or endure . . . pecuniary damage" (Veblen 1904: 32). On other occasions, pecuniary advantage might best be served not by "cutthroat competition" but by working with other businessmen to coordinate activities by "collective selling ('collective bargaining')" (Veblen 1904: 258). The tendency for businessmen to work 'collaboratively' was certainly a feature of industrial organisation during Veblen's time (and still sometimes today), as evidenced by the trust-busting activities that were put in force to combat it. But whatever methods are chosen, the businessman's "midsection of effort", whether in the form of aggressive rivalry or cartel behaviour, comes at the community's expense (Veblen 1904: 65). In both cases production is cast in business terms for financial gain, not industrial proficiency.

With the fuller development of the industrial system, the businessman's scope for profit is expanded. Newer means for accumulating wealth are made possible because of the nature of the modern industrial system. This system comprises a series of firms that operate at various points in a continuous sequence of production. In this system we might find a mythical Firm C combining pinheads produced by Firm A and wire produced by Firm B to make pins. The means by which Firm C obtains its inputs from Firms A and B is via transactions. The nature of these transactions is that of the business transaction or "deal".[39] Being business transactions, they are controlled and determined by businessmen.

In earlier times, the businessman whose livelihood depended on the firm would have been motivated to ensure smooth production. But in a system characterised by absentee ownership and corporations, we see a separation of the businessman's pecuniary advantage and the health of a firm and the wider industrial system. Concatenated industry and the multitude of transactions that take place between its firms now provide the businessman with the means for "differential advantage" and financial gain from a "disturbance" to the various industrial "sub-processes" (Veblen 1904: 25). The businessman's focus shifts from technically efficient operation of industrial plant to "gain or loss through business relations simply"; in other words, through efforts to 'play' and speculate on business transactions (Veblen 1904: 24). His incentive for this type of activity is also heightened by his ability to increase capitalisation and earnings through manipulation of "intangible" assets.[40] To do this, he is supported by various financial structures, and so we see the appearance of securities markets, underwriters and other such financial instruments (Sweezy 1958: 183). The community's interest is heightened by an industrial system that runs as smoothly and as technically efficiently as possible, but to the businessman, whether a "disturbance" makes for "heightened facility" or "widespread hardship" matters not (Veblen 1904: 28). His aim is profit, and he cares not whether his "traffic affects the system advantageously or disastrously" (Veblen 1904: 29):[41]

> The economic welfare of the community at large is best served by a facile and uninterrupted interplay of the various processes which make up the industrial system at large; but the pecuniary interests of the business men in whose hands lies the discretion in the matter are not necessarily best served by an unbroken maintenance of the industrial balance. . . . The outcome of this management of industrial affairs through pecuniary transactions, therefore, has been to dissociate the interests of those men who exercise the discretion from the interests of the community.
>
> (Veblen 1904: 27, 29)

At their core, the modern businessman's pecuniary motives represent a desire to accumulate wealth, which in turn can be brought back to invidious comparison and a desire to maintain status. Absentee ownership "rests not on a natural right of workmanship" that was prevalent during the handicraft era but from a "feudalistic ground of privilege and vested interest" (Veblen 1923: 50–51). This lineage caused Veblen to compare the modern absentee owners of capitalism to the "absentee princes" of old (Veblen 1923: 35). Veblen's businessman is thus of ancient origin, and those at the helm of the modern industrial system are simply the spiritual heirs of the predatory surplus raiders who arose at the closure of the savage era and who ushered in the barbarian period. The modern captain of industry is the modern incarnation of this predatory spirit.[42] As with his forerunners, his motivation is the accumulation of wealth, but, in his case, wealth is accumulated through the practice of modern business. Since the industrial system is under the control of predatory capitalists, we find that prosperity itself comes to be recast to align with his scheme:

> This visible difference between the old order and the new is closely dependent on the difference between the purposes that guide the[m]. . . . Under the old order, industry . . . was a quest of livelihood; under the new order industry is directed by the quest of profits. Formerly, therefore, times were good or bad according as the industrial processes yielded a sufficient or an insufficient output of the means of life. Latterly times are good or bad according as the process of business yields an adequate or inadequate rate of profits. Prosperity now means, primarily, business prosperity; whereas it used to mean industrial efficiency. . . . The material necessities of a group of workmen or consumers . . . [are] therefore, not competent to set aside, or indeed to qualify, the natural freedom of the owners of these processes to let work go on or not, as the outlook for profits may decide. Profits is [*sic*] a business proposition, livelihood is not.
>
> (Veblen 1904: 178, 276)

In the modern industrial system, the community loses in two ways. First, it loses control of its 'communal memory', which now falls to the predatory business class. Similarly, the level and the type of production that this technology is used for is not directed to maximising the community's needs and welfare, but rather to the pecuniary considerations of the businessman. The needs of the community are secondary; they are subordinated to those of the businessman. But more so, it occurs that the community accepts the pecuniary standard as the correct 'common sense' standard. So with control of the industrial system in the hands of large corporations, everyone – community and smaller noncorporate producers – is "subject[ed] to the discretion of the larger" (Veblen 1914: 352). The large-scale corporate businessman's influence is:

> decisive even for . . . outlying portions of the field, for he is the only large self-directing economic factor . . . as near as it may be said of any human power in modern times, the large business man controls the exigencies of life under which the community lives. Hence, upon him and his fortunes centres the abiding interest of civilized mankind.
>
> (Veblen 1904: 2–3)

Veblen's analysis certainly accords with his view that in a hierarchical society, the direction of power is from above to those below. In this analysis, it makes sense to think that the business practices and mores of those in control of large-scale industry become universally accepted and adopted. The situation is akin to the canons of taste and the trickling-down from the leisure class to lower grades. The rub, however, is that such a large-scale technically complex industrial system should come under the control of businessmen who do not have the technical expertise to operate it. Given the businessmen's lack of technical expertise, the industrial system is instead run according to precepts that they do understand and are comfortable with, those of predatory business. In an industrial system owned and run by those who do not have the appropriate technical expertise, it is unsurprising that Veblen sees it failing the test of industrial or technical efficiency.

7.4 Engineers to the rescue?

In Chapter 6, I discussed Veblen's four epochs of human development and showed that Veblen considered human development to take place through the interplay between the two dominant themes of predation and workmanship. At various points, one becomes more assertive than the other. The catalyst for this to-and-fro is technology.

In Veblen's conception, even periods dominated by predatory characters have some measure of workmanship, and so even the capitalistic machine age, dominated and owned by predatory capitalists, has an 'echo' of workmanship about it. The presence of this echo means that even capitalists who are motivated by predatory gain and pecuniary advantage have their behaviour tempered by workmanship. As a result, the productive output of the industrial system has some measure of community serviceability about it (Veblen 1904: 51). The result, as Veblen recognised, is that the lot of much of humanity had improved considerably:

> the system of industrial competition . . . has brought about, or has at least co-existed with, the most rapid advance in average wealth and industrial efficiency that the world has seen. Especially can it fairly be claimed that the result of the last few decades of our industrial development has been to increase greatly the creature comforts within the reach of the average human being.
>
> (Veblen 1891: 60)

In Veblen's conception, the prime heirs of the workmanship traditions in the modern machine industry are society's workmen and its engineers. Their roles and function have the overt character of workmanship. In the modern machine era, it becomes their role to manage the productive processes of society. The pecuniary businessmen, recognising their own inability, give the role of industrial management to the "efficiency engineers" (Veblen 1914: 345).

The nature of engineers' roles exposes them to the matter-of-fact nature of the machine process, much more so than their pecuniary overlords. This exposure, coupled with the greater freedom that can be devoted to idle curiosity and scientific pursuits (ironically made possible by the productive bounty of the machine age, which has led to the already mentioned improvement in their lot), mean that their "uncritical habitual faith" in society's "institutional scheme" begins to "crumble" (Veblen 1914: 343). A growing exposure and adherence to the machine process ethos of efficient cause makes them uneasy at the existing inefficient business methods by which society's productive forces and technology are put to use. This unease makes them question the current regime and grow restless at the obvious waste. Is this restlessness enough to see the current pecuniary regime replaced by an 'industrial' regime? Veblen answered no, at least for the time being:

> By settled habit the technicians, the engineers and industrial experts, are a harmless and docile sort, well fed on the whole, and somewhat placidly content with the "full dinner-pail" which the lieutenants of the Vested Interests habitually allow them. It is true, they constitute the indispensable General Staff of that industrial system which feeds the Vested Interests; but hitherto at least, they have had nothing to say in the planning and direction of this industrial system, except as employees in the pay of the financiers. They have, hitherto, been quite unreflectingly content to work piecemeal, without much of an understanding among themselves, unreservedly doing job-work for the Vested Interests; and they have without much reflection lent themselves and their technical powers freely to the obstructive tactics of the captains of industry.
>
> (Veblen 1921: 128)

The nature of institutional development and the lag that occurs causes the engineers to see the current scheme as common sense. In this, they are no different from many other sectors of society, and so this helps to explain their 'docility'. However, constant exposure to the machine process further inculcates an appreciation for the scientific method that causes engineers and technocrats to increasingly question the "imbecile" institutions by which society is ordered. How then to explain their acquiescence? It is because the force that the machine process casts upon these men is countered by the force of pecuniary institutions that are also working upon them. Social development has always been a process whereby the forces of workmanship and those of predation are constant fellow travellers. The presence of predation means that, in the short term at least, the technocrats' understanding of efficiency is also imbued with the capitalists' pecuniary paradigm.

In time, as the methods of production increasingly follow the methods of the machine, and as its underlying scientific ethos comes to dominate thinking and make its presence felt in more and more of societal function, activities and processes that are based on ceremony and predation become increasingly questioned. The power of workmanship will increasingly reassert its authority and cast aside predation. But is it enough to cause a rearrangement of the operation and control of the industrial system? Is it possible that the industrial system will be ordered not according to pecuniary gain, but instead according to technical efficiency? Veblen was equivocal on this and made no concrete predictions, but he certainly thought it possible:

> the technicians and their advice and surveillance are essential to any work whatever in those great primary industries on which the country's productive systems turn, and which set the pace for all the rest. And it is obvious that so soon as they shall draw together, in a reasonably inclusive way, and take common counsel as to what had best be done, they are in a position to say what work shall be done and to fix the terms on which it is to be done. In short, so far as regards the technical requirements of the case, the situation is ready for a self-selected, but inclusive, Soviet of technicians to take over the economic affairs of the country and to allow and disallow what they may agree on; provided always that they live within the requirements of that state of the industrial arts whose keepers they are, and provided that their pretensions continue to have the support of the industrial rank and file; which comes near saying that their Soviet must consistently and effectually take care of the material welfare of the underlying population.
>
> (Veblen 1921: 149)

Veblen's "Soviet of technicians" is an unfortunate term given the course of political development in the twentieth century, but one which probably betrays the colour of his politics. The 'Soviet' comprises the engineers and technocrats whose role it would be to order society's productive system were it to be refashioned in industrial efficiency terms. It is the engineers who take the lead and usher in this altered state of organisation. To be sure, casting the engineers as society's 'saviours' seems an odd choice. It is likely that Veblen's choice was based on his view that the engineers' direct exposure to the machine process would make their minds less sullied by predation than other members of society. Veblen's intuitionalist contemporary John R. Commons considered that Veblen's choice was the inevitable culmination of "tendencies" long since present in Veblen's work, including his never-ending search for an agent of social change (Tilman 1992: 138–139). After disappointment with the social apathy he found in traditional agents of change such as "blue collar workers" and "Bellamyite Nationalist organisations", Veblen relied on the last group available: the "engineer and technician" (Tilman 1992: 138).

While Veblen's choice may seem odd today and was clearly considered dubious even by some contemporaries, during its day it had some notable adherents. The 1920 formation of the Technical Alliance (which was led by the engineer Howard Scott and had the economist Stuart Chase among its members) and the 1932 formation of the Alliance's technocracy movement successor are attributed to Veblen's influence (Segal 2005: 121; 255).[43] Indeed, Veblen was not alone among his contemporaries in his preference for engineering to be the basis for the organisation of society's productive forces, as evidenced by the novelist Harold Loeb's suggestion that "how best to produce and distribute the products of man's efforts is an engineering problem for each detail of which there is always a right answer" (Loeb in Burris 1993: 31; Segal 2005: 121).

Whatever the motives for his choice, Veblen's 'solution' has led some to claim that Veblen had replaced pecuniary elitism with a form of technical elitism (Riesman 1953: 98, 157; Bell 1963: 4). To be sure, the engineers' knowledge of the industrial system would make other members of society become dependent on them. Their esoteric knowledge of technical production processes gives them a source of power that would render them modern age 'Pythagoreans'. Others, like the conservative Chicago economist Abram Harris, considered that Veblen failed to "consider how individual freedom is to be preserved and extended in his technocracy" and argued that the "market mechanism whereby consumers freely express their choices" would be replaced by "authoritarian" technocrats (in Tilman 1992: 63). Hardly the saviours, the engineers instead supplant the leisure class elite, making themselves a new engineering elite.[44] However, arguments like Harris's that are rooted in notions of free market expression neglect a pivotal point raised by Veblen: that emulation and the social nature of consumption impacts, directs, and even curtails the so-called free expressions of consuming agents (Tilman 1992: 63).

While Harris's attack came from the right, Veblen also sustained criticism from the left. The economist Paul Sweezy argued that Veblen "inverts the relationship of engineers to capitalists", transforming what is a relation of "dependence" (namely of the engineer on the capitalist) to one of "conflict" (Sweezy in Tilman 1992: 213). If the relationship were indeed one of dependence and not conflict, then there would be little to drive the engineers to wrest control of the industrial system from the predatory capitalists. As already shown, Veblen himself considered the engineers "harmless and docile" (Veblen 1921: 128), hardly the words one would use in an attempt to convey conflict! Perhaps, as Tilman again notes, Sweezy saw conflict because he read Veblen with Marxist goggles firmly in place. Further, it is possible that Sweezy took Veblen's suggestion regarding the "potential revolutionary class consciousness of engineers . . . literally" and missed the satirical muse that inspired *The Engineers and the Price System* (Tilman 1992: 212). This latter point seems a common refrain from Tilman: that, like Sweezy, so many readers have failed to recognise *The Engineer and the Price System's* "tongue-in-cheek" manner and appreciate Veblen's humour (Tilman 1992: 62).

Tilman (1996: 171) has also argued that many of the criticisms miss Veblen's central point. They fail to recognise that the engineers are not of a predatory character; they are driven by workmanship and efficient cause, and so, unlike the leisure class whose motivation is and always has been predation, the engineers and technocrats commence their actions from a workmanship wellspring. With society guided by such men and women, and with their devotion to science and abhorrence of ceremony, workmanship exerts its influence upon *all* of society. Eventually, workmanship becomes the common sense scheme in the same way that pecuniary institutions are today. The workmanship ethos eventually transforms society from one based on predatory gain to one organised according to technical excellence and efficiency for community gain. It could be said that Veblen's solution is a return to the savage era, characterised as it was by workmanship, but obviously in a far more technologically advanced form.

Veblen's choice of the engineers may seem an odd one, and his 'prognosis' dubious. I personally have many reservations about it. If we accept Veblen's dualistic assertions, then the ever-present predation proclivities would bar the development of such a society. There will always be forces in a 'society of engineers' that undermine its workmanship proclivities. It also seems to have a 'culmination' that would be understandable from a scholar who has chosen to base his thought on a teleological construct like the Hegelian dialectic but seems odd coming from a scholar who claimed to adhere to Darwinian blind chance and abhor teleological notions. It is as though Veblen considered that once the engineers take charge the ceremonial forces will, at last, be forever in abeyance. Again, this seems more a Hegelian viewpoint than a Darwinian one. Perhaps Tilman is correct, and the confusion is a result of Veblen's famous satire being missed in readings of *The Engineers and the Price System*, although why the celebrated Veblenian satire that is so readily appreciated and recognised in Veblen's other works has been missed by so many in this one work is a mystery.

Despite these reservations and the debates regarding the merits of Veblen's 'prediction', I have chosen to present his idea of the engineers for two purposes. The first is to give some sense of Veblen's solution and to show how it fits with his central dichotomy. The second stems from my own self-interest. Society's artists could be considered to be devoted to the production of art in the same way that Veblen's engineers are devoted to an efficient industrial scheme. It is not my intention to present artists as societal saviours but simply to consider the idea that artists are driven by similar workmanship motivations as Veblen's famed engineers. In Chapter 8, I will consider the arts and artists in many different ways, and one of these will be to consider the motivations of artists to produce art with hopes and desires akin to those that Veblen considered his engineers would hold for society's industrial system.

7.5 Conclusion

This chapter has presented various aspects of Veblen's ideas regarding production and consumption. My aim has been to present Veblen's key ideas on both of these areas of economic activity. My choice has been informed by a clear purpose: I have deliberately chosen those areas that I think will, first, give a general sense of what Veblen had to say on these topics and, second, provide a basis for consideration of public subsidy and support to the arts from a Veblenian perspective in Chapter 8.

Veblen's ideas on production and consumption are not so rigidly dichotomous. His characterisation of both production and consumption is as a veritable 'feedback loop' where we see production decisions being tempered and informed by consumption and, similarly, consumption shaped by decisions made in the productive sphere.

His world is not one where the activities of various economics actors invariably combine to achieve maximum welfare. Rather, Veblen's conception of production and consumption is one that recognises the importance of power and the use of said power. Those who have this power are the leisure class and the businessmen, who, in the machine age, are one and the same. Their mores and priorities dominate discourse, method and purpose in all matters of societal function, including production and consumption. The acceptable and respectable patterns of both consumption and production come from them and cascade to those below. They determine the settled habits of those below them. While Marx believed that class consciousness would lead to a revolution that would sweep such an exploitative order away, Veblen showed how the power of ceremonial institutions, such as emulation, ownership and "patriotic fervour", could serve to mute the development of said consciousness (Hunt 1979a: 132). The power of institutions explains why "workers not only endure exploitation and alienation, but also frequently and repeatedly support the very institutions, laws, governments, and general social mores that create and perpetuate their own exploitation and degradation" (Hunt 1979a: 132).

The institutional basis of the elite's power and their desire to maintain their status and position means that efforts for change are slow and subject to resistance. In a world characterised by such hierarchies and power arrangements, it is unlikely that those who have power will wish to see the basis of that power tested and eroded. Of course, this power is subject to technological changes that amend society's institutions, so that even those with power may eventually and over time need to capitulate and accede to the overarching force and 'authority' of institutional natural selection.

The work in this chapter and Chapter 6 will be used to consider public support for the arts, to determine whether Veblen's ideas can provide a different, novel way to understand its existence and, with this, whether some rationale can be found for its existence. I will consider public support for the arts from two general perspectives. The first is to consider public support as an institution in and of itself. The second will be to consider how many of the features and institutions elaborated upon in this chapter have affected and shaped its development.

Notes

1 I have omitted an exploration of Veblen's analysis of credit markets and of business cycles since I will not use either of these in my analysis of public support for the arts.
2 *Positional* goods are goods that we desire in order to maintain our relative rank. With *nonpositional* goods, our relative position is unimportant. *Expenditure cascades* refers to a situation where a shift in income and wealth equality causes a shift in consumption behaviour along all incomes. Veblen's influence in the development of Frank's ideas is visible in Frank (1985), where Frank references *Leisure Class* (Frank 1985: 116) and notes that Veblen "emphasised" the social aspects of consumption, which cause "some people" to be "actively concerned about how the amount of leisure they consume compares with the amounts consumed by their peers" (Frank 1985: 101).
3 The reason for this casting out is generally (and many might say rightly) considered to be due to the inability of the labour theory of value to deal effectively with Smith's water-diamonds paradox. However, some suggest that it was a response to the direction the labour theory had been taken by Marx. By removing any manual or human labour from the determinants of value and instead relying on notions of utility, Marx's opponents could neutralise arguments against capitalism and assure the legitimacy of income accruing to the owners of capital (Hamilton 1987: 356–359; see also Routh 1975).
4 John Dewey, Veblen's University of Chicago colleague and one of the founders of modern psychology and pragmatist philosophy, caricatured economics and its pleasure-pain foundations as "the science of phenomena due to one love and one aversion" (Dewey 1922: 132).
5 See Chapter 3, section 3.3.1 to see how Becker's z theory has adapted this into modern neoclassical interpretations.
6 It is worth highlighting that classical economics was alone among the social sciences in its continued use of the hedonistic calculus (Hamilton 1973: 201). Veblen was not alone in rejecting this model of man and was supported by John Dewey, who expressed frustration with economics' adherence to an approach that portrayed man as existing "naturally in a state of rest so that he requires some external force to set him into action. The idea of a thing intrinsically wholly inert in the sense of absolutely passive is expelled from physics and has taken refuge in the psychology of current economics. In truth man acts anyway, he can't help acting. In every fundamental sense it is false that a man requires a motive to make him do something. To a healthy man inaction is the greatest of woes. Any one [*sic*] who observes children knows that while periods of rest are natural, laziness is an acquired vice – or virtue. While a man is awake he will do something, if only to build castles in the air" (Dewey 1922: 118–119).
7 However, Veblen notes that this distinction is, at the early stages of the barbarian period and leisure class, more apparent (ceremonial) than actual. The predatory pursuits in this period include such things as hunting. Hence, while these have the character of predation, they also serve the wellbeing and furtherance of the community by, for example, contributing to the food supply (Veblen 1899: 27–28). The important point is one of 'spirit' or attitude. For the leisure class, their activities do not have the colour of workmanship but rather predation. Their activities are apprehended in such terms.
8 This is an important point that will be elaborated upon later in the chapter in the discussion on the relationship between economic scarcity, conspicuous consumption and leisure.
9 In the United Kingdom, one might also hear the alternative, where one is accused of being 'common' for displaying poor behavior or consumption choices. The intention in this case is the same as in the case of 'classy'. However, in this case, one is directly accused of consumption or behaviour associated with the lower classes, as opposed to being chastised for not conforming to or meeting the mores of some putative superior class.
10 It may seem silly to think that goods that are 'obviously' good or 'obviously' noxious have social determinants, but even here, the social can be seen to play a role. Recall

from Chapter 6 that society's institutions are a means to pass information and knowledge from generation to generation. Take the case of a poison like arsenic. We avoid its consumption because we know it is bad for us, but we do not need to find that out by individually consuming it. Instead, we know it is bad for us because, through our immersion in society, we come to understand that arsenic consumption will kill us. A similar argument can be made for something 'intrinsically good', like honey. Hence, in this way, we can say that even goods that are 'obviously' good or 'obviously' bad for us have a social element in determining our taste for them.

11 So, for example, we in the West are not born with the taste in clothing that dictates that women wear dresses and men wear pants, but this scheme of acceptable clothing is something that is handed to us through society's institutions. Our tastes in these matters of dress are institutionally determined and subject to change (for example, it is now acceptable in Western societies for women to wear pants).

12 In reality, there is also likely to be intraclass hierarchy. Take an aristocracy. In this case, the monarch or emperor is likely to be at the summit, the other members of the royal family would follow, and so on until we reach the 'lowly' baronet. In modern societies, we often speak of old money and the nouveau riche. The former 'old money' group includes those who have supposedly established their social cachet and have proven their worth as those to be emulated. The latter are the younger or new rich, and as such are still to prove their emulatory worth. One might find that that one way that the latter earn esteem is by following the established trails toward honour forged by old money, in other words, by emulating old money. Indeed, the old money rich, when they were the new money, could be said to have garnered honour by developing behavior modelled on those of the previous bearers of 'high office', the aristocracy, albeit their own interpretation. That this was the approach they used is visible through such things as their building of large mansions and country estates, or the holding of dinner parties and fancy balls, each of which adopted the practices and manners of the aristocracy. Indeed, the Vanderbilts were known to adopt aristocratic methods by such extremes as dressing as Louis XIV and a Venetian princess (see Diggins 1999: 6 for this and more examples; see also Veblen 1899: 52).

13 Consider a literary illustration. In *Jude the Obscure*, Thomas Hardy's protagonist, despite being gifted, is essentially barred from obtaining an 'Oxbridge' style education from the fictitious Christminster because he is not of the appropriate class. Instead, he is forced to undertake training and employment in an area considered more suited to his class, that is, as a stonemason. It should be pointed out that prohibition of consumption and action also affects the upper classes. Veblen gives the example of a French king who after being placed in front of an open fire is said have lost his life by 'toasting' for refusal to lose his good form and move his person himself, since this role belonged to a lower functionary (Veblen 1899: 30).

14 For example, couple or two-person dancing was once associated with the lower working classes. The upper classes instead preferred social forms of dancing. One of the reasons is that the working class forms of dancing were seen to be vulgar, as blatant eroticism. In time, the higher classes adopted an amended form of this style of dance so as to make it more palatable to their canons of taste. Thus, with couple dancing, we see an activity that commenced with the lower classes moving into the upper classes (Illouz 1997: 61).

15 To Veblen goes the kudos for recognition of these conspicuous phenomena, but John Rae wrote of an idea that is very similar in thrust 65 years before Veblen. In *New Principles of Political Economy* (1834), Rae introduces the idea that some articles or goods are consumed in order to provide a sense of "superiority over others", going on to say that such "articles of which the consumption is not conspicuous, are incapable of gratifying this passion [for superiority]" (Rae 1834: 265, 267). Rae did not consider this to be a modern phenomenon associated only with capitalism but suggested that it

has had a long presence in human society, pointing to examples of such practice in the time of ancient Rome (Rae 1834: 266–267).

16 However, Tilman (1992: 183) has argued that Schneider's conclusion is possible because he misses a key element of Veblen's analysis. Efficiency measured in technical terms is just one manifestation of a society that operates to accord with workmanship, but the advent of such a manifestation would probably be accompanied by a wholesale workmanship amendment across the "continuity of life" (Tilman 1992: 183). In the event that such an amendment occurs, Schneider's assertion that technology would be the locus of value would not come to pass, since it would be accompanied by a comprehensive workmanship reorganisation of society's institutions, including those that determine value. In other words, *what* should be produced would be determined not by the ceremonial predilections that are the hallmarks of a predatory capitalist society (such as invidious rank) but by the institutions of a society operating under workmanship proclivities.

17 As will be seen in section 7.3, it is not simply that the industrial system produces goods to satiate individual ceremonial needs but that the way production itself is organised accords with a predatory, ceremonial bent.

18 Another more common example can be found in the lower classes, where vicarious leisure is visible in the ability of a husband to maintain a domiciled wife. Such a wife need not work or sell her labour and can instead devote her time to personal pursuits, such as charity work, or even to tending the home. While the latter kind of activity could be said to involve drudgery, the vicarious leisure is by virtue of the fact that this man obtains status by his ability to maintain his wife and home without the aid of the sale of her labour. In fact, the head of such a household may actually forgo any "pretense of leisure" so as to enable his "middle-class wife [to carry] on the business of vicarious leisure, for the good name of the household and its master" (Veblen 1899: 55).

19 However, it should be noted this does not exclude the possibility that the servant might also feel some benefit from wearing such costly clothing. It is possible for his master to benefit vicariously and the servant directly; they are not necessarily mutually exclusive. The same could be the case for vicarious leisure, meaning that the servant might also gain some sense of status from his being in his master's employ.

20 The need for overt displays of consumption often means that goods that are conspicuously wasteful come to "commend themselves as more serviceable, nobler and more beautiful than such goods as do not embody such a margin of waste" (Veblen 1914: 217).

21 This topic has been considered by modern economists, including the earlier mentioned Robert Frank (2007). Fred Hirsch also considered it in his well-known book *Social Limits to Growth* (1995). Using the positional goods idea, Hirsch considers the existence of social scarcities. In essence, Hirsch says that as capitalism developed, the material or physical necessities of life have in large part been made available to a bulk of the populace, but with the satiation of physical necessities, a greater importance has been placed on the attainment of socially determined positional goods.

22 For example, take the location of a corporate head office. This head office could be placed in any number of locations, and yet often the choice of where to locate is often tainted with ceremonial considerations, such as being in the most desired street in a city. Continuing with this example, the office of a corporate CEO could be equipped with functional furniture and office items, and yet examples abound of offices that contain furniture and conveniences of such extravagance that one cannot help but think these were not production decisions but instead decisions designed to fulfil ceremonial conspicuous consumption. The redecorated office of former Merrill Lynch CEO John Thain is an example of one that contained such extravagances. Among the items in his office were a US$1,400 bin, US$87,000 rug and US$68,000 credenza

(From http://dealbook.nytimes.com/2009/01/22/thains-office-overhaul-said-to-cost-12-million/?scp=2&sq=john%20thain%20trash&st=cse accessed 28 February 2012).

23 That the neoclassical view is taxonomic was explained in Chapter 6. In the case of production, the taxonomic predilections meant that it was less concerned with any process of production but instead diverted time to understanding the features that correlate with this end: to ascertain the payments made to each factor at the 'unavoidable' fated equilibrium.

24 However, recent neoclassical models have sought to endogenise technology to account for growth (see Romer 1994).

25 Again, it could be said that the neoclassical view is an example of its taxonomic inclinations. Since technology does not receive a payment, it does not enter the focus of analysis. Only those elements in production that receive a payment are analysed. Hence, neoclassical economics' analysis of production is actually a classification of property rights in production and not of the process of production. In this way, it is taxonomic.

26 Veblen's idea of a reward to capital based on 'coercion' has analogies with Marx. In Volume 1 of *Capital*, Marx referred to "primitive accumulation", which is not the result of the capitalistic mode of production but its "starting point" (Marx 1867: 309, 359). Like Veblen, Marx rejects notions that trace ownership to rewards accruing to a "diligent, intelligent, and, above all, frugal elite" (Marx 1867: 359); rather, he traces them to the "expropriation of the agricultural producer, of the peasant, from the soil", in other words, to what Veblen might term 'force' or 'fraud' (Marx 1867: 360). Whether Veblen's choice was based on Marx's views or not is unclear; however, it can be said with certainty that Veblen was familiar with Marx's notions of primitive accumulation, since he makes explicit reference to the concept in his work on the origin of capital (Veblen 1908a: 534).

27 The American writer and political economist Henry George also considered rents to be a reflection of the increased productive power of the land resulting from the community's activities. As an example, consider George's story of the "unbounded savannah", where he shows how the community together transforms this wild plain into a mighty city and increases its "productiveness" (George 1886: 235, 239). As a consequence, rents have "increased accordingly", which "the landowner can claim" (George 1886: 240, 241). The point being that it is the community's efforts to create a city where there was once an empty savannah and the benefits that accrue from this that is the source of the landlord's gain (George 1886: 235–243).

28 See section 7.3.2 for Veblen's discussion of one of the means used to claim these payments, namely, the use of patents.

29 Veblen's "on the aggregate" caveat recognises that some tangible assets might be used for less than serviceable purposes, meaning that they would not be considered "materially productive". He does not introduce the possibility that an "intangible" asset might be productive but does go so far as to say that these assets might be "indifferent" with respect to their contribution to or detraction from productive activity (Veblen 1908b: 115–116).

30 To be sure, a patent giving ownership over a technology could be said to have a technological basis, but the income deriving from the patent is not from the use of the technology, it is simply from having a recognised claim to ownership over the technology.

31 The idea of intangible assets was also considered by the Australian economist Elizabeth Webster in *The Economics of Intangible Assets* (1999). The work, which resulted from her doctoral dissertation, analyses intangible assets from a post-Keynesian perspective. Whereas the neoclassical paradigm perceives investment as a means to raise a firm's physical productive capacity, the post-Keynesian view considers investment as a means to "enhance profits and to gain control over the business environment" (Webster 1999: 2). In this post-Keynesian understanding, the incentive for intangible

investment comes from three possible sources, including "as a competitive weapon, . . . to contain . . . a level of fundamental uncertainty, . . . or to enhance . . . productive capacity" (Webster 1999: 2). Webster refers to the "embryonic and belated recognition of intangible forms of capital in the literature" and makes no reference to Veblen in her work, suggesting that she was probably unaware that Veblen had considered such forms of investment at least as early as 1904 (Webster 1999: 2).

32 I am referring to the Aleutian islanders Veblen uses as an example in his critique of John Bates Clark's economics, where he sarcastically wrote that a "gang of Aleutian Islanders slushing about in the wrack and surf with rakes and magical incantations for the capture of shell-fish are held, in point of taxonomic reality, to be engaged in a feat of hedonistic equilibration in rent, wages, and interest" (Veblen 1908c: 160).

33 Although, as will be shown later, the workmanship aversion to futility in production is 'thwarted' by the predatory nature of those who own it.

34 Veblen was not alone in recognising the interdependent nature of modern industrial production. Veblen's '*bête noir*', Alfred Marshall, also spoke of industrial " 'integration' ", by which he meant the "growing intimacy and firmness of the connections between the separate parts of the industrial organism" (Marshall 1890: 241). The use of the term organism indicates Marshall's acceptance of the advances made in biology, particularly by Darwin, and their usefulness in the study of economics (Marshall 1890: 240). Veblen was certainly aware of Marshall's view and of this passage, as evidenced by his explicit reference in *The Theory of Business Enterprise* to the chapter from which Marshall's quote is drawn (Veblen 1904: 95).

35 The impact of the clock upon the ways and means of life was considered by the English writer and historian E. P. Thompson in his article *Time, Work-discipline and Industrial Capitalism* (1967). Thompson undertook a study of the development and adoption of the timepiece and its impact upon the function and organisation of society, tracing it from feudal and Renaissance times onward. In an industrial capitalist society, the timepiece is not limited to the operation of the industrial system but makes its presence felt in all manner of life, from the "factory or workshop discipline" to its "impingement upon social and domestic life" (Thompson 1967: 83).

36 Fordism refers to mass production techniques that were characterised by "moving assembly lines, standardised products, extreme division of labour [and] low skill levels" (Jackson 2006: 449–450). By contrast, post-Fordism is said to comprise "less standardised production" (Jackson 2006: 450; see also Amin 2008). From an output perspective, the difference is between "mass production" in the Fordist period and "flexible specialization" in the post-Fordist era (Williams et al 1987: 406). There is some debate as to whether one can confidently pronounce a shift from an era of mass production (Fordism) into one of flexible production and the return of the so-called artisan producer (post-Fordism) (see Williams *et al* 1987; see also Krishan 2009: chapter 4).

37 While Adam Smith is famous for his assertion regarding the greater good that arises from the "invisible hand" (Smith 1776: 19, 364), he is also known for his arguments regarding class conflict. Smith spoke of "two parties", of "workmen" and "masters", the former wishing to "get as much, the masters to give as little, as possible" (Smith 1776: 60). Their incongruent aims lead to a "dispute" where the 'master' class, due to its relatively limited numbers, has the ability to organise and "force the other into a compliance with their terms" (Smith 1776: 59–60; see also Rima 1998). Similarly, David Ricardo refers to three classes that make up society whose share of the produce is in the form of "rent, profit and wages" (Ricardo 1817: 5). Ricardo goes on to say that the "principal problem in Political Economy" is to "determine the laws which regulate this distribution" (Ricardo 1817: 5). Implied in Ricardo's statement is an interdependence between the three classes but also the potential for differences and misalignment in their claims for their 'reward'. This latter point provides a source of

class conflict (see Wolff 2002). The inclusion of notions of conflict by both Smith and Ricardo suggests that classical economists envisaged the possibility that the functioning of capitalism may create tension, meaning that capitalism's operation may be less than harmonious and its outcomes anything but benevolent.

38 Although, as Veblen notes and recognised, the technological methods of industry had long since moved beyond the businessman's apprehension (Veblen 1914: 354).

39 Veblen claimed that the word 'deal' was appropriated by businessmen from gaming slang (Veblen 1904: 33). I have not been able to validate his claim, but the word deal itself appears to be of far older heritage and is actually from an Old High German word "teil" which goes further to Old Norse "delid", both meaning a part or a share. Whatever the case, Veblen's claim serves to give some indication regarding the esteem in which he held the directors and owners of the industrial system.

40 Recall that intangible assets are of a ceremonial provenance and do not increase physical production or output, but they can increase the firm's earnings.

41 Veblen considered that insensitive and 'bloody minded' behaviour by capitalists was made possible because of the disconnection between producer and consumer. The handicraft era was such that the "personal contact" between a "producer and his customer was somewhat close and lasting". Such close contact made the possibility of "personal esteem and disesteem" a considerable factor in "controlling the [behaviour of] purveyors of goods and services". Failure to comport oneself in a proper and honourable manner carried real consequences, including loss of reputation (Veblen 1904: 52). The increasingly impersonal nature of production was a point noted by Marshall too when he said that the "personal relations between shopkeeper and customer are becoming more distant" (Marshall 1890: 288).

42 It is unsurprising that Veblen adopted the martial "captain of industry" terminology to refer to the heirs of the first exploitative class, although the term predates Veblen's use, as evidenced by Book 4, Chapter 4 of Thomas Carlyle's work *Past and Present* (1843), which bore the title "Captains of Industry".

43 The Technical Alliance had among its activities a nationwide survey of the industrial system to expose the waste of the capitalist system and help create an industrial system organised according to technical engineering precepts (Burris 1993: 28). Its technocracy movement successor considered that human progress should be measured by the ability to produce and use energy, since energy is the 'blood' of the modern industrial system that enables its machines to function (Segal 2005: 121).

44 In *The Managerial Revolution*, the American political philosopher James Burnham presented a scenario that is in many respects analogous to that presented by Veblen. Whereas Veblen gives the role of 'saviour' to the engineers, Burnham chooses a managerial class, the 'managers', who will "exercise . . . control over the instruments of production and gain preference in the distributions of products" (Burnham 1941: 68). Burnham's managers are "not to be confused with engineers and technicians, although they may be both" (Sweezy 1942: 3). They are those who have "charge of the actual technical process of producing", and they comprise those whose "job [is] to organize the materials, tools, machines, plant, facilities and labour" required for production (Burnham 1941: 72). Whereas under capitalism, control of the industrial system is guaranteed by a system of "property rights vested in . . . [capitalists] as individuals" (Burnham 1941: 64), the power the managers have over the industrial system will be by virtue of the "technical nature of . . . modern production" and the "institutions which comprise the state" (Burnham 1941: 64, 80). Like Veblen, who considered that the shift to the engineers would be supported by an alignment in the institutional structure, Burnham considered that the managers' control would be "guaranteed by appropriate political institutions, analogous to the guarantee of bourgeois dominance under capitalism by the bourgeois political institutions" (Burnham 1941: 65).

8 The Veblenian duality and public support for the arts

8.1 Introduction

In the Veblenian construct, social evolution takes place through the interaction of two prime forces. These forces are workmanship, which includes the group-regarding predilections of man, and predation, which comprises the self-regarding inclinations of the species. It is the relationship between these two forces, moulded by technological change, which determines the timbre of society. When workmanship dominates, society is characterised as one where group-regarding characters come to the fore. On the other hand, where predation dominates, self-regarding behaviour wins out. In time, this interaction leads to a process of evolution, which manifests itself in the very institutions that guide and direct society. To borrow a Marxist term, the play between these two forces determines the nature of the social 'superstructure'. Importantly, because the process is one of evolution, it is unknown whether the future course and shape of society will be one that leans more in favour of predation or will align to meet workmanship.

What if this duality could be applied to gain an understanding of public support for the arts? It would suggest that to understand public support for the arts, one would need to appreciate the force and impact of both workmanship and predation in matters of art. The strength of either force will determine whether the arts and public support can be characterised as serving workmanship desires or whether they are in the service of the predatory. It is the aim of this chapter to apply the Veblenian duality to gain an understanding of public support for the arts, and to determine whether this approach might also yield a rationale for its support.

Two possible approaches will be considered. The first of these will be to treat public support for the arts as an institution. This approach would treat public support in the same way as an institution like ownership or the leisure class. Just as Veblen outlined how the leisure class and ownership arose through the interplay of workmanship and predation triggered into action by technological change, this approach would consider public support as the most recent incarnation of an institution that has a long pedigree.

Unlike the first approach, the second will consider the impact of the two forces on the very nature of art itself. To achieve this, a case study will be considered, that of contemporary (visual) art. This choice has been made because of recent concerns expressed by 'cultural leaders' of an apparent shift that, they believe, now sees the visual arts judged and operated not on artistic grounds but on financial foundations, as an investment, the assertion being that the art resulting from this is somewhat inferior to that which was produced under 'pre-investment' circumstances. It is my assertion that many of the developments said to have occurred in contemporary art could be viewed within the Veblenian perspective as the ascendancy of predatory/ceremonial institutions in the operation of contemporary art. As such, public support would be warranted on the basis that it might enable the arts to occur without predatory intrusion, or at the very least reduce it.

However, as will be seen, it may be possible for a programme of public support for the arts that is nominally designed to counter ceremonial proclivities still to be contaminated by ceremonial or predatory aspirations. Therefore, to balance the argument, I will present examples of how a 'nobly' designed system of support and subvention could turn out to be the outlet by which predatory institutions assert a presence. If this is the case, then arguments in favour of public support would need to be reconsidered or tempered.

8.2 The institution of public support: Heir to patronage?

In earlier chapters, it was shown that Thorstein Veblen considered the leisure class to be an institution with a long heritage whose origins could be traced to the earliest barbarian era. Along with ownership, this institution was the defining feature of that era, and its initial appearance was explained as a product of institutional evolution set in train by technological change. The modern capitalist at the helm of the modern capitalist industrial system is in essence the most recent form of this ancient institution.

Suppose for a moment that public support for the arts is also an institution. If so, then, like the leisure class, the modern form of public support for the arts can be explained through a process of evolution taking place over centuries. Just like the institution of the leisure class, public support for the arts might be traced back to an earlier ancestor. The disbursement of public support and funding to the arts through bodies like the Australia Council, the US National Endowment for the Arts (NEA) or the Arts Council of England is thus merely the outcome of the most recent step in the evolution of an older institution, namely, an institution of arts patronage.

Any analysis based on this approach would seek to trace the evolution of the institution from its earliest forms to its most recent manifestations. Like all institutions, the evolution of public support for the arts must be appreciated within the totality of social institutional development. Institutions work in tandem, they touch and blend and overlap and develop co-dependently, so that a development or change in one institution can have effects across the wider system of institutions. The result is that the evolution of other institutions is also affected. And so, to understand evolution in public support for the arts, we would need to identify other relevant institutions and understand their evolution.

Before proceeding on this kind of analysis, I would firstly like to attend to a definitional matter. In general, most discussion implies that public support for the arts occurs when resources and funding are provided to the arts by democratic governments. However, this need not be the case, and so for this section, the definition of public support will be *explicitly* broadened. By public support, it is meant funding or resources provided for the production and support of art by the government or ruler of a region or nation, democratic or otherwise. Support that is provided for the production of art by a democratic government thus fulfils this criterion, but so too does support provided by a suzerain, emir, feudal lord, prince, monarch, pope or emperor. This is not an unreasonable definition, for it reflects the fact that democratic government as commonly appreciated in the West is historically atypical in the ways of human governance. The broadened definition recognises and enables an analysis built on this historical reality. With this definitional matter now resolved, it is possible to develop an analysis that treats public support as an institution. In particular, public support for the arts can be viewed as the descendant of a far older system of *public arts patronage*.

Arts patronage is a system whereby a patron provides support in the form of privilege or financial backing to an artist. The artist is essentially in the patron's employ, and his role is to produce works on the patron's behalf. Coupled with the newly explicit definition of public support, *public* arts patronage thus occurs when a patron, in the form of a ruler, democratic or otherwise, commissions an artist to produce works of art. Since the ability to commission public works rests with those who have the political authority, arts patronage thus reflects a society's centre of economic and political power (Hollingsworth 1994: 1–2). In evolutionary terms, it reflects and is tempered by the evolution of the institutions of power and government. To trace its development would require concomitant tracing of the seats of power.

Consider feudal Europe. Its strictly formal class divisions meant that economic, social and political power rested with the church, aristocracy and nobility. As such, the nature of public arts patronage during this period was one that saw the power to commission art works resting with aristocratic and clerical rulers. During perhaps the most famous period of arts patronage, the Italian Renaissance, public support occurred when a prince, pope or monarch commissioned works to be produced at his bequest. In the case of the Florentine republic, wealthy bankers and merchants like the famous Medici (who were in essence aristocrats of a sort) were found at its head, and it was through them that public patronage occurred (Hollingsworth 1994: 3). Thus, the Italian Renaissance form of public arts patronage was highly intertwined with and directed by the period's leisure class.

It is common among art scholars to consider Italian Renaissance art to be the product of free artistic exploration (Hollingsworth 1994: 1). However, its patronage and control by the Italian Renaissance leisure class would cause Veblen scholars to be immediately sceptical of this claim. Indeed, the overtly leisure class character of Italian Renaissance patronage gives an indication regarding the expectations and role of art. Far from free artistic expression enabled by enlightened patrons who stood out of the artist's way, fifteenth century art was commissioned by patrons who were "active consumers", not "passive connoisseurs", so much so that it was the patron who controlled the final form of artistic output, not the artist (Hollingsworth 1994: 1). The need to maintain control can be related to leisure class needs. Art's chief role was to evoke images of "wealthy, powerful and ambitious patrons" (Hollingsworth 1994: 2). Art patronage was thus a form of "conspicuous expenditure", a form of "propaganda" where "architecture, sculpture and painting were seen as potent tools in the fabrication of images of wealth and power" (Hollingsworth 1994: 3).

The Renaissance forebear of public support suggests that the institution of public support has a predatory past. The strong presence of predation during the Renaissance meant that art's chief role was as a display of wealth in the creation of the patron's 'image'. So powerful was this need that 'meddling' Renaissance patrons "kept careful control of the craftsmen who carried out their commission" (Hollingsworth 1994: 6). It would not be unreasonable to suppose that, given control by the then leisure class, public patronage's origin might have been predatory and traceable to the earliest forms of this class, implying that it is a predatorily inspired institution. But a Veblenian evolutionary analysis would need to take into account the impact of the forces of *both* workmanship and predation. The constant interplay between workmanship and predation means that the presence of either would 'see-saw' over different periods. An overtly predatory institution might at other times be tempered, so that predation is muted and workmanship amplified.

One way in which a rise in workmanship would be felt is in a recalculation of the relationship between artist and patron. Unlike the tightly controlled output of the Renaissance artist, a system of patronage with greater workmanship would probably give the artist greater control over the final output. Greater control suggests that the patron's desire for prestige would be less dominant in deciding the final output. Indeed, the rise in the ability of the artist to assert himself would be met with a diminution in the stature, reverence and opinions of the patron. So, when Samuel Johnson famously and sardonically responded to Lord Chesterfield's overtures that a patron is "one who looks with unconcern on a man struggling for life in the water and when he has reached ground encumbers him with help", we see evidence of change in attitude. Similarly, when Emperor Joseph famously told Mozart that his opera *Die Entführung aus dem Serail* had too many notes, Mozart's defiant reply, "there are just as many notes as there should be", suggests that the unchallenged deference to the patron was waning. It is unlikely that an artist would have responded so boldly to a Renaissance overlord, and so this could be interpreted as the all-powerful predatory needs of the Renaissance patron moderating in favour of the artistic workmanship bents of the artist.

Johnston's attitude to Lord Chesterfield and Mozart's response to the Emperor are also reflective of a change in the nature of the institution of the leisure class. Once an institution built on notions of unassailable inherited divine rights, workmanship causes a revision, so that hitherto held notions of a divine hereditary natural order are seen in a new, sceptical light. In terms of public arts patronage, it means that the Renaissance notion of an "absolute ruler [who] dominated the cultural life of the city" (Hollingsworth 1994: 2) was supplanted to eventually become the modern Australia Council and NEA, built on democratic foundations. The interactive and overlapping nature of institutions means that the shift in the leisure class institution forces a shift in related institutions like public patronage.

As mentioned earlier, public patronage is tightly linked with the institutions that inform and organise government and the centres of power. Thus, that Italian Renaissance public arts patronage was directed by capricious princes, monarchs and popes is no surprise. This method of patronage reflects the feudal institutions of government prevalent at the time, and so it was logical for the art produced during that era to be ordered under the divinely anointed authority of the feudal princes and the temporal power of the popes. Since Renaissance times, government institutions have evolved. In the West, government institutions have morphed into the institutions of representative democratic government. It is not unexpected, then, for modern forms of public arts patronage to reflect democratic 'reforms'. When democratic governments like those in Australia, the United Kingdom and the United States establish bodies like the Australia Council, the Arts Council of England and the NEA, it is a reflection of public patronage amended to fit within amended government institutions. The evolution of public patronage reflects the gradual shift in the institutions of government in the West. With this shift, public patronage, which was once necessarily and *sufficiently* an expression of the needs and desire of the prince, monarch or pope, now necessarily expresses the needs and desires of the democratic region or state.

Evolutionary change, whether social or biological, has within it evolutionary hang-ons or vestiges.[1] These hang-ons or vestiges mean that all institutions, including patronage, are burdened with the flotsam of their ancestral forms. The origin of public arts patronage with the predatory leisure class ensured that among its key aims was status aggrandisement and maintenance. In other words, a clear motivation was that of ceremonialism. If public support is indeed an heir to predatorily inspired leisure class patronage, then we should find some remnant of its predatory origin in its modern manifestations. The predatory vestiges should have a presence within the goals and methods of the modern institution of public support.

Indeed, this will be the basis of some of the analysis to follow, where I outline ways in which predatory characters may be present within modern public support programmes putatively designed for artistic workmanship. One of these aligns with the status-craving aims of princely patronage, and it will be shown that a nation or region might shape its public support policies to earn prestige. Thus, like the Italian Renaissance princes, modern public cultural policy could at least partly be about maintaining an appearance or earning prestige. The difference between older forms of public patronage and modern types is that the benefit once enjoyed by the prince is in the modern form 'enjoyed' by the greater region or nation. Thus, the predatory origins of the institution of public patronage impose themselves in the modern practice of public support. If public support is indeed the heir to older forms of artistic patronage motivated by ceremonial/predatory aims, and if institutions are weighed down with the dross of ancestral institutions, then it may be unavoidable that modern systems of public support, putatively designed to promote artistic workmanship, will be at least partly directed by predatory characteristics.

The treatment of public support for the arts as the descendant of an ancient institution of public patronage has important implications. The institutional appreciation of public support as the modern manifestation of public arts patronage suggests that public support may have been present in society in one form or another for centuries. Thus, traditional neoclassical analyses of public support that begin with the question "is there a rationale for public support of the arts?" would need to be recast, for implied within this question is the supposition that the absence of public support is the 'normal' state of affairs. However, it might be possible that the situation is otherwise, that the presence of public support is, historically speaking, the 'normal' state, and that modern calls for its abolition do not recognise this 'reality'.

The analysis in this section is by no means exhaustive. Further work is needed to determine if public support for the arts does indeed have institutional antecedents. A thorough and definitive analysis would require a far more extensive and thorough consideration of the system of patronage than has been presented here. However, this section shows potential avenues for future research into public support for the arts that would treat public support as an institution with a longer heritage than is commonly thought. In time, this new line of research could perhaps cause a recalculation and change in the apprehension of public support for the arts.

8.3 The case of contemporary art

Consider the possibility that the Veblenian duality could be not only applied to consider the development of an institution of public patronage but also to trace the impact of workmanship and predation upon the very pattern and shape of the arts. Just as in the case of the institution of public patronage and support, the shape of art would be affected by whether the period in question is one where predatory forces are bolder or where workmanship has a greater hand. At different periods of social development, the relative strength of the two will change, and so we would expect the nature of the arts to reflect these ever-changing circumstances.

In periods where art is dominated by predation, its purpose would be primarily to serve predatory institutions. Chief among these are the institution of the leisure class and its fellow institution of ownership. On the other hand, when workmanship plays the greater part, we should experience a flourishing of artistic output that accords with 'artistic canons', and the prime motivation for artistic production should be artistic expression.

This approach could be applied to any number of historical periods. But the purpose of this book is to understand public support and to determine if rationales can be made for its existence. As such, it makes sense to focus on the development of art and gauge the impact of workmanship and predation in the modern twentieth and twenty-first century capitalist age. To consider this, a case study will be presented, namely that of the contemporary visual arts. The purpose will be to determine whether contemporary art has developed in a way that can be explained by Veblen's model for economic and social development. To begin with, I will outline the course that has been witnessed in contemporary art, as outlined by various art historians and critics, over the course of the past 50 years or so. From there, I consider whether this course can be understood using the Veblenian paradigm, and from this whether a rationale for public support can be obtained.

8.3.1 The development of 'null' contemporary art

In 1996, the French social theorist Jean Baudrillard caused a stir when he declared that modern art had ceased to have a reason to exist, that it was empty (Baudrillard 2005: 10):

> The adventure of modern art is over. . . . Nothing differentiates it from technical, advertising, media and digital operations. There is no more transcendence, no more divergence, nothing from another scene: it is a reflective game with the contemporary world as it happens. This is why contemporary art is null and void.
>
> (Baudrillard 2005: 89, 91)

Art had become null, empty and without function because the "purpose of art" had shifted (Baudrillard 2005: 77). Art was originally concerned with "a whole other scene; inventing something other than reality" and "never concerned itself with the question of reality in its right form" (Baudrillard 2005: 77–78). But art had morphed so that it no longer presented an alternative but instead "turned to reality" (Baudrillard 2005: 78). The result is art that "has become a terminal, an image-feedback to reality" (Baudrillard 2005: 77–78). Nothing differentiated modern art from reality, and so Baudrillard pronounced art empty. Even 'active' nullity, the idea that the emptiness of art is a calculated and purposeful reflection by artists of the 'insignificance' or 'meaningless' of modern life, is simply a "duplicity" to give *ex post facto* purpose to that which Baudrillard considered to be intrinsically "null and void" (Baudrillard 2005: 27).

The renowned Australian art critic Robert Hughes has expressed views regarding the state of contemporary art that mirror the emptiness described by Baudrillard, albeit less sanguinely and with greater melancholy. However, Hughes traces the 'problems' of contemporary art to its increasing commercialisation and subjugation to the vagaries of an artistically uninformed market. Hughes makes his claims regarding the 'vacuity' of contemporary art in his 2008 UK Channel 4 documentary *The Mona Lisa Curse* (Chang and Hughes 2008). In his inimitable imperious style, Hughes proclaims that art is no longer valued according to artistic criteria, to "make us feel more clearly and more intelligently" or to "give us coherent sensations which otherwise we would not have had" (Hughes in Chang and Hughes 2008), but is instead appraised and venerated according to financial motive and profit:

> [There has been] a giant shift in the art world . . . [and] that shift is all about money. It's a story that I've watched unfold over the last 50 years. I've seen

> with growing disgust the fetishisation of art, the vast inflation of prices and the effect of this on artists and museums. The entanglement of big money with art has become a curse on how art is made, controlled and above all in the way in the way it's experienced. And this curse has infected the entire art world.
>
> (Hughes in Chang and Hughes 2008)

Hughes traces the "giant shift", the pivot from artistic to financial, to two events. The first is the 1962 New York City tour of Da Vinci's *Mona Lisa*. This "emblematic event" transformed Leonardo's work from art into an "icon of mass consumption" (Hughes in Chang and Hughes 2008). As a result of the tour, works like the *Mona Lisa* are no longer 'experienced' in artistic terms, but are consumed "like a photo in a magazine . . . to be scanned and quickly discarded" (Hughes in Chang and Hughes 2008). Footage of the 1962 tour shows people filing past the work, each spending perhaps no more than a few minutes in front of the piece in large groups that would surely affect and limit the perspective by which the work could be appreciated. In such a scenario, even the most adamant art lover would struggle to view the work in all its glory and take artistic sustenance from it. The point of such a visit seems to be not to experience art but to earn the right to say one has seen a work. One goes to see the *Mona Lisa* for the same reason one goes to listen to the Beatles at Shea Stadium, to be able to say one was there. [2] Hughes reckons that the *Mona Lisa* tour cultivated a new "cult of the celebrity masterpiece" that has cast a "curse" over the future development and apprehension of all art (Hughes in Chang and Hughes 2008). Art is no longer be treated or judged on artistic terms but is instead seen as something to be consumed in a 'throwaway' manner.

The second event or pivot point is the auction of the Robert and Ethel Scull collection by Sotheby Parke Bernet (now Sotheby's) on 18 October 1973. The auction, aided by a "calculated campaign of press agentry and P.R. worthy of the building of a movie star's career",[3] amassed a then-record $2.2 million for the Sculls (Rose 1973: 80, see also Kirschenbaum 1979: 50). Notable items included Jasper Johns' *Double White Map*, purchased for $10,200 in 1965 and selling for $240,000, with similar then-record profits obtained for many other works, including those by Rauschenberg and Warhol (Kirschenbaum 1979: 50; Sayre 1974).

The importance of the Scull auction for the future of art was recognised even at the time. In 1973, the art critic and historian Barbara Rose described the auction as the night the "art market collapsed" (Rose 1973: 80). It might seem strange to an economist to call a night that produced record art prices one of market collapse, and yet the collapse Rose refers to is actually a creation, namely the creation or birth of an art world that judges art in profit and investment terms. Art was on its way to becoming a commodity, sought after not for its artistic achievement but for its potential as an investment. The auction was to be the catalyst for a reappraisal of the purpose of art, which would increasingly be seen as a vehicle for financial gain. As Robert Scull himself admitted, art would be judged not according to an artistic or aesthetic credo but by business principles:

> Art is supposed to be such a fine, toney, cultured thing, y'know, and suddenly people are bidding wildly like it was a commodity just like any other. And I think at Parke Bernet, that's art without the floss of culture. Over there it is hard, cold money and business and, man, over there you've gotta write a check out. There's no fooling around and talking about the aesthetics of art. There they just talk about the money of art.
>
> (Robert Scull, originally said in 1973, quoted in Kirschenbaum 1979: 52)

Hughes would say that the nullity Baudrillard identified is inevitable when art is judged and produced primarily with profit and commercial considerations in mind. In such a scenario, art comes to be "stripped of everything but its market value" (Hughes in Chang and Hughes 2008). Since art is credited on financial terms, price comes to take on greater symbolic value, so that the greater the price, the better the art. Price creates a celebrity around the art, makes it enter into the popular apprehension and makes it desirable. Damian Hirst's *For the Love of God*, a platinum cast of a human skull encrusted with 8,601 diamonds, is given celebrity and significance primarily because of its $100 million price (Graw 2009: 36–38).[4] The symbolic significance of this price is in its ability to 'compel' us to accept Hirst as an artist of reckoning. He must be, since his work can command such high prices. The price functions to "strike you blind so that you can't make your own judgments" and to limit one's ability to judge the art on anything other than financial criteria (Hughes in Chang and Hughes 2008).

Hughes does not deny that money has always played a role in art, but his thesis is that while it may have played *a* role, it is now *the* role. While the art produced in the past *might* have yielded a profit,[5] his suggestion is that profit was not *the* motive or purpose of art. Any profit occurred not by intent, but by accident. Now, profit is *the* key motive: It occurs not by accident but by intent and is the initial motivator, the inciting event and primary force behind the development and production of art.

It would of course be folly to unquestioningly and uncritically take the views of a single art critic and historian, even one with Hughes's gravitas and respect. Yet Hughes is not alone. The English art critic John Berger made similar suggestions regarding the impact of the market in his 1972 documentary series *Ways of Seeing*, predating the Scull auction by a year and Hughes by 36 years. Basing his documentary on a Marxist narrative[6] that was in part a response to the traditional views of art presented by Kenneth Clark in his earlier documentary series *Civilisation*, Berger noted that a work by Leonardo had "acquired a kind of new impressiveness. . . not because of what it shows . . .. . .[but] because of its market value" (John Berger in Dibb and Berger 1972: Episode 1). By 1989, the market shift had become so pronounced that Whitney Biennial[7] curators Richard Armstrong, Richard Marshall and Lisa Phillips were noting that "wealth is the only agreed-upon arbiter of value" and that "capitalism has overtaken contemporary art, quantifying and reducing it to the status of a commodity" (in Velthuis 2008: 307). Since then, in an echo of Hughes's thesis, the cultural critic James Panero has said "the point of sale, rather than the point of creation . . . [has come] to take precedence in determining the primary meaning for certain works of art" so that price has taken on a "more prominent concern in evaluating all works of art" (Panero 2009: 27). The art historian Isabelle Graw has also identified "the market's increased power of definition over what is regarded as a meaningful work of art" so that "economic data" are now "confused with artistic achievement" (Art Forum 2008: 294 and Graw 2009: 19).[8] The market, once "viewed as a necessary means of making sadly inevitable financial transactions", had changed "by the dawn of the twenty-first century . . . to the status of an end in itself" (Graw 2009: 57). The view that the market determines artistic value is not confined to 'quixotic' art historians and critics. The art market's 'doyen', Sotheby's Tobias Meyer, infamously lauded the role of the market when he said that the "best art is the most expensive, because the market is so smart" (in Panero 2009: 29).

The financial paradigm by which art is measured has resonated and imposed its methods across a number of aspects of contemporary art. Market and financial dominance even affects the very language of art. This was the vision of the future that concerned the art historian Leo Steinberg, who as early as 1968 was lamenting the increasing encroachment of business aims, methods and language into the world of what was then called avant-garde art:

> Avant-garde art . . . is for the first time associated with big money. And this is because its occult aims and uncertain future have been successfully translated into homely terms. For far-out modernism we can now read 'speculative growth stock'; for apparent quality, 'market attractiveness', and for an adverse change of taste, 'technical obsolescence'. A feat of language to absolve a change of attitude. Art is not, after all, what we thought it was; in the broadest sense it is hard cash. The whole of art, its growing tip included, is assimilated to familiar values. Another decade, and we shall have mutual funds based on securities in the form of pictures held in bank vaults.
>
> (Steinberg in Stallabrass 2004: 100)

Hughes's lament is the realisation of Steinberg's warning. While Steinberg's mutual funds of art do seem to have come to pass, Hughes and others would say that the financial paradigm and association with "big money" has made its presence felt in other ways, including in the way art is produced, the way art is experienced and the calculus by which art is judged.

8.3.2 The dominance of predatory forces?

What has happened to contemporary art, and can we account for it using a Veblenian construct? The 'weeping' by Hughes and others regarding the state of contemporary art would suggest that the production of great art is incompatible with capitalism. The underlying notion is that capitalism and its profit-seeking mandates produce art that is barren, without purpose, colour or depth.

Such a notion has far earlier antecedents than the likes of Hughes. Indeed, it is a theme raised in works by those who adhere to Marxist philosophies. For example,

Marx's notion of *alienation*, referring to the loss of control one has over one's life resulting from the loss of control over one's labour, was used by William Morris in his 1884 work *Art and Socialism* to account for the deleterious effects of capitalism upon art. Marx described alienation as the "mutilating [of] the labourer into a fragment of a man" that "degrade[s] him to the level of an appendage of a machine" (Marx in Solomon 1973: 40–41). The result is that the act of labour becomes a "hated toil", so that alienation "destroy[s] every remnant of charm in . . . work" (Marx in Solomon 1973: 40–41). For Morris, "art is man's expression of his joy in labour", what Marx referred to as 'charm' (Morris in Solomon 1973: 85). But alienation means that this joy is lost, rendering capitalism "incompatible with the existence of healthy art" (Morris in Solomon 1973: 84). The capitalist sees this lack of joy in labour and considers it "natural, inevitable, and on the whole desirable" (Morris in Solomon 1973: 84). The socialist, on the other hand, "sees in this obvious lack of art a *disease* peculiar to modern civilisation and hurtful to humanity" (Morris in Solomon 1973: 84, his italics; see also Upchurch 2005).

In the 1960s, the Austrian Marxist and art historian Ernst Fischer espoused a line of analysis, also based on the idea of alienation, that mirrors Morris somewhat. Fischer argued that capitalism "is not . . . a social force that is well-disposed to art or that promotes art" (Fischer 1964: 51). On the contrary, "capitalism turned everything into a commodity" (Fischer 1964: 49). The pre-capitalist worker was an artisan who had control over his product and held a direct relationship with the consumer of his goods. By contrast, the worker in the capitalist era produces goods anonymously, and his *commoditised* outputs are "swallowed up in the competitive flood and carried away into uncertainty" (Fischer 1964: 49). Fischer considered that the impact of this impersonal market would be an increase in alienation, where the fruits of a worker's labour are subjected more and more to the laws of the impersonal market (Fischer 1964: 49). Art was not immune to this change, and the impact of "capitalist competitive forces" soon did away with the system of arts patronage based on a personal and direct relationship between the artist and patron (Fischer 1964: 49). As a consequence, the artist was no longer subjected to the whims of a known patron with whom he can interact but to the faceless market and its "laws of competition" (Fischer 1964: 49). The result is an artist transformed into a "commodity producer" (Fischer 1964: 49). In an echo of Veblen's idea of social status attainment, Fischer claims that "insofar as the average capitalist needs art at all, he sees it as an embellishment of his private life or as a good investment" (Fischer 1964: 51).

Another important Marxist approach was outlined by the art historian Clement Greenberg in his seminal 1939 essay *Avant-Garde and Kitsch.* Greenberg's central assertion is that 'kitsch', the 'poorer' cousin of the superior forms of art represented by 'avant-garde', is a product of the capitalist "industrial revolution" (Greenberg 1939: 11). While avant-garde pursuits result in superior works, like a poem by "T. S Eliot", kitsch is "mechanical and operates by formulas", leading to 'inferior' outputs like a "Tin Pan Alley" song (Greenberg 1939: 5–6, 12). Unlike avant-garde art, which requires time for contemplation and understanding, the producer of kitsch "predigests art for the spectator" so that it can be enjoyed "without effort" (Greenberg 1939: 16–17, 19). This relative immediacy of enjoyment makes kitsch more attractive to the newly urbanised labouring masses that "did not win the leisure and comfort necessary" to enjoy avant-garde art and traditional cultural pursuits (Greenberg 1939: 12). As such, the 'snap' appeal of kitsch means that it is more appealing to a time-poor mass than more demanding and 'superior' avant-garde art. But the larger mass of consumers for kitsch output and the relative ease by which it is produced means that it is also more likely to result in "enormous profits", especially as compared with avant-garde. These profits become "a source of temptation to the avant-garde" artist to switch to the production of "ersatz culture" (Greenberg 1939: 12). Indeed, many of the avant-garde practitioners fail to resist the financial temptation, and the result is a loss for art (Greenberg 1939: 13).

Clearly, at least some of the developments laid out by Hughes could be explained using a Marxian approach. But is it possible to account for the trajectory of contemporary art on Veblenian foundations? Veblen was clearly influenced by Marx, a point made in Chapter 5. However, despite these influences, a Veblenian-based analysis would proceed from a different point and along a different path, being framed not in terms such as alienation but in evolutionary terms, and in particular using the frequently cited duality between workmanship and predation.

As was noted in previous chapters, Veblen considered human social and economic development to have occurred over four broad periods. These periods are marked by the to and fro between workmanship and predation, and the ability of one or the other to assert itself more fully in the development of the institutions that guide society. When predation dominates, the organisation of large-scale machine production is designed to fit with the motivation and needs of the predatory class who control it. In the Veblenian apprehension, it is a predatory capitalist leisure class who control the tools of production. Their goals and aims are wealth accumulation and the quest for profit. Other pursuits, in particular industrial efficiency, are relegated in favour of financial gain. Indeed, where industrial efficiency threatens the potential for financial gain, Veblen's businessmen may even ruthlessly and willingly 'sabotage' the system so as to maintain financial advantage. The imposing scale of modern industry is such that its pecuniary methods and purpose are cast upon all aspects of societal organisation and function, including those that do not lend themselves readily or directly to the adoption of newer technologies and techniques. As was shown in Chapter 7, even seemingly 'insulated' industries come to be infected by the mores of the predatory capitalist age. Importantly, however, this state of affairs, this way of viewing things, becomes the 'natural' way of seeing things. As Veblen noted, even the engineers, putatively guided by workmanship, come to appreciate efficiency not in technical but in pecuniary terms (see Chapter 7). To view things otherwise simply goes against 'common sense'.

Similarly, Veblenian analysis of consumption considers the role of a good in terms of its serving predatory or workmanship needs. A good may serve both workmanship and predation, and some goods that begin life with a workmanship role may become infected with predatory inclinations.[9] Thus, with Veblen, consumption is understood by appreciating that it has a social function, including the desire to display and maintain one's position and rank. Our tastes and desires and our final consumption decisions are determined by these social requirements, which are in turn forged by the interplay between workmanship and predation. Importantly, in a society where predatory forces dominate, our modes of consumption would bend to predatory/ceremonial needs.

Moving from this, the developments that have occurred in the case of contemporary art appear to suggest that the period in question is one where predatory forces have proven to be more dominant. The imposition of the financial paradigm and the seemingly amplified ceremonial role of art allude to such a predatory situation.[10] The question is how to determine whether the period referred to by Hughes is in fact one where predatory forces have come to dominate.

During periods of predatory dominance, we would expect less wealth and income equality. This is because, just as the predatory-dominated barbarian era saw a leisure class control the booty and outputs of production and claim an unequal share of output, a modern period of predation would see the modern leisure class claiming an increasingly greater share of society's income and wealth. Therefore, one way to determine whether predatory forces have become more assertive over the period in question would be to consider measures of equality and the distribution of wealth and income. If predation has indeed come to dominate, we would find the share of income and wealth for those at the top to have risen. On the other hand, if workmanship has dominated, then these shares would be more equalised.

Income and wealth shares could also be used to offer a more 'mainstream' explanation. According to such a mainstream view, in times where the distribution of wealth and income is more equal, we would expect the disposable income and resources available for expenditure on luxuries such as art to be lower, and so prices for art would fall. When it is less equal, wealth is concentrated in fewer people, and so the reverse is true. Moving from this, the dominance of finance in art and art's rising prices would be explained as the result of a society that has experienced such a shift in income and wealth distributions. With wealth skewed so that it is in the hands of a relative few, the ability to lavish expensive works of art on oneself is increased.

Such a mainstream explanation need not contravene or compete with a Veblenian analysis and could be conceived as upholding it. For, as mentioned, such a shift in wealth and income equality might be interpreted as a shift in the dominance of the twin forces that shape society. Further, a Veblenian analysis could add to a mainstream analysis, since it is one thing to suggest that increased wealth shares for those at the top increases their ability to consume art, but this does not answer *why* they would want to purchase the art in the first place. To make a point made by Veblen and highlighted in Chapter 6, on its own, this view could be said to amount to a taxonomical analysis, for it does not seek to determine the cultural and social factors or forces that impact upon and determine the consumption of art. In the Veblenian model, these social forces include, among other things, the desire for accumulation and the ceremonial need for status attainment.

Given this, consider Figures 8.1 to 8.5, which provide various measures of equality over the course of the twentieth and early twenty-first centuries in

Australia, the United States and the United Kingdom.[11] These measures include the Gini and Pareto-Lorenz coefficients,[12] and the share of income enjoyed by the top one, five and 10 per cent of income earners. On the basis of the Gini coefficient (Figure 8.1), each of these three countries has seen a trend towards greater income inequality since the 1960s and 1970s, a finding reinforced by the Pareto-Lorenz coefficient data shown in Figure 8.2. Examination of equality through the share of income enjoyed by the top one, five and 10 per cent of income earners, shown in Figures 8.3, 8.4 and 8.5,[13] supports the findings in Figures 8.1 and 8.2. These indicators suggest that Australia, the United Kingdom and the United States have seen a 'skewing' of the income distribution, so that those at the top now claim a larger share of the 'prize'. In each of these three countries the post-Second World War period was one of a "Great Compression", a term developed by Goldin and Margo (1992) to describe the period of wage structure equalisation that occurred from the 1940s where the "rich got dramatically poorer while workers got considerably richer" (Goldin and Margo 1992: 1; Krugman 2006: paragraph 6). But by the 1960s, the compression began to unravel, and in its place was a period of "widening", where income shares began to skew in favour of the richer members of

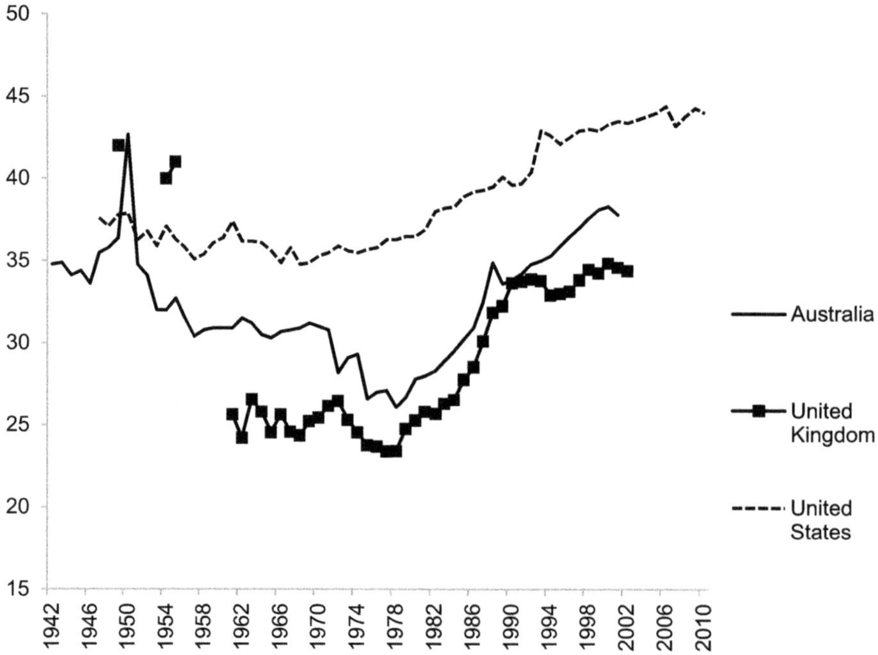

Figure 8.1 Gini coefficients (%) for the United States (since 1947), United Kingdom (since 1949) and Australia (since 1942)

Source: US Census Bureau Current Population Survey, Annual Social and Economic Supplements, Historical Tables. Retrieved 28 June 2012 from http://www.census.gov/hhes/www/income/data/historical/inequality and UNU–WIDER

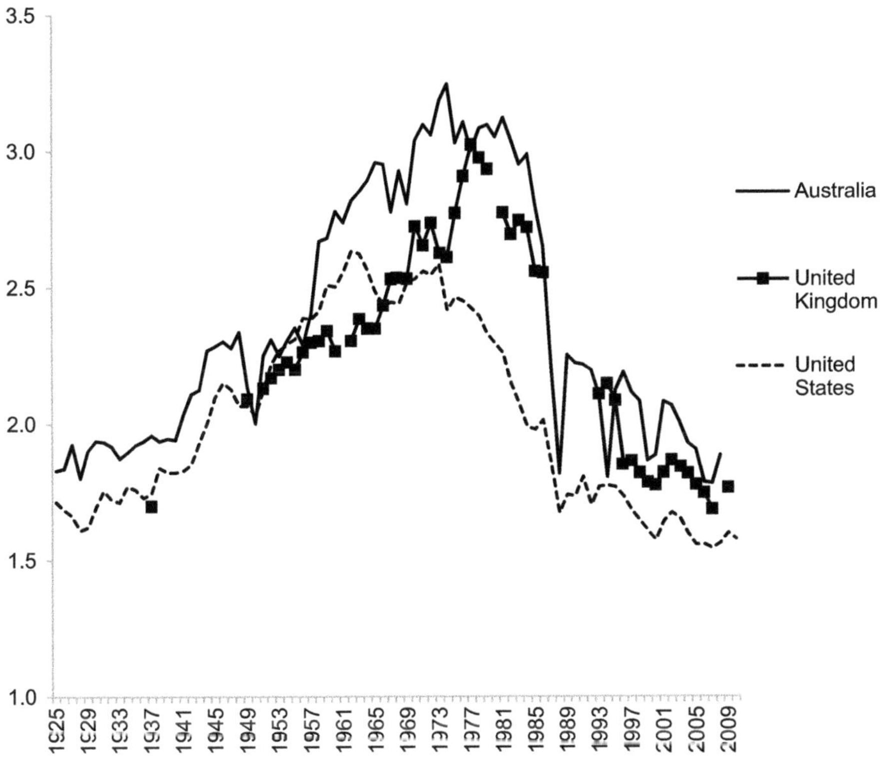

Figure 8.2 Pareto Lorenz coefficients for the United States (since 1952), United Kingdom (since 1937) and Australia (since 1926)

Source: Alvaredo, Facundo, Anthony B. Atkinson, Thomas Piketty and Emmanuel Saez, The World Top Incomes Database. Retrieved 28 June 2012 from http://g-mond.parisschoolofeconomics.eu/topincomes

society, so that by the 2000s "the concentration of income at the top had reached levels not seen since 1929" (Goldin and Margo 1992: 1; Krugman 2012: paragraph 1).[14]

In Veblenian terms, the shift in income equalities over the period could be interpreted as predation and its institutions of ownership and the leisure class asserting a greater influence. But shifting income distribution in favour of the rich is only one manifestation of a society that is predatory. If indeed the shift in income and wealth measures referred to earlier represents an increase in the strength of predatory forces, then we would expect a recalculation in many if not all aspects of society, so that they increasingly align with a predatory mind-set. Importantly, for an analysis of art, it means that art too would be subjected to the predatory paradigm, so that it too comes to be grasped and judged through the prism of predatory forces and its 'client' institutions of ownership and the leisure class.[15]

Indeed, the shift that Hughes and others say has occurred in contemporary art is one where artistic mores have been replaced with those of profit, which is

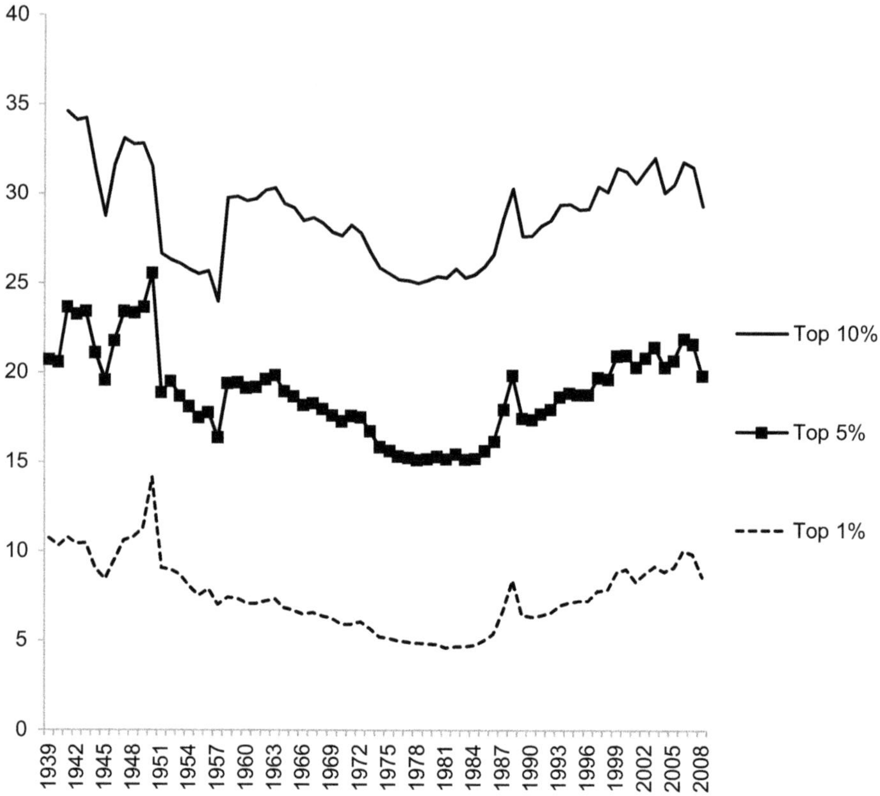

Figure 8.3 Share of income in Australia by the top 10, 5 and 1 per cent of income earners since 1939

Source: Alvaredo, Facundo, Anthony B. Atkinson, Thomas Piketty and Emmanuel Saez, The World Top Incomes Database. Retrieved 28 June 2012 from http://g-mond.parisschoolofeconomics.eu/topincomes

indicative of predatory forces. Just as capitalist large-scale production is organised not to yield maximum industrial efficiency and optimal community welfare but rather profit, so too contemporary art is now produced to achieve profit, not artistic innovation or the optimal 'artistic welfare' of the community. 'Artistic efficiency' has been discarded (or at the very least taken second place) in favour of art produced to accord with the financial paradigm of a modern predatory capitalist society. The profit-oriented market is now all-powerful in matters of art, so that:

> it is neither the official academies – certainly not the art schools – nor the Church, but rather the institutions of the market that exert the dominating influence on art. The market's power is acknowledged without question. . . . You cannot work outside of, and in opposition to, the market because unlike the academies, it is universal in its influence.
>
> (Timms 2004: 48–49)

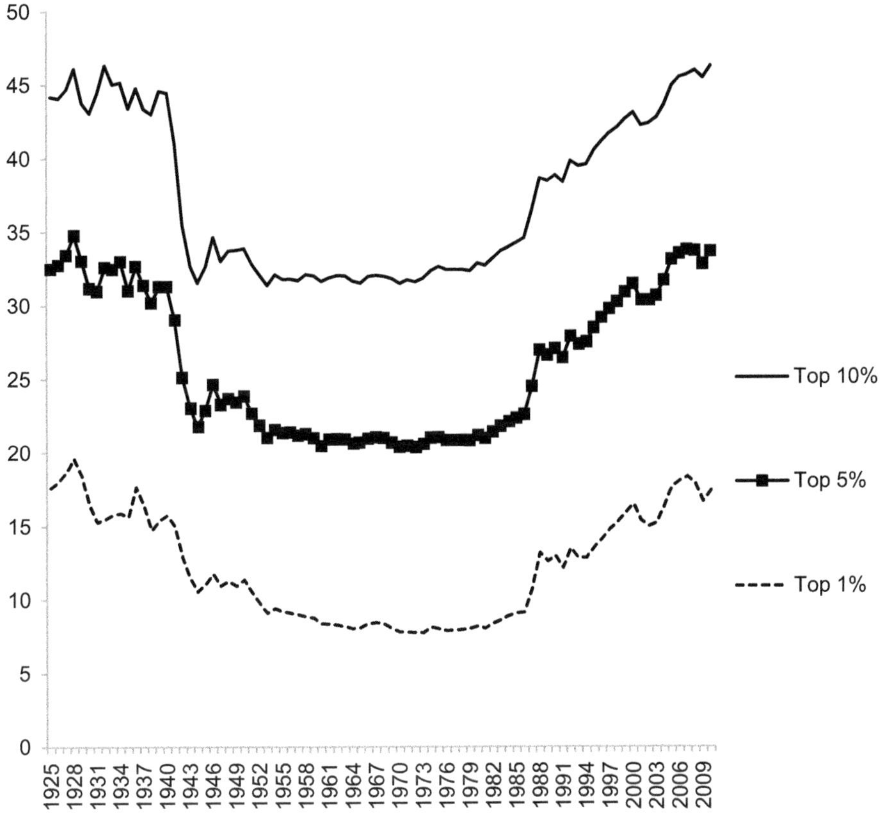

Figure 8.4 Share of income in the United States by the top 10, 5 and 1 per cent of income earners since 1925

Source: Alvaredo, Facundo, Anthony B. Atkinson, Thomas Piketty and Emmanuel Saez, The World Top Incomes Database. Retrieved 28 June 2012 from http://g-mond.parisschoolofeconomics.eu/topincomes

The dominance of predation in current society means that the human endeavour of art is no longer driven primarily to answer questions such as: Why am I here?; What is my purpose?; or, What does this all mean? Instead, art's "job is to sit on the wall and get more expensive" (Hughes in Chang and Hughes 2008). This is in essence the basis of the Hughes argument, that art has been increasingly produced for the purposes of profit, presumably to enable greater wealth accumulation. In Veblenian terms, the leisure class and ownership institutions have made an increasing impact on the development of art, so that art's role is now primarily to serve predatory, not workmanship institutions.

However, as mentioned elsewhere, including in Chapters 6 and 7, it is the case that workmanship and predation are fellow travellers, and neither is ever fully banished. The difference lies in the level and power by which these forces permeate society and, hence, the fabric of art. In the current scheme, it would

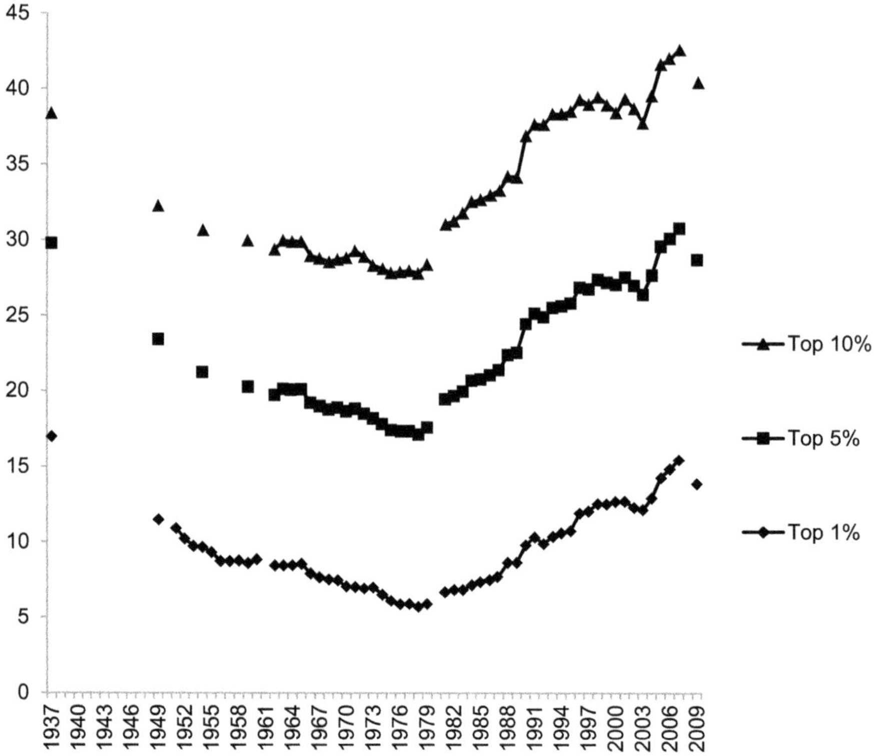

Figure 8.5 Share of income in the United Kingdom by the top 10, 5 and 1 per cent of income earners since 1937

Source: Alvaredo, Facundo, Anthony B. Atkinson, Thomas Piketty and Emmanuel Saez, The World Top Incomes Database. Retrieved 28 June 2012 from http://g-mond.parisschoolofeconomics.eu/topincomes

seem that art is dominated by the predatory, but with social evolution it might one day be driven by workmanship. Indeed, it is probable that predatory forces held sway over the development of art in the past, an assertion that could be easily derived from a Veblenian reading of the passage by Timms.[16] Thus, while Hughes laments the trajectory of contemporary art as though such a thing had never before occurred, a Veblenian view would appreciate that art has always been subjected to both predatory and workmanship forces, suggesting that even in times past, art may have been subjected to overt predation.

In reference to this latter point, consider an example which is admittedly very simple but which nonetheless serves to illustrate the point. In *Signs of Change* (1888), William Morris complained of the deleterious effects that industrial capitalism was wreaking on Victorian society and art, claiming that the "world is everywhere growing uglier and more commonplace" (Morris 1888 71). Could this increased ugliness be attributable to an increase in predation? The general apprehension of Victorian Britain is indeed of a society that was brutal, unfair and cruel, as any reading of Dickens would affirm. On this simple basis, it seems that nineteenth century Britain[17] was a society directed by predation, and this may at least partly explain Morris's lament. It also implies a constant presence for the forces of predation and, further, indicates that predatory dominance in art has precursors to the current contemporary art period.

While predation has a constant presence in society, and hence, art, the nature of institutional evolution means that the way in which it appears would be amended to fit within the evolving institutional scheme. In section 8.2, it was shown that during the Italian Renaissance, art was subjected to predatory forces that manipulated it, so that art's primary role was to display rank and earn honour for its possessor. Thus, while the investment role of art may not have been present, the art that was produced during the period nonetheless operated to serve predatory desires. But amended institutions mean that the modern leisure class must make its predatory desires real through modern institutional incarnations.

Take the institution of ownership. Entry to this institution was once limited to booty from raids and wars, aristocratic inheritance or participation in priestly duties. But the modern form of this institution means that it is now possible to gain entry through other means, including commercial ventures and the quest for profits. The modern desire for art as an investment would thus be envisaged as part of a recalculation of the ancient institution of ownership, a predatory institution that has broadened its means of accumulation from the sacerdotal and martial to also include commercial outlets.

It would seem, therefore, that it is neither novel, nor without precedent, for art to be subjected to the service of predatory forces. That contemporary art is subjected to predatory forces would need to be appreciated within the context of a broader social evolution that has, in the current capitalist scheme, seen predatory elements come to the fore. However, returning to the point made earlier and elsewhere, the continued presence of workmanship suggests that even in such periods all would not be 'lost', and workmanship might be able to manifest itself. For even predatory societies like Victorian Britain produced great artists like Morris and Dickens, both of whom produced what, in the Veblenian construct, would be considered art that aligns with, is driven by and is produced according to workmanship.

8.3.3 The manifestation of predatory forces in contemporary art

It was contended earlier that what has occurred in the world of contemporary art could be appreciated within the Veblenian paradigm as the result of a period where predatory forces have gained an upper hand. To determine whether predatory forces have indeed usurped workmanship, income and wealth equality indicators were considered. These indicators suggested that the period in question could be construed as one where predation is stronger than workmanship.

If contemporary art is indeed subject to predatory forces, the next challenge is to determine how these forces might appear and impact upon it. There are a number of possible ways this could occur, but in the interests of brevity, I will limit my analysis to three areas. The first of these is to consider the way in which museums and galleries have responded to the new financial paradigm. I then outline how participants in the contemporary art world have sought to manipulate prices, which I bring back to a Veblenian account of intangible assets. Finally, I outline how the canons of art come to be shaped to fit predatory paradigms.

The 'traditional defenders' of art and the financial paradigm

If the situation described by Hughes and others was simply between private buyers and artists, then we might reject the idea that the art world had changed. The situation would instead be caricatured as a case of 'Elmer Gantry' type artists 'fleecing' rich businessmen who are too stupid to know good art from bad: in other words, a case of the occasional philistine businessmen falling prey to the charms of clever (con) artists. If this were the case, then we would probably find the financial view of art limited to these parties. However, that a new predatory financial standard has been more widely adopted is evidenced by the change in the goals, strategies and methods of reputable museums and galleries.

Once, the museums and galleries would be described as the 'defenders' of artistic values, basing their collections not on market value or popular whim but on artistic credibility. However, many museums and galleries now choose to sell pieces from their traditional collections in order to obtain a single high-priced piece of contemporary art (Panero 2009: 29). The aim of such activity seems to be the desire by museums to base their collections on art that is popular or has celebrity. The celebrity surrounding these pieces enables museums to mount exhibitions that provide high financial returns.

The celebrity view of art is visible in the attitude of the former Guggenheim director Thomas Krens. Krens has suggested that "museums and cultural institutions have an obligation to be populist institutions" (Thomas Krens in Chang and Hughes 2008). Krens is noted for introducing exhibitions based on works by fashion designers such as Giorgio Armani (Vogel 1999) and opening the Guggenheim to showcase the wares of industrial firms. The latter led to the "Art of the Motorcycle" show, which exhibited the two-wheeled machines of BMW and Honda, among others (Green 2005).

Krens is heir to a populist transformation in museum culture that commenced with the 1967 appointment of Thomas Hoving as the director of the Metropolitan Museum of Art in New York (the Met). Hoving is credited with the creation of the 'blockbuster' exhibit, designed to draw crowds and transform the Met from an impenetrable "elitist, stiff [and] gray" organisation, considered the plaything of the privileged, into an institution with wider community engagement (Hoving in Kennedy 2009: paragraph 43).

Others, however, have described the Hoving-Krens change in less than flattering terms. For example, Krens's New York Met counterpart, Phillippe De Montebello, has described the pursuit of populism and the quest for profit as a "betrayal of public trust" (in Klebnikov 2001: paragraph 2). In its quest for populism and profit, the Guggenheim had resorted to exhibiting not art, but entertainment. In shades of

Greenberg's kitsch/avant-garde divide, De Montebello described entertainment as the "rapid gratification of an immediate desire", adding that in his view institutions like the Met and the Guggenheim "are definitely not in the entertainment business" (in Klebnikov 2001: paragraph 11). Hughes has recast the Hoving-Krens view into more 'direct' terms, saying that "to popularise the museum is a euphemistic and more palatable way of saying" that the "market transforms the museum into a commercial model" (Hughes in Chang and Hughes 2008).

The adoption of a commercial paradigm in the museum world has been implemented beyond the boundaries of New York City. Since Krens, many other museum directors have happily adopted the Guggenheim approach. It is a point noted by the arts journalist Tyler Green in a scathing summation of the Krens commercial legacy:

> The Krens Era showed that museum directors could wander far from the traditionally ethical as long as their boards were compliant. While many of Mr Krens' peers copied his "innovations," many more watched and said nothing. The Association of Art Museum Directors – a strong candidate for the most spineless, useless industry association in America – never sanctioned, censured or formally criticized Mr Krens in any way. Mr. Krens' most lasting legacy is this: He made the building of synergies between non-profit art museums and for-profit corporations acceptable to his peers.
>
> (Green 2005: paragraphs 2–3)

A thought game might help to better consider the implications of the Hoving-Krens view and contextualise the concerns expressed by Green, Hughes and De Montebello. The Hoving-Krens model suggests that artists who do not receive popular praise would be rejected or placed lower in ranking in favour of artists who do. In the modern scheme, popular praise is based on the ability to earn income for the museum. But popular praise may have little to do with artistic merit, and indeed it might be the reverse. Consider a case I am more familiar with, namely, music. It is undoubtedly so that for many the music of Madonna is preferred to and is hence more popular than Mozart. A quick glance at the number of viewers of a Madonna or Mozart YouTube clip confirms this, with a Madonna clip easily receiving more viewers in one day than a Mozart clip receives over its lifetime. Does this mean that the musical equivalent of the galleries and museums, such as the conservatoriums of music, should base their activities on the works of Madonna? Few would answer in the affirmative, and yet this seems the inevitable end of the Krens-Hoving view.

Of course, despite the 'brouhaha' from the likes of Hughes, De Montebello and Green, it should be recognised that there may be cases where artistic merit and popular praise and profitability meet, where commercial desires and artistic principles coincide. Something may be popular and yet also artistically rich. The point, however, is that in a world where the predatory paradigm is asserted, popular praise and the ability to earn income trumps artistic merit; the former is the factor upon which museums make their collection and exhibition choices. Importantly, however, in cases where a disconnect exists between popularity and artistic merit, predatory realities mean that popular praise and the ability to earn profits for the museum would be the dominant factor. To reiterate a point made elsewhere, pecuniary efficiency replaces technical or industrial efficiency as the 'common sense' definition of efficiency, so that profit-minded museum directors adopt a financial paradigm by which to value and judge art and make their exhibition and collection choices.

However, one final point needs making. Earlier, it was noted that Thomas Hoving sought to turn the Met from an elitist organisation to one attractive to a mass public, and the Krens agenda is seen as heir to this change. The suggestion by Hughes and others is that because of this the museum has become commercial; in a Veblenian paradigm, it is seen as the predatory marking its presence in the museum. However, it is possible that the transformation of the museum has merely seen one set of predatory flavours replace another. Hoving is right, in that, traditionally, such bodies were seen as elitist. If so, it suggests that the museums and galleries may have long been subject to predatory forces and a leisure class that predates both Hoving and Krens. This older form of the leisure class may have operated according not to profit but to other predatory desires. The Hoving-Krens revolution could thus be viewed as a force that helped replace one set of older predatory archetypes with a modern capitalist version. The clamour that is heard regarding the increasing commercialisation of the museum, could, in my view, thus be appreciated as the cries from an older, fading leisure class and its 'outdated' predatory traditions being cast aside to make room for a newer, profit-oriented, capitalist replacement.

Inflating through the manipulation of intangible assets

A corollary of the predatory financial paradigm and the quest for profit is the incentive for both artist and collector to undertake measures to raise the price of art. There are a number of ways in which this is achieved. One is by manipulating the prices obtained for art, either at auction or through a dealer. Artists, auction houses and dealers have been known to employ intermediaries like public relations or advertising firms to build an artist's or an individual piece's profile through such things as marketing or advertising strategies designed to create a 'buzz' around an artist or work (Graw 2009: 53). Such a strategy was used by the Sculls at their seminal 1973 auction (Rose 1973: 80).

Prices can also be manipulated and inflated by associating a work or artist with a highly respected museum or gallery. Association with esteemed bodies lends the work gravitas. It confirms its place as serious art. Stephen Cohen, owner of Damien Hirst's *The Physical Impossibility of Death in the Mind of Someone Living*, otherwise known as Hirst's 'Shark', probably had this at least partly in mind when he loaned the work to the Met (Smith 2007). Some may claim that the work's credibility is based not on artistic grounds but on its notoriously high price tag, said by some to be $12 million (Thompson 2008). But association with the Met serves to refute such assertions and reinforce the market's proclamation that the work is to be taken as serious art, making it an object worthy to covet.

Recall from Chapter 7 that in Veblen's theory of business enterprise, capital value was said to comprise the stock of machines but also the value of intangible assets. These intangibles include such things as good will and reputation. By bolstering intangibles through activities such as advertising and public relations, firms can increase their capitalisation value. Veblen characterised intangibles as having a ceremonial origin, and so when artists and collectors adopt the businessman's intangible asset strategies and seek to inflate the price of art through such means, we see ceremonialism and predation in art. Alberto Mugrabi, a wealthy collector whose family holds a collection of Warhols, second only in number to the Warhol Museum in Pittsburgh (Konigsberg 2009), has openly admitted to the art as investment view and to 'supporting' artists and the value of his art investments by "promoting them" (Alberto Mugrabi in Chang and Hughes 2008). Mugrabi sees this as a way of "controlling" his investments and "influence[ing] other people into liking the art" (Alberto Mugrabi in Chang and Hughes 2008). The practice is also recognised by the respected New York art dealer Richard Feigen, who has noted that a "menu of certain favoured artists has gotten expensive because they have been promoted", and argues that the resulting recognition "has very little to do with how important they are [as artists]" (Richard Feigen in Chang and Hughes 2008). While not employing Veblenian terms, Feigen's analysis and Mugrabi's tactics amount to the manipulation of intangibles as a means to raise the price of art.

Exploiting intangible assets is not an activity limited to artists or rich collectors, but has also been used by museums and galleries. A key method used by museums and galleries is to sell the advantage associated with their own 'brand'. As an illustration, there is now an arm of the Louvre planned for Abu Dhabi as well as multiple Guggenheims already dotted around Europe, with another planned for Abu Dhabi. By selling the right to use their brand, museums lend credibility to a collection that might otherwise be considered below par. Similarly, museums and galleries can lend their goodwill to build the reputation or credibility of a single artist or work. The Hirst *Shark* loan to the New York Met is just such a case. The esteem of these institutions and the potential for benefit gives the museums and galleries the power and incentive to seek a payment for the privilege of association. It is not difficult to see that the collection and exhibition choices made by museums could come to be based not on artistic distinction but on the ability of collectors and artists to pay for an exhibition.[18] Museums now have it within their scope the ability to impart the gravitas associated with their good name for a price. Those who can afford to pay get a space in the museum and the benefit of its reputation, whereas others are 'shut out'.[19] In this way, the methods of business enter and dominate the practical vernacular of the traditional establishments of art.

The financial canons of art

The imposition of the predatory element in contemporary art stretches beyond the museum, artist and collector and affects the canons of taste and views regarding artistic merit in the wider society. If the auction houses and dealers and their awe-inspiring prices are not enough to convince of the merit of particular artists or work, then the respect that cultural institutions still hold serves to reinforce the predatory market view of art and challenges and undermines the ability of those who reject or are suspicious of the market's ability to determine quality. If a work is housed within the walls of a respected institution such as the Guggenheim or the Tate, then it challenges the assertions of those who argue that the work is artistically base. Damien Hirst's *Shark* must be great art, because the Met has deemed it worthy to place within its walls. Collectors may seek the imprimatur and assistance of respected cultural institutions to elevate the price of works in their collections, but the effect is also is to make "choices for everyone by bringing the influence of their own taste into the museum" (Hughes in Chang and Hughes 2008).

Since the calculus upon which such collectors judge art is pecuniary, we would find that in time, abetted by the museums and galleries, the investment collectors impose their investment view of art on the wider public, so that the public too comes to judge art by a financial calculus. In their quest to exploit the advantage conferred to them by their intangible assets, museums become accomplices to savvy collectors and artists and cause a recalculation of artistic canons. In Veblenian terms, we see the canons of taste determined by an art 'leisure class' who are driven by 'predatory pecuniary' motives. The power of this class to determine the exhibit choices made by museums makes them the ultimate arbiters on matters of art. They are the canon setters with respect to artistic merit.

The effect of the new financial norm comes to be reflected in the very patterns and production choices of art, so that the topics and media of art affirm predatory pecuniary canons. As an illustration of this, the Australian art critic Peter Timms has noted that since the 1980s, Australian sculpture has experienced a renaissance. He attributes the resurgence not to artistic motivation but to increasing financial support provided by corporate interests to the sculptural medium, including a National Sculpture Prize funded by Macquarie Bank. To win such a competition, the sculptor would likely choose artistic themes and sculptural methods that serve "the interests of commercial institutions" (Timms 2004: 51). It is unlikely, for example, that we would find sculptures that pay homage to Marx winning praise from corporations like Macquarie Bank, and so it is unlikely that a sculptor would base his work on such subjects.[20]

It is a point recognised by Stallabrass too in reference to the increasing role that corporate collecting has played in art since 1945. Figures on the level of corporate collecting are difficult to determine, since many deals are undertaken in secret, but one 1990 study referenced by Stallabrass suggests that corporate collectors account for up to 30 per cent of all sales in New York (Stallabrass 2004: 128). It is probable that with the growth in corporate size and power since that time that this figure has shown some growth. Stallabrass notes that corporate collectors generally purchase art that is "congruent with the company image" and aligns with their view of the world (Stallabrass 2004: 127). In response, given the considerable share of the market taken by corporate collectors, artists produce works that reinforce and affirm the corporate view (Stallabrass 2004: 128; Timms 2004: 51). Corporate credos and whims now affect the pattern of art, but as Timms sardonically notes, for the purposes of artistic endeavour and progress, we should "question the extent to which we want to allow real-estate developers to determine the course of art practice" (Timms 2004: 51). Recast in Veblen's language, do we want art determined by those motivated by 'artistic efficiency' and workmanship or predatory financial effectiveness?

8.3.4 Developing an argument for public support

The discussion of the path of contemporary art suggests that it has developed to accord with a predatory paradigm. The question however is whether we can derive a rationale for public subsidy and support for art from this analysis.

One argument for support would be to provide a means for art to take place that is not subjected to or reliant on a market organised to service predatory institutions. The art that would be produced would be 'cocooned' from such predatory forces, so it could presumably be produced in accordance with artistic workmanship imperatives. At the very least, public support might moderate the predatory forces that operate in art. It would remove, for example, the financial imperative that sees museums falling for the 'charms' of the financial when choosing their collections and instead see them base their choices solely on artistic merit. Any decision to provide support or subsidy would presumably be constructed so that art would be produced to fulfil not financial imperatives but instead those of art: in more colourful Veblenian language, to have art that is produced to the beat of a workmanship and not a predatory drum.

This is admittedly a normative argument, a question of opinion by which we say that one form of art is preferable to another, that art that is financially 'inspired' is inferior to that produced for other reasons.[21] It is based on the idea that art should have certain characteristics that would not otherwise occur in the absence of support; that the measure of art should be based not on financial but on traditional artistic grounds, and that support would give 'oxygen' to allow such art activity to occur.[22]

This argument requires that we acquiesce to the idea that one can apply a 'scientific' eye to matters of art so that one can objectively determine whether one art is superior to another. But as Stallabrass notes, "there can be no pretence to scientific objectivity in any account of art" (Stallabrass 2004: 151). While Hughes, Panero, Graw, Rose and Steinberg are art historians and critics of high esteem whose views should be respected and taken seriously, it must be admitted that no analysis of art can be completely impartial or objective in the way that analysis of the function of light by physicists can be objective.[23] Others might see what Hughes considers to be barren art in different, positive terms; where Hughes sees 'pecuniary motive', others see 'industrial efficiency'. That said, it is not unreasonable to grant more authority to the views of those who have devoted their energies and developed an expertise in the history and matters of art; and as was shown earlier, whether one is a lover or hater of the output of contemporary art, few deny the increasing role of the market and financial decisions in art. As such, for the purposes of this work, let us defer to the expertise of writers such as Hughes and

Graw, and indeed the pronouncements of Tobias Meyer and Robert Scull, and take it as given that art now operates to a different, predatory, financial beat.

The case study presented here of contemporary art could readily be applied to many other fields of artistic pursuit. Replace contemporary art with music, with writing, with performance, with drama. Examples exist in each of these fields, to greater or lesser degrees, where the predatory profit motive could be said to have replaced the workmanship artistic motive. Consider what might occur when the primary purpose of the arts is to make a profit. In music, the lustrous sounds of an Igor Stravinsky would recede, and the resulting vacuum filled with the manufactured piffle of 'boy bands'. Absent the next wave of great French and Italian cinema, we are limited with the formulaic dross of Hollywood. Few would disagree that boy bands and the formulaic outputs of Hollywood are naked pursuits of profit, not artistry. But if unbridled profit continues to be the key driver, then this might be the future state of all art, whether visual, performing or otherwise. Support and subsidy for artistic pursuit might[24] allow the development of art and performing art that operates for artistic purposes.

However, one final caveat needs to be made before proceeding. As has been mentioned throughout, and indeed in this chapter, it is the case that social development is subject to both workmanship and predation. One or the other is never fully absent but is muted, and it is possible that that muted force will prove more assertive in the future. Consequently, even in predatory periods, workmanship is not fully banished, and, indeed, it plays a role in directing much of human effort. Thus it is possible that in the current predatory period great works of art could be produced even in the absence of public support. Consider that Hughes himself notes the presence of Robert Rauschenberg during the contemporary art period, an artist for whom he has expressed great respect and admiration (Hughes in Chang and Hughes 2008). And it is interesting to note that, at the height of Morris's predatory Victorian Britain, the pre-Raphaelites, a writer of the calibre and talent as the already mentioned Dickens, and indeed Morris himself, were able to flourish. Importantly, that persons in the form of Hughes, Graw and Panero exist at all suggests that there will also continue to be those who apply a workmanship eye to matters of art. Thus, it seems, it is *possible* even in periods of workmanship ebb and predatory amplification for great art to be produced and for it to be appreciated not in financial but in artistic terms. Public support would be thus be provided, it seems, not to *enable* great art to be produced but to *ensure* that great workmanship inspired art is produced during periods of predatory dominance.

8.4 Public support and ceremonial infection

The argument in favour of public support that was presented earlier suggests that public support and subsidy would be warranted if it enables the development of art and performing art that is driven by workmanship. The assumption behind this is that the design, operation and management of a support mechanism would be such that it promotes only artistic endeavours that are at their base motivated by artistic pursuit and merit, not profit, and that workmanship inclinations direct such schemes. However, consider the possibility that a programme notionally designed and initiated to support the arts comes to be driven not by workmanship but by predation. While the 'deleterious' effects of the profit motive might be quarantined, it is possible that art supported by and produced through public programmes would merely displace profit and enable other ceremonial imperatives to take its place. We should at the very least recognise this possibility and consider how it might play out.

Two possible routes for the entry of predatory/ceremonial flavours into public support for the arts will be considered. The first will be the possibly that public support becomes 'sullied' by predatory or ceremonial emulation. The second will be to consider that arts funding and support reflect the canons of those at the peak of society. In a world where the peak comprises a leisure class, art support merely and primarily confirms and makes real the tastes of the predatory leisure class. Of course, these two possibilities are by no means exhaustive, but serve as examples. It is however acknowledged that there may be other avenues through which predatory forces may manifest themselves.

8.4.1 Ceremonial emulation and national hierarchies

The first predatory 'fly in the ointment' to be considered is that of predatory emulation. As was shown in Chapter 6, predatory emulation causes individuals to act for their own self-regard, if necessary at the expense of the group. Predatory emulation, coupled with the ability to compare oneself with one's peers, is the root cause of activities such as conspicuous consumption, conspicuous waste and vicarious consumption. The ability to compare ourselves with others makes us copy and emulate those who are of higher social rank, and we adopt the behaviour and practices of our social betters in order to meet appropriate social standards and earn respect.

Now take this argument and carry it from the individual to the national or regional level, so that, just like individuals, nations and regions act through the motive of predatory emulation. Implied in this is that there exists a social rank of nations and regions, where lower-ranked nations and regions seek to mimic or emulate and adopt the practices of 'superior' or 'elite' nations and regions. Similarly, 'elite' nations and regions work to maintain their superior rank, to jealously guard their position against potential competitors.

In terms of public cultural policy, predatory emulation would affect the development of policies so that they are at least partly[25] crafted to improve or cement a nation or region's rank and status within the hierarchy. Its primary function is not for the sake of art but for the benefit of national or regional prestige. The choices as to which art forms to support are based on an ability to earn status, not artistic merit; and so, within cultural policy, we would find lower-ranked nations and regions adopting the cultural practices, copying the patterns of art and emulating the cultural activities of those considered the elite. Higher-ranked nations, on the other hand, develop cultural policies to ensure their status in the vanguard. Since the aim of such activities is to convey and earn status and advertise a nation or region's 'civilised' character, it is likely that supported cultural activities would be those that are conspicuous and ensure that the nation receives the proper acknowledgement. Since newer types of art are untested in terms of this ability, it means that arts funding would likely be directed to art forms with proven records in conveying status – in general, to the older, established arts.

If this is the case, if art support is designed not for the sake of art but to maintain a ceremonial face, then the argument in favour of support presented in the case study of contemporary art could be difficult to justify. For if public support designed to militate against art produced solely for profit comes instead to be dominated by other predatory institutions, we find that art is again 'slave' to the predatory, making the arguments developed in section 8.3 less compelling.

It is one thing to posit a theoretical possibility, but do examples exist of art policy driven by regional or national predatory emulation? To determine this, I will consider emulation between nations. As with individuals, we find that lower-ranked nations seek to adopt the cultural practices of those ranked higher. This approach implies a hierarchy, and requires that one outline which are the higher- and lower-ranked nations. As such, for the purposes of this analysis, it is assumed that the elite nations are those of the West. It should be noted that by elite it is not meant that Western nations are better or superior, and there is no implication that the West and its cultural and artistic traditions are superior to others. This qualification is offered not from some sense of political correctness or a desire to avoid effrontery but from a Veblenian perspective. For Veblen, hierarchies have little to do with being better or more able; on the contrary, they are simply a reflection of power. In his portrayal of the leisure class, Veblen showed that superiority stems from the power that accrues to that class from their stock of wealth.[26] The same measure of power from wealth can be applied to nations. Since, economically and culturally speaking, Western nations have dominated the course of economic and social development over the course of at least the past three hundred years, it seems logical that we define the nations of the West as the elite nations. In the Veblenian argot, the West comprises a 'leisure class' of nations.

If the West comprises the elite, then other, lower-ranked nations would seek to emulate the cultural traditions of the 'superior' West. Consider the case of opera and classical or symphonic music. Opera can be traced to around the sixteenth century and is said to have begun in Italy with Monteverdi's *Orfeo*. Its development occurred mostly in Germany and Italy, although France too has excellent examples of operatic work, particularly in the nineteenth century. As for symphonic music, its origins are in the Renaissance, in the 'consorts' of that period, a term used to describe a grouping of musicians. The consorts eventually evolved into the orchestras, and Monteverdi is again sometimes credited with the modern formalisation of these groupings when, around 1600, he dictated the exact number and type of instruments he wished to accompany his *Orfeo*.

Clearly, whatever the minute details of their origins, both opera and symphonic music are Western traditions. They are not out of place within Western nations, being merely a reflection of Western cultural canons.[27] Yet a host of non-Western nations have chosen to establish opera companies and symphony orchestras. It is not enough for these nations to enjoy an occasional or even regular tour by a Western-based company or orchestra; they go further and actually found opera companies and symphony orchestras of their own.

Take, for example, the nations of East Asia. Table 8.1 provides a list that I have compiled of East Asian nations that have companies that perform Western opera, while 8.2 gives a list of symphony orchestras.[28] The tables show that in some cases, these nations have multiple opera companies and symphony orchestras. How does one account for the presence of publicly funded Asian symphony orchestras and opera companies?

One explanation might attribute their existence to a Western colonial hangover. Opera companies and symphony orchestras are therefore the cultural remnants of former European masters. The musical and performance traditions of opera and symphonic music have been left behind in the same way that civic buildings were left behind. While this might (at least partly) explain the presence of publicly supported opera companies and symphony orchestras in places like Singapore and Hong Kong, it fails in countries that, like Thailand and South Korea, had no Western colonial past.

Another way to account for the existence of Asian opera companies and symphony orchestras that can be applied more commonly is by use of the idea that cultural policy is driven by ceremonial emulation and the related desire to earn status. One kind of analysis built on this platform would acknowledge the major economic advancement experienced by many Asian nations during the late twentieth and early twenty-first centuries. To display their improved wealth and claim their rightful rank and position, these nations adopt the appropriate cultural markers. Since the world is one of Western economic and cultural hegemony, it is the cultural and artistic traditions of the West that serve this purpose; and if the purpose of such cultural policies is to convey esteem, it makes sense for nations to develop cultural policies that earn esteem in the most conspicuous and high manner. Opera and symphonic music serve this purpose very well.

Table 8.1 Western opera companies in Asian countries

Country	*Opera Company*
Hong Kong	• Opera Hong Kong
Japan	• Fujiwara Opera
	• New National Theatre Tokyo
	• Nihon Opera Kyokai
	• Tokyo Opera Nomori
Korea	• Seoul Opera
Singapore	• Singapore Lyric Opera
Thailand	• Bangkok Opera

Table 8.2 Symphony orchestras in Asian countries

Country	*Symphony orchestra*
Cambodia	• Angkor National Youth Orchestra
China	• China National Symphony Orchestra
	◦ China Philharmonic Orchestra
	◦ China Broadcasting Orchestra
	◦ China NCPA Concert Hall Orchestra
	◦ Beijing Symphony Orchestra
	◦ Guangzhou Symphony Orchestra
	◦ Guiyang Symphony Orchestra
	◦ Hangzhou Philharmonic Orchestra
	◦ National Ballet of China Symphony Orchestra
	◦ Qingdao Symphony Orchestra
	◦ Shanghai Broadcasting Symphony Orchestra
	◦ Shanghai Symphony Orchestra
	◦ Shanghai City Symphonic Orchestra
	◦ Shenzhen Symphony Orchestra
	◦ Sichuan Symphony Orchestra
	◦ Tianjin Symphony Orchestra of China
	◦ Xiamen Philharmonic Orchestra
Hong Kong	• City Chamber Orchestra of Hong Kong
	• Hong Kong Chamber Orchestra
	• Hong Kong Chinese Orchestra
	• Hong Kong Philharmonic Orchestra
	• Hong Kong Sinfonietta
	• Pan Asia Symphony Orchestra
	• SAR Philharmonic Orchestra
Macao	◦ Macao Orchestra
India	• Delhi Symphony Orchestra
	• Goa Symphony Orchestra
	• Indian Philharmonic Orchestra
	• Symphony Orchestra of India
Indonesia	◦ The Jakarta Symphony
Japan	• Hiroshima Symphony Orchestra
	• Japan Philharmonic Orchestra
	• Kanagawa Philharmonic Orchestra
	• Nagoya Philharmonic Orchestra
	• New Japan Philharmonic
	• NHK Symphony Orchestra
	• Orchestra Ensemble Kanazawa
	• Osaka Philharmonic Orchestra
	• Tokyo Metropolitan Symphony Orchestra
	• Tokyo Philharmonic Orchestra
	• Tokyo Symphony Orchestra
Malaysia	• Yomiuri Nippon Symphony Orchestra Malaysia
	• Malaysian Philharmonic Orchestra
	• Malaysian Philharmonic Youth Orchestra
	• Penang State Symphony Orchestra and Chorus
	• KLPac Sinfonietta
North Korea	◦ National Symphony Orchestra of Korea
South Korea	• KBS Symphony Orchestra
	• Seoul Philharmonic Orchestra
	• Bucheon Philharmonic Orchestra
	• Ensemble TIMF

Country	*Symphony orchestra*
Philippines	◦ Manila Symphony Orchestra ◦ Manila Philharmonic Orchestra ◦ Philippine Philharmonic Orchestra ◦ San Miguel Philharmonic Orchestra ◦ DLSU Pops Orchestra ◦ DLSZ Symphony Orchestra
Singapore	• Braddell Heights Symphony Orchestra • Orchestra of the Music Makers • Singapore Symphony Orchestra • Singapore National Youth Orchestra
Sri Lanka	◦ Symphony Orchestra of Sri Lanka
Taiwan	• Chimei Philharmonic Orchestra • Evergreen Symphony Orchestra • Kaohsiung City Symphony Orchestra • National Symphony Orchestra (Philharmonia Taiwan) • National Taiwan Symphony Orchestra • Philharmonia Moment Musical • Taichung City Symphony Orchestra • Taipei Century Symphony Orchestra • Taipei Philharmonic Orchestra • Taipei Symphony Orchestra
Thailand	◦ Siam Philharmonic Orchestra ◦ Thailand Philharmonic Orchestra

The respect arising from the provision of these two art forms stems not only from the ability to present or mount productions or concerts but in all the trappings that come with them. There is, to be sure, much gravitas associated with the ability to mount an entire production of Wagner's *Ring*,[29] but nations earn respect from corollary activities too, such as the building of grand concert halls or imposing opera houses. These sorts of activities again serve to differentiate the nation from those that are incapable of providing such monuments to art and cultural activity.

As a concrete example, consider China. While not yet establishing its own permanent Western opera company, China has been working feverishly in other ways to ensure that Western opera has a stronger presence in the Middle Kingdom. As part of this, China is currently building 50 opera houses, and despite having its own operatic tradition (made famous in the West in the 1993 Palm D'Or winning film *Farewell My Concubine*), its musicians now compose works within the Western operatic tradition (Krich 2011). According to the renowned Chinese opera singer and New York Metropolitan Opera regular Tian Hao Jiang, the Chinese "consider this [Western opera] the highest art form" (in Krich 2011: paragraph 4). By mimicking the artistic and cultural practices of the powerful, namely the West, China is alerting the world to its place and "new membership in the world's cultural elite" (Krich 2011: paragraph 4).

It is interesting to note that while China adopts the Western operatic tradition, no similar adoption of Chinese opera is occurring in the West, or elsewhere, as far as I know. There is, for example, no similar programme to construct buildings devoted to Chinese opera. This is not to say that non-Western art forms do not make their presence felt in the West.[30] It is merely to note that Western absorption is not of the style or scale that is seen in Asian nations with respect to Western opera and symphonic music.

No doubt, the reasons for this are likely to be multifarious, but in the vein of this analysis, one cause would be traced to the lack of honour obtained by the presence of a regular Chinese opera company in the West. Some might object that the absence of a regular Chinese opera company is more about lack of interest, that low audience numbers for this art form would make such a company a financially prohibitive option in the West. Yet the lack of financial viability has not hindered the presence of Western opera, which even in its traditional Western home is notoriously financially stricken and would struggle without government support.[31] In other words, if governments and the public considered a regular Chinese opera company a worthy pursuit, then such a company would be underwritten in the same way that Western opera is underwritten. As for lack of interest, as Veblen would probably say, interest, or as it is otherwise known, taste, is a socially determined thing. The West's cultural and social dominance makes it the ultimate canon setter with respect to matters of taste. The lack of interest in Chinese opera in the West (and indeed elsewhere) is in effect a reflection of Western-determined canons, and the interest shown in Western opera in China and elsewhere in Asia is also an expression of Western cultural dominance and canons.

It is clear from this brief analysis that a public programme for the support for the arts could turn out to be a vehicle for the predatory forces of society. When this occurs, cultural policy is built not on a platform of workmanship and the desire to see artistic pursuit and innovation flourish but with a desire to earn social status and promote nationalist ends.

The argument developed here could be applied to any number of art forms. Consider the discussion of the contemporary visual arts in section 8.3. There it was revealed that the Louvre has entered an agreement with the government of Abu Dhabi to locate a branch of the famed French museum in that emirate. There is little argument regarding the respect that the Louvre name holds, which undoubtedly provides benefits (such as increased tourism) that probably contributed to Abu Dhabi's desire to be to be the location of the Middle Eastern branch of this esteemed body. But in the spirit of the analysis in this section, could it also be that Abu Dhabi covets the Louvre as a means to earn cultural prestige, making it ceremonially inspired?

To determine its workmanship *bona fides*, consider that an arrangement struck in the spirit of workmanship artistic endeavour would not prohibit a similar Louvre from appearing elsewhere in Middle East. If another nation or region was willing and able to meet the requirements for a Louvre museum, and if artistic endeavour and innovation would result from this, then an agreement struck under a 'workmanship star' would view such a development positively. However, that ceremonial inclinations play their part is evident in the exclusivity clauses contained in the Abu Dhabi agreement. These clauses prohibit the building of another Louvre elsewhere in the Middle East (Cocks 2008).[32]

As the only Middle Eastern nation with a Louvre, Abu Dhabi is thus given the 'right' to make a profound cultural statement, namely that the elite French nation has recognised and confirmed Abu Dhabi as *the* Middle Eastern nation with a cultural and artistic pedigree worthy of association with the mighty Louvre. With France's blessing, Abu Dhabi can confidently claim its place among culturally advanced nations.[33] But as the then-French Culture Minister Renaud Donnedieu de Vabres noted, the arrangement also provides "a way of enhancing our country's image" (in Riding 2007: paragraph 7). The minister's statement reminds us that cultural policy can be crafted not only as a means for lower-ranked nations and regions to earn higher prestige, but also as a vehicle for elite nations to maintain and guard their own.

8.4.2 Public support and leisure class canons

Some 10 or so years ago, I saw a report broadcast on the Australian Broadcasting Corporation's (ABC) *Lateline* programme that dealt with the issue of arts funding. The report gave details of an announcement by the then-New South Wales Minister for the Arts of a new programme to provide public support and funding for rock and roll music. What struck me about the report were the repeated passionate statements by the minister that rock and roll is art, a statement echoed by others who were interviewed. It seemed that the minister and others saw a need to defend rock and roll's legitimacy as an art form. Interestingly, it seemed that the reason for the ABC report was the novelty of providing public funding for rock and roll music. Perhaps the novelty of the announcement is that the new funding programme challenged generally held ideas that view rock and roll and its variants not as serious art. Unlike 'unimpeachable' and 'serious' art forms like opera, ballet or classical music, rock and roll does not immediately spring to mind as an appropriate or valid candidate for public support. Indeed, the repeated statements throughout the report from the minister and others suggest that the proponents of rock and roll funding also felt a need to justify such activity as legitimate art. For if rock and roll is not legitimate art, then it would be difficult to justify public patronage. Behind this is the idea that public patronage should be limited to 'high art' or 'high culture' and not be extended to 'low art' or 'low culture'.

This example has been presented to show how the canons of taste can shape social views and impact upon policy decisions. That rock and roll is considered low art is a reflection of the social canons of taste. In essence, rock and roll has not entered the accepted canons of taste as high art. On the other hand, high art activities like opera and symphonic music are socially accepted as legitimate, confirming their membership of the appropriate canons. Their entry into this canon renders their artistic value beyond question. It is part of the common apprehension to view opera and symphonic music as art, whether one consumes it or not, and so public support provided to these two art forms is beyond question.

In the Veblenian construct, these canons of taste are determined by the apex class. This class sets the parameters that are followed and adapted by lower classes throughout society. Through their activities and in their practices, the leisure class establishes the parameters and determines what is (un)acceptable, (un)desirable and (il)legitimate, including in matters of art. If an activity does not enter the dominant class' canon as an accepted art form or activity, then the activity struggles to obtain this status in the wider society. The canons of taste, as directed and shaped by the leisure class, have deemed opera and symphonic music to be legitimate high art activities, and so the response towards its public support is accompanied by less controversy than in the case of 'lowly' rock and roll.

But why should rock and roll not be venerated in the same way as opera and symphonic music? How is it that rock and roll comes to be deemed vulgar, low art, while classical music and opera enter the pantheon of high culture? In other words, why is rock and roll not within the canons of taste? To answer this, recall that, as was shown in Chapter 7, the canons of taste are moulded by a very important social need: to convey status and earn esteem. Thus the canons of taste follow accepted paths towards honour. Innovations or newer activities, unproven in their ability to earn status, are treated with scepticism or even disdain. The result is a canon of taste that has within it an inherent conservatism, where innovations find difficulty in entering the realm of the acceptable:

> conservatism is a characteristic of the wealthier and therefore more reputable portion of the community, it has acquired a certain honorific or decorative value. . . . Conservatism, being an upper-class characteristic, is decorous; and conversely, innovation, being a lower-class phenomenon, is vulgar. . . . Innovation is bad form. . . . The fact that the usages, actions, and views of the well-to-do leisure class acquire the character of a prescriptive canon of conduct for the rest of society, gives added weight and reach to the conservative influence of that class. It makes it incumbent upon all reputable people to follow their lead . . . [and] acts to greatly stiffen the resistance of all other classes against any innovation.
>
> (Veblen 1899: 132)

The conservative nature of the canons of taste means that artistic innovations are treated sceptically. Their ability to convey honour is not proven, and so the canons of taste in art would come instead to covet proven, established art forms. This helps to explain the difficulty of a relatively new art form such as rock and roll to earn the status of legitimacy.[34] But if this is the case, then it presents implications for public support; for if public support for the arts is a reflection of the ceremonial canons of a dominant leisure class, then we would find the choices regarding which art to support determined not by artistic merit and workmanship but by ceremonially dictated taste. In other words, public art and cultural policy, supposedly provided to enable the arts to flourish and be innovative, become instead tools for the tastes of the dominant class to be made real. As a result, choices regarding which activities to support are not based solely on artistic merit but rather on their acceptance within the dominant predatory canons of the leisure class.

That public cultural policy comes to reflect the canons of a dominant class is easily understood in the case of nondemocratic nations. Public support and the whims of a dictator or upper class are one and the same. So, for example, when Abu Dhabi provides public funding to have its own Louvre, it is a direct reflection of the decisions and hence canons of the ruling emir. But in democratic nations, there is no such obvious mechanism by which a leisure class makes its canons and sentiments clear. Two questions arise: Does this class dictate matters of public funding? And if so, how?

As was shown in Chapters 2 and 4, democratic nations generally provide public support and funding to the arts in two ways. One is by providing incentives through the tax code for private donations to arts organisations. These incentives are designed to motivate individuals and corporations to make donations to artistic activities. Among Western nations, this approach is more common in the United States. The second approach is to fund the arts through general taxation revenues. Governments often establish bodies headed by experts and esteemed persons who then determine how, to what and to whom funds should be directed. Sometimes, governments use a combination of these two approaches.

It is often claimed that funding provided through tax code incentives results in conservative art. The large donors are, by virtue of the size of their contributions, given greater power over the art that is produced with their money. The implication is that established art forms are preferred to newer or innovative works or mediums, and so we find that the art that is produced travels well-beaten paths (Rushton 2008). So, for example, when the NY Metropolitan Opera receives a sizeable donation from wealthy 'benefactor A', it does so under the proviso that it produces three 'Mozarts' and two 'Verdis' over a given season. Newer works would struggle to enter the repertoire. Veblen would say that the approach ensures that the conservative canons of the predatory leisure class leads to art that aligns with predatory taste canons and worldviews. While the transmission mechanism in this case is more subtle than that of a dictatorship or nondemocratic nation, this approach still provides an obvious means by which a dominant class might come to impose its artistic mores upon the wider public.

But what of the alternate, general taxation revenue case? Arts funding provided through general revenue should avoid the 'perils' of funding provided through tax code incentives. Since funding to the arts in this case is from general taxation revenue, the whims of a single benefactor do not determine the kind of art that is produced. Further, many nations using this approach establish arts bodies whose role is to manage and direct public support and funding. Those at the head of these bodies generally include those who are chosen for their supposed expertise and leadership in matters of art, so that, at least in theory, funding goes towards activities whose primary function is to advance the cause of art. But what about in practice?

It is tempting to consider that the latter approach used in democratic nations avoids the pitfalls of the others, that it results in the provision of public support to art activities that advance artistic innovation – in Veblenian language, that the art that is produced with public support is driven and shaped by the spirit of artistic workmanship. But democratic government and its various policy instruments and bodies are not immune from societal patterns, and when these societal patterns are set by a leisure class motivated by pecuniary gain and the need to display esteem, we find that:

> Representative government means, chiefly, representation of business interests. The government commonly works in the interest of the business men with a fairly consistent singleness of purpose . . . with the sanction of the great body of the people, even including those who have no pecuniary interests to serve in the matter, constitutional government has, in the main, become a department of the business organization and is guided by the advice of the business men. . . . It seldom happens, if at all, that the government of a civilized nation will persist in a course of action detrimental or not ostensibly subservient to the interests of the more conspicuous body of the community's business men.
>
> (Veblen 1904: 286–287)

The views expressed by Veblen in this passage are by no means novel or innovative, and no doubt similar views have been expressed by others, both before and since. But what it tells us is that the dominance of the leisure class means that it determines the very fabric and purpose of government itself, so that democratic government accedes and organises to accord with ceremonial leisure class values. In the case of the arts, arts bodies, purportedly designed to dole out funding on an artistic basis, come to be infected by the dominant leisure class paradigm, so that the funding provided by such bodies serves the leisure class by acting within the parameters it sets. Thus, those who head the bodies established to disburse public funding and support for the arts reflect the canons and patterns of the dominant class.

If public support for the arts is indeed determined by the dominant predatory class, we would expect it to have a few characteristics. First, we would expect much if not all public support to go to established art forms; second, we would find that newer art forms struggle to gain access to public resources, especially as compared with established art; and, finally, we would find an overrepresentation of those who consume the established art outputs to come from the dominant class.

In order to properly consider the first of these characters, it is necessary to make an assumption regarding established art forms. In the spirit of the preceding section, and for obvious reasons, opera and symphonic music have been chosen as the representatives of established art. With this in mind, consider Figure 8.6, which is a snapshot of funding provided by the Australia Council to its seven art form boards and two committees between 2008 and 2010. The art form boards and committees provide advice on arts policy development and administer the Australia Council's grant programs for various art forms. Further information on the role of each of the boards has been provided in Table 8.4.

As can been seen, the area receiving the great bulk of Australia Council funding during this period was the Major Performing Arts Board. This board provides core grants and funding to Australia's major performing arts organisations, including its opera companies, orchestras, ballet and theatre companies. Interestingly, the funding provided through the Major Performing Arts Board was very much greater than the sum total of funding granted through the remaining eight art form boards and committees.

Now consider Table 8.3, which separates the figures displayed in Figure 8.6, so that the funding provided to the established art forms of opera and the orchestras[35] (classical music) is clearer to see. Clearly, opera alone received roughly double the amount of funding given to its nearest 'rival', the Community Partnerships Section, while the other boards and committees did not come near the level of public funding provided to opera. So it seems that Australia Council funding decisions during this period were directed primarily in favour of the established art forms of opera and symphonic music. In the spirit of section 8.4.1, they were directed towards activities that have a high conspicuous value, designed to advertise Australia's membership of the 'civilised' group of nations.

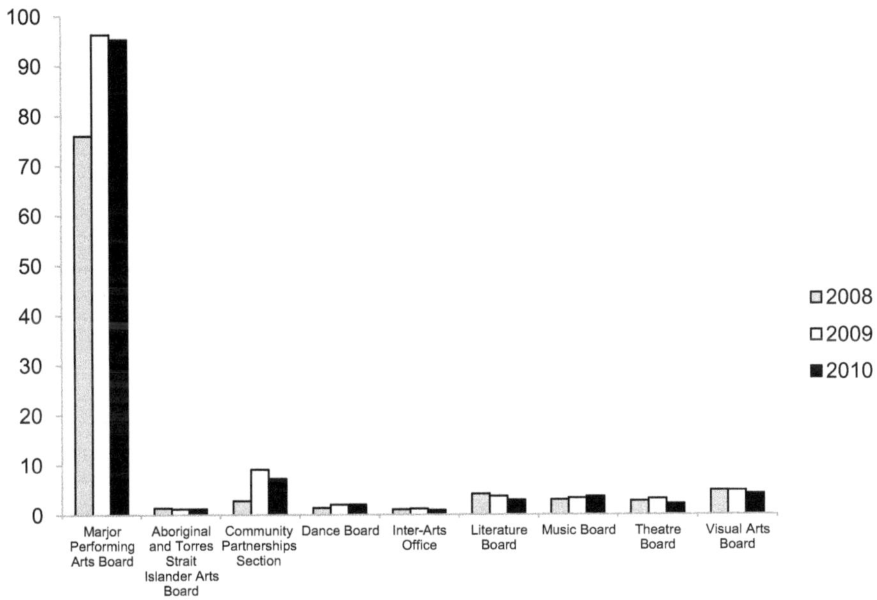

Figure 8.6 Australia Council Grants calendar year 2008–2010 (Australian $million)

Source: Retrieved 24 April 2012 from https://online.australiacouncil.gov.au/GrantsList

Table 8.3 Australia council funding to opera and orchestras calendar year 2008, 2009 and 2010 (Australian $million)

	2008	*2009*	*2010*
Opera	$16.6	$20.7	$21.0
Orchestras	$44.8	$53.0	$53.9
Total Major Performing Arts Board	$76.0	$96.3	$95.3
All Artform Boards/Committees	$97.1	$124.5	$119.5

Source: https://online.australiacouncil.gov.au/GrantsList accessed 24 April 2012

It should be admitted that mounting opera productions and maintaining regular symphony orchestras is a costly exercise, especially when compared to other art forms. Thus, the large funds directed to these activities could be reflective of this reality. However, this does not contradict the central point made in this section and may serve to confirm it. Consider that there are other art forms that are similarly costly to run but which the Australian government does not choose to fund. Take the jazz big bands that were so common during the earlier half of the twentieth century. Given the number of musicians involved (often 17 or more), the costs associated with maintaining a big band would be considerable. And yet, while there is a plethora of Australian publicly funded symphony orchestras, there is no regular publicly funded Australian big band. Clearly, the Australian government is willing to undertake the financial burden of maintaining regular opera companies and symphony orchestras but shows no such willingness in the case of big bands. Perhaps this is because big bands do not serve a ceremonial function in the way that opera and symphonic music do. They are not part of the leisure class canons, and, going back to the discussion in section 8.4.1, they do not earn status or esteem for nations in the way that opera does. The result is that Australia

Table 8.4 Australia Council for the Arts: Artform Boards and Committees

Board/Committee	*Role*
Aboriginal and Torres Strait Islander Arts Board	To assist and determine funding for traditional and new arts by Aboriginal and Torres Strait Islanders.
Community Partnerships Committee	Provides support to artists, community arts and cultural organisations and communities for community based art and culture including for community cultural development.
Dance Board	Responsible for Australia Council programs to encourage the growth and development of Australian contemporary dance.
Inter-Arts Office	Provide Australia Council support for new artistic practices, including those that span art forms or are interdisciplinary.
Literature Board	Supports and promotes the development of Australian literature, including book, magazine and online publishing.
Major Performing Arts Board	Supports Australia's Major dance, music, opera or theatre companies through core grants. To be eligible for the support, a company must be: • an international company • an Australian flagship company – resident or touring • a specialist company • a state flagship company.
Music Board	Responsible for supporting and directing Australia Council activities in the area of music.
Theatre Board	This board supports Australian contemporary theatre.
Visual Arts Board	Supports the visual arts through a range of visual media. These include craft, design, new media arts and visual arts.

Source: http://www.australiacouncil.gov.au/about_us/our_structure/artform_boards (accessed 24 April 2012)

is unwilling to bear the financial burden associated with the maintenance of this art form.

The reliance on the data presented in Figure 8.6 and Table 8.3 is also open to the charge that the direction and size of funding is confused with artistic innovation. While opera is undoubtedly an art form with a long heritage, it is possible that opera funding is directed to innovative works and to newer manifestations. If Australian opera funding were directed in this way, then it would challenge the notion that Australia Council funding choices are a manifestation of conservative leisure class canons.

One way to resolve this is to consider the production decisions of Opera Australia, Australia's national opera company. Table 8.5 lists the operas mounted by Opera Australia between 2008 and 2010. As the table shows, the composers whose works dominated these three seasons are Puccini, Mozart and Verdi. There have been examples of productions based on modern works, including the wholly new opera *Bliss* by the Australian composer Brett Dean in 2010. But as the table shows, the Dean opera managed only six performances out of a total 165 for the 2010 season.[36] The low number is shared by other modern operas, including those by the twentieth-century composers Benjamin Britten, Richard Strauss and Dmitri Shostakovich. The modern nature of these works certainly fulfils the innovative characteristic, and so it is possible to view the lower number of performances devoted to these newer composers as evidence of their difficulty of entry within the canons. At the very least, we might say that they have a far lower rank within the canons of taste.

Some might object that Opera Australia bases its production choices on works that are popular. It might mount other, less popular works, but unless it wishes to ensure its financial demise and enter the annals of opera company martyrdom, it must mount productions that have an audience. A question immediately arising from this is what makes works popular? Why does a Mozart opera have an audience while a work by Dean struggles? This is a complex question, but in keeping with the Veblenian analysis, popularity is a reflection of socially determined taste. Mozart is popular because he has entered the canons of taste. Why has Mozart achieved this while others like Dean struggle? In the Veblenian view, the consumption of Mozart is proven in its ability to convey civility and learning and therefore to earn esteem, while Dean's work is not. Thus, in the Veblenian paradigm, Mozart has been accepted within the dominant canons because its consumption achieves status in a better fashion than the works of Dean. Of course, it is possible that Mozart is performed because his works are beautiful. But as Veblen said and as was noted in Chapter 7, a thing may be intrinsically beautiful and yet still not be coveted. Returning to the earlier point, what is coveted is determined by the canons of taste, which are driven by the ability to earn status and prestige. Hence, to say that Opera Australia mounts works that are popular is to say that it mounts works that are part of the canons of taste.

The aversion to innovation is not limited to the performing arts but can be witnessed in the visual arts too. As an example, consider that in 2005, Arts Victoria, the government agency that until very recently[37] was charged with encouraging and managing the arts in the Australian state of Victoria, awarded funding to the Australian artist Konstantin Dimopoulos. Dimopoulos is known for painting trees blue, the purpose of which, he claims, is to raise awareness of our arboreal friends and the role they play in sustaining life. At the time of the funding, a huge outcry was heard from Victorian civic leaders, resulting in the cancellation of the funding and the trees escaping Dimopoulos's artistic 'fard'. Leaving aside opinions regarding the value and nature of Dimopoulos's art, this episode serves to highlight the attitudes towards newer arts and the provision of public funding.[38] But, more than this, it suggests that when public arts agencies like Arts Victoria seek to support works that step outside the accepted canons, they risk the possibility of community wrath and ire. The Arts Victoria decision to fund Dimopoulos did not adhere to accepted canons. Hence, the social element of public arts funding decisions is made more apparent. As was shown in Chapter 7, consumption and production decisions are necessarily shaped by the social institutional construct and canons of taste; and as the Dimopoulos example suggests, so too is this the case in matters of publicly supported art.

Table 8.5 Productions mounted by Opera Australia 2008, 2009 and 2010

Year	*Opera*	*Composer*	*Number of Performances*
2008	La Bohème	Puccini	26
	La Cenerentola	Rossini	9
	Carmen	Bizet	20
	Un Ballo in Maschera	Verdi	9
	Arabella	R. Strauss	5
	My Fair Lady	Lerner and Lowe	14
	Don Giovanni	Mozart	18
	Otello	Verdi	8
	Lucia di Lammermoor	Donizetti	10
	Orlando	Handel	8
	The Pearlfishers	Bizet	12
	Billy Budd	Britten	7
	The Makropulos Secret	Janáček	6
2009	Madama Butterfly	Puccini	23
	Cavalleria Rusticana/ Pagliacci	Mascagni/Leoncavallo	10
	The Magic Flute	Mozart	17
	Lady Macbeth of Mtsensk	Shostakovich	7
	Werther	Massenet	6
	Aida	Verdi	20
	Manon Lescaut	Puccini	8
	Fidelio	Beethoven	10
	I Capuleti e i Montecchi	Bellini	8
	The Mikado	Gilbert and Sullivan	27
	Così fan tutte	Mozart	14
	Peter Grimes	Britten	6

Year	*Opera*	*Composer*	*Number of Performances*
2010	Tosca	Puccini	21
	Manon	Massenet	8
	La Traviata	Verdi	19
	A Midsummer Night's Dream	Mendelssohn	10
	Bliss	Dean	6
	A Little Night Music	Sondheim	12
	The Marriage of Figaro	Mozart	22
	La Fanciulla del West	Puccini	8
	La Sonnambula	Bellini	9
	The Pirates of Penzance	Gilbert and Sullivan	27
	Rigoletto	Verdi	15
	Der Rosenkavalier	R. Strauss	8

Source: Opera Australia 2008, 2009 and 2010 Annual reports (http://www.opera-australia.org.au/aboutus/opera_australia/annual_reports accessed 24 April 2012)

While it is true that Australia Council funding is largely directed towards established art forms, this alone is not enough to indicate adherence to leisure class patterns. It might be that the choices made by bodies like the Australia Council do not signal adherence to a leisure class canon but are merely a reflection of those who head these organisations. One way to determine this would be to analyse audience make-up. If public support is a vehicle for the manifestation of leisure class canons, then those who consume its product should primarily be from this class. The problem is that, in the absence of a strictly formalised class structure, determining class membership and hence measurement of class consumption and production activities is problematic. In modern societies with less official class structures, it requires use of indirect measurement through the use of proxies. Two proxy measures that serve this purpose are income and highest level of educational attainment. Income has been chosen for obvious reasons. As for educational level, its choice is based on the premise that it reliably serves as a measure of socio-economic status and class membership.[39]

Tables 8.7 and 8.8 present figures for Australian attendance at musicals and opera and classical musical performances, organised according to income and educational attainment. Clearly, the higher the qualification held, the higher attendance at both opera and classical music concerts. A person is five times more likely to attend a classical musical performance if he or she has a postgraduate qualification than if the highest education level is Year 10 or below. Bachelor degree qualified persons are twice as likely to attend a classical music concert than someone with a Year 12 qualification. In the case of opera and musicals, the figures show that a person with a Year 10 or below level of education is three times less likely to attend an opera or musical than one with a postgraduate qualification.

Annoyingly, Australian figures group opera and musical theatre attendance together, so that one cannot make as definitive a statement about opera attendance as one can for classical music. Thankfully, the Australia Council's US counterpart, the NEA, undertakes regular surveys of participation in the United States that allow for direct measurement of opera attendance. The NEA's 1992 survey found that 79.2 per cent of operagoers had university qualifications. Further, this research found that those with postgraduate qualifications were 10 times more likely to attend an opera than the group who had some high school education or no high school education and twice as likely than those whose highest qualification was a high school diploma (Cherbo and Peters 1992: 26). The 1992 figures were repeated in the 2008 update of this survey (NEA 2008: 20: 83; Table 8.6).

Income level figures found a greater preponderance of those with higher incomes in Australian classic music and opera and musical audiences. As Table 8.7 shows, those in the highest income quintile are three times more likely to attend classical music performances than those in the lowest. In the case of opera and musicals, those in the highest quintile are two and half times more likely to consume opera than the lowest. Again, the co-measurement of attendance at operas and musicals makes it impossible to gain an exact picture of Australian opera attendance. Turning again to the NEA, in 1992, those with the highest incomes were more than twice as likely to attend as those on the lowest income levels (Cherbo and Peters 1992: 23). In 2008, those on the highest income level were 24 times more likely to attend an opera and eight times more likely to attend a classical music concert (NEA 2008: 20; Table 8.6).

What may not be immediately apparent from the audience data is the over-representation of wealthier persons in opera and classical music audiences. One way to understand this is to analyse the NEA data presented in Table 8.6. First, consider that the NEA notes that more than half those who attended opera in the United States in 2008 had incomes of $75,000 or more and two-thirds had either a college or graduate degree (NEA 2008: 83). This means that, based on income, more than half the US opera audience is drawn from only 30 per cent of the total US population, while using the education measure, two-thirds come from a cohort that comprises 27 per cent of the total US population.

The implications of this analysis should be taken carefully and are by no means definitive, but they do suggest that it is plausible that public support and subsidy is used to make the canons of taste of a wealthier class tangible. The examples drawn from the Australia Council, Opera Australia and Arts Victoria suggest that traditional art is favoured over newer works. Further, audience participation data reinforce the idea that opera and classical music audiences are mostly drawn from wealthier classes. This suggests the possibility that public support comes to be directed to serve and make real the patterns of taste and consumption of the wealthier class. In other words, it provides the means by which this class can meet its ceremonially dictated needs. As in the case of section 8.4.1, if this is the case, then the arguments developed for support in section 8.3 need to be tempered or reappraised. For if public support is driven not by artistic workmanship but by ceremonial canons, if its purpose deviates so that it does not serve

Table 8.6 United States opera and classical music attendance 2008 by education and income level (%)

Education			
Highest Level of Education	*US Population*	*Classical Music*	*Opera*
Grade School	5.0	1.0	0.5
Some High School	9.8	2.5	2.5
High School Grad	30.4	10.3	9.5
Some College	27.3	26.8	21.3
College Graduate	18.3	32.9	35.3
Graduate School	9.1	26.6	31.0
Income Level			
Annual Income	*US Population*	*Classic Music*	*Opera*
Less than $10K	5.8	2.4	0.8
$10K to $20K	9.6	3.9	3.8
$20k to $30K	11.7	5.3	8.0
$30K to $40K	11.3	8.0	5.9
$40K to $50K	9.3	8.4	6.9
$50K to $75K	20.3	20.1	20.1
$75 K to $100K	13.5	16.5	13.2
$100K to $150K	10.7	16.5	16.5
$150K and over	8.0	18.9	18.9

Source: National Endowment for the Arts: 2008 Survey of Public Participation in the Arts, http://www.nea.gov/research/2008-SPPA.pdf (accessed 24 April 2012)

Table 8.7 Australian musical and opera and classical music concert attendance by highest level of educational attainment (%)

	Postgrad degree	*Graduate diploma or graduate certificate*	*Bachelor degree*	*Advanced diploma or diploma*	*Certificate*	*Year 12*	*Year 11*	*Year 10 or below*
2005–06								
Classical music concerts	25.7	23.2	16.4	15.0	6.8	8.3	7.6	5.1
Musicals and operas	24.7	33.5	25.3	23.1	12.4	15.5	17.0	11.1
2009–10								
Classical music concerts	26.1	21.9	15.4	13.0	5.6	6.5	6.1	4.6
Musicals and operas	30.6	32.0	26.5	23.1	12.0	12.9	14.8	10.1

Table 8.8 Australian musical and opera and classical music concert attendance by equivalised* gross household income quintiles (%)

	Lowest Quintile	*Second Quintile*	*Third quintile*	*Fourth quintile*	*Highest quintile*	*Could not be determined***
2005–06						
Classical music concerts	5.3	6.6	8.8	9.7	15.3	9.7
Musicals and operas	9.5	10.2	15.6	18.8	25.6	16.4
2009–10						
Classical music concerts	6.0	6.6	8.0	9.5	13.7	—
Musicals and operas	9.0	10.7	16.3	20.0	25.9	—

* Equivalised income estimates have been adjusted by equivalence factors to standardise the income estimates with respect to household size and composition.
** 'Could not be determined' category was not included in 2009–10 data
Source for Tables 8.6 and 8.7: Australian Bureau of Statistics, Attendance at Selected Cultural Event and Venues, Australia, Cat no. 4114.0

the sake of art but serves the need for status aggrandisement and conveyance of one's position in the hierarchy, then workmanship-based rationales would need to be reconsidered.

8.5 Conclusion

This chapter has been presented with a single purpose, to apply Veblen's framework to determine if we can obtain a better understanding of public support for the arts. My approach has sought to avoid the nineteenth century relics present in Veblen's analysis and focus instead on what I consider to be the crux of Veblen's approach, the duality between workmanship and predation. There is no reliance on outdated notions of instincts, but there is a reliance on the idea that human social evolution takes place through the interaction of self-regarding and group-regarding forces. For ease, and in keeping with Veblen's construct, I have continued to use the workmanship and predatory/ceremonial nomenclature.

To begin with, Veblen's evolutionary institutional framework was applied in a 'direct' manner. Like ownership and the leisure class, this approach cast public support for the arts as an institution. A brief analysis suggested that public support might be the heir to the far older institution of public arts patronage. The discussion suggested that the older form of arts patronage might have evolved into the modern variant of public support. Patronage was seen as an institution initially motivated by predatory forces serving leisure class aims. However, it was shown how the forces of workmanship might come to exert a greater influence, so that workmanship has a greater presence. The co-dependence of institutions and the need to consider institutional development *in toto* was highlighted. It was suggested that any analysis of public support using an institutional method would need to recognise this co-dependence and accept that the evolution of an institution of public arts patronage would be affected by evolutionary changes and modifications to other institutions, like ownership and the leisure class. In time, this new line of research might yield an improved understanding of public support.

This was followed by an analysis of the effects of the workmanship-predation duality on the very nature of art itself. To consider this, I resorted to the use of a case study, that of contemporary art. I commenced by laying out the developments in contemporary art over the past 50 years or so as reported by a number of leading art historians and critics. The claims made by these historians amount to the idea that contemporary art and capitalism are irreconcilable, that you cannot have great art when it is subjected to the forces of the market. This was then interpreted within the Veblenian duality. Using indicators that measure equality, it was suggested that the period in question could be interpreted as one where predatory forces are dominant. The strength of the predatory in a capitalist society means that art is produced to satisfy not artistic workmanship but ceremonial needs. From there, it was shown through tangible examples how these predatory forces have appeared in the world of art. Finally, an argument in favour of public support was developed. This argument amounted to the notion that public support could lead to art that is produced to accord with workmanship aims and not predation. Public support would enable art to be quarantined from the vagaries of the predatory capitalist economy and enable the production of art driven by artistic workmanship bents. At the very least, it might reduce the force of predation. Importantly, however, the constant presence of workmanship, even in predatory periods, meant that such support would not be *required* to enable workmanship-inspired art to occur, but to *ensure* it occurred.

However, the argument in favour of public support was followed by a caveat. In essence, this caveat recognised an issue raised by Veblen himself long ago, that the co-presence of workmanship and predation means that both forces simultaneously exert a presence on human activities. As a result, while an institution or activity might appear to be obviously predatory and serve predatory ends only, the presence of workmanship means that its predatory tendencies would be tempered by workmanship. Similarly, a workmanship institution or activity is moderated by predatory forces. Thus a public support programme that is supposedly designed to enable the production of art driven by workmanship could become infected by predation. The result is that public support could at the very least partly serve predatory ends. If this is the case, then arguments in favour of public support would need to be reconsidered.

It seems, given the caveats, that any programmes to support artistic workmanship would need to quarantine all predatory elements. At the very least, the predatory forces should, if possible, be minimised. The difficulty is in the ability to achieve this, given that it might not be possible fully to appreciate and identify the full extent of predatory forces. In addition, even if one was able to identify the potential predatory forces, it still needs to be recognised that public support programmes are developed or delivered not in a vacuum, but within the wider society. Thus it is likely that public support will inevitably contain within it predatory elements.

Finally, it should be noted that, given social evolution, any argument for support would need to be considered within the context of the broader society. It might be the case that public support is warranted in societies where predation is amplified, like our own. But the possibility that predation may wane sometime in the future means that arguments in favour of support based on the need to quarantine predation lose their lustre. For if society does indeed come to be directed by workmanship, then the justification made previously would no longer hold. Public support would not quarantine art from the overt predatory bents, because in a workmanship-directed society, these bents have already been attenuated. Hence any argument in favour of support would need to recognise this evolutionary possibility.

Notes

1 See Chapter 6, section 6.3.2, for information and discussion on these hang-ons and institutional vestiges.

2 It seems that few would have gone to see the Beatles at Shea Stadium for any other reason. The music of that famed 1965 concert was piped through the stadium's public address system, designed to transmit not music but public announcements. This ensured that the sound quality was second rate and inaudible to many if not all of the 55,000 attendees, particularly when competing over the sound of screams. The Beatles' drummer, Ringo Starr, has said of the event "I never felt people came to hear our show, I felt they came to see us. . . . The volume of screams would just drown everything out" (Ringo Starr in Godley, Smeaton and Wonfor 1995: Episode 5).

3 Veblen might say that this was designed to bolster the value of the Sculls's intangible assets. More on intangibles later in the chapter.

4 The importance of its price to its notoriety and celebrity is revealed by the media reports that invariably mention the work's price (Graw 2009: 38).

5 For example, the works of French nineteenth century painter Gustave Courbet yielded a profit during his life, a point Courbet himself noted when he wrote: "Last year, either I or those who held my paintings sold twenty-five thousand francs worth of my paintings. Consequently yours are already worth more than a hundred thousand francs" (in Graw 2009: 36).

6 The Marxist pedigree of Berger's documentary is best appreciated by the fact that Berger explicitly declared that the first of the four-part series owed its ideas to the 1936 essay *The Work of Art in the Age of Mechanical Reproduction* by the German cultural critic and Marxist Walter Benjamin (Dibb and Berger 1972: Episode 1).

7 The Whitney Biennial is an exhibition of contemporary American art at the Whitney Museum of American Art in New York City.

8 Interestingly, Panero (2009) and Graw (2009) also highlight the importance of the Scull auction.

9 The most obvious example of this is clothing. Originally intended to protect the body from the elements and so serving workmanship needs, it has become a means to display rank and status, serving a ceremonial function.

10 Correspondingly, while a presentation of 'pre-contemporary' art case analysis has not been presented, it would be fair to suggest that Hughes's argument suggests that the

period preceding the 'decline' in contemporary art is one where workmanship had an increased presence.

11 These nations have been chosen for two reasons. First, they were chosen because of the author's familiarity with them and their language; but second, they were chosen because each of these is known to have fervently followed a 'free-market' philosophy. In the United States and the United Kingdom, this was expressed as Reaganomics and Thatcherism, while in Australia the term economic rationalism was adopted.

12 A society with greater income equality would have a Gini coefficient closer to zero, while a society characterised as unequal would return Gini figures closer to 1 (note that Figure 8.1 presents these coefficients in multiples of 100). The Pareto-Lorenz coefficient measures the concentration of wealth in the hands of the rich. The higher the Pareto-Lorenz coefficient, the lower the level of inequality (Atkinson 2006: 2). It should be noted that consistent Gini data for the United Kingdom were not available. As such, there is a break in the data at 1961 in Figure 8.1. Pre-1961 United Kingdom observations are based on data derived using tax unit income shares, while post-1961 data are based on data on household income shares. All Australian estimates are based on gross taxable income from tax records, while United States data are the Gini ratio for families.

13 The United Kingdom data in Figure 8.5 have a break in 1989. Pre-1989 data are based on income share per tax unit, while post-1989 data are based on income share per adult.

14 The Nobel laureate Paul Krugman has developed a very good analogy to describe the widening that has occurred in the United States: "imagine a line of 1,000 people who represent the entire population of America. They are standing in ascending order of income, with the poorest person on the left and the richest person on the right . . . the richer they are, the taller they are. Start with 1973. If you assume that a height of six feet represents the average income in that year, the person on the far left side of the line – representing those Americans living in extreme poverty – is only sixteen inches tall. By the time you get to the guy at the extreme right, he towers over the line at more than 113 feet. Now take 2005. The average height has grown from six feet to eight feet, reflecting the modest growth in average incomes over the past generation. And the poorest people on the left side of the line have grown at about the same rate as those near the middle – the gap between the middle class and the poor, in other words, hasn't changed. But people to the right . . . [are] now 560 feet tall, almost five times taller than his 1973 counterpart" (Krugman 2006: paragraphs 10–12).

15 Examples of the predatory paradigm dominating art are available from Veblen's own age. In *The Robber Barons* (1934), the American author Matthew Josephson describes how the Gilded Age capitalist required his "own private art collection and . . . art gallery" (Josephson 1934: 341). The mammoth desire for art from this newly rich "American baronial caste" was such that they purchased art "by the yard" (Josephson 1934: 341). Josephson recounts how, as a consequence, the price for art objects rose to a level that would once have been "balked at" (Josephson 1934: 341). While a motivation for Robber Baron art purchases was the desire to mimic the actions of their European leisure class contemporaries and lavish their homes with objects that conveyed their status and power (Josephson 1934: 341), the art as investment view was also at play. Josephson recounts how the millionaire William Henry Vanderbilt referred to his art purchases as "money "well invested" as paintings "increase in value with age and especially after the death of the artists" (Vanderbilt and Josephson in Josephson 1934: 343). The demand for art as investment saw some paintings increase in value a "hundred, a thousand fold more rapidly than the certificates of the best managed joint-stock companies" (Josephson 1934: 343). The impact of this activity affected the activities of artists, who more and more produced art to satiate Robber Baron demand, with the result that the art that was produced was said to be "so similar" that "one would think they were all painted by one man" (Josephson 1934: 343).

16 Consider that Timms refers to the power that the Church once had over art. As Chapters 6 and 7 showed, Veblen considered liturgical duties, and hence the Church, to have a predatory origin.

17 This is a point recognised by Veblen in his analysis of this period, which he called the machine age (See Chapter 6).

18 This was the allusion made in the *New York Times* regarding a Guggenheim exhibition of the Italian fashion designer Giorgio Armani. As the *Times* pointed out, the exhibition took place some eight months after a sizeable $15 million donation by the Armani Company to the Guggenheim (Vogel 1999). The implication is that the Armani exhibit occurred as a result of the payment and that financial considerations dictated the decision made by the Guggenheim, an allegation denied by the Guggenheim.

19 We can see with this that we create a tier system of museums and galleries. Those like the Guggenheim or the Tate that can command higher prices would be at the apex, and so it would cascade down to more 'provincial' museums. While once the tier or ranking would have been based on the artistic value of the collections possessed by these institutions, now it is based on the level that can be charged in order for a collector or artist to have work exhibited within the museum space. Ironically, it is the artistic credibility that these organisations have developed (sometimes over centuries) that enables them to command such high prices.

20 See also English (2014), who presents an interesting analysis of the impact of cultural awards.

21 Although it should be noted that neoclassical economics too is not immune from normative pronouncements. Indeed, the stylised nature of neoclassical economics is itself a display of normative bias, in that the "purpose of the theory" is to "demonstrate . . . social optimality if the real world were to resemble the model" (Eichner and Kregel 1975: 1309).

22 There is a similar argument made in the case of public support for science, where an oft-heard argument is that public funding should be provided to enable and support fundamental science. In the absence of such funding, the only science that would occur is that which makes a profit. While the idea that the market should be the sole determinant of the topics of scientific inquiry is often rejected and arguments for its subsidy generally accepted, it seems that similar arguments are harder to accept for many in the case of art.

23 The same lack of objectivity could be said to apply to economics, which, as Alfred Marshall himself noted, "cannot be compared with the exact physical sciences" (in Heilbroner 1953: 317) because of the mercurial and unpredictable nature of its human subjects.

24 I say might because, as will be seen in section 8.4, it is not certain that any support would be used to promote artistic endeavour but might be used to service ceremonial and predatory ends.

25 I say partly because there would probably be other factors that have an input to cultural policy, such as tourism and the expected gains from being the location of respected cultural bodies.

26 Indeed, as was shown in Chapters 6 and 7, Veblen considered that the origins of this class could be said to be less than morally beyond repute, coming as it did from a combination of 'force' and 'fraud'.

27 Although it should be noted that this is not strictly the case, and in a sense the argument treats Western civilisation in a monolithic manner. As stated earlier, while opera has deep roots in Germany and Italy, they are more tenuous in places like Spain or the United Kingdom. Indeed, as a reflection of this, in a very funny episode of the BBC comedy *Yes Minister*, the Minister refers to opera as the heritage of the "Axis powers". It is possible to consider the presence of opera around Europe as an effort to earn esteem by the competing nations of Europe. For ease of exposition however, I have treated Western civilisation as a whole, and so have chosen to focus on emulation between lower-ranked nations and the higher-ranked nations of the West.

28 The tables were produced through a desktop study by visiting the websites of various national cultural bodies, from opera.stanford.edu (accessed 24 April 2012) and http://orcheseek.fc2web.com/o-asia.html (accessed 3 July 2012) as well as through a Google search. It is possible that the tables are not complete, so that some opera companies and symphony orchestras are absent from the list. Whatever the case, the tables serve to show that opera companies and orchestras whose purpose is to present Western traditions exist in non-Western nations.

29 Wagner intended that the four operas that form the series be performed in sequence. As a result, mounting Wagner's *Ring* is a notoriously difficult and resource-consuming task for even the most experienced Western opera company. Given this daunting task, it is unsurprising to find that when Thailand's Bangkok Opera (a relative newcomer to the group of opera companies, founded only in 2001) mounted South-East Asia's first ever production of the *Ring*, critic Desmond Chewyn from the *Financial Times* described it as "an event of significance for Asian arts and culture" (Chewyn 2007: paragraph 1)

30 For example, the works of French composer Claude Debussy have been noted for drawing their inspiration from the Gamelan orchestral music of Indonesia. Debussy is said to have seen such an orchestra and become fascinated by its cyclical musical style at the Exposition Universelle held in Paris in 1889. Similarly, jazz is a Western musical development made possible by melding Western musical traditions with the musical traditions of Africa, particularly African rhythmic and percussive elements.

31 Krich (2011) notes that opera companies in the art form's Italian birthplace are struggling to stay afloat. Paarlberg (2012) has highlighted a similar problem with symphonic music, noting a NEA report that found a decline in US attendance at symphony orchestra concerts of 28 per cent since 1982.

32 To be sure, part of the motivation for such a clause is the incentive to protect and ensure the pecuniary advantage that is gained by being unique, as one of only a handful of Louvres in the world and certainly the only one in the Middle East. In either case, it serves to show that ceremonial considerations are present in cultural and art policy decisions.

33 This approach is not limited to places like Abu Dhabi and has been adopted by 'lower-ranked' regions within the 'elite' West too. Some years ago the City of Geelong in Victoria, Australia, a city often maligned as a 'cultural backwater', sought to establish an arm of the Guggenheim so as to appropriate the cultural standing of that respected institution and use it to raise Geelong's own status (ABC 2002).

34 It also helps to explain why avant-garde music, such as the works of Schoenberg, struggles to gain acceptance. Performances of Schoenberg's works, even of *Pierrot Lunaire*, are a rare occurrence. Similarly, while the Australia Council provides irregular funding to jazz musicians, there is no permanent Australian jazz orchestra. Both of these art forms represent an innovation and so have not readily entered the appropriate canons. This point will be elaborated upon in the discussion on opera production choices made by the Australia Council. That said, innovations that can serve this role might quickly enter into the canons. Since the primary aim is to earn esteem, any new activity or art form that shows itself capable of doing this will gain entry into the canons. Consider the case of modern or contemporary art. Its modernity has not militated against its being desired. The rapid entry of this class of art into the canons can be explained by the extraordinarily high prices paid for such works. The high prices paid for them provide a ready means to convey status. Hence, contemporary art fulfils the function of status conveyance.

35 The orchestra figure includes funding to chamber groups, including the Australian Chamber orchestra and Musica Viva.

36 On this point, it is interesting to note that Mozart's *Don Giovanni*, now often lauded as perhaps the greatest opera yet written and a regular in opera schedules, was at first a dismal failure, managing only five performances at its Vienna debut in 1788. Perhaps the low number of performances can be attributed to *Don Giovanni's* then-innovative nature, making it a difficult candidate for entry into the canons of the eighteenth century aristocratic leisure class.

37 See Chapter 2, section 2.2.1 for more information on Arts Victoria and its replacement with Creative Victoria.

38 Interestingly, Dimopoulos has since been awarded funding to produce his work abroad, and, ironically, the same Melbourne media that objected to the Arts Victoria funding now write articles about Dimopoulos in a positive light, of a 'local boy done good' abroad. It seems only after Dimopoulos received approval in the United States could his work be appreciated. Perhaps this is a case of the rejected proverbial prophet, or perhaps it is a case of ceremonial emulation as discussed in section 8.4.1. Only after approval from 'elite' nations (from the Australian perspective) does Dimopoulos's work receive acceptance in Australian canons of art (see Herald Sun 2012 and Minchin 2005).

39 Take what is considered to be perhaps the most prestigious of qualifications, the medical degree. Studies from New Zealand, the United Kingdom and North America confirm that those undertaking medical qualifications tend to come from high socio-economic backgrounds. For example, one study in New Zealand found that 69 per cent of New Zealand medical students come from affluent backgrounds (AMWAC 1997: 7).

9 Conclusion

In the religion of ancient Rome, responsibility and power over gates and doorways was given to the god Janus. Like Christianity and the 'mystery' of its trinity, Janus is made up of two figures, a 'binity', if you will, comprising 'Janus Patulcius' and 'Janus Clusivus'. Janus Patulcius has authority over *open* gates or doorways, while Janus Clusivus takes over when gates or doorways are *closed.*

In many respects, the process and operation of research follows the form of the Roman god, for research is both an explicit attempt to close doors and an implied attempt to open them. Research explicitly closes doors when it obtains answers to the questions that it poses, but answering these questions has consequential outcomes, so that the very same process that closes doors almost unwittingly (implicitly) opens new ones, creating new questions. The aim of this final chapter is to close and summarise the findings of this work and also to highlight some of the new doors that have, as a consequence, opened to potential new lines of research.

Firstly to questions answered and doors closed. In Chapter 1, I stated that my intention was to consider and answer two key questions. The first of these asked 'What is the nature and origin of public support for the arts?' while the second and related question asked 'Is there a rationale for such support?'

In Chapter 4, existing approaches to understand public support were presented. Each of these is built on a neoclassical platform and is focused entirely on the second question. With the first question unanswered and implicitly taken as given, neoclassical approaches have instead sought to find justifications for public support for the arts by identifying the economic 'pathogens' that cause market failures. Public support is thus justified as a means to address market failures. However, as was noted, neoclassical rationales for support can be easily overturned since the very source of market failure is often open to question.

The 'weakness' of the neoclassical approach led to the consideration of public support through an alternative paradigm: the economic construct of Thorstein Veblen. In Chapters 5–7, I outlined the major influences in the development of Veblen's constructs, the foundations of his economic paradigm and his approach to understanding consumption and production. As was shown, Veblen was heavily influenced by the discoveries of Darwin and natural selection and proposed a duality of competing social forces that drive and shape social evolution and the natural selection of social institutions. These forces include group-regarding forces, which Veblen termed workmanship, and self-regarding forces, which Veblen called ceremonial, predatory or even sportsmanship. The interplay between these forces shapes and moulds the institutions that guide society. At some moments, the predatory forces have the upper hand, and so the institutions of society reflect a predatory paradigm; during others, workmanship is more powerful, and so society and its institutions have a workmanship character. Which of these forces is more prevalent during any given time is largely determined by technology. Veblen traced the interaction of these two groups of forces through four periods of human development. Our current period, the capitalist age, which Veblen referred to as the machine age, is one where the predatory has a greater influence than workmanship.

In Chapter 8, the Veblenian construct was used to understand the origin and nature of public support. The crux of this analysis was the Veblenian duality, and a number of methods using the duality were canvassed.

Firstly, public support for the arts was treated as an institution, as an heir to a far older institution of arts patronage. Public support given to the arts in modern capitalist societies was seen as the most recent manifestation of an ancient institution of arts patronage that had evolved over centuries. Given the overlap, interdependence and interaction between society's institutions, it was shown that analysis of an institution of public support or patronage needs to take into account the role and development of society's institutions *in toto*. Key among the institutions pertinent to such an understanding are ownership and the leisure class. Further, in accord with general social development, the evolution of the institution of public support has been subject to both predatory and workmanship forces and reflects the power and influence of workmanship and predation at any particular point. It was shown that at some points, the institution of public support 'served' overtly predatory aims, while at others, it was more in accord with workmanship.

Having established grounds for public support to be considered from institutional foundations and demonstrated that public support is subject to predatory and workmanship forces, the next step was to consider the impact of both workmanship and predation on the nature of the arts themselves. A case study was presented, based on concerns expressed by the Australian art critic Robert Hughes and other leading art historians, about the impact of capitalism on contemporary art. These arguments amounted to the idea that the fabric of contemporary art was being damaged by capitalist market forces that were more interested in valuing art as an investment than in appraising and valuing it according to artistic canons.

The 'Hughes' argument was then cast in Veblenian terms as contemporary art acquiescing to the power of the predatory institutions of modern capitalism. However, to see if this is the case, it was first necessary to determine whether the period Hughes refers to is one where predatory forces dominated. During times of predation, one would expect wealth and power in the hands of relatively few. However, during workmanship, the reverse would hold, and wealth and power would be more evenly shared. On the basis of income distribution and wealth equality data (such as the Gini and Pareto-Lorenz coefficients), it was discovered that contemporary art developed during a period of predatory domination. The arguments of Hughes and others regarding the so-called inferior quality of contemporary art could thus be explained as a consequence of its being made to serve predatory capitalist aims at the expense of artistic (workmanship) canons.

From this, an argument in favour of public support for the arts was developed, predicated on the idea that public support would enable the arts and artistic activity to occur in the absence of the pressures of the predatory institutions of capitalism. In other words, public support could be justified in order to 'quarantine' art from the aims of predatory institutions, such as ownership and the leisure class. However, as was noted, while one of Veblen's two forces may have a greater hand during a given period, the other is never fully banished. Our own age may be one ordered to fit a predatory mould, but workmanship still has some influence on the nature and structure of society. This helps to explain the appearance of a contemporary artist like Robert Rauschenberg, a man who produced art during a predatory-dominated period and for whom Hughes expressed high esteem and respect. It seems, therefore, that even a predatory age can produce art that is driven by artistic canons. If this is the case, then the argument in favour of public support requires amendment. Public support would thus be provided not to *enable* great art to be produced but to *ensure* that it is produced.

Despite this Veblenian justification for support, a caveat was presented. It was shown that public support programmes designed to support workmanship ends might instead advance the predatory. This is because ceremonial elements could 'infect' public support programmes. Two examples of how this might occur were given. The first showed that public support could be influenced by the ceremonial desire to achieve or cement one's rank. The approach showed how different nations use their public arts support programmes to fund artistic activities that appear not to be about advancing art but about 'advertising' their status as a 'civilised' nation. In other words, public support is a means for invidious ceremonial emulation on a national level. The other avenue for ceremonial infection that was presented is the possibility for public support to be used to support activities that reflect the tastes and canons of the ruling class. The activities that are supported are based not on artistic merit or the ability to advance the arts but on their entry in the leisure class canons. In both cases, the caveats to support amount to the idea that public support that is designed to enable artistic workmanship succumbs to the predatory, so that even a system of support putatively designed to advance art instead advances predatory aims.

The Veblenian justification is thus that public support for the arts would *ensure* that workmanship inspired art is produced. But such a programme is justifiable only if the possibility of predatory entry into public support programmes is eliminated or, at the very least, minimised. However, given the nature of social development and institutions, the Veblenian approach showed that it is probable that any workmanship-inspired programme of public support would invariably contain predatory elements within it.

Veblen once said that "the outcome of any serious research can only be to make two questions grow where one grew before" (Veblen 1908d: 133). Given Veblen's inspiration for this book, it is fitting that I now 'defer' to his pronouncement and outline two new 'questions' that have arisen as a consequence of this work. First, while Chapter 8 presented two avenues by which predatory forces might enter public support programmes, it is possible that others exist. It would therefore be worthwhile investigating how workmanship forces manifest themselves in such programmes. The findings from this research would enable the design of support programmes that maximise the entry of the latter and minimise the passage of the former. Related to this, Chapter 2 summarised five models that have been used to provide public support for the arts. It would therefore be useful to determine which of these best aligns with workmanship aims, if any. Alternatively, this research may suggest the abandonment of previous approaches and suggest a wholly new model that would better advance workmanship aims. On related point, the Veblenian approach in Chapter 8 could also be extended to an analysis of public support programmes in other areas, such as universities, public research and sport.

As noted above and in Chapter 8, public support for the arts could be considered the successor to an ancient institution of arts patronage. This brings us to the second new 'question'. Due to word limitations, the analysis in Chapter 8 was brief and presented only the salient points of such an approach. Future research could develop these ideas further. This would entail a more detailed historical understanding of the system of patronage. It would also require the development of a richer understanding of the development and evolution of related institutions, including, but not only, the leisure class and ownership. The shape of each of these institutions at various points would be considered, and the lineage of the modern institutions of public support would be traced to their antecedents. One possible approach would be to choose five periods in history, such as Ancient Rome, feudal Europe, Renaissance Italy, classical Europe and the modern capitalist age, and to compare how patronage and the various institutions manifested themselves within each. Such an approach would draw heavily on other disciplines, such as art history.

Bibliography

4Food (2009 (March 6)), *Heston's Feasts: Eating Insects – Channel 4* [video file], accessed from http://www.youtube.com/watch?v=XLW4CKIy6VY on 8 February 2012.

Abbing, Hans (1980), 'On the Rationale of Public Support to the Arts: Externalities in the Arts Revisited', in Towse (Ed.) (1997), Volume 2: 538–546.

ABC (2002 (22 April)), 'Geelong dreams of a Guggenheim Gallery' [transcript], *7.30 Report* [television series], Australian Broadcasting Corporation, accessed from http://www.abc.net.au/7.30/content/2002/s537640.htm on 24 April 2012.

ABC (2010 (1 March)), 'Art, Power and Passion' [transcript], *Q&A* [television series], Australian Broadcasting Corporation, accessed from http://www.abc.net.au/tv/qanda/txt/s2827132.htm#transcript on 6 June 2010.

Alcalá, Francisco and Gonzale-Meastre, Miguel (2012), 'Artistic Creation and Intellectual Property: A Professional Career Approach', *Journal of Economics and Management Strategy*, 21(3): 633–672.

ALP Platform 2014, *Victorian Labor Platform 2014*, Melbourne, Australian Labor Party Victorian Branch, accessed from https://www.viclabor.com.au/wp-content/uploads/2014/05/Victorian-Labor-Platform-2014.pdf on 3 April 2015.

Alvaredo, Facundo, Atkinson, Anthony B., Piketty, Thomas and Saez, Emmanuel, *The World Top Incomes Database*, accessed from http://topincomes.g-mond.parisschoolofeconomics.eu/ on 28 June 2012

Ambirajan, S. (1959), *Malthus and Classical Economics*, Bombay, India, Popular Book Depot.

Amin, Ash (2008), *Post-Fordism: A Reader* [eBook], Hoboken, New Jersey, John Wiley and Sons.

AMWAC (1997 (December)), *Characteristics of Students Entering Australian Medical Schools: 1989 to 1997* (AMWAC Report 1997.7, AIHW cat HWL 6), North Sydney, NSW, Australia, Australian Medical Workforce Advisory Committee and Australian Institute of Health and Welfare, accessed from http://www.ahwo.gov.au/documents/Publications/1997/The%20characteristics%20of%20medical%20students%20entering%20medical%20schools.pdf on 3 May 2012.

Anderson, Karl L. (1933), 'The Unity of Veblen's Theoretical System', *The Quarterly Journal of Economics*, 47(4): 598–626.

Antonelli, Paola (2012 (November 29)), "Video Games: 14 in the Collection, for Starters" [blog article], *Inside/Out*, New York City, Museum of Modern Art, accessed from http://www.moma.org/explore/inside_out/2012/11/29/video-games-14-in-the-collection-for-starters on 6 May 2015.

Arora, Payal and Vermeylen, Filip (2013), 'Art Markets', in Towse and Handke (Eds.) (2013): 1–12.

Art Forum (2008), 'Art and Its Markets: A Roundtable Discussion', *Artforum international*, 46(8): 293–303.

Arts Council of Ireland (2000), *A Comparative Study of Levels of Arts Expenditure in Selected Countries and Regions*, Dublin, Arts Council of Ireland, accessed from http://www.artscouncil.ie/Publications/A_Comparative_study_pf_levels_of_arts_expenditure.pdf on 21 January 2013.

Arts Council of New Zealand Toi Aotearoa Act (1994), New Zealand.

Arts Victoria Act (1972), Victoria, Australia.

Atkinson, A. B. (2006 (December)), *Concentration Among the Rich* (Research Paper No. 2006/151), Helsinki, Finland, UNU-World Institute for Development Economics Research.

ATO (2010), *Taxation Statistics 2010: Charitable Gifts and Donations*, Australian Taxation Office, accessed from http://www.ato.gov.au/corporate/content.aspx?menuid=0&doc=/content/00305922.htm&page=44&H44 on 13 May 2012.

ATO (2015), 'Table 10: Individuals – selected deductions, 2009–10 to 2011–12 income years', *Taxation Statistics 2011–2012*, Australian Taxation Office, accessed from https://www.ato.gov.au/About-ATO/Research-and-statistics/Previous-years/Tax-statistics/Taxation-statistics-2011–12/?page=8#Table10 on 8 March 2015.

Austen-Smith, David (1994), 'On Justifying Subsidies to the Performing Arts', *Journal of Cultural Economics*, 18(3): 239–249.

Australia Council (2004), *Making Cross-country Comparisons of Cultural Statistics: Problems and Solutions* (Working Paper 2), Sydney, Australia, Australia Council for the Arts, accessed from http://www.australiacouncil.gov.au/__data/assets/pdf_file/0020/32627/Making_Crosscountry_Comparisons_of_Cultural_Statistics__Problems_and_Solutions.pdf on 13 June 2012.

Australia Council (2010), *Australia Council for the Arts Annual Report 2009–2010*, Strawberry Hills, NSW, Australia, Australia Council for the Arts, accessed from http://www.australiacouncil.gov.au/news/media-centre/reports/on 8 March 2015.

Australia Council (2011), *Australia Council for the Arts Annual Report 2010–2011*, Strawberry Hills, NSW, Australia, Australia Council for the Arts, accessed from http://www.australiacouncil.gov.au/news/media-centre/reports/on 8 March 2015.

Australia Council (2012 (26 March)), *Australia Council Review Survey: A Research Report*, Strawberry Hills, NSW, Australia, Australia Council for the Arts, accessed from http://culture.arts.gov.au/sites/default/files/australia-council-review/australia-council-review-survey-report.pdf on 13 January 2013.

Australia Council (2013), *Australia Council for the Arts Annual Report 2012–2013*, Strawberry Hills, NSW, Australia, Australia Council for the Arts, accessed from http://www.australiacouncil.gov.au/news/media-centre/reports/on 8 March 2015.

Australia Council (2014), *Australia Council for the Arts Annual Report 2013–2014*, Strawberry Hills, NSW, Australia, Australia Council for the Arts, accessed from http://www.australiacouncil.gov.au/news/media-centre/reports/on 8 March 2015.

Australia Council Act (1975), Australia.

Australia Council Charter, 'Charter of Operations' [web page], Surry Hills, NSW, Australia, Australia Council for the Arts, accessed from http://www.australiacouncil.gov.au/about/corporate_information/charter_of_operations on 3 January 2012.

Australia Council for the Arts, 'Artform Boards' [web page], accessed from http://www.australiacouncil.gov.au/about_us/our_structure/artform_boards on 24 April 2012.

Australia Council for the Arts, *Australia Council Grants List*, accessed from https://online.australiacouncil.gov.au/GrantsList on 24 April 2012

Australian Bureau of Statistics, *Arts and Culture in Australia: A Statistical Overview*, Cat. no. 4172.0.

Australian Bureau of Statistics, *Attendance at Selected Cultural Event and Venues, Australia*, Cat. no. 4114.0.

Australian Bureau of Statistics, *Cultural Funding by Government, Australia*, Cat no. 4183.0.

Australian Business Arts Foundation (ABAF) (2010 (June)), *Australian Business Arts Foundation Survey of Private Sector Support, Measuring private sector support for the arts in 2008–09*, accessed from http://www.abaf.org.au/Media/docs/AbaF-Survey-of-Private-Sector-Support-2010-Summary-b87493a2-cc2e-4c9f-b232-da5a066d0134–0.pdf on 2 June 2012.

Australian Business Arts Foundation (ABAF) (2011 (July)), *Submission to the Mitchell Review of Private Sector Support for the Arts*, accessed from http://arts.gov.au/sites/default/files/submissions/private-sector/pdf/AbaF-submission.pdf accessed 8 March 2015.

Australian Film Commission (2006 (August)), *Submission to the Department of Communications, Information Technology and the Arts Review of Australian Government Film Funding Support*, accessed from http://arts.gov.au/sites/default/files/pdfs/70-australian-film-commission.pdf on 10 May 2012.

Australian Government (2013), *Creative Australia: National Cultural Policy*, Canberra, Australia, Commonwealth of Australia, accessed from http://creativeaustralia.arts.gov.au/assets/Creative-Australia-PDF.pdf on 9 March 2015.

Ayres, Clarence E. (1958), 'Veblen's Theory of Instincts Revisited', in Dowd (Ed.) (1958): 25–38

Ayres, Clarence E. (1962), *The Theory of Economic Progress: A Study of the Fundamentals of Economic Development and Cultural Change*, New York City, New York, Schocken Books.

Balibar, Etienne (1995 [2007]), *The Philosophy of Marx*, London, United Kingdom, and New York City, New York, Verso.

Banfield, Edward C. (1984), *The Democratic Muse: Visual Arts and the Public Interest*, New York City, New York, Twentieth Century Fund.

Banks, John and Cunningham, Stuart (2013), 'Games and Entertainment Software', in Towse and Handke (Eds.) (2013): 416–427.

Barnes, Russell (director) and Dawkins, Richard (writer) (2006), *The God Delusion (The Root of All Evil)* [television documentary series], Glasgow and London, United Kingdom, IWC Media.

Barsdate, Kelly (2007), *Public Funding to the Arts: 2011 Update*, Seattle, Washington, accessed from http://www.giarts.org/sites/default/files/22–3_Vital-Signs.pdf on 30 May 2012.

Bartley, Russell H. (1997), 'In Search of Thorstein Veblen: Further Inquiries into His Life and Work', *International Journal of Politics, Culture and Society*, 11(1): 129–173.

Bartley, Russell H. and Bartley, Sylvia E. (2000), 'Stigmatizing Thorstein Veblen: A Study in the Confection of Academic Reputations', *International Journal of Politics, Culture and Society*, 14(2): 363–400.

Bateman, Bradley W. (2004), 'Why Institutional Economics Matters as a Category of Historical Analysis', *Research in the History of Economic Thought and Methodology*, 22(1): 193–201.

Baudrillard, Jean (2005), *The Conspiracy of Art: Manifestos, Interviews, Essays*, Cambridge, Massachusetts, and London, United Kingdom, Semitext(e).

Baumol, W.J. (1986), 'Unnatural Value: Or Art Investment as Floating Crap Game', *American Economic Review*, 76(2): 10–14, reprinted in Towse (Ed.) (1997), Volume 2: 549–553.

Baumol, W.J. (1993), 'Health Care, Education and the Cost Disease: a Looming Crisis for Public Choice', *Public Choice*, 77(17–28), reprinted in Towse (1997a): 510–521.

Baumol, W.J. (1995), 'The Case for Subsidizing the Arts', *Challenge*, 38(5): 52–56.

Baumol, W.J. (1996), 'Symphony Orchestra Economics: The Fundamental Challenge', *Harmony*: 52–54, accessed from http://polyphonic.org/harmony/2/Orchestra_Economics_Baumol.pdf on 23 April 2010.

Baumol, W.J. and Bowen, W.G. (1965), 'On the Performing Arts: The Anatomy of their Economic Problems', *American Economic Review*, 50(2): 495–502.

Baumol, W.J. and Bowen, W.G. (1966), *Performing Arts, the Economic Dilemma: A Study of Problems Common to Theater, Opera, Music and Dance*, New York City, New York, Twentieth Century Fund.

Baumol, W.J. and Oates, M.I. (1972), 'On the Economics of the Theater in Renaissance London', *Swedish Journal of Economics*, 74:136–160, reprinted in Towse (Ed.) (1997), Volume 2: 3–27.

Baumol, W.J. and Oates, W.E. (1972), 'The Cost Disease of the Personal Services and the Quality of Life', *Skandinaviska Enskilda Banken Quarterly Review*, 2(44–54), reprinted in Towse (Ed.) (1997a): 82–92.

Becker, G.S. (1998), *Accounting for Tastes*, Cambridge, Massachusetts, Harvard University Press.

Beer, Gillian (1983), 'Darwin, Instinct and Ethology', *Journal of the History of Behavioral Sciences*, 19(1): 68–80.

Bell, Daniel (1963), 'Introduction', in Veblen (1921 [1963]): 2–35.

Benhamou, F. (1996), 'Is Increased Public Spending for the Preservation of Historical Monuments Inevitable? The French Case', *Journal of Cultural Economics*, 20(2): 115–131, reprinted in Towse (Ed.) (2007): 322–338.

Benhamou, F. (2003), 'Artists' Labour Markets', in Towse (Ed.) (2003): 69–75.

Benhamou, F. (2003a), 'Heritage', in Towse (Ed.) (2003): 255–262.

Benhamou, F. (2004), 'Who Owns Cultural Goods? The Case of Built Heritage', in Ginsburgh (Ed.) (2004): Chapter 12.

Benhamou, F. (2015), 'Fair Use and Fair Competition for Digitized Cultural Goods: the Case of eBooks', *Journal of Cultural Economics*, 39(2): 123–131.

Benjamin, Walter (2008), *The Work of Art in the Age of its Technological Reproducibility, and Other Writings on Media*, Cambridge, Massachusetts, Belknap Press of Harvard University Press.

Berger, John (1972), *Ways of Seeing*, Harmondsworth, United Kingdom, Penguin.

Berle, Adolf A, Jr., and Means, Gardiner C. (1932 [1950]), *The Modern Corporation and Private Property*, New York City, New York, The Macmillan Company.

Berleant, Arnold (1980), 'Subsidization of Art as Social Policy', *Journal of Cultural Economics*, 4(2): 63–72.

Bhattacharjee, Ken and Mendel, Toby (2001), *Local Content Rules in Broadcasting*, Article 19, London, United Kingdom, accessed from http://www.article19.org/data/files/pdfs/publications/local-content-rules.pdf on 10 June 2012.

Bille, T. and Schulze, G. (2006), 'Culture in Urban and Regional Development', in Ginsburgh and Throsby (Eds.) (2006), Volume 1: 1051–1099.

Blaug, Mark (Ed.) (1976), *The Economics of the Arts*, Boulder, Colorado, Westview Press.

Blaug, Mark (1978), 'Why Are Covent Garden Seat Prices So High?' *Journal of Cultural Economics*, 2(1): 1–20, reprinted in Towse (Ed.) (1997), Volume 1: 302–321.

Blaug, Mark (Ed.) (1992), *Thorstein Veblen (1857–1929)*, Aldershot, Hants, England, Edward Elgar.

Blaug, Mark (2001), 'Where Are We Now in Cultural Economics?' *Journal of Economic Surveys*, 15(2): 123–143.

Boakes, Robert A. (1984), *From Darwin to Behaviourism: Psychology and the Minds of Animals*, Cambridge, United Kingdom and New York City, New York, Cambridge University Press.

Borowiecki, Karol J. and Prieto-Rodriguez, Juan (2014), 'Video Games Playing: A Substitute for Cultural Consumptions?' [online journal article], *Journal of Cultural Economics*, published online on 8 September 2014.

Borreau, Marc, Gensollen, Michel, Moreau, François and Waelbroeck, Patrick (2013), '"Selling Less of More?" The Impact of Digitization on Record Companies', *Journal of Cultural Economics*, 37(3): 327–346.

Boyle, Melissa, Nazzaro, Stacy and O'Connor, Debra (2010), 'Moral rights protection for the visual arts', *Journal of Cultural Economics*, 34(1): 27–44.

Broadcasting Services (Australian Content) Standard (2005), Australia.

Brumby, John (2009 (13 July)), 'Mary Poppins to Fly in with Spoon Full of Sugar' [media release], Victorian Government, accessed from http://archive.premier.vic.gov.au/newsroom/7505.html on 4 July 2012.

Burke, Simon (2011, 30 June), "Australian Stories Need to be Told by Our People" [web opinion article], Melbourne, *The Age*, accessed from http://www.nationaltimes.com.au/opinion/society-and-culture/australian-stories-need-to-be-told-by-our-people-20110630–1gsn9.html on 29 March 2012.

Burnham, James (1941 [1945]), *The Managerial Revolution, or What Is Happening in the World Today?*, Harmondsworth, England, Penguin.

Burris, Beverly H. (1993), *Technocracy at Work*, Albany, New York, State University of New York.

Callahan, Gene (2001 (April 27)), 'De Gustibus Non Est Disputandum' [web article], *Mises Daily*, Auburn, Alabama, United States, Ludwig von Mises Institute, accessed from http://mises.org/daily/666/ on 31 June 2010.

Callinicos, Alex (2011), *The Revolutionary Ideas of Karl Marx* [eBook], Chicago, Illinois, Haymarket Books.

Cameron, S. (1990), 'The Demand for Cinema in the United Kingdom', *Journal of Cultural Economics*, 14(1), reprinted in Towse (Ed.) (1997), Volume 1: 241–253.

Canada Council for the Arts (2004, last updated 4 March 2004), 'History of the Canada Council' [web page], accessed from http://www.canadacouncil.ca/aboutus/Background/kd127229037949843750.htm#45 on 31 May 2012.

Canada Council for the Arts Act (1985), Canada.

Carlyle, Thomas (1843 [2004]), *Past and Present* [eBook], Oxford, Mississippi, Project Gutenberg, accessed from http://www.gutenberg.org/files/26159/26159-h/26159-h.htm on 10 December 2012.

Caserta, M. and Cuccia, T. (2001), 'The Supply of Arts Labour: Towards a Dynamic Approach', *Journal of Economic Issues*, 25(3): 185–201.

Casson, Mark (2006), 'Culture and Economic Performance', in Ginsburgh and Throsby (Eds.) (2006), Volume 1: 360–397.

Caves, Richard E. (2000), *Creative Industries: Contracts Between Art and Commerce* Cambridge, Massachusetts, and London Harvard University Press.

CBO (2011 (March)), *Reducing the Deficit: Spending and Revenue Options*, Washington, D.C., Congressional Budget Office, Congress of the United States, accessed from http://www.cbo.gov/sites/default/files/cbofiles/ftpdocs/120xx/doc12085/03–10-reducingthe-deficit.pdf on 31 May 2012.

CBO (2013 (March)), *Options for Reducing the Deficit: 2014 to 2023*, Washington, D.C., Congressional Budget Office, Congress of the United States, accessed from https://www.cbo.gov/sites/default/files/cbofiles/attachments/44715-OptionsForReducingDeficit-3.pdf on 8 March 2015.

Center of Philanthropy at Indiana University (2009), *Overview of Arts and Culture Giving*, Indianapolis, Indiana, United States, Center on Philanthropy at Indiana University.

Challenge (2008), 'Lessons from Behavioural Economics: Interview with Robert Frank', *Challenge*, 51(3): 80–92.

Champarnaud, Luc, Ginsburgh, Victor and Philippe, Michael (2008), 'Can Public Arts Education Replace Arts Subsidization?', *Journal of Cultural Economics*, 32(2): 109–126.

Chang, Mandy (director) and Hughes, Robert (writer) (2008), *The Mona Lisa Curse* [television documentary], London, United Kingdom, Oxford Film and Television.

Chartrand, Harry Hillman and McCaughey, Claire (1989), *The Arm's Length Principle and the Arts: An International Perspective – Past, Present and Future*, originally in Cummings, M. C., Jr. and J. Schuster, J. Mark Davidson (Eds.) (1989), *Who's to Pay? for the Arts: The International Search for Models of* Support, New York City, New York, American Council for the Arts, accessed from http://www.compilerpress.ca/Cultural%20Economics/Works/Arm%201%201989.htm on 17 May 2012.

Cherbo, Joni Maya and Peters, Monnie (1992), *American Participation in Opera and Musical Theater: 1992* (Research Division Report #32), Washington, D.C., National Endowment for the Arts, accessed from http://www.nea.gov/research/reports/NEA-Research-Report-32.pdf on 3 May 2012.

Chewyn, Desmond (2007 (6 December)), "Valkyries over Bangkok" [web article], *The Financial Times*, accessed from http://www.ft.com/cms/s/0/a6d0d320-a39f-11dc-b229–0000779fd2ac.html#axzz1sv01SNAq on 24 April 2012.

Clark, John Bates (1899 [1908]), *The Distribution of Wealth: A Theory of Wages, Interest And Profits* [eBook], London, United Kingdom, Macmillan and Company, accessed from http://files.libertyfund.org/files/329/Clark_Wealth0190_Bk.pdf on 23 February 2012.

Coase, Ronald H. (1960), 'The Problem of Social Cost', *Journal of Law and Economics*, 3(1): 1–44.

Coase, Ronald H. (1966), 'The Economics of Broadcasting and Government Policy', *American Economic Review*, 56(2), reprinted in Towse (Ed.) (1997), Volume 1: 427–434.

Coats, A. W. (1954), 'The Influence of Veblen's Methodology', *Journal of Political Economy*, 62: 529–537.

Cocks, Anna Somers (2008 (June)), 'Revealed: Details of Contract Between Abu Dhabi and France' [web article], *The Art Newspaper*, Issue 192, accessed from http://www.theartnewspaper.com/articles/Revealed-details-of-contract-between-Abu-Dhabi-and-France%20/8553 on 24 April 2012.

Colander, David (2000), 'The Death of Neoclassical Economics', *Journal of the History of Economic Thought*, 22(2): 127–143.

Colapietro, Vincent (2000), 'Charles Sanders Peirce: Introduction – Peirce's Life: Cultural Context and Philosophical Background', in Stuhr (Ed.) (2000): 43–53.

Collier, Andrew (2008), *Marx: A Beginner's Guide* [eBook], Oxford, United Kingdom, Oneworld.

Commonwealth of Australia, House of Representatives (1974), *Second Reading Speech, Australia Council Bill (Official Hansard)*, accessed from http://parlinfo.

aph.gov.au/parlInfo/genpdf/hansard80/hansardr80/1974–07–23/0053/hansard_frag.pdf;fileType=application%2Fpdf on 31 May 2012.

Cooke, A (1994), *The Economics of Leisure and Sport*, London, United Kingdom, Routledge.

Copyright Law of the United States, US Code Title 17 Chapter 1, section 2(b) "Subject matter of copyright: In general" (2011 (December)), United States of America.

Council of Europe/European Institute for Comparative Cultural Research, 'Compendium of Cultural Policies and Trends in Europe' [web page], accessed from http://www.culturalpolicies.net on 10 May 2012.

Courty, P. (2003), 'Some Economics of Ticket Resale', *Journal of Economic Perspectives*, 17(2): 85–97, reprinted in Towse (Ed.) (2007): 151–163.

Cowen, T. (1989), 'Are All Tastes Constant and Identical: A Critique of Stigler and Becker', *Journal of Economic Behavior and Organization*, 11: 127–135, reprinted in Towse (Ed.) (1997), Volume 1: 139–147.

Cowen, T. (1996), 'Why Women Succeed, and Fail, in the Arts', *Journal of Cultural Economics*, 20(2): 93–113, reprinted in Towse (Ed.) (2007): 448–468.

Cowen, T. (2008), 'Why Everything has Changed: the Recent Revolution in Cultural Economics', *Journal of Cultural Economics*, 32(4): 261–273.

Cowen, T. (2011), 'Creative Economy', in Towse (Ed.) (2011a): 120–124.

Craik, Jennifer (1996), 'The Potential and Limits of Cultural Policy Strategies', *Culture and Policy*, 7(1): 177–204.

Craik, Jennifer (2006), *A Horse with No Name: Arts and Cultural Policy in Australia*, Paper presented at the Australasian Political Studies Association Conference, University of Newcastle, 25–27 September 2006, accessed from http://www.newcastle.edu.au/Resources/Schools/Newcastle%20Business%20School/APSA/MEDIAPOP/Craik-Jenni.pdf on 17 May 2012.

Craik, Jennifer (2007), *Re-Visioning Arts and Cultural Policy: Current Impasses and Future Directions* [eBook], Canberra, Australia, ANU E Press, accessed from http://epress.anu.edu.au/revisioning_citation.html on 17 May 2012.

Creative Victoria (2015 (April 16)), 'Meet the Minister' [web page], accessed from http://creative.vic.gov.au/About_Us/People_and_Structure/Meet_the_Minister on 3 May 2015.

Cwi, David (1980), 'Public Support for the Arts: Three Arguments Examined', *Journal of Cultural Economics*, 4(39–62), reprinted in Towse (1997), Volume 2: 514–537.

Cwi, David and Lyall, Katharine (1978), *Economic Impact of the Arts and Cultural Institutions: A Model for Assessment and a Case Study in Baltimore*, Washington, D.C., National Endowment for the Arts.

Darwin, Charles (1859 [1929]), *The Origins of Species by Means of Natural Selection*, London, United Kingdom, Watts and Co.

Darwin, Charles (1871 [1875]), *The Descent of Man and Selection in Relation to Sex* [eBook], New York, D. Appleton and Company.

DCMS (2001), *Creative Industries Mapping Documents 2001*, Department for Culture, Media and Sport, Government of the United Kingdom, London, accessed from https://www.gov.uk/government/publications/creative-industries-mapping-documents-2001 on 3 April 2015.

De Marchi, N. (1999), 'Economic Engagements with Art: Introduction', *History of Political Economy*, 31(Supplement): 1–30.

De Marchi, N. (2004), 'Auctioning Painting in Late Seventeenth-Century London: Rules, Segmentation and Prices in an Emergent Market', in Ginsburgh (Ed.) (2004): Chapter 7.

De Marchi, N. and Greene, J.A. (2005), 'Adam Smith and Private Provision of the Arts', History of Political Economy, 37(3): 431–54.

De Marchi, N. and Van Miegroet, Hans J. (2000), 'Rules versus Play in Early Modern Art Markets', *Recherches Economiques de Louvain*, 66(2): 145–165.

De Waal, C. (2005), *On Pragmatism*, Belmont, California and London, United Kingdom, Thomson Wadsworth.

Deal Book (2009 (January 22)), 'Thain's Office Overhaul Said to Cost $1.2 Million' [web article], *The New York Times*, accessed from http://dealbook.nytimes.com/2009/01/22/thains-office-overhaul-said-to-cost-12-million/?scp=2&sq=john%20thain%20trash&st=cse on 28 February 2012.

DeBoer (1985), 'Is Rock 'n' Roll a Symptom of Baumol's Disease', *Journal of Cultural Economics*, 9(2): 48–59.

Department of Regional Australia, Local Government, Arts and Sport, 'Film – Tax Incentives 10BA and 10B' [web page], accessed from http://arts.gov.au/film-tv/tax-incentives on 4 June 2012.

Dewey, John (1910), 'The Influence of Darwinism on Philosophy', in Wilson (Ed.) (1967): 198–210.

Dewey, John (1922), *Human Nature and Conduct: An Introduction to Social Psychology* [eBook], New York City, New York, Henry Holt and Company, accessed from http://ia600304.us.archive.org/15/items/humannatureconduOOdeweiala/humannatureconduOOdeweiala.pdf on 20 February 2012.

Dewsbury, D.A. (1993), 'William James and Instinct Theory Revisited', in Donnelly (Ed.) (1993): 263–291.

Dibb, Mike (Director) and Berger, John (Writer) (1972), *Ways of Seeing* [television documentary series], London, United Kingdom, British Broadcasting Corporation.

Dickenson, V. (1992), 'Museum Visitor Surveys: An Overview, 1930–1990', originally in Towse, Ruth and Khakee, Abdul (Eds.) (1992), *Cultural Economics*, Berlin and Heidelberg, Springer-Verlag: Chapter 14, reprinted in Towse (Ed.) (1997), Volume 1: 272–281.

Diggins, John Patrick (1999), *Thorstein Veblen: Theorist of the Leisure Class*, Princeton University Press, Princeton, New Jersey.

Donnelly, M.E. (Ed.) (1993), *Reinterpreting the Legacy of William James*, Washington, D.C., American Psychological Association.

Dorfman, Joseph (1934 [1961]), *Thorstein Veblen and His America*, New York, Augustus M. Kelly.

Dowd, Douglas F. (Ed.) (1958), *Thorstein Veblen: A Critical Reappraisal*, Ithaca, New York, Cornell University Press.

Dugger, William M. (1979), 'The Origins of Thorstein Veblen's Thought', *Social Science Quarterly*, 60(3): 424–431, reprinted in Tilman (Ed.) (2003), Volume 1: 3–10.

Dugger, William M. (1984), 'Veblen and Kropotkin on Human Evolution', *Journal of Economic Issues*, 18(4): 971–985.

Dugger, William M. (2007 (12 August)), 'Veblen the Red' [web article], *MRZine*, accessed from http://mrzine.monthlyreview.org/2007/dugger081207.html on 28 October 2012.

Edgell, Stephen (2001), *Veblen in Perspective*, Armonk, New York, M.E. Sharpe.

Edgell, Stephen and Tilman, Rick (1989), 'The Intellectual Antecedents of Thorstein Veblen: A Reappraisal', *Journal of Economic Issues*, XXIII(4): 1003–1026, reprinted in Tilman (Ed.) (2003), Volume 1: 77–100.

Eichner, Alfred S. and Kregel, J.A. (1975), 'An Essay on Post-Keynesian Theory: A New Paradigm in Economics', *Journal of Economic Literature*, 13(4): 1293–1314.

Ekelund, R.B. and Ritenour, S. (1999), 'An Exploration of the Beckerian Theory of Time Costs: Symphony Concert Demand', *American Journal of Economics and Sociology*, 58(4): 887–899.

Ekelund, R.B., Jr., Ressler, R.W. and Watson, J.K. (2000), 'The "Death-Effect" in Art Prices: A Demand-Side Exploration', *Journal of Cultural Economics*, 24(4): 283–300, reprinted in Towse (Ed.) (2007): 363–383.

English, James F. (2014), 'The Economics of Cultural Awards', in Ginsburgh and Throsby (Eds.) (2006), Volume 2: 120–142.

Farchy, Joëlle, Gansemer, Mathilde and Patrou, Jessica (2013), 'E-book and Book Publishing', in Towse and Handke (Eds.) (2013): 344–352.

Fayazmanesh, Sasan (1998), 'On Veblen's Coining of the Term "Neoclassical" ', originally in Fayazmanesh, Sasan and Tool, Marx (Eds.) (1992), *Institutionalist Method and Value: Essays in Honour of Paul Dale Bush*, Cheltenham, United Kingdom, Edward Elgar, Volume 1: Chapter 4, reprinted in Tilman (Ed.) 2003, Volume 1: 486–510.

Fehr, Ernst and Gächter, Simon (2000), 'Cooperation and Punishment in Public Goods Experiments', *The American Economic Review*, 90(4): 980–994.

Feld, Alan L., O'Hare, Michael and Schuster, J. Mark (1983), *Patrons Despite Themselves: Taxpayers and Arts Policy*, New York City, New York, New York University Press.

Feldman, W.T. (1968), *The Philosophy of John Dewey: A Critical Analysis*, New York City, New York, Greenwood Press.

Filer, R.K. (1986), 'The "Starving Artist" – Myth or Reality? Earning of Artists in the United States', *Journal of Political Economy*, 94(1): 56–75, reprinted in Towse (Ed.) (1997), Volume 2: 227–246.

Film Act (2001), Victoria, Australia.

Film Victoria (2008), *Film Victoria Annual Report 2007–08*, Melbourne, Victoria, Australia, Film Victoria, accessed from http://www.film.vic.gov.au/__data/assets/pdf_file/0019/991/FV_2007–08_Annual_Report.pdf on 13 June 2012.

Fischer, Ernst (1964), *The Necessity of Art: A Marxist Approach*, Harmondsworth, England, Penguin.

Florida, Richard (2002), *The Rise of the Creative Class, and How it's Transforming Work, Leisure, Community and Everyday Life*, New York City, New York, Basic Books.

Florida, Richard (2002a (May)), "The Rise of the Creative Class: Why Cities Without Gays and Rock Bands are Losing the Economic Development Race" [magazine article], *Washington Monthly*, accessed from http://www.washingtonmonthly.com/features/2001/0205.florida.html on 19 May 2015.

Foley, Martin (2015 (April 16)), 'Minister Unveils Taskforce to Steer Future of Creative Industries' [media release], accessed from https://4a5b508b5f92124e39ff-ccd8d0b92a93a9c1ab1bc91ad6c9bfdb.ssl.cf4.rackcdn.com/2015/04/150416-Minister-Unveils-Taskforce-To-Steer-Future-Of-Creative-Industries.pdf on 20 May 2015.

Francis, Hannah and Grubb, Ben (2015 (April 16)), "Dallas Buyers Club tells downloaders to 'name price' for pirating their film" [web article], *The Sydney Morning Herald*, accessed from http://www.smh.com.au/action/printArticle?id=98411380 on 15 May 2015.

Frank, Robert (1985), 'The Demand for Unobservable and Other Nonpositional Goods', American Economic Review, 75 (1): 101–16

Frank, Robert (2005), 'Positional Externalities Cause Large and Preventable Welfare Losses', AEA Papers and Proceedings Papers and Proceedings of the One Hundred

Seventeenth Annual Meeting of the American Economic Association, Philadelphia, *The American Economic Review*: 95(2): 137–141.

Frank, Robert (2007), *Falling Behind: How Rising Inequality Harms the Middle Class* [eBook], Berkeley, California, University of California Press.

Frank, Robert (2011), *The Darwin Economy: Liberty, Competition and the Common Good* [eBook], Princeton, New Jersey, and Oxford, United Kingdom, Princeton University Press.

Frey, Bruno S. (1994), 'Art: The Economic Point of View', in Peacock, A. and Rizzo, I. (Eds.) (1994): Chapter 1, reprinted in Towse (Ed.) (1997), Volume 1: 37–50.

Frey, Bruno S. (1994a), 'Cultural Economics and Museum Behavior', *Scottish Journal of Political Economy*, 41(3): 325–335, reprinted in Towse (Ed.) (1997), Volume 1: 376–386.

Frey, Bruno S. (1994b), 'The Economics of Music Festivals', *Journal of Cultural Economics*, 18(1): 29–39.

Frey, Bruno S. (2003), *Arts and economics: Analysis and Cultural Policy*, New York City, New York, Springer.

Frey, Bruno S. (2011), 'Festivals', in Towse (Ed.) (2011a): 220–228.

Frey, Bruno S. and Eichenberger, R. (1995), 'On the Return of Art Investment Return Analyses', *Journal of Cultural Economics*, 19(3): 207–220, reprinted in Towse (Ed.) (1997), Volume 1: 489–502.

Frey, Bruno S. and Pommerehne, Werner W. (1989), *Muses and markets: Explorations in the Economics of the Arts*, Oxford, United Kingdom, and New York City, New York, B. Blackwell.

Friedman, Milton (1962 [2009]), *Capitalism and Freedom: Fortieth Anniversary Edition*, Chicago, Illinois, University of Chicago Press.

Fullerton, Don (1991), 'On Justifications for Public Support of the Arts', *Journal of Cultural Economics*, 15(2): 67–82, reprinted in Towse (1997), Volume 2: 559–574.

Galbraith, John Kenneth (1960), 'Economics and Arts', in *The Liberal Hour* [eBook], London, United Kingdom, Hamish Hamilton: 52–79, accessed from http://ia700204.us.archive.org/4/items/liberalhour031268mbp/liberalhour031268mbp.pdf on 10 January 2013.

Galbraith, John Kenneth (1973 (April)), 'A New Theory of Thorstein Veblen', *American Heritage Magazine*, 24 (3), accessed from http://www.americanheritage.com/print/52989 on 29 September 2012.

Gallie, W.B. (1946 [1952]), *Peirce and Pragmatism*, Harmondsworth, United Kingdom, Penguin Books.

Gapinski, J.H. (1980), 'The Production of Culture', *Review of Economics and Statistics*, 62(4): 578–586, reprinted in Towse (Ed.) (1997), Volume 1: 285–293.

George, Henry (1886 [1979]), *Progress and Poverty: An Inquiry Into the Cause of Industrial Depressions and of Increase of Want with Increase of Wealth; The Remedy*, New York City, New York, Robert Schalkenbach Foundation

Ghiselin, Michael T. (1969), *The Triumph of the Darwinian Method*, Berkley and Los Angeles, California, University of California Press.

Ghosh, Syamal K. (1984), 'On the Validity of Veblen's Criticisms of Economic Orthodoxy: An Analysis of His Positions in Light of Current Conditions and Economic Thought ', *American Journal of Economics and Sociology*, 43(2): 235–246, reprinted in Tilman (Ed.) (2003), Volume 1: 474–485.

Gillispie, C.C. (1960 [1967]), *The Edge of Objectivity: An Essay in the History of Scientific Ideas*, Princeton, New Jersey, Princeton University Press.

Gilman, Nils (1999), 'Thorstein Veblen's Neglected Feminism', *Journal of Economic Issues*, 33(3): 689–711.

Ginsburgh, V.A. (Ed.) (2004), *Economics of Art and Culture: Invited Papers at the 12th International Conference of the Association of Cultural Economics International*, Amsterdam, The Netherlands, Elsevier.

Ginsburgh, V. A and Throsby, David (Eds.) (2006), *Handbook of the Economics of Art and Culture* [eBook], Volume 1, Amsterdam, The Netherlands, Elsevier Science.

Ginsburgh, V. A and Throsby, David (Eds.) (2014), *Handbook of the Economics of Art and Culture* [eBook], Volume 2, Amsterdam, The Netherlands, Elsevier Science.

Girard, Augustin (1981), 'A Commentary: Policy and the Arts: The Forgotten Cultural Industries', *Journal of Cultural Economics*, 5(1): 61–68).

Giving Institute, 'About' [web page], accessed from https://givinginstitute.org/about/ on 5 January 2013.

Giving USA (2010), *Giving USA 2010: The Annual Report on Philanthropy for the Year 2009 (Executive Summary)*, Chicago, Illinois, Giving USA Foundation.

Giving USA (2011), *Giving USA 2011: The Annual Report on Philanthropy for the Year 2010 (Executive Summary)*, Chicago, Illinois, Giving USA Foundation.

Giving USA (2012), *Giving USA 2012: The Annual Report on Philanthropy for the Year 2011 (Executive Summary)*, Chicago, Illinois, Giving USA Foundation.

Giving USA Data Tables (2014), 'Data Tables for Charts in the Numbers', *Giving USA: The Annual Report on Philanthropy 2014*, Chicago, Illinois, Giving USA Foundation.

Giving USA Reports: A Public Initiative of the Giving Institute, 'About' [web page], accessed from http://www.givingusareports.org/about.aspx on 5 January 2013.

Godley, Kevin, Smeaton, Bob and Wonfor, Geoff (directors) (1995), *The Beatles: Anthology* [television documentary], London, United Kingdom, Apple Corps.

Goldin, Claudia and Margo, Robert A. (1992), 'The Great Compression: The Wage Structure in the United States at Mid-Century', *The Quarterly Journal of Economics*, 107(1): 1–34.

Gornostaeva, G. and Pratt, A.C. (2006), 'Digitisation and Face-to-face Interactions: The Example of the Film Industry in London', International Journal of Technology, Knowledge & Society, 1(3): 101–108.

Goodwin, Craufurd D. (2005), 'Kenneth Clark: His Case for Public Support of the Arts', *History of Political Economy*, 37(3): 557–592.

Gordon, Christopher (2009), 'Augustin Girard (1926–2009): A Personal Tribute', *International Journal of Cultural Policy*, 15(3): 363–364.

Grampp, William D. (1989), *Pricing the Priceless: Art, Artists, and Economics*, New York City, New York, Basic Books.

Grampp, William D. (1989a), 'Rent-seeking in arts policy', *Public Choice*, 60: 113–121, reprinted in Towse (Ed.) (2007): 51–59.

Graw, Isabelle (2009), *High Price: Art Between the Market and Celebrity Culture*, Berlin, Germany, and New York City, New York, Sternberg Press.

Gray, Asa (1860), 'Review of Darwin's Theory on the Origin of Species', in Wilson (Ed.) (1967): 20–37.

Gray, Leila (2011 (September 19)), "Gamers Succeed where Scientists Fail" [online article], *UW Today*, Seattle, Washington, the University of Washington, accessed from http://www.washington.edu/news/2011/09/19/gamers-succeed-where-scientists-fail/ on 30 May 2015.

Green, Tyler (2005 (3 October)), "Krens Relinquishes The Ramps! Ms. Dennison to Feed Starved Gugg" [opinion article], *The New York Observer*, accessed from http://observer.

com/2005/10/krens-relinquishes-the-ramps-ms-dennison-to-feed-starved-gugg/ on 11 July 2012.

Greenberg, Clement (1939), '*Avant-Garde* and Kitsch', in O'Brian (Ed.) (1986): 5–22.

Griffiths, Teresa (Director) and Hughes, Robert (Writer) (2003), *Visions of Space* [television documentary series], London, United Kingdom, Oxford Film and Television.

Grimmer-Solem, Erik (2003), *The Rise of Historical Economics and Social Reform in Germany, 1864–1894*, Oxford, United Kingdom, and New York City, New York, Clarendon Press.

Hamilton, David B. (1973), 'What has Evolutionary Economics to Contribute to Consumption Theory?' *Journal of Economic Issues*, 7(2): 197–207.

Hamilton, David B. (1987). 'Institutional Economics and Consumption', *Journal of Economic Issues*, XXI(4): 1531–1554, reprinted in Tilman (Ed.) (2003), Volume 1: 352–375.

Hamlin, Alice Julia (1897), 'An Attempt at a Psychology of Instinct', *Mind*, 6(21): 59–70.

Han, Angela (2009), 'Public Funding for the Arts: 2009 Update' [web article], Seattle, Washington, United States of America, Grantmakers in the Arts, accessed from http://www.giarts.org/article/public-funding-arts-2009-update on 30 May 2012.

Han, Angela (2010), 'Public Funding for the Arts: 2010 Update' [web article], Seattle, Washington, United States, Grantmakers in the Arts accessed from http://www.giarts.org/article/public-funding-arts-2010-update on 30 May 2012.

Hansen, Trine Bille (1997), 'The Willingness-to-Pay for the Royal Theatre in Copenhagen as a Public Good', *Journal of Cultural Economics*, 21(1): 1–28.

Hansmann, H. (1981), 'Nonprofit Enterprise in the Performing Arts', *Bell Journal of Economics*, 12(2): 341–361, reprinted in Towse (Ed.) (1997), Volume 2: 393–413.

Hartley, John, Potts, Jason, Cunningham, Stuart, Flew, Terry, Keane, Michael and Banks, John (2013), *Key Concepts in Creative Industries*, London, United Kingdom, Sage Publications.

Hayek, Friedrich A. von (1944 [2001]), *The Road to Serfdom*, London, United Kingdom, Routledge.

Heilbroner, Robert (1953 [2000]), *The Worldly Philosophers* (seventh edition), London, United Kingdom, Penguin Books.

Heilbrun, James (2003), 'Baumol's Cost Disease', in Towse (Ed.) (2003): 91–101.

Heilbrun, James and Gray, Charles M. (2001), *The Economics of Arts and Culture* (second edition), Cambridge, United Kingdom, and New York City, New York, Cambridge University Press.

Hendon, William S. and Shannahan, James L. (Eds.) (1983), *Economics of Cultural Decisions* Cambridge, Massachusetts, Abt Books.

Herald Sun (2012 (April 5)), "Australian Artist Painting Trees Blue to Highlight Deforestation" [web article], *Herald Sun*, accessed from http://www.heraldsun.com.au/news/victoria/australian-artist-painting-trees-blue-to-highlight-deforestation/story-e6frf7lf-1226318641145 on 24 April 2012.

Hesmondhalgh, David (2002), *The Cultural Industries*, London, United Kingdom, Sage.

Hesmondhalgh, David and Pratt, Andy (2005), 'Cultural Industries and Cultural Policy', *International Journal of Cultural Policy*, 11(1): 1–14.

Hill, Forest G. (1958), 'Veblen and Marx', in Dowd (Ed.) (1958): 129–150.

Hiller, R. Scott (2015), 'The Importance of Quality: How Music Festivals Achieved Commercial Success', *Journal of Cultural Economics*, published online on 23 April 2015.

Hirsch, Fred (1995 [2012]), *Social Limits to Growth* [eBook], Hoboken, New Jersey, Routledge.

Hitchens, Christopher (2007), *God is Not Great: How Religion Poisons Everything*, New York City, New York, and Boston, Massachusetts, Twelve.

Hobson, J.A. (1936), *Veblen*, London, United Kingdom, Chapman and Hall.

Hodder, H.J. (1956), 'The Political Ideas of Thorstein Veblen', *The Canadian Journal of Economics and Political Science*, 22(3): 345–357.

Hodgson, Geoffrey M. (Ed.) (1994), *Economics and Evolution: Bringing Life Back Into Economics*, Cambridge, United Kingdom, Polity Press.

Hodgson, Geoffrey M. (1998), 'On the Evolution of Thorstein Veblen's Evolutionary Economics', *Cambridge Journal of Economics*, 22(4): 415–431.

Hodgson, Geoffrey M. (Ed.) (1998a), *The Foundations of Evolutionary Economics, 1890–1973*, Cheltenham, United Kingdom, Elgar.

Hodgson, Geoffrey M. (2001), *How Economics Forgot History: The Problem of Historical Specificity in Social Science*, New York City, New York, Routledge.

Hodgson, Geoffrey M. (2004), *The Evolution of Institutional Economics: Agency, Structure and Darwinism in American Institutionalism*, London, United Kingdom, and New York City, New York, Routledge.

Hodsdon, Barrett (1995), 'Flagship Culture and Commercial Chimera: Government Involvement in Australian Film', in Sabine (Ed.) (1995): 172–197.

Hojman, David E. and Hiscock, Julia (2010), 'Interpreting Suboptimal Business Outcomes in Light of the Coase Theorem: Lessons from Sidmouth International Festival', *Tourism Management*, 31(2): 240–249.

Holding, Tim (2009 (30 November)), 'Musical Provides Wicked Boost to Victoria' [media release], Melbourne, Australia, Victorian Government, accessed from http://archive.premier.vic.gov.au/newsroom/8893.html on 4 July 2012.

Holding, Tim (2010 (17 March)), 'Sydney Falls Further Behind Melbourne on Tourism' [media release], Melbourne, Australia, Victorian Government, accessed from http://archive.premier.vic.gov.au/newsroom/9833.html on 4 July 2012.

Hollander, Samuel (1985), *The Economics of John Stuart Mill*, Oxford, United Kingdom, Blackwell.

Hollingsworth, Mary (1994), *Patronage in Renaissance Italy: From 1400 to the Early 16th Century*, London, United Kingdom, J. Murray.

Homan, Paul T. (1927), 'John Bates Clark: Earlier and Later Phases of His Work', *The Quarterly Journal of Economics*, 42(1): 39–69.

Honan, William H. (1988, 15 May), "Book Discloses That Reagan Planned To Kill National Endowment for Arts" [web book review], *The New York Times*, accessed from http://www.nytimes.com/1988/05/15/arts/book-discloses-that-reagan-planned-to-kill-national-endowment-for-arts.html on 4 June 2012.

Howard, M.C. and King, J.E. (Eds.) (1976), *The Economics of Karl Marx: Selected Readings of Exposition and Criticism*, Harmondsworth, United Kingdom, Penguin.

Hughes, Robert (1980 [2002]), *The Shock of the New: Art and the Century of Change*, London, United Kingdom, Thames and Hudson.

Hunt, E.K. (1979), *History of Economic Thought: A Critical Perspective*, Belmont, California, Wadsworth.

Hunt, E.K. (1979a), 'The Importance of Thorstein Veblen for Contemporary Marxism', *Journal of Economic Issues*, 13(1): 113–140.

Hunt, E.K. (2002), *History of Economic Thought: A Critical Perspective* (updated second edition), Armonk, New York, M.E. Sharpe.

Hunt, E.K. (2003), *Property and Prophets: The Evolution of Economic Institutions and Ideologies*, Armonk, New York, and London, United Kingdom, M.E. Sharpe.

Hutter, Michael and Thorsby, David (2008), *Beyond Price: Value in Culture, Economics and the Arts*, Cambridge, United Kingdom, Cambridge University Press.

Illouz, Eva (1997), *Consuming the Romantic Utopia: Love and the Cultural Contradictions of Capitalism*, Berkeley, California, University of California Press.

International Federation of Arts Councils and Culture Agencies (IFACCA) (2012), 'Current Members' [web page], accessed from http://www.ifacca.org/membership/current_members/ on 20 May 2012.

Jackson, William A. (2006), 'Post-Fordism and Population Ageing', *International Review of Applied Economics*, 20(4): 449–467.

James, Patricia (1979), *Population Malthus: His Life and Times*, London, United Kingdom, Routledge and Kegan Paul.

James, William (1890 [1950]), *The Principles of Psychology* (Volume 2), New York City, New York, Dover Publications, Inc.

James, William (1898), 'Philosophical Conception and Practical Results', *University Chronicle*, I(4): 287–310, accessed from http://ia700500.us.archive.org/16/items/philosophicalcon00jameuoft/philosophicalcon00jameuoft.pdf on 5 January 2012.

James, William (1904), 'What Pragmatism Means', in Stuhr (Ed.) (2000): 193–202.

JCT (2011 (October 14)), *Present Law and Background Relating to the Federal Tax Treatment of Charitable Contributions*, Washington, D.C., Joint Committee on Taxation, Congress of the United States, accessed from https://www.jct.gov/publications.html?func=startdown&id=4371 on 30 May 2012.

JCT (2011a (March 9)), *Background Information On Tax Expenditure Analysis And Historical Survey of Tax Expenditure Estimates*, Washington, D.C., Joint Committee on Taxation, Congress of the United States, accessed from https://www.jct.gov/publications.html?func=startdown&id=3740 on 30 May 2012.

JCT (2013 (February 11), *Present Law and Background Relating to the Federal Tax Treatment of Charitable Contributions*, Washington, D.C., Joint Committee on Taxation, Congress of the United States, accessed from https://www.jct.gov/publications.html?func=startdown&id=4506 on 8 March 2015.

Jevons, William Stanley (1871 [1965]), *The Theory of Political Economy* [eBook], (fifth edition), New York City, New York, Sentry Press.

Johanson, Katya (2008), 'How Australian Industry Policy Shaped Cultural Policy', *International Journal of Cultural Policy*, 14(2): 139–148.

Jones, Eric L. (1987), *The European Miracle: Environments, Economics and Geopolitics in the History of Europe and Asia* (second edition), Cambridge, United Kingdom, Cambridge University Press.

Jorgensen, Elizabeth and Jorgensen, Henry (1999), *Thorstein Veblen: Victorian Firebrand*, Armonk, New York, M. E. Sharpe.

Josephson, Matthew (1934 [1962]), *The Robber Barons: The Great American Capitalists 1861–1901*, New York City, New York, A Harvest Book.

Kauffman, Bill (1990 (August 8)), *Subsidies to the Arts: Cultivating Mediocrity* (Cato Policy Analysis No. 137), Washington, D.C, Cato Institute, accessed from http://www.cato.org/pubs/pas/pa137.html on 2 May 2010.

Kennedy, Randy (2009 (December 10)), "Thomas Hoving, Remaker of the Met, Dies at 78" [web obituary], *The New York Times*, New York City, New York, accessed from http://www.nytimes.com/2009/12/11/arts/design/11hoving.html?pagewanted=all&_r=0 on 28 January 2013.

Keynes, John Maynard (1936 (26 August)), 'Art and the State', in Moggridge (Ed.) (1982): 341–349.

Keynes, John Maynard (1936a [1997]), *The General Theory of Employment, Interest and Money*, Amherst, New York, Prometheus Books.

Kirschenbaum, Baruch D. (1979), 'The Scull Auction and the Scull Film', *Art Journal*, XXXIX(1): 50–54.

Klamer, Arjo (Ed.) (1996), *The Value of Culture: On the Relationship between Economics and Arts*, Amsterdam, The Netherlands, Amsterdam University Press

Klebnikov, Paul (2001 (8 January)), 'Museums Inc.' [web article], *Forbes*, accessed from http://www.forbes.com/global/2001/0108/032.html on 11 July 2012.

Knoedler, Janet T. (1997), 'Veblen and Technical Efficiency', *Journal of Economic Issues*, 31(4): 1011–1026.

Konigsberg, Eric (2009 (February 27)), "Is Anybody Buying Art These Days?" [web article], *The New York Times*, accessed from http://www.nytimes.com/2009/03/01/magazine/01Brothers-t.html?pagewanted=all on 13 April 2012.

Koslowski, Peter (1995), 'Economics as Ethical Economy in the Tradition of the Historical School', in Koslowski (Ed.) (1995): 1–11.

Koslowski, Peter (Ed.) (1995a), *The Theory of Ethical Economy in the Historical School: Wilhelm Roscher, Lorenz von Stein, Gustav Schmoller, Wilhelm Dilthey, and Contemporary Theory*, Heidelberg, Germany, and New York City, New York, Springer-Verlag.

Krabbe, J. J. (1996), *Historicism and Organicism in Economics: The Evolution of Thought*, Dordrecht, The Netherlands, and Boston, Massachusetts, Kluwer.

Krich, John (2011 (15 August)), 'As Opera Struggles in West, an Art Form Flourishes in China', *Time*, accessed from http://www.time.com/time/printout/0,8816,2086143,00.html on 18 April 2012.

Krishan, Kumar (2009), *From Post-Industrial to Post-Modern Society: New Theories of the Contemporary World* [eBook], Hoboken, New Jersey, Blackwell Publishing.

Krugman, Paul (2006 (November 30)), 'The Great Wealth Transfer' [opinion article], *Rolling Stone*, accessed from http://www.rollingstone.com/politics/story/12699486/paul_krugman_on_the_great_wealth_transfer on 3 July 2012.

Krugman, Paul, (2012 (May 3)), "Plutocracy, Paralysis, Perplexity" [opinion article], *The New York Times*, accessed from http://www.nytimes.com/2012/05/04/opinion/krugman-plutocracy-paralysis-perplexity.html on 3 July 2012.

Kushner, Roland J. and Cohen, Randy (2009), *National Arts Index 2009: An Annual Measure of the Vitality of Arts and Culture in the United States*, Washington, D.C., and New York City, New York, Americans for the Arts, accessed from http://www.americansforthearts.org/pdf/information_services/art_index/NAI_full_report_print_quality.pdf on 29 January 2012.

Landes, William M. (2001), 'What Has the Visual Artist's Rights Act of 1990 Accomplished?', *Journal of Cultural Economics*, 25(4): 283–306.

Landes, William M. (2003), 'Copyright', in Towse (Ed.) (2003): 132–142.

Landes, William M. (2011), 'Copyright', in Towse (Ed.) (2011a): 100–112.

Landes, William M. and Posner, Richard A. (1989), 'An Economic Analysis of Copyright Law', *Journal of Legal Studies*, 18(2): 325–63.

Landes, William M. and Levine, Daniel B. (2006), 'The Economic Analysis of Art Law', in Ginsburg and Throsby (Eds.) (2006), Volume 1: 211–251.

Lebergott, Stanley (1964), *Manpower in Economic Growth*, New York City, New York, McGraw-Hill.

Leichentritt, Hugo (1951 [1965]), *Musical Form*, Cambridge, Massachusetts, Harvard University Press.

Lévy–Garboua, L. and Montmarquette, C. (1996), 'A Microeconometric Study of Theatre Demand', *Journal of Cultural Economics*, 20(1): 25–50, reprinted in Towse (Ed.) (2007): 177–202.

Liebowitz, Stan J. (2014), 'How Much of the Decline in Sound Recording Sales is Due to File-sharing?' [online journal article], *Journal of Cultural Economics*, published online on 28 September 2014.

Liebowitz, Stan J. and Zentner, Alejandro (2012), 'Clash of the Titans: Does Internet use Reduce Television Viewing?', *The Review of Economic Statistics*, 94(1): 234–245.

Liebowitz, Stan J. and Zentner, Alejandro (2015), 'The Internet as a Celestial TiVo: What Can We Learn from Cable Television Adoption?' [online journal article], *Journal of Cultural Economics*, published online on 25 March 2015.

Loton, D.J. and Lubman, D.I. (2015), 'Just One More Level: Identifying and Addressing Internet Gaming Disorder within Primary Care', *Australian Family Physician*, in press.

Louv, Richard (2003 (July 13)), "Building Cities with the Creative Class" [newspaper column], *The San Diego Union* Tribune, accessed from http://legacy.utsandiego.com/news/metro/louv/20030713–9999_mz1e13louv.html on 3 May 2015.

Lovejoy, Arthur O. (1908 [1963]), *The Thirteen Pragmatisms, and Other Essays*, Baltimore, John Hopkins Press.

Lovejoy, Arthur O. (1936 [1960]), *The Great Chain of Being: A Study of the History of an Idea*, New York City, New York, Harper and Row.

MacDonald, G.M. (1988), 'The Economics of Rising Stars', *American Economic Review*, 78(1): 166–166, reprinted in Towse (Ed.) (1997), Volume 2: 206–217.

Maloney, Richard G. and Wassall, Gregory H. (2013), 'A Case Study in Cultural Economic Development: The Adams Arts Program in Massachusetts', Rushton (Ed.) (2013): 60–79.

Maltby, Richard (2003), *Hollywood Cinema* (second edition), Malden, Massachusetts, Blackwell Publishing.

Mandel, Benjamin R. (2014), 'Investment in Visual Art: Evidence from International Transactions', in Ginsburgh and Throsby (Eds.) (2006), Volume 2: 233–260.

Markusen, Ann, Nicodemus, Anne Gadwa and Barbour, Elisa (2013), 'The Arts, Consumption, and Innovation in Regional Development', in Rishton (Ed.)(2013): 36–59.

Marshall, Alfred (1890 [1961]), *Principles of Economics*, London, United Kingdom, Macmillan and Co.

Marshall, Alfred (1897), 'The Old Generation of Economists and the New', *The Quarterly Journal of Economics*, 11(2): 115–135.

Marshall, Alfred (1920), 'Principles of Economics: Preface to the Eighth Edition', in Marshall (1890): xii–xvii.

Martin, F. (1994), 'Determining the Size of Museum Subsidies', *Journal of Cultural Economics*, 18(4): 255–270.

Marx, Karl (1843), 'Critique of Hegel's Philosophy of Right', in O'Malley (Ed.) (1970): 129–142.

Marx, Karl (1867), *Capital: A Critique of Political Economy* (Volume I) [eBook], Moscow, Progress Publishers, accessed from http://www.marxists.org/archive/marx/works/download/pdf/Capital-Volume-I.pdf on 20 February 2012.

Marx, Karl (1894 [1959]), *Capital: A Critique of Political Economy* (Volume III) [eBook], New York, International Publishers, accessed from http://www.marxists.org/archive/marx/works/download/pdf/Capital-Volume-III.pdf on 7 December 2012.

Marx, Karl (1973), *Grundriss: Foundations of the Critique of Political Economy (Rough Draft)*, Middlesex, England, Penguin Books.

Marx, Karl (1977), *A Contribution to the Critique of Political Economy*, Moscow, Russia, Progress Publishers.

Marx, Karl and Engels, Friedrich (1888 [2004]), *The Communist Manifesto*, Peterborough, Ontario, Canada, Broadview.

Marx, Karl and Engels, Friedrich (1976), *The German Ideology*, Moscow, Russia, Progress Publishers.

Mattson, V. and Tilman, Rick (1987), 'Thorstein Veblen, Frederick Jackson Turner, and the American Experience', *Journal of Economic Issues*, 21(1): 219–235.

Mayhew, Anne (1987), 'The Beginnings of Institutionalism', *Journal of Economic Issues*, XXI(3): 971–998, reprinted in Tilman (Ed.) (2003): 11–38.

Mayr, Ernst (1991), *One Long Argument: Charles Darwin and the Genesis of Modern Evolutionary Thought*, Cambridge, Massachusetts, Harvard University Press.

MCC (2015), 'Adams Art Program' [web page], Boston, Massachusetts, Massachusetts Cultural Council, accessed from http://www.massculturalcouncil.org/programs/adamsarts.asp on 3 March 2015.

McCaughey, Claire (2005 (October)), *Comparisons of Arts Funding in Selected Countries: Preliminary Findings*, Ottawa, Canada, Canada Council for the Arts, accessed from http://www.americansforthearts.org/NAPD/files/11620/Comparisonsofartsfunding27Oct2005.pdf on 4 May 2012.

McCormick, Ken (2006), *Veblen in Plain English*, Youngstown, New York, Cambria Press.

McGuiness, R. (2004), 'Music as a Commodity: Creating a Market in Eighteenth-Century London', in Ginsburgh (Ed.) (2004): Chapter 8.

McKenzie, Jordi and Walls, W. David (2013), 'File Sharing and Film Revenues: An Empirical Analysis', *The University of Sydney, Economics Working Paper Series*: 2013–14, accessed from http://econ-wpseries.com/2013/201314.pdf on 3 April 2015.

McNertney, E.M. and Waits, C.W. (1988), 'The Incomes of Cultural Providers: A Review of Current Research', originally in Shaw, D., Hendon, W. and Owen, V (Eds.) (1988), *Cultural Economics 88: An American Perspective*, Akron, Ohio, Association for Cultural Economics: 41–49, reprinted in Towse (Ed.) (1997), Volume 2: 275–283.

Mei, J. and Moses, M. (2002), 'Art as an Investment and the Underperformance of Masterpieces', *American Economic Review*, 92(5): 1656–1668, reprinted in Towse (Ed.) (2007): 353–365.

Melbourne (2011), *City of Melbourne Annual Report 2010–11*, Melbourne, Victoria, Australia, City of Melbourne, accessed from http://www.melbourne.vic.gov.au/AboutCouncil/PlansandPublications/AnnualReport/Documents/AnnualReport2010_11.pdf on 4 January 2013.

Mencken, H.L. (1921), *Prejudices: First Series* [eBook], London, United Kingdom, Jonathan Cape, accessed from http://ia601207.us.archive.org/25/items/prejudicesfirsts00menc/prejudicesfirsts00menc.pdf on 27 November 2011.

Micklethwait, John and Wooldridge, Adrian (2003), *The Company: A Short History of a Revolutionary Idea*, London, United Kingdom, Weidenfeld and Nicholson.

Mill, John Stuart (1863), 'Utilitarianism', in Mill (1906): 111–172.

Mill, John Stuart (1906 [1992]), *On Liberty and Utilitarianism*, New York City, New York, Alfred A. Knopf.

Minchin, Liz (2005 (24 August)), "Blue Trees Get the Axe" [web article], *The Age*, accessed from http://www.theage.com.au/news/national/blue-trees-get-the-axe/2005/08/24/1124562901897.html on 24 April 2012.

Mirowski, Philip (1987), 'The Philosophical Bases of Institutionalist Economics', *Journal of Economic Issues*, XXI(3): 1001–1038, reprinted in Tilman (Ed.) (2003), Volume 1: 39–76.

Misak, Cheryl (Ed.) (1999), *Pragmatism*, Calgary, Alberta, Canada, University of Calgary Press.

Moeran, Brian and Pedersen, Jesper Strandgaard (Eds.) (2012), *Negotiating Values in the Creative Industries: Fairs, Festivals and Competitive Events*, Cambridge, United Kingdom, Cambridge University Press.

Moggridge, Donald (Ed.) (1982), *The Collected Writings of John Maynard Keynes* (Volume XXVIII), London, United Kingdom, Macmillan Cambridge University Press.

Moggridge, Donald (2005), 'Keynes, the Arts and the State', *History of Political Economy*, 37(3): 535–555.

Montias, J.M. (1979), 'Statistical Evidence on the Economic Status of Artists and Artisans in Delft in the 17th Century', *Journal of Cultural Economics*, 3(1): 1–29, reprinted in Towse (Ed.) (1997), Volume 2: 69–97.

Montias, J.M. (2004), 'Art Dealers in Holland', in Ginsburgh (Ed.) (2004): Chapter 6.

Moore, Gregory C.G. (2005), 'Evangelical Aesthete: Ruskin and the Public Provision of Art', *History of Political Economy*, 37(3): 483–508.

Moore, T. (1968), 'Reasons for Subsidizing American Theater', in Blaug (Ed.) (1976): 25–41.

Moreland (2011), *Moreland City Council Annual Report 2011*, Coburg, Victoria, Australia, City of Moreland, accessed from http://www.moreland.vic.gov.au/mccwr/publications/reports/annual%20report%202011.pdf on 3 January 2013.

Morris, William (1883), 'Art Under Plutocracy', in Morton (Ed.) (1984): 57–85.

Morris, William (1884), 'Art and Socialism', in Morton (Ed.) (1984): 109–133.

Morris, William (1888 [2002]), *Signs of Change* [eBook], Oxford, Mississippi, Project Gutenberg, accessed from http://www.gutenberg.org/ebooks/3053.epub.noimages on 10 January 2013.

Morrison, W.G. and West, E.G. (1986), 'Subsidies for the Performing Arts: Evidence of Voter Preference', *Journal of Behavioral Economics*, 15: 57–72, reprinted in Towse (Ed.) (1997), Volume 2: 647–662.

Morton, A.L. (Ed.) (1984), *Political Writings of William Morris*, London, United Kingdom, Lawrence and Wishart.

Murphy, John P. (1990), *Pragmatism: From Peirce to Davidson*, Boulder, Colorado, Westview Press.

National Assembly of State Arts Agencies, 'About State Arts Agencies' [web page], Washington, DC, accessed from http://www.nasaa-arts.org/About/About-State-Arts-Agencies.php on 2 June 2012.

National Cultural Policy Discussion Paper (2011), Barton, ACT, Australia, Office for the Arts, Department of the Prime Minister and Cabinet, Commonwealth of Australia, accessed from http://culture.arts.gov.au/sites/default/files/discussion-paper/national-cultural-policy-discussion-paper.pdf.

National Foundation on the Arts and the Humanities Act (1965), United States of America.

National Humanities Alliance (2015 (20 May), 'National Endowment for the Humanities' [web page], Washington, D.C., National Humanities Alliance, accessed from http://www.nhalliance.org/advocacy/funding-priorities/national-endowment-for-the-humanities-fy2013.shtml on 8 March 2015.

NEA (1965), *National Endowment for the Arts, Annual Report, 1964–1965 (First Annual Report of the National Council for the Arts 1964–1965)*, Washington, D.C., National

Endowment for the Arts, accessed from http://www.nea.gov/about/AnnualReports/NEA-Annual-Report-1964–1965.pdf on 3 May 2012.

NEA (2000 (January)), *International Data on Government Spending on The Arts*, Washington, D.C., National Endowment for the Arts, accessed from http://www.nea.gov/research/notes/74.pdf on 2 January 2012.

NEA (2007 (January)), *How the United States Funds the Arts*, Washington, D.C., National Endowment for the Arts, accessed from http://ia700806.us.archive.org/28/items/howunitedstatesf00nati/howunitedstatesf00nati.pdf on 3 March 2012.

NEA (2008), *2008 Survey of Public Participation in the Arts* (Research Report #49), Washington, D.C., National Endowment for the Arts, accessed from http://www.nea.gov/research/2008-sppa.pdf on 24 April 2012.

Netzer, Dick (1978), *The Subsidized Muse: Public Support for the Arts in the United States*, Cambridge, United Kingdom, and New York City, New York, Cambridge University Press.

Ng, B. D. and Weimer-Hastings, P. (2005), 'Addiction to the Internet and Online Gaming', *CyberPsychology and Behavior*, 8(2): 110–113.

Nguyen, Godefroy Dang, Dejean, Sylvain and Moreau, François (2013), 'On the Complementarity between Online and Offline Music Consumption: the Case of Free Streaming', *Journal of Cultural Economics*, 38(4): 315–330.

O'Brian, John (Ed.) (1986), *Clement Greenberg: The Collected Essays and Criticism* (Volume I), Chicago, Illinois, University of Chicago Press.

O'Hagan, John (1996), 'Access to and Participation in the Arts: The Case of those with Low Incomes/Education Attainment', *Journal of Cultural Economics*, 20(4): 269–282.

O'Hagan, John (2003), 'Tax Concessions', in Towse (Ed.) (2003).

O'Hara, Phillip Anthony (2000), *Marx, Veblen and Contemporary Institutional Political Economy: Principle and Unstable Dynamics of Capitalism*, Cheltenham, United Kingdom, Edward Elgar.

O'Malley, Joseph (Ed.) (1970), *Karl Marx: Critique of Hegel's 'Philosophy Of Right'*, Cambridge, United Kingdom, Cambridge University Press.

Oldroyd, D. R. (1980), *Darwinian Impacts: An Introduction to the Darwinian Revolution*, Milton Keynes, United Kingdom, The Open University Press.

Opera Australia (2008), *Opera Australia Annual Report 2008*, Surry Hills, NSW, Australia, Opera Australia, accessed from http://www.opera-australia.org.au/res/pdfs/Opera_Australia_Annual_Report_2008.pdf on 24 April 2012.

Opera Australia (2009), *Opera Australia Annual Report 2009*, Surry Hills, NSW, Australia Opera Australia, accessed from http://www.opera-australia.org.au/res/pdfs/Opera_Australia_Annual_Report_2009.pdf on 24 April 2012.

Opera Australia (2010), *Opera Australia Annual Report 2010*, Surry Hills, NSW, Australia, Opera Australia, accessed from http://www.opera-australia.org.au/res/pdfs/OA%20 2010_annual%20report%20_Part%201.pdf on 24 April 2012.

Opera Glass, 'Opera Company Pages on the World Wide Web' [web page], accessed from http://opera.stanford.edu on 24 April 2012.

Orcheseek: Global Portal of Symphony Orchestras, 'Orcheseek Orchestra Link – Asian Countries', accessed from http://orcheseek.fc2web.com/o-asia.html on 3 July 2012.

Orme, Tylor (2014), 'The Short- and Long-term Effectiveness of Anti-piracy Laws and Enforcement Actions', *Journal of Cultural Economics*, 38(4): 351–368.

Osborne, William (2004), "Marketplace of Ideas: But First, The Bill, A Personal Commentary On American and European Cultural Funding" [web article], *ArtsJournal.com*, accessed from http://www.artsjournal.com/artswatch/20040311–11320.shtml on 19 June 2012.

Paarlberg, Michael Ahn (2012 (February 2)), 'Can Asians Save Classical Music?', *Slate Magazine*, accessed from http://www.slate.com/articles/arts/culturebox/2012/02/can_asians_save_classical_music_.single.html on 24 April 2012.

Palma, María Luisa, Palma, Luis and Aguado, Luis Fernando (2012), 'Determinants of Cultural and Popular Celebration attendance: The Case Study of Seville Spring Fiestas', Journal of Cultural Economics, 37(1): 87–107.

Panero, James (2009), 'The Art Market Explained', *The New Criterion*, 28(December): 26–29.

Paulus, O. (2003), 'Measuring Museum Performance: A Study of Museums in France and the United States', *International Journal of Arts Management*, 6(1): 50–63, reprinted in Towse (Ed.) (2007): 269–282.

Peacock, Alan (1969), 'Welfare Economics and Public Subsidies to the Arts', *Manchester School of Economic and Social Studies*, 4(December): 323–335, reprinted in Towse (1997), Volume 2: 501–513.

Peacock, Alan (1976), 'The "Output" of the London Orchestras, 1966–75', *The Musical Times*, 117(1602): 641–644, reprinted in Towse (Ed.) (1997), Volume 1: 298–302.

Peacock, Alan (1992), 'Economics, Cultural Values and Cultural Policies', originally in Towse, Ruth and Khakee, Abdul (1992) (Eds.), *Cultural Economics*, Berlin and Heidelberg, Germany, Springer-Verlag: Chapter 1, reprinted in Towse (1997), Volume 2: 547–558.

Peacock, Alan (1993), *Paying the Piper: Culture, Music and Money*, Edinburgh, Scotland, Edinburgh University Press.

Peacock, Alan (1994), 'A Future for the Past: The Political Economy of Heritage', *Proceedings of the British Academy*, 87: 189–226, reprinted in Towse (Ed.) (1997), Volume 1: 387–424.

Peacock, Alan and Godfrey, C. (1974), 'The Economics of Museums and Galleries', *Lloyds Bank Review*, 111: 17–28, reprinted in Towse (Ed.) (1997), Volume 1: 364–375.

Peacock, Alan and Rizzo, Ilde (Eds.) (1994), *Cultural Economics and Cultural Policies*, Dordrecht, The Netherlands, and Boston, Massachusetts, Kluwer Academic Publishers.

Pearson, Heath (1999), 'Was There Really a German Historical School of Economics?', *History of Political Economy*, 31(3): 547–562.

Peirce, Charles Sanders (1877), 'The Fixation of Belief', in Stuhr (Ed.) (2000): 67–76.

Peirce, Charles Sanders (1878), 'How to Make Our Ideas Clear', in Stuhr (Ed.) (2000): 77–87.

Peters, E., Unur, S., Clark, J. and Schulze, W.D. (2004), 'Free-riding and the Provision of Public Goods in the Family: A Laboratory Experiment', *International Economic Review*, 45(1): 283–299.

Philanthropy Australia (2011), *Strategies for Increasing High Net Worth and Ultra High Net Worth Giving: Final Report*, accessed from http://www.philanthropy.org.au/pdfs/papersreports/PA-High-Net-Worth-Giving-Report-170211.pdf on 3 June 2012.

Phillips, Rhonda (2004), 'Artful Business: Using the Arts for Community Economic Development', *Community Development Journal*, 39(2): 112–122.

Plekhanov, Georgi (1910), 'Fundamental Problems of Marxism', in Plekhanov (1976): 117–183.

Plekhanov, Georgi (1976), *Selected Philosophical Works* (Volume III), Moscow, Russia, Progress Publishers.

Polinsky, A. Mitchell (2003), *An Introduction to Law and Economics*, New York City, New York, Aspen Publishers.

Potts, Jason (2011), *Creative Industries and Economic Evolution: New Horizon in Institutional and Evolutionary Economics*, Cheltenham, United Kingdom, Edward Elgar.

Potts, Jason, Cunningham, Stuart and Hartley, John (2008), 'Social Network Markets: a New Definition of the Creative Industries', *Journal of Cultural Economics*, 32(3): 167–185.

Priddat, Birger P. (1995), 'Intention and Failure of W. Rocscher's Historical Method of National Economics', in Koslowski (Ed.) (1995a): 15–35.

Public Broadcasting Service (2009), 'Keeping Score: Shostakovich's Symphony No. 5' [web page], Public Broadcasting Service, accessed from http://www.pbs.org/keepingscore/shostakovich-symphony-5.html on 10 August 2012.

Rae, John (1834 [1964]), *Statement of Some New Principles on the Subject of Political Economy*, New York City, New York, A. M. Kelley.

Ricardo, David (1817 [2001]), *On the Principles of Political Economy and Taxation* [eBook], Kitchener, Ontario, Canada, Batoche Books.

Riding, Alan (2007 (January 13)), "Abu Dhabi Is to Gain a Louvre of Its Own" [web article], *The New York Times*, accessed from http://www.nytimes.com/2007/01/13/arts/design/13louv.html on 24 April 2015.

Riesman, David (1953), *Thorstein Veblen: A Critical Interpretation*, New York City, New York, Scribner.

Rima, Ingrid Hahne (1991), *Development of Economic Analysis* (fifth edition), Homewood, Illinois, and Boston, Massachusetts, Irwin.

Rima, Ingrid Hahne (1998), 'Class Conflict and Adam Smith's "Stages of Social History" ', Journal of the History of Economic Thought, 20(1): 103–113.

Romer, Paul M. (1994), 'The Origins of Endogenous Growth', *The Journal of Economic Perspectives*, 8(3): 3–22.

Rose, Barbara (1973 (5 November)), 'Profit Without Honor' [web article], *New York Magazine*: 80–81, accessed from http://books.google.com.au/books?id=JucCAAAAMBAJ&pg=PP2&dq=5+november+1973&hl=en&sa=X&ei=AcoFUe6pBeTxmAX3jYGQDg&ved=0CDcQ6AEwAQ#v=snippet&q=scull&f=false on 26 March 2012.

Rosen, S. (1981), 'The Economics of Superstars', *American Economic Review*, 75(1): 208–212, reprinted in Towse (Ed.) (1997), Volume 2: 187–200.

Rosen, S. and Rosenfield, A. M. (1997), 'Ticket Pricing', *Journal of Law and Economics*, 60(2): 351–376, reprinted in Towse (Ed.) (2007): 125–150.

Rosselli, J. (1989), 'From Princely Service to the Open Market: Singers of Italian Opera and their Patrons, 1600–1850', *Cambridge Opera Journal*, 1(1): 1–32, reprinted in Towse (Ed.) (1997), Volume 2: 37–68.

Routh, Guy (1975), *The Origin of Economic Ideas*, London, United Kingdom, Macmillan.

Ruse, Michael (1979), *The Darwinian Revolution*, Chicago, Illinois, and London, United Kingdom, The University of Chicago Press.

Ruse, Michael (Ed.) (2009), *Philosophy After Darwin: Classic and Contemporary Readings*, Princeton, New Jersey, Princeton University Press.

Rushton, M. (2008), 'Who Pays? Who Benefits? Who Decides?' *Journal of Cultural Economics*, 32(4): 293–300.

Rushton, M. (Ed.) (2013), *Creative Communities: Art Works in Economic Development*, Washington, D.C, Brookings Institution Press.

Ruskin, John (1890), *St Mark's Rest: The History of Venice* [eBook], New York City, New York, John Wiley and Sons, accessed from http://archive.org/details/stmarksresthisto00ruskiala on 21 January 2013.

Sabine, William (Ed.) (1995), *A Century of Australian Cinema*, Port Melbourne, Victoria, Australia, William Heinemann Australia.

Samuels, Warren J. (1999), 'Review of Elizabeth Watkins Jorgensen, and Henry Irvin Jorgensen *Thorstein Veblen: Victorian Firebrand*', *Journal of the History of Economic Thought*, 21(4): 465–467.

Santagata, Walter (2011), 'Cultural Districts', in Towse (Ed.) (2011a): 146–157.

Saram, P.A. (1999), 'The Vanishing Subtitle in Veblen's "Leisure Class"', *International Journal of Politics, Culture and Society*, 13(2): 225–240.

Sawers, David (1993), *Should the Taxpayer Support the Arts?* (Current Controversies No. 7), Westminster, London, United Kingdom, Institute of Economic Affairs, accessed from http://www.iea.org.uk/sites/default/files/publications/files/upldbook405pdf.pdf on 4 November 2011.

Sayre, Nora (1974 (October 17)), "Movie Documents Auction of Scull's Art" [film review], *The New York Times*, accessed from http://select.nytimes.com/gst/abstract.html?res=FB0B15FE395E1A7493C5A8178BD95F408785F9 on 26 March 2012.

Schmoller, Gustav von (1900), *Grundriss der allgemeinen Volkswirtschaftslehre (Outline of General Economics)*, Leipzig, Germany, Duncker & Humblot.

Schneider, Friedrich and Pommerehne, Werner W. (1983), 'Private Demand for Public Subsidies: A Study in Voting and Expenditure Theory', originally in Hendon, William S. and Shanahan, James L. (Eds.) (1983), *Economics of Cultural Decisions*, Cambridge Massachusetts, Abt Books: 192–206, reprinted in Towse (Ed.) (1997), Volume 2: 632–646.

Schumpeter, Joseph (1912 [1954]), *Economic Doctrine and Method: An Historical Sketch (Epochen der Dogmen: und Methodengeschichte)* [eBook], New York City, New York, Oxford University Press, accessed from http://library.mises.org/books/Joseph%20Schumpeter/Economic%20Doctrine%20and%20Method%20An%20Historical%20Sketch.pdf on 2 February 2011.

Scitovsky, Tibor (1983), 'Subsidies for the Arts: the Economic Argument', in Hendon and Shannahan (Eds.) (1983): 6–15.

Screen Australia, 'Producer Offset' [web page], accessed from http://www.screenaustralia.gov.au/producer_offset/ on 4 June 2012.

Screen Australia (2009), *Screen Australia Annual Report 2008–2009*, Woolloomooloo, NSW, Australia, Screen Australia, accessed from http://www.screenaustralia.gov.au/about_us/Corporate-Information.aspx on 8 March 2015.

Screen Australia (2010), *Screen Australia Annual Report 2009–2010*, Woolloomooloo, NSW, Australia, Screen Australia, accessed from http://www.screenaustralia.gov.au/about_us/Corporate-Information.aspx on 8 March 2015.

Screen Australia (2011), *Screen Australia Annual Report 2010–2011*, Woolloomooloo, NSW, Australia, Screen Australia, accessed from http://www.screenaustralia.gov.au/about_us/Corporate-Information.aspx on 8 March 2015.

Screen Australia (2013), *Screen Australia Annual Report 2012–2013*, Woolloomooloo, NSW, Australia, Screen Australia, accessed from http://www.screenaustralia.gov.au/about_us/Corporate-Information.aspx on 8 March 2015.

Screen Australia (2014), *Screen Australia Annual Report 2013–2014*, Woolloomooloo, NSW, Australia, Screen Australia, accessed from http://www.screenaustralia.gov.au/about_us/Corporate-Information.aspx on 8 March 2015.

Screen Australia Act (2008), Australia.

Seaman, B.A. (1981), 'An Assessment of Recent Applications of Economic Theory to the Arts', *Journal of Cultural Economics*, 5(1): 36–51.

Seares, Margaret and Gardiner-Garden, John (2011 (June)), *Cultural Policies in Australia*, Australia Council for the Arts, accessed from http://www.australiacouncil.gov.au/__data/assets/pdf_file/0003/107715/Seares_2011_Cultural_policies_in_Australia.pdf on 13 January 2013.

Segal, Howard P. (2005), *Technological Utopianism in American Culture* [eBook], Syracuse, New York, Syracuse University Press.

Sheehan, Peter (1996), 'Economics Beyond the Neoclassical Synthesis: Rediscovering Keynes's Enterprise', *History of Economics Review*, 25(Winter/Summer): 45–66.

Shimp, Kaleb (2009), 'The Validity of Karl Marx's Theory of Historical Materialism', *Major Themes in Economics*, 11: 35–56.

Shionoya, Y. (2005), *The Soul of the German Historical School: Methodological Essays on Schmoller, Weber, and Schumpeter* [eBook], New York City, New York, Springer.

Singer, Peter (2000), *Marx: A Very Short Introduction*, Oxford, United Kingdom, Oxford University Press.

Skinner, Sarah J., Ekelund, Robert B., Jr. and Jackson, John D. (2009), 'Art Museum Attendance, Public Funding, and the Business Cycle', *American Journal of Economics and Sociology*, 68(2): 491–516.

Slater, Don (1997), *Consumer Culture and Modernity*, Oxford, United Kingdom, Polity Press.

Smith, Adam (1776 [2005]), *An Inquiry into the Wealth of Nations* [eBook], Pennsylvania, Pennsylvania State University.

Smith, Roberta ((2007 (October 16)), "Just When You Thought It Was Safe" [web article], *The New York Times*, accessed from http://www.nytimes.com/2007/10/16/arts/design/16muse.html on 13 April 2012.

Snowball, J. D. (2005), 'Art for the Masses? Justification for the Public Support of the Arts in Developing Countries – Two Arts Festivals in South Africa', *Journal of Cultural Economics*, 29(2): 107–125.

Snowball, J. D. (2007), *Measuring the Value of Culture: Methods and Examples in Cultural Economics* [eBook], Berlin and Heidelberg, Germany, Springer.

Solomon, Maynard (1973), *Marxism and Art, Essays Classic and Contemporary: Selected and with Historical and Critical Commentary by Maynard Solomon*, New York City, New York, Alfred A. Knopf.

Spencer, David A. (2004), 'Deconstructing the Labour Supply Curve', *Metroeconomica*, 55(4): 442–458.

Spencer, David A. (2009), *The Political Economy of Work*, London, United Kingdom and New York City, New York, Routledge.

Sraffa, Piero (Ed.) (1952 [1962]), *The Works and Correspondence of David Ricardo* (Volume V), London, United Kingdom, The Syndics of Cambridge University Press.

Stalin, Joseph (1940), *Dialectical and Historical Materialism*, New York City, New York, International Publishers.

Stallabrass, Julian (2004), *Art Incorporated*, Oxford, United Kingdom, and New York City, New York, Oxford University Press.

Stigler, G. J. and Becker, G. S. (1977), 'De Gustibus Non Est Disputandum', *American Economic Review*, 67(2): 76–90, reprinted in Towse (Ed.) (1997), Volume 1: 112–126.

Stiglitz, Joseph E. (1994), *Whither Socialism?* Cambridge, Massachusetts, The MIT Press.

Streeten, Paul (2006), 'Culture and Economic Development', in Ginsburgh and Throsby (Eds.) (2006), Volume 1: 399–412.

Stubbs, Ryan (2012), 'Public Funding for the Arts: 2013 Update', Grantmakers in the Arts Reader, 25(3): 8–9, reprinted in *Arts Funding Snapshot: GIA's Annual Research on*

Support for Arts and Culture, Seattle, Washington, Grantmakers in the Arts, accessed from http://foundationcenter.org/gainknowledge/research/pdf/artsfunding_2012.pdf on 8 March 2015.

Stubbs, Ryan (2013), 'Public Funding for the Arts: 2013 Update', Grantmakers in the Arts Reader, 25(3): 8–9, reprinted in *Arts Funding Snapshot: GIA's Annual Research on Support for Arts and Culture*, Seattle, Washington, Grantmakers in the Arts, accessed from http://www.giarts.org/sites/default/files/24–3_Vital-Signs.pdf on 8 March 2015.

Stubbs, Ryan (2014), 'Public Funding for the Arts: 2014 Update', Grantmakers in the Arts Reader, 25(3): 8–10, reprinted in Arts Funding Snapshot: *GIA's Annual Research on Support for Arts and Culture*, Seattle, Washington, Grantmakers in the Arts, accessed from http://foundationcenter.org/gainknowledge/research/pdf/artsfunding_2014.pdf on 8 March 2015.

Stuhr, John J. (Ed.) (2000), *Pragmatism and Classical American Philosophy: Essential Readings and Interpretive Essays* (Second edition.), New York City, New York, and Oxford, United Kingdom, Oxford University Press.

Sweezy, Paul M. (1942), 'The Illusion of the "Managerial Revolution"', *Science and Society*, 6(1): 1–23.

Sweezy, Paul M. (1958), 'Veblen on American Capitalism', in Dowd (Ed.) (1998): 177–198.

Szostak, Rick (1999), *Econ-art: Divorcing Art from Science in Modern Economics*, London, United Kingdom, Pluto Press.

Tadayoni, Reza and Henten, Anders (2013), 'Has Digitization Delivered? Fact and Fiction in Digital TV Broadcasting', in Towse and Handke (Eds.) (2013): 134–151.

Talisse, Robert B. and Aikin, Scott F. (2008), *Pragmatism: A Guide for the Perplexed* [eBook], New York City, New York, Continuum.

Thompson, Don (2008), *The $12 Million Stuffed Shark: The Curious Economics of Contemporary Art*, New York City, New York, Palgrave MacMillan.

Thompson, E. P. (1967), 'Time, Work-Discipline, and Industrial Capitalism', *Past and Present*, 38(December): 56–97.

Thompson, Eric, Berger, Mark, Blomquist, Glenn and Allen, Steve (2002), 'Valuing the Arts: A Contingent Valuation Approach', *Journal of Cultural Economics*, 26(2): 87–113.

Throsby, David (1994), 'The Production and Consumption of the Arts: A View of Cultural Economics', *Journal of Economic Literature*, 32(1): 1–29, reprinted in Towse (Ed.) (1997), Volume 1: 51–79.

Throsby, David (1994a), 'A Work-Preference Model of Artist Behaviour', originally in Peacock, A. and Rizzo, I. (Eds.) (1994), *Cultural Economics and Cultural Policies*, Dordrecht, The Netherlands, Kluwer: Chapter 6, reprinted in Towse (Ed.) (2007): 397–408.

Throsby, David (1997), 'Seven Questions in the Economics of Cultural Heritage', originally in Hutter, M. and Rizzo, I. (Eds.) (1997), *Economic Perspectives on Cultural Heritage*, Basingstoke and London, Macmillan: Chapter 2, reprinted in Towse (Ed.) (2007): 285–302.

Throsby, David (2001), *Economics and Culture*, Cambridge, United Kingdom, Cambridge University Press.

Throsby, David (2001a), *Public Funding in the Arts – 1900 to 2000* (Year Book Australia), Canberra, Australia, Australian Bureau of Statistics, accessed from http://www.abs.gov.au/Ausstats/abs@.nsf/0/ed192b5a87e90dbeca2569de0025c1a6?OpenDocument on 17 May 2012.

Throsby, David (2010), *The Economics of Cultural Policy* [eBook], Cambridge, New York, Cambridge University Press.

Throsby, David and Withers, Glenn (1979), *The Economics of the Performing Arts*, Melbourne, Australia, Edward Arnold.

Throsby, David and Withers, Glenn (1985), 'What Price Culture?' *Journal of Cultural Economics*, 9(2): 1–34, reprinted in Towse (Ed.) (1997), Volume 2: 577–610.

Tilman, Rick (1992), *Thorstein Veblen and His Critics, 1891–1963: Conservative, Liberal and Radical Perspectives*, Princeton, New Jersey, Princeton University Press.

Tilman, Rick (1996), *The Intellectual Legacy of Thorstein Veblen*, Westport, Connecticut, and London, United Kingdom, Greenwood.

Tilman, Rick (Ed.) (1993), *A Veblen Treasury: From Leisure Class to War, Peace, and Capitalism*, Armonk, New York and London, United Kingdom, M. E. Sharpe.

Tilman, Rick (Ed.) (2003), *The Legacy of Thorstein Veblen* (3 volumes), Cheltenham, United Kingdom, Edward Elgar.

Timms, Robert (2004), *What's Wrong with Contemporary Art?* Sydney, Australia, University of New South Wales Press.

Tool, Marc (1977), 'A Social Value Theory in Neoinstitutional Economics', *Journal of Economic Issues*, XI(4): 823–846, reprinted in Tilman (Ed.) (2003), Volume 1: 450–474.

Towse, Ruth (1994), 'Achieving Public Policy Objectives in the Arts and Heritage', in Peacock, A. and Rizzo, I. (Eds.) (1994): 143–165.

Towse, Ruth (Ed.) (1997), *Cultural Economics: the Arts, the Heritage and the Media Industries* (2 volumes), Cheltenham, United Kingdom, Edward Elgar.

Towse, Ruth (Ed.) (1997a), *Baumol's Cost Disease: the Arts and Other Victims*, Cheltenham, United Kingdom, Edward Elgar.

Towse, Ruth (1997b), 'Introduction', in Towse (Ed.) (1997), Volume 1: xiii–xxi

Towse, Ruth (Ed.) (2003), *A Handbook of Cultural Economics*, Cheltenham, United Kingdom, Edward Elgar.

Towse, Ruth (2006), 'Copyright and Creativity: An Application of Cultural Economics', *Review of Economic Research on Copyright Issues*, 3(2): 83–91.

Towse, Ruth (2006a), 'Copyright and Artists: A View from Cultural Economics', *Journal of Economic Surveys*, 20(4): 567–585

Towse, Ruth (Ed.) (2007), *Recent Developments in Cultural Economics*, Cheltenham, United Kingdom, Edward Elgar.

Towse, Ruth (2008), 'Why has Cultural Economics Ignored Copyright?', *Journal of Cultural Economics*, 32(4): 243–259.

Towse, Ruth (2010), *A Textbook of Cultural Economics*, Cheltenham, United Kingdom, Edward Elgar.

Towse, Ruth (2010a), 'Creativity, Copyright and the Creative Industries Paradigm', *Kyklos*, 63(3): 461–478.

Towse, Ruth (2011), 'Creative Industries', in Towse (Ed.) (2011a): 125–131.

Towse, Ruth (2011a), *A Handbook of Cultural Economics* (second edition), Cheltenham, United Kingdom, Edward Elgar.

Towse, Ruth (2014), *Advanced Introduction to Cultural Economics*, Cheltenham, United Kingdom, Edward Elgar.

Towse, Ruth and Handke, Christian (Eds.) (2013), *The Digital Creative Economy*, Cheltenham, United Kingdom, Edward Elgar.

Towse, Ruth, Handke, Christian and Stepan, Paul (2008), 'The Economics of Copyright Law: A Stocktake of the Literature', *Review of Economic Research and Copyright Issues*, 5(1): 1–22.

Tresch, Richard W. (2002), *Public Finance: A Normative Theory*, London, United Kingdom, Academic Press.

Tubadji, Annie, Osoba, Brian J. and Nijkamp, Peter (2014), 'Culture-based Development in the USA: Culture as a Factor for Economic Welfare and Social Well-being at a Country Level' [online journal article], *Journal of Cultural Economics*, published online 30 September 2014.

Tucker, A. (Ed.) (1996), *The Value of Culture: On the Relationships Between Economics and Arts*, Amsterdam, The Netherlands, Amsterdam University Press.

Tucker, K.A. (1977), *Economics of the Australian Service Sector*, London, United Kingdom, Croom Helm Ltd.

Tuttle, Frank W. and Perry, Joseph M. (1970), *An Economic History of the United States*, Cincinnati, Ohio, South-western Publishing Co.

UNCTAD (2008), *Creative Economy Report 2008 The Challenge of Assessing the Creative Economy: Towards Informed Policy-making*, United Nations Conference on Trade and Development, New York, United Nations, accessed from http://unctad.org/en/Docs/ditc20082cer_en.pdf on 3 April 2015.

UNESCO (1969 (May)). *UNESCO-ANU Seminar on Public Support for the Performing Arts, Canberra*, Canberra, Australia, Australian National University Central Printing Pool.

UNESCO (2006), *Understanding Creative Industries: Cultural Statistics for Public-policy Making*, United Nations Educational, Scientific and Cultural Organization, New York, United Nations, accessed from http://portal.unesco.org/culture/en/ev.php-URL_ID=29947&URL_DO=DO_TOPIC&URL_SECTION=-465.html on 3 May 2015

United States Census Bureau, *Historical Income Tables: Income Inequality*, accessed from http://www.census.gov/hhes/www/income/data/historical/inequality/ on 28 June 2012

UNU–WIDER (United Nations University – World Institute for Development Economics Research), *World Income Inequality Database*, accessed from http://www.wider.unu.edu/research/Database/en_GB/database/ on 28 June 2012

Upchurch, Anna (2004), 'John Maynard Keynes, the Bloomsbury Group and the Origins of the Arts Council Movement', *International Journal of Cultural Policy*, 10(2): 203–217.

Upchurch, Anna (2005), 'William Morris and the Case for Public Support of the Arts', *History of Political Economy*, 37(3): 509–534.

Utah Division of Arts and Museums, Department of Heritage and Arts, 'What We Do' [web page], Utah, United States, accessed from http://arts.utah.gov/about_us/what.html on 2 June 2012.

Van Loon, Ruben, Gosen, Tom and Rouwendal, Jan (2014), 'Cultural Heritage and the Attractiveness of Cities: Evidence from Recreation Trips', *Journal of Cultural Economics*, 38(3): 253–285.

Veblen, Thorstein (1891), 'Some Neglected Points in the Theory of Socialism', *Annals of the American Academy of Political and Social Science*, 2(November): 57–54.

Veblen, Thorstein (1892), 'Boehm-Bawek's Definition of Capital, and the Source of Wages', *The Quarterly Journal of Economics*, 6(2): 247–250.

Veblen, Thorstein (1898), 'Why is Economics Not an Evolutionary Science?' *The Quarterly Journal of Economics*, 12(4): 373–397.

Veblen, Thorstein (1898a), 'The Instinct of Workmanship and the Irksomeness of Labor', *American Journal of Sociology*, 4(2): 187–201.

Veblen, Thorstein (1898b), 'The Beginnings of Ownership', *American Journal of Sociology*, 4(3): 352–365.

Veblen, Thorstein (1899 [2005]), *The Theory of the Leisure Class*, United States, Dodo Press.

Veblen, Thorstein (1899a), 'The Preconceptions of Economic Science' (Part 1), *The Quarterly Journal of Economics*, 13(2): 121–150.

Veblen, Thorstein (1899b), 'The Preconceptions of Economic Science' (Part 2), *The Quarterly Journal of Economics*, 13(4): 396–426.

Veblen, Thorstein (1899c), 'The Barbarian Status of Women', *American Journal of Sociology*, 4(4): 503–514.

Veblen, Thorstein (1900), 'The Preconceptions of Economic Science' (Part 3), *The Quarterly Journal of Economics*, 14(2): 240–269.

Veblen, Thorstein (1901), 'Gustav Schmoller's Economics', *The Quarterly Journal of Economics*, 16(1): 69–93.

Veblen, Thorstein (1904 [2005]), *The Theory of Business Enterprise*, New York City, New York, Charles Scribner's Sons.

Veblen, Thorstein (1906), 'The Place of Science in Modern Civilisation', *American Journal of Sociology*, XI(5): 585–609.

Veblen, Thorstein (1906a), 'The Socialist Economics of Karl Marx and His Followers' (Part 1), *The Quarterly Journal of Economics*, 20(4): 575–595.

Veblen, Thorstein (1907), 'The Socialist Economics of Karl Marx and His Followers' (Part 2), *The Quarterly Journal of Economics*, 21(2): 299–322.

Veblen, Thorstein (1908), 'Fisher's Capital and Income', *Political Science Quarterly*, 23(1): 112–128.

Veblen, Thorstein (1908a), 'On the Nature of Capital' (Part 1), *The Quarterly Journal of Economics*, 22(4): 517–542.

Veblen, Thorstein (1908b), 'On the Nature of Capital: Investment, Intangible Assets, and the Pecuniary Magnate' (Part 2), *The Quarterly Journal of Economics*, 23(1): 104–136.

Veblen, Thorstein (1908c), 'Professor Clark's Economics', *The Quarterly Journal of Economics*, 22(1): 147–195.

Veblen, Thorstein (1908d), 'The Evolution of the Scientific Point of View', in Veblen (1919): 32–55.

Veblen, Thorstein (1909), 'Fisher's Rate of Interest', *Political Science Quarterly*, 24(2): 296–303.

Veblen, Thorstein (1909a), 'The Limitations of Marginal Utility', *Journal of Political Economy*, 17(9): 620–636.

Veblen, Thorstein (1914 [2006]), *The Instinct of Workmanship and the State of the Industrial Arts*, New York City, New York, Cosimo Classics.

Veblen, Thorstein (1915 [2003]), *Imperial Germany and the Industrial Revolution* [eBook], Kitchener, Ontario, Canada, Batoche Books, accessed from http://socserv.socsci.mcmaster.ca/econ/ugcm/3ll3/veblen/ImperialGermany.pdf on 4 April 2012.

Veblen, Thorstein (1917), *An Inquiry Into the Nature of Peace & the Terms of Its Perpetuation* [eBook], New York City, New York, The Macmillan Company, accessed from http://ia600401.us.archive.org/10/items/inquiryintothena005294mbp/inquiryintothena005294mbp.pdf on 3 September 2012.

Veblen, Thorstein (1918 [1957]), *The Higher Learning in America: A Memorandum on the Conduct of Universities by Business Men*, New York City, New York, Hill and Wang.

Veblen, Thorstein (1919), *The Place of Science in Modern Civilisation* [eBook], New York City, New York, B. W. Huebsch, accessed from http://fax.libs.uga.edu/HB34xV395/1f/place_of_science_in_modern_civilisation.pdf on 10 January 2012.

Veblen, Thorstein (1921 [1963]), *The Engineers and the Price System*, New York City, New York, Harcourt, Brace and World.

Veblen, Thorstein (1923 [1997]), *Absentee Ownership and Business Enterprise in Recent Times: The Case of America*, New Brunswick, New Jersey, Transaction Publishers.

Velthuis, Olav (2008), 'Accounting for Taste: Olav Velthuis on the Economics of Arts', *Artforum international*, 46(8): 305–309, 316.

Victor A. Ginsburgh, Victor A. and Menger, Pierre-Michel (Eds.) (1996), *Economics of the Arts: Selected Essays*, Amsterdam, The Netherlands, and New York City, New York, Elsevier.

Victorian Government Innovation Statement (2002 (October)), *Victorians. Bright Ideas. Brilliant Future: Victorian Government Innovation Statement*, Melbourne, Australia, Victorian Government.

Vogel, Carol (1999 (December 15)), "Armani Gift to the Guggenheim Revives Issue of Art and Commerce" [web article], *The New York Times*, accessed from http://www.nytimes.com/1999/12/15/arts/armani-gift-to-the-guggenheim-revives-issue-of-art-and-commerce.html?pagewanted=all&src=pm on 12 April 2012.

Von Ungern-Sternberg, Thomas and Von Weizsäcker, Carl Christian (1985), 'The Supply of Quality on a Market for "Experience Goods" ', *The Journal of Industrial Economics*, XXXIII(4): 531–540.

Walker, Donald A. (1977), 'Thorstein Veblen's Economic System', *Economic Inquiry*, XV(2): 213–237, reprinted in Tilman (Ed.) (2003), Volume 2: 51–75.

Webster, Elizabeth (1999), *The Economics of Intangible Investment*, Cheltenham, United Kingdom, Edward Elgar.

Weintraub, Judith (1971 (March 22)), "Germaine Greer – Opinions That May Shock the Faithful" [interview], *The New York Times*, accessed from http://www.nytimes.com/books/99/05/09/specials/greer-shock.html?_r=2 on 19 August 2012.

West, Cornel (1989), *The American Evasion of Philosophy: A Genealogy of Pragmatism*, Madison, Wisconsin, University of Wisconsin Press.

West, Edwin G. (1986), 'Arts Vouchers to Replace Grants', *Economic Affairs*, 6(3): 9–11 and 16, reprinted in Towse (1997), Volume 2: 665–668.

West, Edwin G. (1988), 'Government Grants to Nonprofit Firms: Still Searching for the Rationale', *Journal of Cultural Economics*, 12(2): 93–95, reprinted in Towse (Ed.) (1997), Volume 2: 431–433.

West, Edwin G. and McKee, Michael (1983), 'De Gustibus *Est* Disputandum', *American Economic Review*, 67(2): 76–90, reprinted in Towse (1997), Volume 1: 112–126.

Wiggins, David (1999), 'C. S. Peirce: Belief, Truth, and Going from the Known to the Unknown', in Misak (Ed.) (1999): 9–30.

Williams, Karel, Cutler, Tony, Williams, John and Haslarn, Colin (1987), 'The End of Mass Production?', *Economy and Society*, 16(3): 405–439.

Wilson, R. J. (Ed.) (1967), *Darwinism and the American Intellectual: A Book of Readings*, Homewood, Illinois, The Dorsey Press.

Withers, Glenn (1980), 'Unbalanced Growth and the Demand for Performing Arts: An Econometric Analysis', *Southern Economic Journal*, 46(3): 735–742, reprinted in Towse (Ed.) (1997), Volume 1: 227–234.

Withers, Glenn (1983), 'The Cultural Influence of Public Television', originally in Shanahan, J., Hendon, W. Hilhorst, I. and van Straalen, J. (Eds.) (1983), *Markets for the*

Arts, Akron, Ohio, Association of Cultural Economics: 31–46, reprinted in Towse (Ed.) (1997), Volume 1: 449–464.

Wolff, Rick (2002), *Why Read Marx Today?*, Oxford, United Kingdom, Oxford University Press.

Zajac, Edward E. (1995), *Political Economy of Fairness*, Cambridge, Massachusetts, The MIT Press.

Index

For Product Safety Concerns and Information please contact our EU representative GPSR@taylorandfrancis.com
Taylor & Francis Verlag GmbH, Kaufingerstraße 24, 80331 München, Germany

www.ingramcontent.com/pod-product-compliance
Ingram Content Group UK Ltd.
Pitfield, Milton Keynes, MK11 3LW, UK
UKHW022013180926
475701UK00003B/335
9780367597405